MORNINGSIDE

The Americano: Fighting with Castro for Cuba's Freedom

MORNINGSIDE

THE 1979 GREENSBORO MASSACRE
AND THE STRUGGLE FOR
AN AMERICAN CITY'S SOUL

ARAN SHETTERLY

AMISTAD

An Imprint of HarperCollins*Publishers*

HarperCollins books may be purchased for educational, business, or sales promotional use. For information, please email the Special Markets Department at SPsales@harpercollins.com.

FIRST EDITION

Library of Congress Cataloging-in-Publication Data has been applied for.

ISBN 978-0-06-285821-4

24 25 26 27 28 LBC 5 4 3 2 1

Morningside *is for my father, Robert, whose work guided me to this story. For my wife, Margot, who makes everything possible. For my son, Giles, who, like all children, inherits our history. And for all the dreamers struggling to build beloved community.*

Nations reel and stagger on their way; they make hideous mistakes;
they commit frightful wrongs; they do great and beautiful things.
And shall we not best guide humanity by telling the truth
about all of this, so far as the truth is ascertainable?

——W. E. B. DU BOIS

CONTENTS

Section I. AMERICA: 1979   *1*

Section II. DREAMS: 1966–1979   *91*

Section III. BACKLASH: 1979–1985   *253*

Section IV. RENEWAL: 1986–2006   *365*

Epilogue   *411*

Acknowledgments   *419*

Notes   *423*

SECTION I

AMERICA: 1979

DEBATE

On the evening of November 2, 1979, the comfortable eight-room bungalow at the corner of Cypress and Yanceyville Streets in Greensboro, North Carolina, hummed with activity. In the kitchen and dining room and in an upstairs office, men and women huddled together, making placards, practicing speeches, and fine-tuning logistics for the march and conference set to take place the following day. Several women sat on the living room's colossal empire couch talking and laughing as they stitched bolts of khaki cloth into Revolutionary Youth League uniforms for the children who were busy chasing one another through the house and across the property's oak-canopied yard. As they laughed and played, their shouts, like hurled incantations, carried past the silhouetted limbs, toward the low clouds that blanketed the city.[1]

The house belonged to a handsome, intellectual couple who'd found each other through radical politics and recently married. Signe Waller held a doctorate in philosophy from Columbia University but quit teaching to commit herself to grassroots political activism. Jim Waller, a physician by training, had been drawn to North Carolina by the offer of a coveted postdoc at Duke University. He'd left the medical profession to become a laborer and a labor organizer. His new colleagues, fellow lintheads at the Haw River Granite Mill, one of the largest corduroy producers in the world, nicknamed the bespectacled, thick-whiskered ex-doctor Blackbeard. They'd come to appreciate his quirky, wry humor and to trust the workplace agitation he encouraged in the interest of their health and quality of life. He was their pirate. After eighteen months, plant management fired Jim for, the managers said, omitting the fact of his medical degree on the application—a pretense, the activists believed, convinced the spooked managers dismissed him for his relentless union organizing.[2]

Jim wasn't the only licensed doctor in the close-knit group. Paul Bermanzohn, Mike Nathan, and Mike's wife, Marty, offered all who asked a short parable about why, after dedicating years to their medical training, they'd shifted their focus beyond the examining room. A doctor sits in his office and people keep hobbling in with broken legs, they'd say. The doctor sets the legs and sends the people back into the world. But they keep returning, their legs fractured once more. Curious about the cause of this epidemic, the doctor looks outside. He sees a big hole and watches as people fall in. The doctor decides to leave the office, pick up a shovel, and fill the hole.[3]

One would have been hard-pressed to encounter a more unusual mix of people in Greensboro or most anywhere in the United States. They were Black and white and brown, men and women, young and middle-aged. Some held degrees from the country's most prestigious universities. Others had never completed high school. And yet they all agreed that "filling the hole" meant inverting the social order, turning power over to the country's working people. If capitalism didn't soon collapse like the rickety house of cards they believed it to be, they'd agitate to dismantle it, textile mill by bank by distant investor. The future society they imagined would prevent byssinosis, the debilitating brown lung disease that cut short the lives of the Piedmont's textile workers; pay living wages; support working mothers; and deliver healthy food to all its citizens regardless of race, culture, or circumstance. These goals might not have sounded terribly radical but seeing how far short society fell of these objectives had broken their faith in the political and business establishments' commitment to the country's poor and working people, to the idea of America's inevitable progress.[4]

The people bustling around Signe and Jim's home were not "Kumbaya"-singing hippies or dropouts. They rarely drank and didn't take drugs. The ideals of the Declaration of Independence—"all men are created equal"—had led them to the melody of a siren song: "From each according to his ability, to each according to his need." It was a hazardous amalgam sprung from American soil. While they weren't controlled or in communication with any foreign power, they did find inspiration in the peasant revolution in China and its charismatic and ruthless philosopher-soldier, Chairman Mao Tse-tung. Mao, possessing a gift for pithy quotes, had said, "If you want to know the taste of a pear, you must change the pear by eating it yourself. . . . If you want to know the theory and methods of revolution, you must take part in revolution. All genuine knowledge originates in direct experience."[5]

When the moment grew ripe for revolt, the men and women in the house on Cypress Street were prepared to taste the pear: what else, they asked, but a well-organized insurrection could overthrow a government that extracted its immense wealth and power from Native American land, the toil of Black slaves, and the exploitation of the working poor? These men and women intended to be agents of history, wading into relentless currents to rudder the United States toward a far and brighter shore.

The next day's Anti-Klan March and Conference would call attention to a new wave of white supremacist and Ku Klux Klan activity percolating around the South. More meaningfully, perhaps, the event aimed to "educate the people" about the peculiar way the country's economics still depended on racial disparities, and how the Klan's racist ideas kept Black and white workers from coming together to make unified demands of the Piedmont's powerful mill owners. With good weather, the event might be the largest labor march in Greensboro since the radical uprisings of the Great Depression, causing the owners of the city's hulking textile mills, which whirred and clacked around the clock churning out cotton fabric, to tremble.[6]

These few dozen activists in North Carolina's textile capital were not alone. They constituted one local cadre of an organization with its headquarters in New York's Chinatown and core groups in Boston, Baltimore, Detroit, Chicago, Denver, San Diego, and Los Angeles. Total membership reached possibly as high as three thousand, though the activists avoided keeping a list of names that might fall into the hands of the FBI or any law enforcement agency antagonistic to the group's revolutionary goals.[7]

Less than a month earlier, the organization had gone by the relatively innocuous name Workers Viewpoint Organization (WVO). At its conference in October, a majority of members agreed that it no longer made sense to obscure their underlying politics. In the depths of America's Cold War with the Soviet Union, they changed their name to the Communist Workers Party (CWP). Addressing the membership, the general secretary of the group, a charismatic Chinese American named Jerry Tung, steeled party members to fight for a new society, which could "only be forged by blood—by sacrificing the most sacred of all things—our lives."[8]

The Anti-Klan March and Conference would be the organization's first significant action under the new moniker *Communist Workers Party.*

❖

In the midst of the Cypress Street excitement, Thomas Anderson, known to all as Big Man, raised a concern. If these brazen organizers were going to provoke the Klan, they would need "expert gunmen, somebody who knows how to shoot" to protect them.[9]

Big Man arrived in Greensboro in 1950 and had been employed in the mills for nearly thirty years. Despite Greensboro's carefully cultivated reputation as a progressive southern city, Big Man's experience led him to a different view. "Greensboro," he believed, "is about the craziest city in the South. It's worser than Mississippi, Alabama, Georgia, and Louisiana." Older than the others in the house, his physical presence as well as his long tenure as a mill worker in Greensboro commanded respect. "It's a lot of things that happens in the South," he said. Growing up Black in Greenwood, South Carolina, in the 1920s and '30s, he'd learned what the Klan was capable of. "If you attack the Klan, you would most certainly, sooner or later, get hurt. . . . I know they has kilt people, drag people down the road and hang 'em up in trees, and shoot them 'til there is nothing left but the rope. And gotten away with it."[10] As the 1970s gave to the 1980s, fear of the Klan still slipped through American time, irreducible and intact, like the slither of a dream-snake through the cerebellum, even for rugged, middle-aged Big Man.

Something else bothered Big Man. He believed some in the group were growing too comfortable with the possibility of violence. They'd picked up a slogan circulating through the South—"Death to the Klan"—and printed it on their flyers and posters. They'd printed an open letter to the Klan calling them "scum," threatening to "chase [them] off the face of the earth."[11] Referring to the Workers Viewpoint Organization's participation in a rally four months earlier that succeeded in interrupting a Klan screening of the racist 1915 film *Birth of a Nation*, Jim Waller had confided, "Big Man, the next time we meet the Ku Klux Klan, we're going to have to be ready to kill." Big Man knew that for all their revolutionary bluster, these radicals, men and women he cared deeply for, weren't prepared to trade shots with the Klan. Three policemen had been at the demonstration against the *Birth of a Nation* screening. That shirt-thin blue line likely prevented the armed Klansmen from opening fire and massacring the hundred raucous demonstrators chanting anti-Klan slogans. Big Man thought the CWP should stay focused on building more powerful unions in the mills, not risk confrontations with the Klan. Their "Death to the Klan" agitation defied his common sense.

People heard Big Man out. Maybe, some suggested, they should request that residents along the march route stand on their porches with guns.[12]

❖

It was growing late when Nelson Johnson, the thirty-six-year-old leader of the local cadre, strode into the house, his five-foot-eight-inch frame tipped forward, a slight hitch in his confident gait. His bright eyes, which could shift in an instant from empathy to defiance, flashed with optimism. This multiracial CWP group in the Carolina Piedmont wouldn't have existed without the Promethean gift of Nelson's hopeful fire, his vision of a more equal future, his resilient network of personal and professional relationships in Greensboro's Black community, and his talent for knitting together coalitions across class and age, among Black professionals, students, and the poor—and, more recently, across race. The respect he commanded derived not only from charisma and astute social analysis, but from the courage he'd demonstrated in confronting powerful people and institutions and winning labor strikes, rent strikes, and political campaigns. Change, he'd learned from experience, didn't just happen; it required pressure and risk.

Many CWP members, not only in Greensboro, but around the country, had followed Nelson into the organization, believing in his leadership and his quest for equality more than any ideology.[13] He'd never been drawn to the secret guerrilla tactics of roaming, underground radicals—Black and white—like the Black Liberation Army or the Weather Underground, who burst into moments of space and time to explode the "establishment's" symbols of power. Instead, he'd chosen the door-to-door, meeting-to-meeting grind of building unity around a vision of how America's vast power and prosperity might be shared with the poor and the marginalized.

Pacing back and forth in the living room, Nelson countered Big Man in a "lawyerly fashion." Like Big Man he'd come to Greensboro from the agricultural Black Belt South. A generation younger, however, he located existential threats in the biased inertia of institutions more than in the angry face of a racist vigilante. The Klan, Nelson believed, wouldn't dare ride into a Black neighborhood in broad daylight. The Klan were night riders, not day raiders, right? Big Man couldn't deny this.[14]

The real threat to the march then, Nelson continued, wasn't the Klan, but the Greensboro Police Department (GPD). He ticked off the list of the department's most recent offenses: When he applied for a parade permit, he'd had no choice but to accept the police demand that the CWP not carry guns during the march, though he believed the stipulation might infringe on the group's constitutional rights. Despite agreeing to these rules, it took two weeks, instead of the standard seventy-two hours, for the permit to be issued. And these weren't the only signs that the police were intent on disrupting the event he and his comrades had been planning for two months. As Nelson's wife, Joyce, and others stuck flyers to electric poles around the city, they noticed the police tailing them and tearing their posters down. A rumor of potential violence caused the church that offered its sanctuary for the postmarch conference to withdraw the invitation. Joyce traced the rumor back to the police department, yet no one at the GPD had warned Nelson or any other CWP members of threats to *their* safety.[15]

No, the enemy they would face the next day, Nelson believed, wasn't the vigilante Klan. The police would be everywhere during the march, he said, looking for a violation of the permit, protecting the interests of the businessmen who ran the city.

If the police couldn't find a violation, they might be willing to stage one, Nelson warned. As the women sat sewing on the living room couch, Nelson demonstrated how a provocateur's jacket might swing open, revealing a weapon, granting the cops an opening to shut down the march, or worse, provoke a riot: "If anyone should come into the march with a weapon, that person is either just an innocent person with a gun or a provocateur, and more likely it's a provocateur . . . immediately pull away from the person and leave him alone, and let the police take him. . . . We [will] not be baited into responding to violence with violence."[16]

Remember, said Nelson, the police get away with murder.

❖

As the 1970s ground to a close, many in America felt their comfortable and optimistic post–World War II assumptions slipping beyond reach. Everyone fretted over the economy. As the country tipped toward recession, everyday people worried about mortgages with 17 percent interest rates, rising unemployment, and whether to buy some gold as a hedge against the weakening dollar. Waiting in long lines to gas up their cars, they conversed in a new, pessimistic language, using terms such as *stagflation* and *price spurts*. With expectations and habits shaped by a quarter century of vertiginous growth and abundance, this shift created confusion. "Anybody who isn't schizophrenic these days just isn't thinking clearly," quipped one of President Jimmy Carter's economic advisers.[17]

The pervasive economic anxiety churned a deluge of other national insecurities: President Nixon resigned in a corrupt, shameful scandal in 1974. The United States had lost the bitterly divisive Vietnam War, exiting Saigon in ignominious fashion in 1975. In 1976, the Senate Select Committee to Study Governmental Operations with Respect to Intelligence Activities—known as the Church Committee after its chairman, Senator Frank Church of Idaho—revealed to the American public brazen illegal activity among the country's law enforcement and intelligence agencies, including the FBI and CIA. These new injuries to the nation's institutions and collective psyche festered with older, still unresolved wounds. The trauma of the 1960s assassinations of President John F. Kennedy, Malcolm X, Martin Luther King Jr., and Robert Kennedy lingered like bad omens, while hope for the transformative power of the civil rights legislation passed that same decade decayed, leaving behind a residue of disillusion.

Even President Carter, or "Peanut Carter" as the CWP called

him,[18] derisively referring to his farming roots, acknowledged this collective "malaise." In an unusually doubtful and self-reflective statement for an American president, Carter admitted that "our people are losing their faith . . . in progress." Carter talked of "wounds" that were "still very deep" and that "have never been healed." America faced, he said, "a turning point in our history" between "narrow interests ending in chaos and immobility" and the "restoration of American values." When President Carter sought the input of regular citizens on how to deal with the crisis, one said to him, "When we enter the moral equivalent of war, Mr. President, don't issue us BB guns."[19]

For the CWP, the right path forward wasn't to restore old American values, but rather to choose renewal: "Against the backdrop of the deepest economic crisis this country has ever seen, the choice . . . for Afro-Americans and all US people is a life and death question, either the destruction of monopoly capitalism . . . or fascism and world war."[20]

Communists weren't the only ones questioning the future of capitalism. To believe that American values could be, as President Carter hoped, restored or reformed without revolution required that Americans, wrote James Baldwin, "set up in themselves a fantastic system of evasions, denials, and justifications, [for a system that] is about to destroy their grasp of reality, which is another way of saying their moral sense."[21] *TIME* magazine and other mainstream periodicals took up the debate, noting that "capitalism, the system that relies on the maximum use of free markets and the minimum of government controls, is today being challenged as at no time since the Great Depression," and wondering if "it [can] be repaired or is . . . fatally flawed?" "The central economic fact of our day," announced one economist, "is the declining vitality and élan of capitalism and capitalists." Even Lee Iacocca, the chairman of the Chrysler Corporation, which the federal government had just bailed out in 1979, stated bluntly, "Free enterprise has gone to hell."[22] Was the American dream, that promise of "ever brighter tomorrows," dying or dead?

❖

In the official "party" speech following the next day's march, Nelson Johnson planned to tie the recent rise of Ku Klux Klan activity around the South to the "decay of capitalism." The Klan, he'd argue, "turn[ed] worker against worker, white against Black, Indian or Chicano, Protestant against Catholic or Jew. The Klan is being promoted to make it harder to fight this capitalist system which is the real source of the problems of the American people." If capitalism needed retrograde vigilantes to protect it, then the Klan was a symptom of the weakness in the American system.[23]

Others in the group took it as their duty to confront what they identified as expressions of evil in the world. As a Black child in rural South Carolina, Willena Cannon had witnessed the Klan burn a Black man to death in a barn. His screams still haunted her nightmares.[24] For Signe Waller—who, like Jim Waller, Paul Bermanzohn, and Mike Nathan, was Jewish—allowing the Klan to maintain the race line through terrorism was "tantamount to standing by and letting Hitler do what he did in Germany."[25] Histories, both personal and collective, had brought them to this place and time.

The activists gave voice to these powerful emotions in their agitprop and in an open letter addressed to "All KKK Members and Sympathizers," written ten days earlier and signed by Nelson. In it they'd not only called the Klan "scum" and "racist cowards" but challenged them "to attend our November 3rd rally in Greensboro." The letter promised the Klan would be "smashed physically" and shown "no mercy." The CWP harbored no hope of convincing the Klansmen to become more tolerant; their evil ideas and attitudes needed to be contained and eliminated.

Some CWP members were still trying to get their heads around what it meant to be openly communist in America. "As long as it was Workers Viewpoint, it was . . . safe. . . . It was respectable," said one member. But "once you said you were a communist, you just isolated yourself from everybody. It was so hard to convince people, even though people knew you weren't any different. . . . A lot of people said, 'couldn't you just not say that.'"[26]

Despite this, any doubts about the organization's name, strategy, or tactics were insignificant in comparison to the respect and loyalty each felt for the other "intelligent, committed people" in the group. "I love these people," one member said, "there's nobody, even family, that you come that close to."[27] At a level more fundamental than any ideological definition, the CWP members in North Carolina found joy in their shared dedication to understanding, facing, and acting against the pain they saw everywhere in the world.

❖

The group finally reached a compromise between those alarmed by Big Man's warning and those who hewed to Nelson's logic. A small security detail of a half dozen trusted people would secretly bring guns to the march in defiance of the police department's stipulations in the parade permit. In the improbable event that the Klan arrived and the need arose for the group to defend themselves, a few shotguns and small pistols would be kept close at hand, stashed in the back seats of cars—out of sight of the police but within easy reach.[28]

It grew late. Preparations were mostly in hand. Early the next morning, Nelson would prepare the venue he'd procured—without, he believed, the knowledge of the police—to replace the church for the conference.

As the night's activity wound down, each might have taken stock of the men and women they'd come to love both as friends and for their dedication to political struggle. Bill Sampson, a Harvard Divinity School graduate, and his wife, Dale, talented organizers working on logistics for the march, were, everyone knew, struggling to conceive a child. Willena Cannon, the former majorette at the North Carolina Agricultural and Technical (A&T) State University in Greensboro, sporting a magnificent Afro, thrilled the children in the Revolutionary Youth League with a surprise box of raspberry berets.

Jim Waller, despite stepping away from the medical profession to organize in the mills, attended to his comrades' and the mill workers' kids free of charge, always treating their various childhood ailments as much with humor as with medicine. The next morning, they all anticipated seeing Sandi Smith, the beautiful and bold mill organizer, recently separated from her husband, auntie to Nelson and Joyce's children, who would drive up from Kannapolis, where she'd begun rallying workers at the imposing Cannon Mills textile plant.

Up the road, at a meeting in Durham, more CWP members prepared for the march, including the doctors Paul Bermanzohn and Mike and Marty Nathan; Bermanzohn's wife, Sally; and Cesar Cauce, a big, jocular Cuban, working toward his PhD in history at Duke.

At the next day's march, they all hoped to demonstrate "leadership in the struggle against racism" among mill workers and members of Greensboro's working class and the city's Black communities. Nelson envisioned an opportunity for "the Party to shine out, to have a militant posture and a high profile, to attract people to join our ranks, to galvanize the movement." He "hoped for a large demonstration that would breathe and be alive with chants and a vibrant presence."[29]

The compromise plan didn't make Big Man feel any safer. He'd already decided to skip the march and likely pull back from his work with the CWP.

With a plan in place, however, the others stopped worrying about what the next day would hold.

Bring the children, they reminded one another.

SHADOWS

Eddie's watch read a few minutes after 11 p.m. Nervously flicking ash into a heavy glass tray on the polished coffee table, he swung his feet onto the tan carpet, turned down the TV, and reached for the telephone receiver. He winced in anticipation of a complaint from his back, still sore after surgery to repair a ruptured disk. The grimace, though, was as much psychic as physical.

A "bad feeling" knotted Eddie's gut. The phone call shattered the night like a starter's pistol, setting in motion something that Eddie hadn't been able to stop and from which he believed he could not extricate himself. He began to wish he'd gone with his wife to visit her family in Roanoke, Virginia, instead of sticking around Greensboro.[1]

Virgil Griffin's Piedmont twang vibrated through the line. His shift at the Buffalo Gas Station in Mount Holly, North Carolina, had just ended.

"We're on our way to Greensboro, Yank," reported the Grand Dragon of the Invisible Knights of the Ku Klux Klan.

Virgil and a couple of fellow Klansmen planned to hit the road by midnight. Three good ol' boys barreling northeast across the undulating Piedmont, through chilly fall air "Straightenin' the curves" and "flattenin' the hills," to quote Waylon Jenning's song for the new hit TV comedy *The Dukes of Hazzard*.[2] In Virgil's white Buick, they'd cover the hundred miles of dark interstate from rural Mount Holly to

Greensboro in an hour and a half, arriving like a bad memory in a city they barely knew. If Nelson Johnson and the CWP felt that the world wasn't moving fast enough toward equality, Virgil and his buddies—along with a loose network of racists spread throughout the country—inspired in part by a white supremacist fantasy novel advocating Anglo-Saxon revolution in America called *The Turner Diaries*,[3] were gathering to resist the changes they believed would plow their white heritage and entitlements under like winter rye in springtime. Virgil and his crew guarded what they described as a southern way of life: family histories rooted in the antebellum South and the Civil War, white culture defined against inferior Black culture, and connections to the land they saw slipping away, out of phase with an evolving America. To preserve these and a place in the world that they believed to be a birthright, they were willing to test the limits of "what the law would allow." And the law, as Big Man observed earlier that evening, had historically been quite generous toward Klan vigilantism that protected the social, political, and economic status quo.

Yank responded to Virgil's call with a thudding affirmative, his northern New Jersey accent an unmistakable tell of his northern roots, even over the phone line, and gave directions to a Waffle House around the corner from where he lived.

With two hours to kill before Virgil's crew showed up, Eddie pried his lean, six-foot-one-inch frame off the couch, grabbed a stack of posters, and slipped out the side door into the autumn night. The Hillsdale Park neighborhood stretched out north, west, and east from where Eddie stood, modest brick ranch homes on quarter-acre lots dotting gently rolling, twenty-year-old streets. The developers had preserved many of the largest oak trees and tulip poplars when they built the development in the late 1950s. Home sites for white working- and middle-class buyers (custom more than outdated covenants prevented the sale of the homes to Negroes) sold quickly. The new owners were enticed by "Greensboro's newest and most exciting location," a perfect symbol of the postwar American dream: urban living in the shade of an idealized pastoral past, to be found in well-equipped stand-alones of 1,100 to 1,500 square feet. One could relax in emerald, light-dappled backyards and dream of an ever-better, ever-richer future.[4]

The neighborhood suited Eddie, who still swooped his hair back into a short, lacquered 1950s-style pompadour. Now he slid into his spacious white Cadillac and eased out of the driveway, turning left, left, left again, and then right, rumbling northeast up Freeman Mill Road and across Florida Street toward Hampton Homes, a mostly Black public housing project. Once he hit Freeman Mill Road, he drove slowly, cigarette dangling from his lips, his gaze sweeping the telephone and streetlight poles.

When he spotted what he was looking for, he'd pull the car over, pick a poster off the leather bench seat, and step out into the shadows. The signs he hunted, the ones the cops hadn't already removed, were pasted about southeastern Greensboro, declaring "Death to the Klan" and announcing an Anti-Klan March and Conference for the next day, November 3. A photograph of a marching and chanting *mob of race mixers*, as Eddie saw it, filled the middle of the flyer. The notice had captured Eddie's attention and that of white supremacists throughout the state of North Carolina. It directed participants to the Windsor Community Center off East Lee Street at 11 a.m. on Saturday morning and, because the poster had been made before Nelson Johnson scrambled to line up a new conference venue, mistakenly advised that the 2 p.m. conversation would be held at the All-Nations Pentecostal Holiness Church at 1800 Freeman Mill Road.

Eddie worked quickly and precisely. He positioned his poster over the "Death to the Klan" placards, leaving only the word *Klan* visible. "Traitors beware," warned Eddie's sign. "Even now the crosshairs are on the back of YOUR necks. It's time for old-fashioned American Justice." Together with these words, the silhouette that now obscured the group photo was of a deep-rooted, old tree, like the oaks in Eddie's neighborhood. From one sturdy branch a man dangled from a rope, silent, alone, and dead: lynched. He'd use the activists' own sign against them, intercepting and redirecting their message, his threat of death canceling theirs. Eddie thought it a clever touch.[5]

When he finished, an articulation of "old-fashioned American Justice"—vigilante, white supremacist justice of a kind that most Americans associated with decades past—concealed a different aspiration, for racial and economic equality, also called *justice* by its partisans. The competing posters, pasted together, represented a struggle as old as America itself about race, class, and the very meaning of the founding American values that all are "created equal" and that there be "justice for all."

❖

Time did fly by. Eddie Dawson had come to live in Greensboro in 1963, the year President Kennedy was killed in Dallas. That's how he remembered arriving in the Tar Heel State, trailing his late wife back to her hometown, half-whipped by the bad choices he'd made, looking older than his forty-four years and ready for a fresh start. After years spent haunting the racetracks and gambling joints of New Jersey, Louisiana, and Florida, chasing the next thrill, the next drink, his marriage—if not his life—depended on a narrower path. As the country mourned, Eddie worked on figuring out who he was going to be in a city where Black college students had sparked a social revolution. After nearly three years of sit-ins and sit-downs, most, but not all, of Greensboro's downtown commercial establishments allowed Negroes across the threshold to shop, eat, or watch a movie, as long as they had enough money in their wallets to pay. Even so, in most other aspects of life—neighborhoods, schools, hospitals, and graveyards—segregation remained the rule rather than the exception in 1963.

Eddie didn't have much of a résumé to work with. Since he'd done time in federal prison for desertion and mouthing off at an Army superior during World War II—"I wasn't cut out" for the military, he would say[6]—he'd survived on bluff, bluster, and odd jobs. He found work with a siding company and began traveling around West Virginia, Virginia, and North Carolina, replacing aluminum siding or wooden clapboards with the latest and greatest technology, vinyl.

Eddie liked to tell the story of how he joined the Klan in 1965: "I was sitting at the counter having coffee and this fellow came up with a piece of literature and he started talking Ku Klux Klan, which I knew, [but] I was very, very limited to my knowledge of what they did or anything else."[7]

During his years in the South, Eddie had known Klansmen, but he'd never joined the organization. He shared their values, though: Eddie didn't "uphold Blacks." The "integration of marriage" made him so angry he could lose control of himself. When he heard this, the Klan recruiter said, "You'd make a good Klansman," and encouraged Eddie to fill out an application and show up at a Klan meeting. Eddie felt flattered.

The next Tuesday evening after work, Eddie drove down to the address the man had given him, a garage on Bessemer Avenue, north of downtown Greensboro. It was a warm summer night. A group of about fifteen men dressed in overalls were gathered outside, enjoying the weather and one another's company as they waited for the meeting to get started. Eddie stepped out of his Cadillac in a suit and tie and said hello in his thick New Jersey accent. The men scattered like roaches when the lights come on. "You'll have to understand how these people feel about a Yankee," Eddie would chuckle later. "When I said hello, everybody disappeared. . . . Just left me standing there. . . . [I thought] . . . they were, you know, strange people. I figured out later that if you come neat and driving the car I was driving, you're an FBI informant."[8]

Eddie overcame that first impression and became a Klansman. Two charismatic men then dominated the United Klans of America in North Carolina. A hard-driving salesman named Bob Jones carried the title the Exalted Cyclops and ran the state operation, while George Dorsett, the Klan's preacher—or Klud in Klan terminology— provided the moral imperative of white Christian supremacy.

Working in tandem, Jones and Dorsett barnstormed the state, setting a torrid schedule of nightly barbecues and ceremonial cross-burnings, attracting crowds that numbered in the thousands.[9]

Bob Jones provided the big picture of how Jews, Blacks, and communists were destroying America.[10] Publicly, at least, he denounced the use of violence, advocating the ballot box as the place to protect the interests of the white man and the virtues of the white woman. If Jones tried to make his bigoted conspiracies sound rational, Dorsett communed with his listeners' lizard brains: "I'm fighting not for myself, but for the children of America, to keep them from being raped, mugged, and knifed. We don't believe in violence, and we're not going to have violence, if we have to kill every n—— in America."[11]

Applications to become dues-paying members poured in after Jones's and Dorsett's performances. By the time Eddie joined, there were as many as two hundred Klaverns, or Klan lodges, around the state, boasting upward of ten thousand members—more, it was believed, than could be flushed from all the other southern states combined. Guilford County and its county seat, Greensboro, claimed several hundred Klansmen, members of about eight Klaverns. These went by anodyne names, such as the Guilford County Booster Club; there, white men of different social stations enjoyed one another's company and organized both public and secret resistance to keep integration from spreading from the downtown lunch counters to white schools and neighborhoods.[12]

Eddie quickly "built up a reputation" as someone who'd "just as soon shoot you as look at you"—someone who, in the face of danger, would "brazen it out," rising quickly through the ranks of the most numerous, powerful state Klan organization in the country.[13] Within months, Jones and Dorsett and other top Klansmen trusted Eddie with an invitation into their Inner Circle. After all the people drove home from the rented cornfields with their handbills and Klan magazines, their bellies full of roast pig and their minds aflame with patriotism and pride in their white, Protestant heritage, a handful of men would jam into a parked car. "And that's the troublemakers,"

Eddie would say. "These people are present at every meeting; they're present at every rally, all activities, street walks, etc."[14] Those big corn-field meetings were "a joke" and bored Eddie to tears. Inside the car, however, the secret group planned and then carried out Klan terror against racial mixing, left-wing politics, the Rothschilds, FBI infiltra-tors, and anyone else who interfered with the supremacy of those who were Protestant and Anglo-Saxon—the essential ingredients, according to the Klan, of being 100 percent American. "This ain't no Boy Scout outfit," Eddie knew. "You wanna be big, you gotta act big."[15] For Eddie, the Klan intrigue replaced the thrill of gambling on the ponies.

After Eddie joined the Klan, he quit the vinyl siding business and went out on his own as a housepainter and handyman. The network helped him get business. For work, Eddie pulled on clean white T-shirts and white painters' pants. On his own time, he still dressed sharp in broad-shouldered suits and skinny ties, like a mob-ster or a gumshoe straight out of the '50s. He drove his signature white Cadillac. What he lacked in schooling he made up for with keen observation, an excellent memory, and a penchant for intrigue. The furrowed brow and lines around his eyes suggested the kind of middle-aged, white male authority that believed itself entitled to im-plicit respect. Eddie's craggy, rather handsome face possessed the malleable gift of a character actor whose role binds a movie's plot, stepping in as cowboy, FBI agent, or Madison Avenue ad executive ready to pitch a new line, a glass of whiskey near at hand. His ability to shape-shift, aided in the South by his New Jersey accent, would serve him well.

In 1967, police in Alamance County, next door to Guilford County, arrested Eddie and his Klan friends for shooting into a store where Black and white people had gathered together. Eddie served nine months in prison. In 1969, shortly after leaving jail for the first of-fense, Eddie and Virgil Griffin provoked a riot with local Black peo-ple in the small North Carolina town of Swan Quarter. This time a court clipped Eddie's wings, sentencing him to five years' probation and a $1,000 fine. When the United Klans of America refused to pay his penalty, Eddie accused the Imperial Wizard, Robert Shelton, of skimming legal fees. In response, the UKA banished him from their ranks.[16]

A short time later, Eddie found himself in the Greensboro FBI office facing a choice between being sent "up the river" or providing information on his fellow white supremacists. FBI operations created rivalries and betrayals, which led to splits. New Klan factions sprouted like mushrooms on a rotten log. So there was always a new Klan group to join. By the late 1960s and early 1970s, the FBI had informants in just about all of the groups. In fact, in some Klaverns, nearly every member passed information along to the Bureau, informants informing on informants.[17] Eddie's Klan friends, some of whom were surely informants, too, didn't know about the deal he made.

❖

Sometime after Nelson Johnson departed Jim and Signe Waller's house to catch a few hours of sleep, Eddie Dawson finished postering and went home. He stretched out on the plaid couch in his wood-paneled den, inhaled one cigarette right after the next, and waited for Virgil.

The paneled walls in the dark room were mostly bare, but a small collection of figurines peeked from a corner shelf. They represented different likenesses of the same character, each staring out from "deep sorrowful wells," as one journalist described Weary Willie's eyes, eyes that pulled attention from the tattered clothes, the red clown nose, white-painted lips, and scruffy beard.

Wandering Civil War veterans and deserters living in a limbo of transient hobo camps during the 1860s came to be known as "Weary Willies." In the 1920s, a trapeze artist named Emmett Kelly reimagined Willie as a circus tramp. As part of his show, Kelly dressed in rags, painted his face, and wielded a broom to sweep the spotlight he both avoided and craved into tidy points of bright light and then under a rug. He'd say of his creation's fast fame: "Maybe it's Willie's attempt at a little dignity in spite of everything that tickles folks. . . . Maybe it's because everyone can feel superior to me. Or maybe when I stare at 'em, it's just nervousness."[18]

Whichever it was, the American people couldn't take their eyes off Willie. Kelly had invented a sad fool who became "the most familiar clown in America," as the *New York Times* reported in the performer's obituary, published seven months earlier, in March 1979. The nostalgia Weary Willie tendered admirers such as Eddie was, perhaps, not so much for a golden age as for a past they could relate to, one fired in hardness and glazed with sentimental humor.

The fifty-nine-year-old Eddie related to something in Weary Willie: An echo of the Great Depression's tough times that shaped him? The costume that both obscured and revealed a man's identity? The lonely eyes, perhaps, that riveted an uneasy audience?

With bits of money that he could spare from his handyman jobs, Eddie picked up the ceramic reproductions when he found them and placed them on the shelf in his den.

Virgil called again, and a few minutes later, Eddie pulled into the parking lot to discover that the Waffle House's canary-yellow sign had gone dark. Eddie collected Virgil and his companions and led them to another all-night café he knew.

It was two in the morning and quiet in Greensboro. The occasional police car floated slowly down the middle of the city streets. A midnight showing of Woody Allen's *Manhattan* let out from the Janus Theater in north Greensboro, along with the weekly screening of *The Rocky Horror Picture Show*. Insomniacs at home could catch the Los Angeles Lakers and Magic Johnson, who along with fellow rookie Larry Bird was busy transforming the National Basketball Association into a commercial juggernaut, or tune in to a classic movie, *Who's Afraid of Virginia Woolf?* at 2:30 or Burt Lancaster in *The Rainmaker* at 2:50.[19]

The predawn embraced those drawn by circumstance or predilection to Greensboro's id hours. All-night partiers set out for private liquor houses in East Greensboro, to find card games, or to search out the ever-growing marketplace of dealers peddling cocaine and heroin. A couple of theaters showing blue movies kept their screens flickering into the wee hours, and the Peacock Massage parlor tantalized from the back pages of the newspaper with offers of "complete massages" just beyond the city limits to the south.

Three weeks earlier, Eddie Dawson had called Virgil on the phone. The two hadn't seen each other in a couple of years, but news of the "Death to the Klan" rally had been spreading like wildfire through North Carolina's white supremacist network, allowing them to look past old grudges and rivalries to focus on the brewing "Jew/communist/n——" conspiracy. Virgil invited Eddie to brief his Klavern on the communist activity in Greensboro and what to expect if they were to confront the November 3 marchers. On October 20, Eddie drove the hundred miles to the Lincoln County fairgrounds and—after the pig roast and speeches, after the cross-burning—followed Virgil, dressed in flowing scarlet robes, into a meeting hall. The diminutive, fiery Virgil introduced Eddie, noting that they'd known each other for more than a decade. Though Virgil was in his thirties and Eddie was on the cusp of sixty, they were both considered members of the North Carolina Klan's old guard. Among the nearly one hundred Kluxers in the room, some had surely heard the rumors that Eddie and Virgil assassinated Klansmen they suspected of snitching to the Feds. That night, Griffin recounted a brawl between Klansmen and local Black people that he and Dawson had participated in, in Morganton, North Carolina, in 1975, when the police hung back and watched the fight. It was up to them, Virgil exhorted his men, to take "the country back from the Communist Party" and "from the n——s" even if "we have to get in the streets and find blood up to our knees by God. . . . Fight for your country!"[20]

Eddie stood up and waved a copy of the CWP's "Death to the Klan" poster at the crowd, as if fanning a campfire to life. He painted a desperate picture of a city under siege by communists disrupting college campuses and production in the mills. "I'm telling you guys right now, it's going to be a knock-down, drag-out fight,"[21] with "big buck n——s."[22] But, Eddie insisted, everyone should go to confront the marchers; it was their "patriotic duty."[23]

Who, Eddie wanted to know, planned to come to Greensboro? Eighty hands shot into the air.

"What about guns?" someone asked. "Should we bring guns?"

"I'm not your father," Eddie responded. The men could bring guns, he said—"you might need them." But he insisted they not conceal their weapons. "There will be wall-to-wall police there. A gun—if it's hidden, a bulge is seen—you will be arrested, and you better have the bond money in your back pocket."[24]

Eddie again asked who planned to come. About forty or fifty men raised their hands, ready to fight.

❖

Now, whether he liked it or not, the first of Eddie's recruits had arrived in Greensboro.[25] With Virgil were two men and a young woman. Coleman "Johnny" Pridmore and Jerry Paul Smith were friends and laborers from Catawba County, both of whom held titled positions in Griffin's Invisible Knights of the KKK. Smith, the Klan faction's chief of security, tall with long stringy hair and a penchant for rough talk, brought along a homemade sign that read "James Earl Ray is my hero."[26] The "girl" with Virgil wasn't the Klansman's wife, which annoyed Eddie. It wasn't that Virgil's virtue—or lack of it— bothered Eddie, but he got the idea that Virgil, whom he'd known as long as he'd been in the Klan, had come up in the middle of the night more to "shack up with the broad" than to make plans for the following day.[27]

After they drank coffee and ate sandwiches, the small group set out to see where the march would end the next day. Virgil and the girl rode with Eddie. They drove past the Windsor Community Center, where the posters directed demonstrators to gather before the start of the anti-Klan march.[28] Then at 1800 Freeman Mill Road, Eddie pulled into the empty parking lot of a small shopping mall. They were in a Black section of town, surrounded by Black people asleep in the houses and apartment buildings nearby. Eddie pointed out the Cosmos Club II, a Black-owned club with an unassuming entrance.

That's where they're going to end up after the march, Eddie told Virgil. This was not the church location printed on the posters that Eddie covered up earlier that night. It was a detail that Nelson Johnson believed he'd kept secret. Eddie would never reveal how he discovered the CWP's plan.

They stayed only a minute or two in the parking lot before heading off again. At three in the morning Eddie dropped Virgil and the girl at a motel. Jerry Paul Smith and Johnny Pridmore climbed into Eddie's Cadillac and rode with him down Randleman Road to a little house with a huge Confederate flag stuck in the yard outside. Brent Fletcher, three-quarters gone, was busy entertaining himself with a gallon bottle of vodka. A half dozen shotguns lay in racks or leaned against the house walls.

The four men sat for a while, talking Klan talk, drinking, admiring Brent's guns, and speculating as to how many Klansmen might show up later that morning.[29]

MORNING

It was still dark on the morning of November 3, 1979, when Nelson Johnson stepped out onto the porch of his home at 1111 Alamance Church Road, just inside the southeastern limits of the municipality, which had been ambitiously annexing county land for forty years, swelling its territory from eighteen to sixty square miles to accommodate some of the largest textile and tobacco factories in the world.[1] Woods, cornfields, and dairy farms surrounded the one-acre property even though it lay less than three miles from Greensboro's struggling downtown and only a couple miles more from the convenient sprawl of new shopping malls.

Built in 1927, the same year Charles Lindbergh visited to break ground on the city's air terminal, the simple bungalow, with its high, broad porch, white clapboard first floor, and gabled, green-shingled second story, had proved a good place to start a family. The owners, professors at Howard University in Washington, DC, supported Nelson and Joyce's activism and didn't pressure the couple for the rent when money grew tight. Nelson made improvements to the house. He built bunk beds for his two daughters and renovated the kitchen, skillfully joining wood recovered from old houses and barns into counters and cabinets until the seams between the various boards vanished. The woodworking relaxed him, and during the hot months he'd plant a few watermelon vines in the backyard, a nod to his youth on the family farm in eastern North Carolina's Halifax County.

The temperature hung in the midforties, and a bitter mist fogged the twilight. Behind him, upstairs in the house, his wife, Joyce, and their two daughters still slept, warmed by heat from a woodstove. In a few hours, he'd be back to collect them.

Nelson pulled on a fall jacket and tugged a wool beret onto his head to ward off the damp autumn chill. Notes tucked into the pocket of his jacket outlined the talk he planned to give that afternoon at the anti–Ku Klux Klan conference, after the march he'd been organizing for months.[2] From the porch he could barely see through the fog to the other side of the street, and he worried that the weather might keep people away from the rally.

He hopped down the eight steps and swung behind the wheel of the '72 Buick station wagon, a hand-me-down from Joyce's mother and stepfather in Richmond. Turning the engine, he automatically spun the radio dial to WEAL and the steady stream of gospel and R & B that banished sleep as well as any cup of coffee. His first stop that morning would be the Cosmos II nightclub on the corner of Freeman Mill Road and Florida Street.

When the Pentecostal Church pastor, frightened by rumors of Klan violence filtering in from the Greensboro Police Department, withdrew his invitation to host the afternoon conference, Nelson reached out to an old friend. Richard Bowling IV, the man who'd "brought disco to North Carolina," agreed to make his nightclub available provided Nelson could bring in lights and sound equipment and find enough chairs to accommodate the crowd.[3] The last-minute inconvenience, Nelson thought, as he set out to turn the dance club into a conference room, was the result of nothing more than "slimy tactics" intended to interfere with the interracial labor organizing that made the police and their bosses uncomfortable. He didn't believe the rumors of violence. He'd said so to his comrades and to the press. No one, not a single police officer, including the handful of Black police officers in the GPD, had warned *him* of any brewing trouble. Given that fact, Nelson chose the club directly across the street from the threatened church so he wouldn't have to alter the march route detailed, turn by turn, in the parade permit finally approved by the police department.

❖

Despite the glum economic news, it promised to be a rather typical fall Saturday in this midsize industrial city. After a long workweek, many planned to stick close to the couch and fridge to watch football. The broadcast of the tilt between the Demon Deacons of Wake Forest from next-door Winston-Salem and South Carolina's Clemson Tigers would flicker into homes at noon. Fitness buffs lined up for the Diet Pepsi 10K and "fun run." Other weekend warriors, including several members of the FBI's Resident Agency in Greensboro, planned to brave the uncertain weather and enter late-season golf and tennis tournaments. Across town, at North Carolina A&T, the tailgating kicked off hours before the pigskin rumble against Tennessee State and their record-setting quarterback, Joe Adams.[4]

Around the city, as coffeepots began to gurgle and puff, newspapers were slipped into mailboxes or chucked onto stoops. To the west and north, boys and girls delivered the Saturday edition of *Greensboro Daily News* (the *Greensboro Record* was the city's evening paper). South of Market Street and east of Murrow Boulevard, youths pitched the weekly *Carolina Peacemaker* onto porches. Many of the *Peacemaker*'s readers also received and read the *Daily News* or the *Record*. Among the fifteen thousand subscribers to the Black newspaper, however, fewer than one hundred white people made a habit of absorbing the view from the other side of the color line or the title quote borrowed from Martin Luther King Jr.: "We must learn to live together as brothers, lest we all die together as fools."[5]

Readers of all three city papers were following Edwin S. "Jim" Melvin's campaign for an unprecedented fifth term as the city's mayor. Melvin, his hair set like a mansard roof over a square, determined face, had spent his adult life tirelessly and optimistically promoting his hometown as a banker, a Jaycee, a faithful congregant of the First Presbyterian Church, a city councilman, and, since 1971, mayor.

Now, for the first time in years, he faced a serious challenge. Sol Jacobs, a sixty-nine-year-old, Jewish, retired delicatessen owner a quarter century Melvin's senior quipped wryly to the *Peacemaker*, "I think [Mayor Melvin] has done a tremendous job from his limited point of view." As a candidate, Jacobs promoted "expanded mass transit and better public access to cable television," issues aimed at improving the lives of Greensboro's poorer voters. It was another issue he championed, however, that vaulted Jacobs into contention.[6]

When Jacobs announced his candidacy, he voiced his support for district-based city council elections. The proposed shift from the at-large voting scheme to one under which councilors would represent specific neighborhoods promised to change the makeup and complexion of the six-person city council from a generally affluent, self-selected gathering of white men to a group that in both class and race more accurately represented Greensboro's population. In a debate that Melvin had tried to avoid, Jacobs hammered at the issue: "I'm for a ward system. . . . City Council is not aware of the needs of the entire city. . . . Ninety percent of all the people who have served on the City Council have been from the Northwest section of the city." No one had to tell Greensboro's citizens that "Northwest" meant affluent and white.[7]

Melvin bristled at the idea that his programs didn't benefit all Greensboro's citizens, lashing out at anyone who suggested he couldn't govern everyone equally, that he couldn't represent Blacks as well as any Black elected official. The economic development plans he pushed, he said, were "color-blind." Changing city council, Melvin complained, would just make his pursuit of progress less efficient. "I have never in my life seen a council so dominated by a mayor, so afraid to make suggestions," observed Sol Jacobs as he campaigned across the city, feeding a sense that Melvin had grown more conservative over time and was losing touch with his own working-class roots. By the late '70s, Melvin was president of a savings and loan bank and had moved his family into a spacious house in the ritzy New Irving Park neighborhood, home to the top managers of the city's big businesses. Even his supporters now described him as "impatient," "sensitive," and "touchy."[8] A *Greensboro Daily News* editorial pointed out Melvin's limitations, admitting that the mayor too often responded to critics with a "hot temper and . . . sharp tongue" and noting that he lacked the "imagination and creativity that makes a well-run city an exciting one." Melvin's energetic optimism, it seemed, had soured, though his personal fortunes as the son of a gas station owner had risen. Perhaps Melvin's impatience was connected to grief. In 1972, two Black men had robbed his father's gas station, shooting the senior Melvin and leaving him to die.

Despite his apparent shortcomings, the editors endorsed Melvin's bid for a fifth term, noting Jacobs's lack of political experience and advising that Melvin had run the city "efficiently and responsibly."[9]

Local Black businessman B. J. Battle didn't mince words, calling the resistance of Melvin and other white leaders to a district voting system "a fear-and-racist campaign." The local branch of the National Association for the Advancement of Colored People (NAACP) and the Greensboro Citizens Association weren't buying Melvin's defense of at-large voting either. Both organizations encouraged their Black constituents to back Jacobs's bid.[10]

During the debate, neither Jacobs nor Melvin was asked what he thought of Nelson Johnson. Both, however, were on the record with their opinions. Jacobs admired Nelson as an unusually gifted community organizer.[11] Melvin, on the other hand, considered Nelson to be not only an adversary, but "dangerous."

❖

If Nelson read his horoscope in the *Carolina Peacemaker* that Saturday morning of November 3, 1979, it didn't give the Taurus a moment's pause: "Everything is against you—and while it's against you, you might as well sit down and pray." He wasn't superstitious or, at this juncture in his life as a self-identified communist, much interested in the metaphysics of prayer. He would have agreed that Jim Melvin and Greensboro's powerful business leaders were aligned against his efforts on behalf of his people and Greensboro's working poor. He knew for a fact that the city's police disliked both him and the planned march. These realities, however, gave him reason to stand up, not sit down.

After setting up at Cosmos II, Nelson drove to Cypress Street, sweeping into Signe and Jim Waller's crowded house already crackling with anticipation. Nelson grabbed coffee and a light breakfast, conferring with Jim about the myriad details—"sound truck, placards, music, leaflets, song leaders, marshals, people showing up on time"—that clamored for attention and order inside his head.[12] They expected several hundred people from Greensboro, scores of arrivals from other North Carolina cities, and even a few folks from southwestern Virginia to join the march against the Klan. As the march organizer, Nelson's goal was to make all the obstacles and last-minute adjustments invisible to the demonstrators so they could immerse themselves in the moment, chanting and singing through Greensboro's streets and neighborhoods.

By the time Nelson left Jim and Signe's, the weather had begun to clear and the temperature to rise. Nelson mentioned "how beautiful the day was turning out" to Jim before he crossed town to collect Joyce and the girls. He dropped them at the Windsor Community Center, the staging area for marchers arriving from out of town, and then drove the half mile to the corner of Everitt Street and Carver Drive.

It wasn't even 10 a.m. when Nelson parked the blue Buick along Everitt Street. Noting that he had arrived before anyone else, he ambled over to the Paradise Drive-Inn for a burger and, perhaps, to recruit a few of the Black workers who frequented the renowned local greasy spoon.[13] There, the workers rubbed shoulders with the neighborhood's "lumpen proletariat," the drug dealers, hustlers, and chronically unemployed attending to their hangovers. Many of the workers and lumpen alike lived in the public housing across the street, Morningside Homes.[14] They were the people with whom Nelson had been working since his mid-1960s arrival in Greensboro, the people he saw as most in need of equality, some fairness, better representation down at city hall, and a break.

❖

When Morningside Homes opened its doors in 1952, Greensboro's Negro community viewed the 380 units as a hopeful endeavor, a government-supported stepping stone to help poor members of the segregated population move from ramshackle poverty toward a dignified, if still segregated, working-class lifestyle. (The Smith Homes development, about three miles west of Morningside, opened for poor white residents just months prior to the completion of Morningside.) At around the same time, mostly white city leaders rezoned the side of Everitt Street opposite Morningside Homes for commercial development, a stretch that would soon fill up with a laundromat, a convenience store, a pool hall, and the Paradise Drive-Inn, which fast became a destination for A&T students in search of savory fatback sandwiches, sausage biscuits, and live jazz.[15]

Twenty-eight years and a civil rights movement later, the Morningside Homes residents were still nearly all Black, and now, rather than appearing in the newspaper's community calendar as the site of teacher conferences and civic association meetings, the units were more likely to be mentioned in the police reports for drug busts and violent crime. Somewhere along the line, the dream hadn't died, exactly, but it had been deferred, run down by cynicism and bitterness. For many, Morningside Homes now represented less a fresh start than a frustrating dead end—or, as one blues-inspired journalist would later call the project, "a colorful patchwork of joy and despair."[16] Joy did exist there, as did community. Neighbors looked after one another's children and nurtured them toward a better future. But to many, whether the best future for Black children in 1979 would be racially integrated or separate, a quarter century after the Supreme Court's *Brown v. Board of Education* decision, remained an open question.

Nelson exited the Paradise Drive-Inn and drove back down to the

Windsor Community Center. About fifty people had gathered there—renewing, as the weather had, his hope that the march and conference would be significant. Joyce activated the crowd, leading songs and chants through a megaphone. Nelson spotted what appeared to be an unmarked police car occupied by a plainclothes cop snapping photographs of the assembly. Ignoring the anticipated surveillance, he collected his daughters and returned to the corner of Everitt and Carver Drive, the slender artery that gave access to Morningside's interior.[17]

By 11 a.m., the parking spaces along both sides of Everitt Street were filling up as people trickled in, milling around the cracked asphalt and fading lawns of Morningside Homes. Nelson Johnson and Alan Blix, a CWP member who'd driven down from Virginia, set to work installing a massive sound system for speakers and singers onto the back of a borrowed flatbed truck, while Dale Sampson pasted "Death to the Klan" flyers—the same posters that Eddie Dawson covered up with his "old-fashioned American Justice" posters—to the truck's sides.[18]

Dale's husband, Bill Sampson, and Jim Waller, concerned primarily with agent provocateurs planted by the police to stir up trouble, conferred about security issues and tested their walkie-talkies. A few of the men in the security detail wore blue hard hats, which made them easy to spot, that would offer a modicum of protection during a brawl. Bill Sampson had wedged an athletic cup into his jockstrap when he dressed that morning, a shield against kicks or well-aimed rocks.[19] He didn't want anything to jeopardize his and Dale's efforts to get pregnant. The few guns they'd brought—the compromise reached during the previous night's debate—remained locked in their owners' cars.

Jim's wife, Signe, picked up a stack of *Workers Viewpoint* newspapers to peddle to marchers for a quarter apiece. Dr. Mike Nathan prepared the first aid kit that he'd carry along in his "beat-up red station wagon"[20] for anyone who might turn an ankle or suffer dehydration during the two-mile walk. The big Cuban graduate student,

Cesar Cauce, unloaded two-by-two-foot picket sticks from the back of a small pickup truck.

Between them, the organizers tallied decades of experience leading militant marches to galvanize community energy. They were like directors of elaborate, provocative street theater, moving people around their communities in an effort, as the German socialist playwright Bertolt Brecht coached, to usher in a new historical reality by making "the familiar strange." One CWP member strummed his guitar and sang, warming up the crowd. The traditional music floated over the neighborhood and drew the curious, who discovered that the words they knew—"We shall not, we shall not be moved"— blended with provocative slogans and lyrics: "We'll smash the Klan, we shall not be moved." Chanted out loud, the new words felt both transgressive and empowering.

Dressed in the khaki shirts their mothers had hand-stitched the night before and new red berets, the surprise gifts of Willena Cannon, the children of the activists conversed with neighborhood kids in Pop Warner football uniforms. The children joked and laughed and took turns poking at a Klan effigy that dangled like bait from the end of a stick. "Well, look at your fashion plates," Nelson teased his two daughters when he spotted them in the bright tams, giving each a quick, proud hug.[21]

Catherine Greenlee, the head of the Morningside Homes resident's council, stood with the singers, keeping a watchful eye on the preparations taking place in her neighborhood.

The tension Nelson Johnson had felt earlier that morning melted away. The weather turned lovely; the energy pulsating in the growing crowd excited him. The scene, he thought, "had charisma."[22]

Just after eleven, Sandi Smith, Joyce's best friend, auntie to Nelson and Joyce's two daughters, and one of the CWP's most electric and committed organizers, arrived in a car carrying mill workers from the JP Stevens Cannon Mills plant in Kannapolis. When Sandi stepped out of her car, something didn't feel quite right. At all the protests and marches she'd ever participated in, there'd always been an oppressive police presence. As the same doubt flickered on the periphery of others' minds, Sandi gave it a voice: "Why ain't there no cops here?"[23]

❖

Eddie Dawson roused himself at 7 a.m., shaking off bleariness like a street dog after an all-night prowl. He then called Detective Jerry "Rooster" Cooper of the GPD to let him know that men were gathering at Brent Fletcher's and that, when he'd dropped Jerry Paul Smith and Coleman Pridmore off there a few hours earlier, there'd been a few guns present.[24]

Before eight, he pulled in at the intersection of South Elm Street and Randleman Road, noting the cars strewn over the patchy yard around Brent Fletcher's outsize Confederate flag as if they'd been dropped by an early morning tornado. A new sign decorated the gathering spot, which read "Black apes, red scum, beware." Men—about fifteen of them by this time—in blue jeans, feed caps, and flannel shirts were filtering in and out of the little house.

Dawson recognized several of them. Eddie's old friend and fellow Klan conspirator James Buck was there. Like Eddie, Buck had drifted down to North Carolina from the North, Wisconsin in his case, like silt to the bottom of a slow-moving river. A Yankee and longtime Klansman, Buck had vouched for Eddie, bringing the Jersey boy into the Klan's Inner Circle. In the 1960s and early '70s, trusted by the "echelon" to do the secret society's dirty work, they'd been enforcers together and arrested together.[25]

Virgil Griffin had already made it over to Brent Fletcher's from the motel room where Eddie had dropped him just four or five hours earlier. The Grand Dragon was operating on as little sleep as Eddie, or perhaps less, given his amorous intentions toward the young woman he'd brought along from Mount Holly.

Inside the three-room house, Fletcher stayed inebriated, a perpetual state for him since he'd returned from Vietnam missing a leg and haunted by nightmares he couldn't shake.[26] There were other veterans among the crowd that morning, including Glenn Miller, a career soldier, who'd recently retired from the Army to dedicate his life to the white power movement.[27] But even those present who hadn't gone overseas felt betrayed by a government that hadn't done everything necessary to win the Vietnam War and by a society that no longer seemed to value the military or to acknowledge the horrors "our boys" had experienced.[28] And then there was the Cold War apparatus, hollowed out by corruption and hypocrisy, that rattled its sabers and sacrificed its youth to the dire threat of international communism, yet allowed homegrown communists to march through city streets chanting "Revolution." Well, if the communists had the First Amendment to protect their ideas, the patriots gathered in Brent Fletcher's house had the Second Amendment to protect white people from having their country snatched away from them.

Eddie didn't know many of the people present: such as the thick, squat man wearing a shapeless hat and a mustache who showed off a model AR-180 semiautomatic rifle, offering to sell the high-powered guns to anyone who wanted one—or the enormous, bearded man who Virgil said needed to talk with Eddie. Virgil took Eddie and the giant into Brent's bedroom. "Tell him what you just told to me," Virgil ordered, craning his neck at the hulking figure.[29]

"I have a tear gas canister," said Roland Wayne Wood, who held the item in a gloved hand so as not to leave fingerprints. He wanted to bring it along to hurl at the marchers. It's a bad idea, said Eddie, explaining that the streets were narrow in the neighborhood where they were going: "We're going to end up with the bad end of the canister."[30]

"Tell that to my lieutenant," responded Wood. When Wood said "lieutenant," rather than "Grand Dragon" or "Klud" or one of the other positions of authority within the Klan, Eddie knew there were Nazis in the crowd, which explained the presence of some of the people he didn't recognize. Just a baby when World War II ended, Virgil, he thought, always had a thing for Nazis. Eddie enlisted in 1941. Though he couldn't tolerate the Army hierarchy, he'd never cottoned to the idea that the Nazis weren't the enemy.[31]

A little before 10 a.m., Eddie told Virgil that he'd forgotten to take his medicine and drove home. Now he called "Rooster" Cooper a second time to let him know that more men with even more guns were staging to confront the communists. (Cooper would later deny both this call and the 7 a.m. call.)[32]

When Eddie returned to Brent Fletcher's house for the third time that morning, he carried a copy of the parade permit, signed by Nelson Johnson. Buck and Eddie stretched a map of Greensboro out on Fletcher's little kitchen table. By this time, more people had shown up, pushing the number of those gathered close to forty. Most of them had driven in from the rural parts of the state, the industrial countryside, where they patched together marginal lives. When their fortunes waned as loggers or long-haul truck drivers, they'd pick up work as lintheads at the big mills, supplementing wage work with truck gardens and a backyard hog pen.[33]

Eddie read the parade permit, and Buck scanned the map for the indicated streets, searching for the intersection of Carver and Everitt, following the directions written out by hand, street by street, turn by turn, from the start of the march to its finish. If they didn't know before, they understood now that Nelson Johnson and the CWP had agreed not to bring guns to the march. They knew that, per their agreement with the police, they would be carrying nothing more dangerous than two-by-two sticks to which they would staple their anti-Klan propaganda.

While Eddie and Buck memorized the route they'd take, Jerry Paul Smith started loading guns into the yellow van and a blue Ford Fairlane. Virgil Griffin stood on Brent Fletcher's front stoop, surveying the activity. A nondescript, tan-colored sedan parked across the road caught his eye. Unmarked cop car, he sensed reflexively. Whether he thought of it as danger or protection, he didn't bother to mention the sedan to Eddie or anyone else.[34]

Just before 11 a.m., Eddie got fidgety, causing the restless crowd to filter out of the house into the yard. "Who's in charge here?" someone else yelled. "I guess he is," Virgil answered, jabbing his thumb at Eddie. It was time, someone shouted, "to kick some god-damned n—— ass."[35]

Eddie turned surly and started rushing everyone into their cars. It's time to get going, he announced, checking his watch. He and his buddy would lead the caravan in Buck's pickup truck. "If anyone jumps you, fight back," Virgil advised as they piled into the minimum number of cars needed to transport thirty-three men and four women.

In their haste, they left a car behind. A teenager had rushed off to pick up a sandwich for his stepfather, Raeford Milano Caudle, the squat man selling automatic rifles. At the on-ramp to I-85, the convoy of eight cars pulled over to wait for the ninth. A few minutes later it caught up to them, and Eddie Dawson, cigarette in hand, strolled back along the line of cars and directed the blue Ford Fairlane with its trunk full of guns into the penultimate spot. It pulled in right in front of Lawrence Morgan's canary-yellow van, which carried eleven men, including Jerry Paul Smith, Coleman Pridmore, and the massive Roland Wayne Wood.[36]

As they paused there beside the highway, none of them seemed to notice the police photographer snapping pictures from a parked car above the ramp driven by Eddie's police handler, Rooster Cooper.

Less than ten minutes later they were rolling again, guided by James Buck and Eddie Dawson toward Morningside Homes in southeastern Greensboro.

Buck turned onto Everitt Street, and Eddie looked back to make sure the others were following. A moment later, they crested a low rise and saw the gathering before them.

Just before 11 a.m., Officer April Wise, one of a small band of women on the GPD, answered a call to a domestic dispute at Morningside Homes. When she parked, she observed "a crowd of people on the south side of Everitt Street across from Carver Drive." The gathering demonstrators, she would note, "appeared quiet and everything seemed calm." Then, minutes after she arrived, she received a radio call from the police dispatcher ordering her to leave the area.[37]

4

SHOOTING

Shortly before 11 a.m., Matt Sinclair and Ed Boyd parked the WTVD Chevy Blazer in the Calvary Baptist Church parking lot across from Morningside Homes. On his way to Greensboro, a cup or two of coffee and a half dozen smokes into the day, Boyd's eyes, perpetually hidden behind a pair of his signature Ray-Bans, had alighted on a maple tree "absolutely ablaze" with fall foliage. The beauty of it lingered in his mind as he surveyed the colorful, boisterous scene before him.

The all-Black news team set to work arranging their equipment. They'd record the songs, the chants, an interview or two, and the start of the march and then hustle back to Durham, edit the video, and have it ready to roll for the evening news. Sinclair was the on-air reporter and Boyd the cameraman, two years into the dream career he'd stumbled on after a stint in the Air Force. "It's not work when you find something you love to do," he'd say, quoting his grandaddy. He ran on nicotine and caffeine, kept a go-bag in his car, and loved the everyday adrenaline of "meeting different people in different situations."[1]

Boyd noted several newspaper photographers and TV crews from Greensboro, High Point, and Winston-Salem, a testament to the organizers' ability to capture media attention with their "Death to the Klan" rhetoric. It all seemed so strange: the Klan, communism, brash language flying on both sides. But it was too intriguing to miss, even if the news directors didn't really know what to make of it all. Boyd believed he understood the activists, however. He'd grown up Black in

Oxford, North Carolina, where in 1970 white men gunned down a Black man in the street and were acquitted of the murder. Boyd could trace the thread of white supremacy in North Carolina history from the bloody 1898 overthrow of a Black and white "fusion" government in Wilmington, through Jim Crow and the civil rights movement, into the restless late 1960s and '70s. Powerful interests continued to resist change, he thought, and racists don't forget how to kill.[2]

"We shall not be moved," the children were singing, when another voice pierced the bright fall morning. "Here comes the Klan!"

When he heard that clarion voice—a young boy's?—Ed Boyd swung his camera to the left, picking up a line of vehicles as they rolled into the neighborhood, filling the narrow lane left open between cars parked on both sides of Everitt Street. Then he saw the Confederate tag, stuck proudly in the place of the front license plate of a Bonneville, and zoomed in. It's a "box canyon," he thought, nowhere to run or hide, the lens of his sunglasses glued to the viewfinder.

Signe Waller, a stack of *Workers Viewpoint* newspapers tucked under her arm, was talking politics with a young man named Percy Sims who appeared inebriated. Perhaps he'd followed Nelson down to the corner from the Paradise Drive-Inn. "The Klan works together with the capitalists," she explained. "And the communists," remarked the addled young man. "No, we're communists," Signe corrected him, "what that means is that we're working for the people. That's why we're out here."[3] Signe smiled, her spirit buoyed by the thought that after the months of work preparing for this day, she and Jim would get a break, a few days at the beach, maybe, away from organizing. Even class traitors deserve a holiday on occasion.[4] Moments earlier, Bill and Jim mentioned that they had picked up Klan talk on their walkie-talkies, but no one knew what it meant.[5] As the cars rolled up on her right, she kept talking and smiling, oblivious to the significance of the sudden traffic.

Cresting the low rise on Everitt Street, Eddie Dawson caught sight of Paul Bermanzohn. Two days earlier, he'd struck up a conversation with Bermanzohn during Nelson Johnson's press conference on the steps of the police department. "Does the Klan really still exist?" Dawson had asked Paul. When he finished his statement, Nelson walked over to where Paul stood with Eddie. "What the hell's this all about? What's this sign 'Death to the Klan'? What are you going to do, kill these people?" Eddie demanded.

"No," said Nelson, "those chicken people won't come off their hill."

"Suppose they do," replied Eddie, "what are you going to do to them?"

"They won't," said Nelson.[6]

Now as Buck's pickup passed Bermanzohn, Eddie rolled down the passenger-side window, leaned his head out, and snarled, "You wanted the Klan, you communist son of a bitch, well you got the Klan."

As the words took shape in the mind of Paul Bermanzohn, the child of two Polish Holocaust survivors, whose mother became known to her persecutors as "the Bird" for escaping the Nazis three times, who grew up longing for murdered relatives he'd never meet, realized that Eddie's weathered face, smoky voice, and lonely eyes were familiar to him.[7]

In a green pickup truck four cars behind James Buck's truck, Ed Boyd's camera focused on a young Klansman loading a pistol.

❖

Hard words percussed the air. "Dirty Kike!" "N—— lover!" "N——!" Then the activists responded, hurling chants of "Death to the Klan" at the passing cars.[8] The reality beyond Signe's big sunglasses—what Ed Boyd could see unfolding through his camera—settled slowly and then instantly into her consciousness. Percy Sims, the drunk young man she'd been talking with, became animated, taunting the Klan in their cars, daring them, imploring them to get out and fight. The Klan car carrying Virgil Griffin veered and lurched at a demonstrator who responded by slamming a heavy piece of wood onto the vehicle's trunk. Another man kicked at the car and missed, then turned and ran.[9]

Nelson Johnson stood across Everitt from the singers when he heard the warning shouts and noticed the cars. He jogged quickly back across the street, adrenaline spiking through his body as he realized what was happening. The Klan caravan moved slowly from west to east. Nelson started walking beside it along the sidewalk. Then up ahead he saw a young man twist his head and shoulders out the passenger-side window of the green pickup truck and into space. The man extended his right arm, aimed a pistol with a long barrel into the sky, and shouted, "You show me a n—— with guts and I'll show you a Klansman with a gun!"[10] A plume of Black smoke spewed from the gun, streaking the clear, fall air, like a sudden exclamation point.

Some thought a firecracker had exploded.[11] But Nelson, who'd seen the gun, shouted for people to get away and began to trot back east along the north side of Everitt, against the traffic. Another shot exploded behind him. And then a third.

The pickup truck driven by James Buck and carrying Eddie Dawson stopped. Behind them the other drivers jammed on the brakes, their forward passage along the narrow street blocked. Their vehicles fishtailed briefly, coming to a rest, and they found themselves surrounded by a shocked and angry crowd, people stunned that Klansmen would be brazen enough to visit a Black neighborhood on a bright Saturday morning.

Sensing fear, or an advantage, or perhaps responding on cue to the signal shots from the long-barreled powder gun, the men in the cars leaped out and rushed the crowd on the sidewalk. Some carried clubs, nunchucks, or hunting knives; others grabbed signposts from the piles arranged for marchers and began attacking people in the crowd.[12]

The marchers fought back. Cesar Cauce held his ground at the edge of the sidewalk in front of Morningside Homes trying to buy time for the women and children to escape deeper into the housing development and to safety. Behind him, Sandi Smith herded all the children she could find, pushing them, running toward the interior of the housing project. Then a cudgel came down with brutal force on her head, shattering her skull.

Nelson saw Frankie Powell—eight months pregnant and known to her friends and comrades by her chosen Swahili name, Chekesha—fall to her knees, blood coursing down her face. Before Nelson could reach her, a man from one of the cars rushed him. Nelson took quick measure of the charging man: he stood 5'7" or 5'8", maybe an inch or so shorter than Nelson, with a "chubby build, dark hair," and in his right hand he held "a medium size butcher knife, the kind used," Nelson knew from his youth on the farm, "to kill pigs."[13]

Before he could react, the man struck with the knife, cutting Nelson's hand. The man lunged a second time and Nelson blocked the blade, suffering another cut on his hand, as the defensive boxing skills he'd picked up in the Air Force punched in.

Behind Nelson and around him now, a steady barrage of shots exploded through the narrow streets, the sounds swarming and echoing off the brick buildings and the cars. For the moment, the noise remained on the periphery of his consciousness as his mind riveted to the immediate task of survival.

Nelson looked into the Klansman's blue eyes and saw fear. It wasn't paralyzing fear but fighting fear, and the man was quick on his feet, clearly intent on injuring or killing the Black man before him. The two men were circling each other when a comrade tossed Nelson a stick. Now he had a tool to keep the man away from his body. He took a swing at the Klansman with the four-foot pole. He missed. He swung again. Lightning quick, the man squatted, the stick whistling above his head. Then he jumped up, using the burst to aim his knife at Nelson's rib cage. Sensing the move, Nelson shot his left arm forward and the knife plunged into his forearm, inches short of its intended target.[14]

Nelson pulled his bloodied arm back and prepared for another attack. But the man turned and ran, disappearing as suddenly as he'd arrived, as if called back to the cars parked on Everitt Street.

Disoriented and still hearing shots, Nelson sprinted across Everitt and dove behind a car to gather himself. A woman reporter who'd sought shelter behind the same car recognized Nelson and panicked, screaming in fear. If the Klansmen came looking for Nelson, she thought, they'd kill her, too.

From the shelter of the news car, Nelson watched as, seconds later, the shooting stopped. Several Klansmen packed guns back into the trunk of the blue Ford Fairlane. The driver gunned the motor and the tires squealed, leaving behind carnage and a wafting cloud of dust in the bright air. A few seconds later, the canary-yellow van took off carrying most of the shooters. A hundred yards down the street, the passengers noticed one straggler sprinting after the van. When the driver slowed so the man could climb in, a policeman stepped into the van's path and raised a shotgun. The van stopped. Then the sirens started.

When he stood up, Nelson saw Jim Waller lying alone, face down on the ground. There were other fallen bodies, but people were running to them. Nelson knelt beside his friend and saw where bullets had entered his back. Not knowing what to do, he spoke to Jim. Getting no response but a ragged exhale, Nelson removed his jacket and draped it over his friend, resting his hand on Jim's back, as if he might still protect him. Then he turned him over. When Nelson looked for a pulse, Jim's eyelids popped up, revealing glassy eyes. His mind flashed to a memory of "Captain Larry Gibson sitting across the table in police headquarters saying 'we are responsible for the safety of this city, including you and the march. Sign this document [agreeing not to bring guns to the march] or you can't get a parade permit.'"[15]

"Is he still alive?" asked a paramedic suddenly beside Nelson, looking at Jim Waller's motionless form on the ground.

"No," said Nelson. "You all killed him."

Nelson stood to give Signe space when she rushed to her husband's side. She gasped and began to rock back and forth as her changed life commenced. Quietly, below the register that could be captured by news cameras, she mumbled, "I can't go on living without Jim." Then her arm shot into the air and she bellowed, "Long live the Commu-. nist Workers Party. . . . We will have Socialist Revolution."[16]

Nelson saw Paul Bermanzohn stretched out on the ground, his leg twitching. Paul, unaware yet of the gravity of his wound, remarked to a comrade hovering nearby that they'd have to improve at armed conflict. In the doorway of one of the Morningside units Nelson caught a glimpse of Sandi Smith, blood streaming over her face. Was she alive? Five minutes earlier Nelson had felt excited for the impact the march and conference would have on Greensboro. He and his comrades had imagined a carefully aimed jab at the nexus of racism and capitalism. Now, the acrid smell of exploded ammunition overwhelmed him, triggering the most hopeless feeling he'd ever experienced.[17]

Only eighty-eight seconds had elapsed from that first shot of black smoke to the peculiar silence after the Klan and Nazi caravan drove away. The world hung suspended between the past and the present, as if unsure whether to go backward or forward. How little time it can take to end or transform a life. How much time comes to bear on that moment. "History," James Baldwin contended, "is the present."[18]

When the cars left and the shooting stopped, Ed Boyd found himself filming from the back seat of the news truck. He'd been recording the shooters when a man with an archaic pistol appeared a few feet in front of him, aiming at the Klansmen. Assuming the Klansmen would turn and obliterate the CWP member with their shotguns and semiautomatic rifles and that he, Boyd, would find himself directly in the line of fire, he panicked, dropped his TV camera, grabbed it again, and hurled himself into the back of the Blazer. But he kept filming. As far as he could tell, the man with the small pistol never fired. In any event, the Klansmen paid no attention to him. Maybe the communist's ancient gun had jammed.

Most of the shooting had taken place right in front of Ed Boyd's position on the south side of Everitt Street. He'd seen the long pistol push dark smoke into the air. He'd watched people run from it. He'd filmed the clattering stick fight as it erupted near the middle of the caravan, and then observed impotently as a group of men from the last car—the canary-yellow van—calmly took weapons from the trunk of the penultimate car, the blue Ford Fairlane that Eddie Dawson had positioned in front of the van, and started firing. Not randomly, Ed thought. It seemed to him they aimed with purpose at specific people in the crowd. The former Air Force enlisted man believed he'd witnessed a well-executed military operation: flush people toward unseen shooters, fight them to slow them down, then pick off the intended targets one by one. By his count, five or six people lay dead or dying.

He kept filming through the new eruption of noise, the crying and shouting, the screaming ambulances and police vehicles arriving one after the other, dozens of suddenly present cops bristling with riot gear. Beside him, a newspaper photographer complained that blood had splattered his camera. Ed wanted to hit him in the head. Instead, he kept filming.

On the way back to Durham carrying three twenty-minute rolls of news footage, and now, evidence, Ed Boyd scanned the highway for the beautiful crimson maple tree he'd seen that morning. Over the coming years, he'd always look for that tree, especially in the fall when its leaves blazed like glorious beacons announcing a terrible history.[19]

❖

As the police cars swarmed to the scene, Nelson wandered the battlefield looking for something to do. He still didn't know who or how many people had been killed. He didn't know where his daughters were or whether they were safe. He didn't know where Joyce was or whether the marchers at Windsor Community Center had been attacked, too.

Nelson saw Captain Trevor Hampton, the highest-ranking Black officer in the GPD, walking toward him. When Nelson was picking up the parade permit at the police department two days earlier, Captain Hampton had told him that the GPD would be at Morning-side to ensure a safe and orderly march. Now Hampton came up to Nelson, grabbed his fellow A&T dropout's injured arm, and asked if he was hurt.

"I'm all right," snapped Johnson, jerking away from the big policeman.[20]

❖

A restless crowd gathered on the south side of Everitt Street. Some had been at the march. Others were drawn by the shots and sirens. Everyone wanted to know what had happened. Nelson approached them, desperate grief and outrage building. Nearby a phalanx of po-lice officers, decked out in riot gear, strutted nervously, worrying that the crowd might direct its fear and anger at them when Nelson be-gan shouting in the resonant voice he'd cultivated to direct large demonstrations, "The police murdered us. It was a setup. The police disarmed us. They wouldn't let us have guns. They let the Klan and Nazis come in and shoot us. This whole system is against the work-ing class. We need a revolution. We declare WAR on them." And with this last line he began roaring like an injured and cornered lion, "This is WAR!"[21]

The crowd grew agitated.

Sensing that the situation could get out of hand, Lieutenant Sylvester Daughtry—another Black officer—conferred for a mo-ment with the GPD lawyer standing beside him. Satisfied with the legal advice, Daughtry gave the order for Nelson to be arrested for inciting a riot.[22] Nearly a dozen officers surrounded Nelson, grabbing at his arms. He resisted, so the police kicked his legs out from under him. As he fell, Nelson reached for a chain-link fence, holding on with all the strength he could muster from his injured hands, blood surging from the stab wounds in his arm. The cops tried to pin Nelson with their feet. Someone kicked him hard in the neck.[23]

Terrified that the police would kill Nelson, Willena Cannon charged the scrum, trying to get between the officers and her friend. A policeman lifted her off the ground as she struggled and placed her under arrest. They shoved Willena and then Nelson into separate cop cars.

The police car carrying Nelson sped for the hospital. The cop in the back with Nelson fidgeted anxiously. "We're going to get blamed for this regardless," he said to his colleague.

"Why did you let it happen?" asked Nelson.

"We didn't think there'd be trouble until the end of the march," the cop responded.[24]

They knew there'd be trouble. The detail reinforced Nelson's growing suspicions that the police had not acted in good faith, but he kept his mouth shut.

Officer April Wise heard an urgent message come across the radio from GPD Communications. Shots had been fired from automatic weapons.[25]

About twenty minutes earlier, she'd obeyed the order to leave Morningside. Now she turned her car back toward the housing project, arriving a few minutes later. As she parked on the east side of Everitt Street and began to climb from the squad car, a Black woman ran up to her shouting, "That's not all of them." The woman assumed the police, represented at this moment by the woman standing in front of her, Officer Wise, would want to know the information she possessed. She continued, "They just went down Gillespie toward Market. They're in a light blue Ford, '64 or '65. The man just put a shotgun in my face and said he'd kill me. Scared me to death."

All Officer Wise knew was what crackled from the radio: shots had been fired. But she understood that the woman could only be referring to fleeing criminals and immediately called in the tip to the police radio. As ambulances screamed to the scene, Officer Wise put on her riot helmet and grabbed a baton. She started directing traffic and then, a short time later, Sergeant W. D. Comer, the man who'd been assigned by Captain Hampton to ensure the safety of the march, ordered her to join the officers securing the crime scene.[26] As she walked to what had been the epicenter of the melee, she witnessed the bodies: Jim Waller's, beside "a flower planter"; Mike Nathan's, still breathing, but resting in a "large blood stain."

Wise approached Signe Waller, but Signe walked away from her, merging with the agitated crowd across the street, where she shouted that the police had "killed her husband."

Wise then tried to speak with Floris Cauce, whose husband, Cesar, lay in a lifeless heap by the flower planter near the Everitt Street sidewalk. In her confusion and shock, Floris wanted to be sure that the police spelled her husband's name correctly: *C-E-S-A-R. C-A-U-C-E.* "He was white," the Black, Panamanian-born woman told the policewoman, perhaps to intercept any confusion that Cesar's big head of curly hair might cause. Though Floris didn't intend to talk with the police officer her fears and anxieties poured out. They'd never had children, she told Officer Wise. There hadn't been time. And how, she worried, "was she to tell [her dead husband's] parents" what had happened?

As Officer Wise walked through the scene, her sense of observation heightened by adrenaline, she noted the "blood spattered poster to the north of" where Mike Nathan lay. In the street she saw a "candle, a Num-chuk [*sic*], a red bandanna still tied together . . . a shotgun shell . . . and a clipboard." She saw a "pair of glasses lying in the street," a "black ink pen, and blood on the pavement." Wise noted "bullet holes in the windows of the community center facing Carver

Drive," casings strewn over the asphalt, and the shattered windows of parked cars, including one emblazoned with the identifying marks of the Channel 12 news team. And she saw a "red beret type hat," resting in the street, lost by one of the fleeing children, who only minutes before had been singing and laughing.

Though it would be some time before she would ever articulate her feelings, Officer Wise left the frightening scene uneasy. Perhaps she empathized with the stunned survivors who'd lost husbands and friends. But a persistent question troubled her and, later, would bother survivors of the shooting when they learned Wise's story: Maybe things would have been different if she hadn't been told to leave Morningside Homes less than half an hour before the Klan caravan arrived. Might her presence—or absence—have been the difference between life and death?

All the objects—the casings, the candle, the clipboard, the glasses, the pen, the beret—and thousands more would be photographed, collected, cataloged, and stored. The bits of inanimate material could never repair what had happened or breathe life back into the bodies strewn across the road and grass. But later, city and federal law enforcement would study, trace, and arrange the evidence, fitting the pieces together to reconstruct, as they saw fit, what transpired at the corner of Carver Drive and Everitt Street.

JURISDICTION

It was almost 2 p.m. when Cecil Moses picked up the telephone in his temporary living quarters to hear the FBI assistant director, Francis "Bud" Mullen, hollering into his ear.

"What's going on in Greensboro?" Bud Mullen demanded.

"How am I supposed to know, Boss? I'm just here in Charlotte doing my laundry."

"Well, get your ass up there," Mullen shouted with the urgency of a messenger feeling pressure from above. "The White House wants to know what's going on."

"What's our jurisdiction?" Moses asked. From an earlier call, he'd learned that a shooting had taken place but didn't yet know with any precision how it had gone down, who had been killed, or whether it fell within the Bureau's purview.

"You figure it out," Mullen said and hung up.[1]

Assistant Special Agent in Charge (ASAC) Moses didn't watch football and hadn't turned on the television in his apartment in Charlotte. Courtesy of the technology fast overtaking slow-developing film, however, video images of the morning's violence at Morningside Homes flickered into homes around the state by 1 p.m., interrupting the Wake Forest–Clemson football game.

The number two FBI man in North Carolina had landed in the

job less than two months earlier after an unanticipated promotion from the Memphis FBI office. His family had remained behind until he could find a house big enough to accommodate his wife and three kids. After endless days spent introducing himself to the state's eight or so FBI agents and making grip-and-grin, get-acquainted visits to his counterparts in federal, state, and municipal law enforcement agencies, Moses had planned to spend his Saturday recovering. His boss, the SAC, had trekked into the East Tennessee hills after deer, beyond the reach of a phone call. The responsibility for organizing the Bureau's response to the shooting in Greensboro, therefore, fell to Cecil Moses.

Moses ended his two-year assignment in Tennessee with a successful hunt for a fugitive named Billy Dean Anderson. After a string of stickups, police shootings, and prison busts, the FBI stuck Anderson into the best PR campaign they'd ever invented, the "Ten Most Wanted List."[2] Anderson made the list in 1975, and his impassive mug, eyes slightly askew, graced post office walls around the country, keeping company over the years with the Native American activist Leonard Peltier and James Earl Ray, the man convicted of assassinating Martin Luther King Jr., who made the list a second time in 1977 when he busted out of a Tennessee prison.

Moses's intuition told him that the "Mountain Man" would take to the woods and caves of his home territory, "a remote, mountainous area inhabited principally by moonshiners, bootleggers, and other outlaws."[3] And so, in early July 1979, Moses told his squad to lace up their boots. They would comb the hills of Fentress County, northeast of Nashville, for traces of the strange, violent iconoclast who'd eluded them for nearly five years.

Up in the hills, Moses and his team caught a tip that the Mountain Man planned to pay a visit to his mother. As dusk fell on the evening of July 7, 1979, the FBI men were tucked back in the hickory forest waiting when the son stepped from his mother's cabin, heading for the cave he called home. An agent ordered the fugitive to drop his weapons and surrender. Moses would report that Anderson whirled around aiming to shoot. But an FBI man fired first, and two rounds of "double ought buck" found their mark. Of the twenty-four pellets, twenty-three burrowed into Anderson's body. Billy Dean Anderson, said Moses, died before he hit the ground.

The homesteaders of Fentress County kept their own accounts of Billy Dean Anderson's reunion with Mr. Death. The man's muscular paintings of Jesus and his talent for escaping prison earned him a place in the hill people's lore. He was their outlaw, after all, writing in his mountain redoubt, "I have seen the beauty of the mountains. I have had a long hard streak. I have seen the beauty of Mother. Mother, I have brought trouble on my folks, but I love them." Speculations about the identity of the snitch who'd ratted Anderson out were braided with tales of FBI deceit. One rumor claimed that the dead man hadn't been armed when the agents shot him. Over the years, his local reputation accumulated, drip by drop, like bootleg whiskey in a copper still beside a secret spring.[4]

Not long after killing Anderson in the mountains, Special Agent Moses visited the Grand Ole Opry in Nashville, where he charmed Glen Campbell and Dolly Parton and entertained the stars' adoring, patriotic fans with a firsthand account of the backcountry hunt for the Mountain Man. The warm reception took Moses back to the days of his youth when, in between Hank Williams songs, *This Is Your FBI* crackled through the transistor radio, carrying the exploits of J. Edgar Hoover and his courageous G-men to the family porch in rural Kentucky.

Despite the shimmer of positive attention that the FBI, and Moses himself, enjoyed following the apprehension of Billy Dean Anderson, the Bureau's glory days seemed like a distant memory. J. Edgar Hoover had tended the Bureau's public image meticulously over his forty-eight years as director, erecting the most popular government agency in America. But by 1977, five years after Hoover's death, analysts described a "tarnished" institution "beset by controversy" after crusading citizens and tough congressional committees uncovered "revelations of abuses of power" and "credible allegations of illegality."[5] In 1976, when asked about Director Clarence Kelley's use of FBI contractors to decorate his private home, presidential candidate Jimmy Carter called the FBI "a disgrace," saying that "when you see the head of the FBI break a little law and stay there, it gives everyone the sense that crime must be OK."[6]

"Morale [at the Bureau]," Moses would say, leaning into his country roots, "was lower than a snake in a wagon rut." The Bureau's critics, from President Carter on down, made Moses angry. He didn't like "being judged by a new generation for what was done in a previous generation." People just didn't understand, he thought, what it took to protect the American system of capitalism and democracy.

Moses threw on a clean suit and, minutes after Bud Mullen hung up, was tearing up I-85 in his Buick at over one hundred miles an hour. He hadn't even thought to pack a suitcase. If the White House and the press cared about what had happened, then it would be a big case. Moses barely knew the names of the agents in the Charlotte Field Office, let alone those who manned the Resident Agencies around the state. But he'd need all hands to kick off the investigation in its first, critical hours. From the car, he radioed ahead, ordering the eight Greensboro agents to work.[7] Within minutes, beepers were buzzing on golf courses and tennis courts, in backyards and woodlots around Greensboro, summoning off-duty agents to the police department.

Cecil Moses jogged into the GPD about an hour after blasting out of Charlotte and encountered a hive of nervous activity, with representatives from various local, state, and federal agencies milling about. The former GPD attorney, Jim Coman, now a brash, first-year prosecutor in the local district attorney's office, reported to the department as soon as he heard the news. Mickey Michaux, the federal attorney for North Carolina's Middle District and the first Black person to hold that position in state history, raced down from Durham.[8] From their accents, ASAC Moses could tell that the

GPD officers, among them a handful of Black policemen, were southerners, mostly from the North Carolina Piedmont. All the FBI agents hustling in were white—not unusual, given that fewer than four hundred agents in the whole country were Black. One attuned to such details would have noted that, since Hoover's day, it wasn't only the public image of the FBI that had changed. The Bureau had relaxed hairstyle protocol, allowing personal coiffures to breach the top of the ear. And the entire Bureau had gained weight. Before 1972, Moses ran and skipped meals to keep his six-foot frame at a trim 172 pounds. After "the Director" died, the allowed upper weight limit for someone Moses's height rose to 198. He and many other agents quickly accommodated themselves to less exercise and bigger lunches. The Greensboro agents' northern accents tipped Moses to the fact that they'd moved south, a vestige, perhaps, of Hoover's inclination to post agents in places where personal ties would be less likely to occlude good judgment. The move to the Piedmont didn't represent a hardship; North Carolina enticed agents with low-cost living, good schools, and nearly year-round golf in a temperate climate. Several of the resident agents had been in North Carolina for years, adapting to life among the "longleaf pines," avoiding transfers—such as the one Moses was in the midst of—that disrupted domestic lives and stretched a Bureau salary.

Mission, as well as comfort, kept the agents in Greensboro. Within the FBI, Greensboro had a reputation as a place where "things started" and spread to other locales.[9] The best example of this had been the movement initiated by the four students at North Carolina A&T who, on February 2, 1960, sat down at the Woolworth's counter on Elm Street and ignited a wildfire of civil disobedience across the South. Their courage ushered in the end to legal segregation and would lead, under the tutelage of brilliant civil rights strategist Ella Baker, to the formation of the Student Nonviolent Coordinating Committee. By the early 1970s, however, the FBI had harassed that organization, better known as SNCC, out of existence.

Under the fluorescent lights in a GPD conference room, Moses called the police officers and Bureau agents to order to plan the investigation of the shooting. Over the years, the GPD and local FBI agents had developed a comfortable working relationship. The primary communications channel ran between the Bureau and the GPD's Criminal Investigations Division. Elsewhere in the building, twelve Klansmen and Nazis were being held for questioning. In the basement parking garage, a young cop guarded the canary-yellow van, the only vehicle in the nine-car caravan to be stopped and confiscated, along with the impressive arsenal packed inside it.[10]

With a laser focus on the jurisdictional question he'd raised with Assistant Director Mullen, Moses fired questions at the assembly. If they were talking about simple murder, then the FBI would have to back away and leave the investigation to state and local authorities. But one pertinent fact emerged: the city had authorized the march when the police department issued Nelson Johnson the parade permit, but the caravan transporting the shooters had no such permission. Moses, who'd started as a clerk in the FBI in 1957, latched on to the existence of the permit. The First Amendment of the Bill of Rights protected the right of "people peaceably to assemble." An infringement of a person's constitutional rights gave the FBI standing. Following Assistant Director Mullen's directive to establish FBI jurisdiction, ASAC Moses opened a civil rights investigation into the shooting, code-named "GreenKil."

Moses called in G-men from around the state to bolster his investigative team and assigned agents to key operational roles. The role of supervising investigator, the FBI's primary liaison to the GPD, the local DA's office, and the Department of Justice, he delegated to Special Agent Thomas Brereton. During his six years at the Greensboro Resident Agency, Brereton—an "officious individual" according to US Attorney Michaux— had earned a reputation as a skilled investigator. He stalked the corridors of the police department, wielding his

Bronx charm to build strong relationships with the local officers and to cement the Bureau's sway with local law enforcement operations. If it fell to Moses to captain the GreenKil operation, Brereton would be its mechanic, tinkering on the engine of justice with all the tools in his bag. Moses then appointed Horace Beckwith, a veteran agent who'd been demoted to the Charlotte Field Office for his involvement in illegal intelligence-gathering operations against leftists, to edit and compile the Bureau's investigative reports.

FBI agents and GPD officers quickly teamed up to interview the men they'd arrested, police officers assigned to the march, and those, like April Wise, who'd been present in the aftermath of the shooting. As transcripts of the interviews trickled in, Moses found no reason to further scrutinize the motives or actions of the Greensboro Police Department that morning. He pointed his GreenKil investigation at the Klansmen, the Nazis, and members of the Communist Workers Party. Moses's investigative priorities would shape how the shooting at Morningside Homes was understood for generations to come.

The evening of November 3, Moses received a call from Lee Colwell, another of Director William Webster's three deputies.[11] Known inside the Bureau as a savant in organizational theory and management, Colwell had climbed from a poor childhood in Hot Springs, Arkansas, to the Bureau's executive floor. An assistant director of the Bureau since 1975, he'd soon become just the second associate director in the Bureau's history, after Hoover's confidant and companion Clyde Tolson. Moses had worked with Colwell during the mid-1970s in the FBI's smallest division, a tiny, internal think tank that came to be known in Bureau lingo as the "Group of 12." The two men became fast friends, discovering they shared southern roots and a love of corn bread. But Moses knew little if anything about the other life this "self-effacing man with a ready smile" led as one of the nation's elite Cold War counterintelligence officers.[12]

"Look," Colwell told Moses, "the director is getting a lot of heat from the White House. He's gonna send in about one hundred outside agents from the Civil Rights Division to take over the case."

"Well, that makes me mad as hell," said ASAC Moses, making no effort to hold back his anger. "I didn't ask to come to Charlotte. I didn't ask for this promotion. If the director doesn't have enough confidence to think I can handle things, then he can send me back to Memphis."

"Hold your temper," said Colwell to his friend. "Don't take it personal."

"Well, I do take it personal. Who in the hell decided this was going to be a civil rights case? When Bud Mullen called me, I asked him what jurisdiction we had. And his word to me was, you figure it out. I'm the one who decided that we'd open a civil rights case because the Communist Workers had a permit to parade, and the Klan interfered with it. Why the hell do they think someone else can do a better job?"

"I'll speak to the director. But don't hold your breath."

The conversation with Colwell only deepened Moses's resentment toward President Carter, who, Moses believed, should never have fired Director Clarence Kelley. The agents gathering in Greensboro all knew that more rode on the GreenKil investigation than the indictments of a few "dumb Kluckers," as ASAC Moses referred to the white supremacists. According to even the restrictive new FBI guidelines, the crime gave them license to freely investigate the Communist Workers Party, to see whether its radical tendrils reached other revolutionary cells around the country. But more than that, a high-profile case such as GreenKil offered a chance to rebuild public trust, demonstrating the Bureau's skill as an investigating agency. It could also present an opportunity to make another argument to lawmakers. Moses and his colleagues wanted the rules restricting their use of informants and undercover agents loosened. The guidelines passed down in reaction to the 1976 Church Committee revelations, they would argue, had tied their hands, preventing them from recruiting informants who could have helped them intercept the deadly violence that erupted at the corner of Everitt and Carver.

No member of the Church Committee had pissed Cecil Moses off more than the senator from North Carolina, Robert Burren Morgan. Senator Morgan had not only questioned the Bureau's judgment and ethics; he'd also committed what FBI agents considered to be an unforgivable transgression. In a 1976 speech at Wake Forest University, Senator Morgan disclosed a Bureau secret: the inflammatory Klan preacher and Greensboro resident George Dorsett, Morgan told his audience—and the hungry press—had for many years been an FBI informant. Moses wouldn't miss any opportunity to embarrass that "real butthole" on the man's home turf.[13]

Colwell called Moses back a few hours later. "The judge is going to back you with the White House. But boy, if you screw up, your career is over."

❖

Five minutes after North Carolina's secretary of crime control and public safety, Burley Mitchell, was informed that there'd been a shooting in Greensboro, he picked up the phone, got the operator, and said, "I need to place an emergency call to Communist China."[14]

"I'm sorry," the operator responded, "we do not show a Communist China."

"Maybe it's the People's Republic of China, but if it's not, it's the country with a fourth of the world's population," said Mitchell, exasperated. "If you can't find that, get me your supervisor."

Half the world away from North Carolina, in the rambling Grand Hotel in Peking, China, a phone rang.[15] Footsteps echoed through the hallways and fists rapped on doors, rousing North Carolina's governor Jim Hunt for the urgent call.

Nearing the end of a three-week trade junket to Asia, Hunt had arrived at the Chinese capital's small airport two days earlier, bustling through the concourse with his staff and a contingent of businessmen to give a quick news conference. Chairman Mao Tse-tung's placid gaze loomed from the mural on the wall behind the podium. At the Great Hall of the People, the governor peddled North Carolina state products, telling China's vice-premier, "It would strengthen the relations between our countries a great deal if the People's Republic of China would begin to purchase our tobacco in the near future."

"I fully agree with you," the vice-premier responded. "This is a very big market for you."[16]

Now, in the middle of the night, Mitchell told the governor, "We've got a helluva mess here. You know the communist groups over at Duke medical? They've gone . . . and got in a shootout with the Klan. We've got a bunch of dead communists in Greensboro." The incongruity of the situation struck Mitchell as the words left his mouth and zipped through the line. He had called into the heart of the communist world with news that self-proclaimed Maoist revolutionaries had been killed in North Carolina. He could be doggone certain that someone in China was listening in on the conversation.

Past midnight, huddled in the hotel, Hunt's staff briefly discussed the idea of jetting back so the governor could attend to the crisis.[17] A darling of the Democratic Party with national aspirations, he'd climbed to the governor's mansion by understanding the limits of progressive politics in North Carolina, especially when they extended to race. He courted business, avoided the left and the extreme right, and pandered to the conservative sensibilities of the old Southern Democrats to keep them from defecting irrevocably to Jesse Helms and the upstart Republican Party.

Hunt certainly had heard the names of Nelson Johnson, Paul Bermanzohn, and Jim Waller from his State Bureau of Investigation briefings and from reading the news. They'd been pestering him for years, nearly upsetting his effort to impose standardized testing on the state's high school students. The attention they brought to the Wilmington Ten case caused the high-profile activist Angela Davis to call North Carolina a "laboratory for new methods of racist repression" for its treatment of the civil rights activists who'd traveled to the coastal North Carolina city to support Black high students being bullied in a newly integrated high school.[18] Taking refuge in a church, the activists had been shot at by white supremacists and then imprisoned for, allegedly, burning down a store. Her opinion probably didn't bother the governor much. But the Wilmington Ten story had jumped the state's borders and the activist press. As national and international media pressure grew, President Carter asked Attorney General Griffin Bell to look into the matter. The Department of Justice filed a brief recommending that the Wilmington Ten's convictions be set aside, suggesting that the prisoners' constitutional rights had indeed been violated. That was embarrassing and politically awkward; a lot of the white people who voted for Hunt would never believe the activist prisoners who'd been languishing in prison for the better part of the decade weren't guilty of something.[19]

No, the agitators who'd been killed and injured in Greensboro were no friends of Jim Hunt. Hunt's instincts, which pointed like a dowsing rod toward the political center, told him to steer clear of a messy situation. He'd keep to his Asian itinerary and finish out the tour. Over the coming weeks and months, he'd generally ignore the whole episode, making only oblique public reference to the shooting. Behind the scenes, he supported his friend Jim Melvin, as Greensboro's mayor hustled to manage the crisis that threatened to tarnish his city's carefully cultivated reputation as a beacon of business-friendly, progressive southern politics.

Mayor Melvin was raking leaves in the front yard of his New Irving Park home when the call came. He immediately summoned white and Black community leaders to city hall.[20] "We cannot let Martin Luther King's dream turn into a nightmare," warned Frank Williams, a Black pastor who, when he'd integrated a white Greensboro neighborhood earlier in the decade, had looked out to see a cross-burning in his front yard. Everyone at the table called for peace and calm. But questions still crackled through the room, threatening the tenuous unity and civility that held them together in a moment of crisis. Nelson Johnson had helped rally the vote to make Henry Frye, in 1968, the first Black elected representative in North Carolina since 1898. Frye, who would later become the first African American chief justice of the North Carolina Supreme Court, asked a pointed question. Why, he wanted to know, hadn't the police stopped the Klan caravan on its way to Morningside Homes if they had it under surveillance? A white man, ignorant of who Frye was, glibly dismissed the question out of hand. "Any lawyer knows why," he said, implying that the police had no legal grounds to stop the Klansmen.[21]

"I'm a lawyer, and a good one," Frye responded tersely, "and I don't know why."[22]

The late-arriving head of the NAACP echoed Frye's question. Said Dr. George Simkins, "We are very much concerned about the police department's failure to take more decisive action to prevent the senseless and brutal murders of innocent people."[23]

Perhaps, for the briefest of moments, Melvin's city—and after so many years in office he did seem to think of it as his personal domain—appeared strange and unfamiliar to him. Maybe in the swirl of fear and Henry Frye's pointed question he found himself on the edge of being, in the words of the southern historian W. J. Cash, "shocked out of the old smugness" and "fumbling for meaning."[24] If so, he gave no public hint of introspection.

Undeterred by the questions raised by Henry Frye or Dr. Simkins, Mayor Melvin settled quickly on a narrative that he pushed like a blade through the cloud of shock and confusion. The shooting "had absolutely nothing to do with race tensions in our city," he informed the press. He went further, saying that "not a single person involved was from our city," leaning into the grooves worn by the old "outside agitator" trope, long used to discredit those who brought trouble to innocent southern communities. As he defended *his* city, the version of it he understood and wished to lead, Melvin stood behind "one of the best police departments in the country."[25]

❖

When police cars flew "screaming with their sirens" up Benbow Road toward Morningside Homes, followed by a paddy wagon, Joyce Johnson thought the "police had found some picayune reason . . . to arrest [us] for a legal march." Then someone shouted, "The Klan's been up there. Came through shooting."[26]

"Let's . . . get away from here," Joyce said. Everyone sped for Signe Waller's house on Cypress Street to take cover and try to learn what had happened a half mile from where they'd been standing.

In 1964, before she turned seventeen years old, Joyce boarded an interstate bus in Richmond, Virginia. When she reached Durham, she carried her cardboard suitcase to a dorm room at Duke University, a new member of the college's second class to admit Negro students. Determined to become a doctor, Joyce, whose mother had worked as a domestic, watched liveried Black servants move some of her new classmates into their rooms. Over the next four years, the university's maids and janitors became her friends as she studied premed and, outside class, immersed herself in the history of America's Black freedom movement. After she'd met Nelson, Joyce connected the Black liberation movement in America to anticolonial struggles in Africa and communist organizing around the world.

Now her mind flickered to the J. Edgar Hoover–led roundups of foreign-born leftists and Black activists during a Red Scare sixty years earlier and the red-baiting of the McCarthy era when she was a girl coming up on Richmond's Southside.[27] She'd grieved Emmett Till in 1955 and nine years later the murders of Voting Rights activists in Mississippi. Then Malcolm in '65, Martin in '68, and the Black Panther Fred Hampton in '69, and so many others rarely named. They'd put Angela Davis in prison and, closer to home, railroaded Ben Chavis and nine others into jail in 1971 for supporting protesting high school students in North Carolina's port city of Wilmington. Standing up for justice and equality got you jailed or killed in America, Joyce thought.

The fear of not knowing what had happened to her husband and daughters overwhelmed her. She headed for Morningside Homes where, from leafleting and campaigning, she knew nearly every door and the people who'd answer each one. During the weeks leading up to November 3, she spent hours sticking up announcements for the anti-Klan march to electric poles in and around Smith Homes, Morningside, Claremont Courts, and the A&T and Bennett campuses. Over the years, she'd learned the alleys and shortcuts, the secrets paths between neighborhoods—knowledge that enabled her to cover more ground in less time, talk to more people.

"Right on!" neighborhood folks called out to her when they'd seen the anti-Klan signs. "We can't go back to this sort of thing," they said, referring to the Klan and the fear the name evoked, like the involuntary shiver arising from an invisible draft of icy air. She'd noticed that some of the posters she'd been placing around town had been removed and others covered up by a terrifying image of a lynched man dangling from a tree with the text "old-fashioned American Justice." Who'd done that? But when the people Joyce saw expressed concern that the Klan might not take this march sitting down, she downplayed their concerns. "Those night riders won't come here," she said. "Bring your families. We'll have lunch and join hands. We've got to get together on this." Some asked if they shouldn't bring "a piece" anyway, just to be safe. She let them know that the police said no guns: "That's just the way it is."[28]

❖

Arriving at Morningside she surveyed the scene before her, the helmeted police, the ambulances, the crowd of restless, angry neighbors edging up to the police tape that had been hastily patched around the scene. She approached a policeman who told her that she couldn't enter the area. Panic rose in her as she pleaded with another cop. She needed to find her daughters. He, too, turned her away. Undeterred, Joyce resorted to the mental map of the neighborhood that had accrued in her mind over the years, a map more precise than any possessed by the police, one that included memories of shared meals, laughter, and conversations about hopes and dreams and trauma. Skirting the police perimeter, Joyce made her way into the development, claiming her own jurisdiction.

Once inside she heard the horrific news. Her best friend, "the little sister [she'd] never had," Sandi Smith, had been killed.[29] Jim, Cesar, and Bill were dead, too. No one knew whether Mike Nathan and Paul Bermanzohn were alive or dead. Nelson, she learned, had been stabbed and then arrested.

She found her children huddled in Catherine Greenlee's apartment, physically safe but traumatized, having witnessed a white man bludgeon their Auntie Sandi as she rushed them to safety. Fellow activist and family friend Lewis Brandon drove Joyce and the girls to his house, and Larry Little, the former head of the Black Panther Party in Winston-Salem, rushed across the Triad to stand guard.

When her girls were safe, Joyce left for the police department. She tried to keep cool at the information desk, despite the terror that gripped her. The police shrugged at her questions, as though she were speaking a foreign language. She left believing that she might never again see Nelson alive.

Joyce knew she had to do something else. She'd never seen anyone, other than Nelson, with Sandi's gifts as an organizer. She'd guarded that friendship through painful personal and political differences, and now Joyce picked up the phone and placed a call to South Carolina. When Sandi's mother answered, Joyce delivered the devastating news. Barely audible through thick grief, a mother's words made their way to her over the line: "But Joyce, you promised me that you would take care of my Sandra."[30]

"Turn grief into strength," Chairman Mao had said. Joyce went to the hospital where the ambulance had taken Paul Bermanzohn and sat for a moment with Sally, whose husband had been rushed into emergency brain surgery. Then Joyce visited Marty Nathan beside

Michael's hospital bed, her husband's body clinging to life even as his brain ceased to function.

By early evening, she'd developed a plan to protect Nelson, who sat in a police cell guarded, Joyce knew, by men who hated him. Running on adrenaline, she gathered Willena Cannon, who'd been released by the Greensboro Police Department; Signe, as Jim's body lay in the city morgue; and Signe's eleven-year-old son, Alex, and headed for the WFMY-TV station.

NARRATIVES

Susan Kidd, the beautiful anchor of WFMY-TV's *PM Magazine* show, greeted Joyce Johnson and her companions in the lobby and then whisked them into a greenroom. A few months earlier, Kidd had reported on a WVO/CWP-led contingent participating in a boisterous Washington, DC, march against South Africa's racial apartheid system. Now she met Joyce and her comrades again as the women's fears and suspicions tumbled out: they described the surveillance of their march preparations, the delayed permit, the rumors of violence that caused the church to retract its offer of space, and the absence of police at Morningside Homes. "Things don't just happen out of the blue, most of the time," Joyce thought, her mind picking through the incidents of the day and the weeks prior to the march, searching for details that might weave the horror into a meaningful narrative.[1]

Since the WFMY cameraman Jim Waters returned from Morningside with a video recording of the shooting, Kidd knew there'd been numerous visits to the station. Pressing local journalists not to "report the incident in a way as to inflame citizens," Mayor Melvin had come through attempting, unsuccessfully, to persuade the news director not to air the violent images.[2] Bill Dill, the young cameraman assigned to Kidd's *PM Magazine* show, had relayed a curious story to his boss. Dill had met Sandi Smith when they were covering the antiapartheid march. Though talk of revolution made him uneasy, he found Sandi

Smith's combination of charisma, beauty, and intelligence mesmerizing. She'd invited him to the Anti-Klan March and Conference. He'd been puttering around his apartment, debating whether to attend the 2 p.m. conference, when news of the shooting flashed on TV. Though it was his day off, Dill hurried the few blocks down Textile Avenue to the WFMY studios.[3]

Shortly after he arrived at the station, Bill watched as four or five men in suits, wearing sidearms, walked into the newsroom. FBI, he assumed. They were met by the news director, and a discussion took place. From Bill's vantage point, it appeared to get heated. Moments later, the news director stalked over to Bill carrying Jim Waters's videocassette. "Play this for them," he instructed Bill, "but don't give them the tape."

The men followed Bill into a small production room and crammed in around him. Bill sat down, jammed the tape into a player, and nervously fumbled with the console controls. The violence that had taken place just hours earlier shimmered into two-dimensional action. "Rewind," one of the men said. "Freeze it," ordered another, as if the young Black man were an extension of the technology he operated. "Rewind again." "Play it slowly." "Pause." Around Dill, the white agents spoke freely, naming the Klansmen and Nazis on the screen. It seemed to Dill that the men weren't watching to discover what had taken place, but to confirm what they already knew. Had they been watching what had happened? he wondered. And if they had been watching or knew as much as they seemed to know, why hadn't they stopped the shooting?[4]

As he sat in that room, listening to the men he believed to be federal agents, he knew in an instant that his sojourn in the South was ending abruptly. Born Black in Buffalo, educated at Oberlin College in Ohio, he'd always known to be careful about the racist "bad apples" who existed among the ranks of law enforcement. However, he'd also believed that, as a policy, the nation's law enforcement institutions protected everyone. The encounter in the tiny production room felt bigger than a few bad apples. His shock would give way to grief, and not only for the death of a woman he'd wanted to know better. He'd worked and learned from good and talented journalists in North Carolina: Craig Sager, Joe Spencer, Mae Israel, and Susan Kidd. Good riddance, North Carolina, he thought. A short time later he drove to Kansas City, the next stop on his road to becoming a celebrated American cinematographer. Despite his own success, what he'd witnessed in Greensboro shook his faith in the good intentions of America's institutions.

After listening to Joyce and her companions, Susan Kidd agreed to preempt her *PM Magazine* show with an on-air interview. As a newsperson, though, she couldn't dispel a concern: "Either they're crazy or people are going to think they are crazy," she thought.[5] The conspiracy that poured out of them implicated Klansmen, police officers, government officials, and textile mill owners. Kidd's team was built to produce two-minute news spots and seven-minute magazine segments. Investigating a complex news event that involved dozens of people from different political groups, elected officials, corporate officers, and law enforcement personnel would be an enormous task. Kidd knew from experience that getting this story right would require extensive shoe-leather reporting, access to documents, and the long, slow cultivation of sources. Neither she nor the WFMY news team possessed the resources to unravel what had happened. The best they could do would be to broadcast Joyce's point of view and let her voice be heard alongside Mayor Melvin's and Police Chief William "Ed" Swing's, which were already shooting out over the airwaves and wires.

Joyce and her friends didn't seek sympathy during the interview; they condemned the government for the "murder of their comrades." "The people are rising up. The capitalists can't kill everybody," said Joyce.[6] The shooting, the women announced, would be "the costliest mistake the bourgeoisie ever made." In the near term, however, she feared the police would kill her husband. "We hold the police accountable for his safety," she said. Signe added, "We're watching what you do with our brother, Nelson."

As Greensboro's citizens processed the news that Klansmen and Nazis had driven by Morningside shooting at communists, most found Joyce and her friends' language surreal, discordant, and foreign. Were the women victims of a deadly crime, or were they guerrilla soldiers at war with a country that bore little resemblance to the one viewers, especially white viewers, believed they knew? The mayor's message, that this had nothing to do with them, felt more reasonable and comforting.

"Are you afraid?" Susan Kidd asked Joyce and her comrades.

No, the women answered.

But they were terrified. Signe went home after the interview and burned coded contact lists of CWP members and the love letters that Jim Waller had written to her.

Through the bars of his cell at the Guilford County Jail, Nelson caught a glimpse of the afternoon *Greensboro Record* headline: "Klan ambush kills 4 WVO people."[7] Jim Waller was dead. Beyond that, Nelson didn't know who else might have been killed. Was Sandi dead or just terribly injured? Were his daughters safe? Big Man had been right, after all; the Klan did come. Self-doubt overwhelmed Nelson. How could he have made such a horrific mistake, such a profound error in judgment?[8]

When Captain Larry Gibson presented Nelson with the unprecedented requirement prohibiting weapons at the march on October 19, Nelson had asked, "Do you know something about the Klan planning to be there? Are you expecting trouble?" "No," responded Gibson.[9] Nelson thought about picking up the parade permit on November 1 and about shaking hands with Captain Trevor Hampton when their paths crossed in the department moments later. Hampton assured Nelson that the police would be at Morningside by 11:30 to go over the march details. No one at the police department had warned him of any potential for violence. And the police *had* arrived by 11:30, but the shooting was already over. Nelson's mind recycled other details—the delay in receiving the permit, the church's withdrawal of its offer to host the conference, the removal of the march posters—which he organized into a narrative of an orchestrated attack involving not only the Klan and Nazi marauders but also the police and the city.

"This man [is] not allowed to make bond for . . . 12 hours after receipt by jail, due to explosive situation in Greensboro, then bond to be $1,000 secured," read the release order. This order would keep Nelson in jail overnight and require him to appear before the district court to face the charges of inciting a riot and resisting arrest. At 9:50 p.m., guards escorted Nelson from the cell to a basement interview room where FBI Special Agent Henry N. Phillips and GPD Detective Welch awaited him. Clicking on a tape recorder, they began asking simple questions.[10]

"What's your name?"

"Talk to my lawyer," Nelson responded, closing his eyes and leaning his chair back against the wall.

The officers threatened to kick the chair out from under Nelson, to tear the bandages off his wounded arm. Your life "wouldn't be worth a wooden nickel" on the street, Nelson heard the FBI agent say. "Whether you realize it or not, you are in a little trouble. There are three hundred to four hundred rednecks out there with your name on their lips."

They'd already lynched Jim, thought Nelson. Exhausted, haunted by thoughts of what had transpired, Nelson willed his mind blank, shifting his focus beyond the room and the throbbing pain in his injured arm, beyond these men he would never trust. They couldn't threaten him into informing on his comrades. He turned his chair around, faced the cement wall, and gave the FBI agent and the detective his back. Eventually they sent him back to the cell. The earth kept turning. Morning would come and, at some point, they would have to release him. As the night wore on, Nelson's hunch that the police absence at Morningside was intentional hardened into certainty.

Late on the night of November 3, one of the police officers on duty at Morningside arrived home. His wife asked how he was. "We didn't get the n——," he responded angrily. Decades later, she'd say she knew her husband was referring to Nelson Johnson.[11]

❖

That same night, in a seedy motel on the outskirts of Greensboro, a pair of FBI agents sat facing two members of the Bureau of Alcohol, Tobacco, and Firearms (BATF).[12]

The Bureau men considered their BATF colleagues to be cowboys running out of an agency that worked fast and loose, and whose recordkeeping was haphazard and informal. Listening to the two BATF men talk did nothing to dispel the Bureau agents' sense of superiority toward the cocky rookie and the slow-witted good ol' boy before them. That said, their interagency colleagues could be useful; the restrictions on the use of provocateurs and informants that hemmed in the FBI's intelligence gathering had not been extended to the BATF.[13]

The senior BATF agent explained again how he'd brought in the short, athletic man sitting beside him to infiltrate the local Nazi group suspected of buying and selling illegal weapons. Though the rookie claimed not to have been at Morningside, members of his Nazi group had just shot and killed four communists. The story the two men told about what they knew of the shooting, however, was peppered with loose ends, inconsistencies, and contradictions. The fact that the Klan and Nazis shot some communists, the FBI men knew, would pale beside the headline that a federal agency possessed intelligence that could have prevented the murders—something the FBI and BATF would publicly deny.

No, the FBI agents didn't like what they were hearing at all. These BATF rubes were in over their heads. "You'd better get your ducks in a row," said one FBI man.[14] Go back, he told them, and write everything down. Create an official version of what you've been doing and what happened. And do so in short order.

With that, two of the FBI agents on Cecil Moses's team walked out of the motel, climbed into their car, and drove back to the local FBI office with no intention to further investigate their BATF colleagues.

Within days, a team of officials and lawyers from BATF headquarters descended on Winston-Salem to construct the official narrative. No one outside of the BATF, a few FBI agents, and an even smaller number of Greensboro policemen knew anything at all about what had been discussed in that motel room. And all of them expected it to stay that way.

❖

As the afternoon of November 3 deepened and descended into twilight, fear enveloped Greensboro like a haze. The fog of anxiety hung thickest in the predominantly Black southeast section of the city. Some of the people living adjacent to Morningside Homes grabbed a few things and fled the city, terrified that the violence might continue either at the hands of white vigilantes or the police, a distinction that wasn't always clear to them. Kids living in Morningside had caught glimpses of Jim, Bill, and Cesar's lifeless white bodies and assumed they were dead Klansmen, adding to decades-long confusion about who'd started the deadly fight on their doorsteps.

Some in the Morningside Homes community vowed "eye for an eye" revenge, improvising weapons such as the jar of acid seen sloshing ominously in the hand of one man. "If we [Black people] had been in their [white] neighborhood, you better believe there would have been cops," said one Morningside resident. "[We're] ready if the Klan comes back," said another.[15]

That afternoon, over at A&T, students were ordered to shelter in their dormitory rooms and to keep the window shades drawn. Hall phones jangled urgently with calls from panicked parents around the country hoping to learn that their children were safe. Every so often a student would sneak out and pick up the receiver to still the ringing and, if they could, assuage the frightened voice coming over the line.[16]

The Klansmen and Nazis who'd fled Morningside after the shooting scattered. Some went home to their families. Virgil Griffin headed across state lines for the swamps behind his sister's house in South Carolina. One shooter set out for Chicago. The AR-180 brandished at Brent Fletcher's house was tossed into a quarry on the outskirts of Winston-Salem.

Eddie Dawson and his friend James Buck watched the news coverage from barstools in a Greensboro saloon. Eventually, Eddie went home, expecting it wouldn't be long before the police—or maybe the FBI—showed up at his door to listen to his version of events. For days, no one came or called the man who'd provided them with inside information on the Klan's plans to confront the march. "They let you go down the drain like a rotten piece of meat," thought Eddie.[17]

The afternoon *Greensboro Record* called the attack a "tactical ambush" by the Klan on the Communist Workers Party. The next morning, however, when the *Greensboro Daily News* hit porches and newsstands, Mayor Melvin's efforts to shape the narrative appeared to be having an effect. The word *ambush* had disappeared from the reporting. "Four Die in Klan-Leftist Shootout," read the headline. The top photo featured a slack-jawed CWP member on one knee beside the body of Jim Waller. A small pistol dangled from the stunned activist's right hand. How could the police prevent violence between two groups intent on attacking each other, Melvin asked rhetorically, saying that "the locale of the shootings was an accident of fate provoked by outside extremists, and . . . it was ironic in light of the city's exemplary record in race relations."[18]

On the inside pages of the November 4 *Greensboro Daily News*, a short article began, "Nelson Johnson, the leader of the protest rally in Greensboro Saturday, is no stranger to violence. His presence at the Saturday violence marked the second time in 10 years Johnson has been a leader in activity that brought death, destruction, and injury." Nelson had "been in and out of jail" in recent years, the article

reported inaccurately, making only cursory mention of his years—
and successes—as an advocate for the city's working poor.[19] However
disparaging, the story contradicted Mayor Melvin's "accident of fate"
statement, offering a glimpse of the relationship between Greensboro's past and its terrible present. It had been only ten years since, in
the wake of a contested student council election at the local Black
high school, National Guard troops surrounded and then stormed
the A&T campus, in the largest military operation on an educational
institution in American history. While this piece of A&T's history
might not have found a place in the nation's collective memory in the
same way that the 1970 shooting at Kent State University did, the
military operation and the unsolved case of the Aggie student who'd
been killed during the conflict lingered as unresolved traumas in
Black Greensboro. Nelson and Joyce Johnson's lives as organizers
were entangled with that event, which took place as a thirty-six-year-
old Jim Melvin assumed a seat on Greensboro's city council for the
first time.

Nelson walked out of prison the next morning and was met, not
by a mob of white supremacists, but with Joyce's embrace. People all
around the country were picking up their local newspapers to read
the shocking headlines. The *New York Times, Boston Globe, Times-
Picayune, Miami Herald, Chicago Tribune, Richmond Times-Dispatch*,
and hundreds more, as well as the major television networks, reported
the news that arrived like an invasion from a past Americans preferred
not to remember and a present they'd rather not see.

NAMESAKE

During that same gloomy fall of 1979, the North Carolina Historical Commission found itself at an impasse. The committee couldn't reach consensus on whether a marker should be erected to honor the twentieth anniversary of the 1960 student sit-ins, only three months away. Martin Luther King Jr. had called the protests against segregation an "electrifying movement of Negro students [that] shattered the placid surfaces of campuses and communities across the South."[1] While many in Greensboro's white community had resigned themselves to sharing public spaces with Blacks, they weren't proud of doing so. They missed their community's "placid surface." One longtime FBI agent remarked that Greensboro's white community "didn't want integration but accepted it with less trouble than anywhere else in the country."[2] He included himself in that characterization. If anything made him proud, it was the idea that the Greensboro Police Department had deftly handled the demonstrations, steering them from the kind of violence that had ripped through Birmingham, Alabama, and other southern cities. Placid surfaces, Melvin and his powerful friends knew, made it easier to run their city and its businesses efficiently and without interference. Why should agitation be publicly celebrated?

On November 1, however, about fifty people had gathered to unveil another state marker acknowledging the founding of the New Garden Friends Meeting and the Quakers' long presence in

Greensboro. "The significance," wrote one journalist, "of 228 years of providing aid to wounded soldiers on both sides at the [American Revolution] Battle of Guilford Courthouse, helping Black slaves escape north via the Underground Railroad, and Friends (Quakers) helping to settle the West, was not elusive."[3]

The Quaker history burnished Greensboro's progressive image. "North Carolina is different from the rest of the South because of the presence of the Quakers," who "served as a conscience which the rest of the region lacked," wrote one historian.[4] When they settled in the area during the eighteenth century, the Quakers set up Manumission Societies, refused to trade products produced by slave labor, and by the early 1800s not only taught enslaved people to read and write but also, under the stealthy guidance of Levi Coffin and his cousin Vestal, spirited them north toward freedom along what came to be known as the Underground Railroad. This history supported Mayor Melvin's boast of the city's "exemplary record in race relations." As is generally the case, the reality was more complex.

In response to the overt and covert abolitionist activities of the Quakers (and Nat Turner's slave rebellion in Virginia), Greensboro's leading citizens organized patrols charged with arresting "all slaves . . . where they do not belong" and passed a law to "render it criminal to teach slaves to read and write."[5] The new 1831 slavery laws, which punished not only the enslaved people who dared dream of freedom but also those who aided and abetted their struggle, became so "oppressive" that many Quakers, including the Coffins, departed North Carolina to continue their abolition work from the relative safety of northern free states.

Quakers remained, however, to found what would become Guilford College, the only Quaker college in the southeastern United States, and to maintain the congregation of the New Garden Friends Meeting. Those who stayed accommodated themselves to the local culture, mores, and economics of white supremacy. The college stayed open during the Civil War and "turned [its back] on the cause of African Americans."[6] Guilford College hosted minstrel shows into the 1950s and would begin to desegregate only in the 1960s, more than a decade after the University of North Carolina admitted Black students. One powerful Guilford College trustee and member of the New Garden Friends Meeting, Robert Frazier, became mayor of Greensboro in the 1950s. A staunch segregationist, Frazier resisted efforts to integrate the Friends Meeting, insisting that "inviting of members of the negro [*sic*] race (who as a group now maintain suitable separate religious meeting places in our community) to attend our regular meetings is to be discouraged."[7]

No Guilford College students participated in the 1960 sit-ins at the Woolworth's lunch counter, though students from the white women's colleges in Greensboro did. As Greensboro eagerly claimed the Quakers in 1979, the full history commemorated by the state-sanctioned plaque was, perhaps, more "elusive" than the *Greensboro Daily News* writer suggested.

The history of how a dissident religion could be grafted to the founding American story might best be examined in the memory of the life and death of the man for whom the city was named, the Revolutionary War general Nathanael Greene.

Nine miles across town from Nelson and Joyce's home, on a hill graced by beech and tupelo trees, hickory and oak, loblolly pine and red maple, sits an outsize facsimile of the "cerebral" revolutionary, Major-General Nathanael Greene. Twenty-seven feet from pedestal to tricorn, astride a bronze steed, monocular in hand, Greene gazes west toward the field where nearly two thousand redcoats formed under the command of Major-General Lord Charles Cornwallis. Greene's faithful stallion bows its finely wrought head, as if gathering courage for the onslaught that would leave the carcasses of nearly a thousand men and beasts strewn across the fields and through the surrounding woods.

Several yards in front of Greene and his horse stands Athena, the Greek goddess of war strategy, a palm branch of peace in one hand, a shield in the other, guiding and protecting his journey into history. A portion of the inscription reads, "[The men who fought here] neither need defense nor eulogy but only just recognition." In fact, however, one eulogy, delivered in 1789, would be critical to establishing Greene's place among the pantheon of American revolutionary heroes.

But before that happened, Greene commanded the southern effort in the Revolutionary War, a task complicated not only by a lack of provisions and resources but also by the opposition of colonists still loyal to the British Crown. Over the years, as the patriotic grip on America's revolutionary history loosened, some historians—searching for facts rather than a unifying narrative—began to describe Greene's southern campaign, and the revolutionary struggle itself, as more than a war between British colonialists and their subjects; they saw in it also a battle between American settlers divided by class, religion, and an increasing economic reliance on the enslavement of Africans.

It rained on March 15, 1781, the day the New Englander Greene and his ragged army of some 4,400 militiamen and veteran Continentals fought over this patch of ground in the village of Guilford Courthouse. Counted among Greene's band of revolutionaries were at least three dozen Black soldiers. After ninety minutes of savage hand-to-hand fighting, Greene ordered a retreat. The British commander, Lord Cornwallis, surveyed the devastating scene as cold rain pummeled the dying and lifeless bodies crumpled over the field. Cornwallis forced Greene's retreat, but at the cost of losing nearly a third of his sharply uniformed men. In the wake of that battle, the will to beat the rebels seemed to abandon the exhausted and starving British and Hessian survivors, their spirits sinking with their feet into the Carolina mud. Seven months later, Cornwallis surrendered to George Washington at Yorktown. Over time, people would begin to connect these two events: the Battle of Guilford Courthouse and the British submission to its former colony. Guilford Courthouse would be called Cornwallis's Pyrrhic victory, one achieved at too great a cost. In the moment, however, even Greene doubted his military effectiveness. A master at logistics who deployed an unusual military strategy—a combination of traditional and guerrilla warfare aimed to inflict both physical and psychological harm on the enemy—he couldn't be certain how much he'd contributed to the ultimate victory. As difficult as it might be to understand that winning a war might require losing battles, explaining Guilford Courthouse as heroic was Sisyphean; the story would require a great deal of repeating.[8]

During 1781 and into 1782, Greene and his Continental charges waited in Charleston, South Carolina, for the peace to be sanctioned. During this time, he personally signed for loans to feed and clothe his men. When the secretary of the treasury didn't pay, the enormous debt fell to Greene personally. Unflattering rumors of Greene's participation in illicit speculation fluttered through the colonies. The major-general sold his property in Rhode Island to cover a portion of what he owed, then hurried his family to an isolated plantation in Georgia granted him by the Georgia General Assembly, a prize for liberating their colony from the Tories.

Greene stood nearly six feet, a tall, sturdy man for his time, with piercing blue eyes and a sharp nose that rose like a shiv from an oval face. From a young age, his keen intelligence and thirst for knowledge fed an ambition that chafed at the limitations caused by his Quaker religion, a lame leg, and the irksome laws and taxes imposed by the British. But now, passing forty, his vigor depleted by eight years of war, instead of basking in the glow of victory, he found himself starting over far from home. Nearly twenty miles upriver from Savannah, Georgia, Greene hoped to squeeze a profit from a steamy floodplain planted in rice and cotton and tended by enslaved workers. In a decade, he'd traveled far from the pacifist and abolitionist values of his New England Quaker childhood and the Black men who'd fought with him against the British.

Greene died suddenly in June 1786. Some said it was heatstroke; others, that the stress of the war debt killed him. His widow, Catharine Littlefield Greene, found herself with five children, her husband's debt, and a low-country plantation hundreds of miles from her friends in New York and Rhode Island, where she'd grown up. She would need the help of these powerful friends to restore her husband's reputation and clear his debt.

Three years later, on the thirteenth anniversary of the publication of the Declaration of Independence, one year after the ratification of the new Constitution, and just two months after George Washington was sworn in as the first president of the new nation, the auburn-haired Alexander Hamilton stepped into the pulpit at St. Paul's Chapel in Manhattan to celebrate the country's founding. Though the president was too ill to attend, the illustrious assembly included members of the Society of the Cincinnati, First Lady Martha Washington, Vice President John Adams and his wife, Abigail, and the entire Senate and House of Representatives. Casting his violet eyes over the assembled US government and Revolutionary War veterans, many of whom had known Nathanael Greene personally, all of them members of the exclusive club now charged with memorializing the struggle for American independence, Hamilton introduced his subject: "For high as this great man stood in the estimation of his Country, the whole extent of his worth was little known."[9]

Hamilton then expounded on Greene's character, his military prowess, and the affection all in the room should feel for his family. "The *name* of *Greene* will at once awaken in your minds the images of whatever is noble and estimable in human nature," predicted Hamilton, though he lamented that Greene's reputation as a statesman and as a soldier "falls far below his desert." In defense of Greene's military strategy, Hamilton asserted that "the art of retreating is perhaps the most difficult in the art of war," calling Greene's movements in the South "a masterpiece of military skill" that should be "revered by a Grateful Country."

"Under a monarchy," the path from Greene's "humble lot of a private citizen" to "a more splendid and ample theater" would have been closed. And so, "animated by an enlightened sense of the value of free government, he cheerfully resolved to stake his fortune his hopes his life and his honor [*sic*]" on "a cause which was worthy of the toils and of the blood of heroes." Greene, through Hamilton's words, comes to embody the declared ideals of the new republic. And from Greene's story Hamilton extracts the essence of patriotism: "We recall the ideas of [Greene's] worth with sensations . . . and feel an involuntary propensity to consider [his] fame our own. We seem to appropriate to ourselves the good [Greene and his like] have acquired and share in the very praise we bestow."

The secretary of the treasury ended his tribute with an appeal to the assembled soldiers and dignitaries on behalf of Greene's five children: "Let us not fail to mingle the reflection that he has left behind him offspring who are the heirs to the friendship which we bore to the father and who have a claim from many, if not from all of us to cares not less than parental."

Everyone in St. Paul's knew about the scandal of Greene's debts from his time in Charleston and that Hamilton's homage was an implicit petition for them to be resolved. If there'd been a single, challenging note in Hamilton's talk, it was his mention of enslaved Africans, whom he described as "bound by all the laws of injured humanity to hate their Masters." Hamilton disliked slavery, but he loved property more and believed it to be the sacred basis of liberty and freedom. Any discomfort the slave owners in the church might have felt when Hamilton mentioned the "humanity" of their human property, or justified the enslaved people's hatred of their masters, was secondary to the eulogy's primary message.

The government assumed Greene's debts. Catharine, liberated from the weight of them, married a young plantation manager and, together, the two started a new slave plantation on Cumberland Island, Georgia.

Catharine made one more contribution that would help determine the industrial and economic future not only of the young nation but also of the city that would become Greensboro, North Carolina. During her last years at Mulberry Grove Plantation outside of Savannah, she was visited by a Yale man named Eli Whitney. Catharine discussed with him the problem she and other plantation owners dealt with that limited the scale of cotton-growing operations: cleaning the seeds from the cotton fibers. Over just a few days, Whitney and Catharine devised a contraption that pulled the white fibers free of the dark seeds fifty times faster than the human hand. They'd invented the cotton gin (engine), which would increase America's production of cotton, grow the textile industry around the world, and stimulate an even more voracious appetite for enslaved workers to tend ever more vast plantations. Eli Whitney's name would be taught to every American student for more than two hundred years, while Catharine's contribution to the world-shaping technology was forgotten.[10]

The story of the Rhode Island Quaker who became a major-general in the Continental Army, confidant to George Washington, and the brilliant military strategist and harasser of Cornwallis, is, then, intimately connected with the compromise of slavery in the land of inalienable rights, the expansion of the slave trade, and US dependence on "King Cotton."

Eighteen years after Hamilton's speech, the citizens of Guilford County, North Carolina, voted to move their county seat to a central location, easily reachable from every corner of the rolling geography they inhabited. Surveyors sent out to put a stake in the precise center of the county soon found themselves "in the middle of a duck pond in a brush thicket." So they placed the new courthouse just off-center, on a high point about a mile from the swamp at what would become the intersection of Market and Elm Streets.[11] In the absence of Hamilton's 1789 intervention on Greene's behalf, establishment of Greene's Guilford Courthouse narrative as heroic, and role in erasing Greene's debt, it's difficult to imagine that the fathers of the new town would have voted unanimously to call it Greensborough. "Consecrated in the affections of their citizens to the remotest posterity," Hamilton said, "the fame of Greene will ever find in them a more durable as well as more flattering Memorial than in the proudest monument of marble or brass."[12]

❖

It took Greensboro and the federal government more than one hundred years to erect a proud memorial to Nathanael Greene. And when they were finally ready to unveil the statue, made not of marble and brass but of granite and bronze, all American history seemed to converge in the North Carolina city: the Revolutionary War, the Civil War, chattel slavery, industry, ideas of freedom, and the iron grip of white supremacy reinforced by half-true narratives disguised as history.

The excitement had been building for months by the morning of July 3, 1915, when people began making their way by horse and automobile from the center of Greensboro to the hill six miles away where Nathanael Greene and his troops had clashed with the British Army. At 9:30 a.m., a military band struck up a lively marching tune, and between ten and twenty thousand people shuffled into formation on the dusty roads that ran through the battleground site. The local paper called it a "gigantic parade," believed to be the largest public gathering in North Carolina history. Among the attendees were official representatives from each of the original thirteen states; two men sporting the "picaresque" uniforms of Rhode Island's Varnum Continentals, the militia cofounded by Greene in 1774; a pair of Greene's "lineal descendants"; and the German-born sculptor who'd spent three years perfecting the monument. Francis Hermann Packer wandered anonymously through the crowd, eavesdropping for reactions to his creation and discreetly snapping images with the cutting-edge technology of the day, Kodak's recently released Vest Pocket camera.

For one journalist, the "unique and beautiful feature" of the parade was the horse-drawn float displaying thirteen young Greensboro ladies, each modeling a flag of one of the colonies. A refreshing shower began to fall, clearing the air of the dust raised by thousands of feet. The reporter's thoughts strayed briefly from the patriotic as his gaze returned to the "lovely young Greensboro women." There "were no further ill effects [from the rain]," he wrote, "than to make the flags cling a little more closely; and nobody who witnessed the spectacle could blame the flags for that."[13]

Attendees listened to a number of speakers offer details and lessons from "the most costly victory that Cornwallis ever won," as George R. Gaither of Baltimore called the Battle of Guilford Courthouse. They were reminded that "Light-Horse Harry" Lee III, father of the "beloved chieftain" Robert E. Lee, had called Greene his "much loved compeer of the Carolinas." Prominent Greensboro businessman A. M. Scales proclaimed the battlefield the "common heritage of the nation."

By the time Rosewell B. Burchard of Rhode Island rose to speak the rain fell steadily. "Rhode Island opens its arms to the South," he bellowed into the weather. Known for his oratorical gifts, the New England state's former lieutenant governor grabbed the attention and affection of his restless audience when he called the Civil War "the Mistake." He reached back prior to the Civil War, to Washington, Thomas Jefferson, Lafayette, "Light-Horse" Lee, and, of course, Greene, invoking the "physical, the mental, and the moral superiority of the men who laid the foundations of this ideal republic," asking, "What names are these to conjure with in the romance and tragedy of the nation's birth?" He continued, "With the young republic destined to wield greater influence in the world's affairs for justice and for peace, it is well for us to keep before us the everlasting and fundamental principles upon which our government was so firmly founded."

Freedom and unity were the words of the day, and Greene its catalyst, the northerner who became the "Savior of the South," the Quaker who, as the speaker from Georgia reminded the audience, "was becoming a southern planter and if he could have lived would have become a real southern planter and a southerner by adoption."[14]

When the speakers finished, Greene's descendants yanked a vast American flag from the statue, revealing it for the first time to the gathered audience.

There's no mention in the reports of any Negroes among the

thousands in attendance, of the Negro revolutionary soldiers who fought bravely against Cornwallis, statements to enlighten readers of a Negro perspective on "American freedom," or what their reaction might have been to calling the Civil War "the Mistake" in the interest of North–South "reconciliation."[15]

The only other event that year to compare with the unveiling of Greene's statue was the November arrival of the "mightiest and most overwhelming theatrical offering ever shown," which required the work of eighteen thousand people and three thousand horses, and was made up of five thousand scenes "ripped from the pages of history" at a production cost of half a million dollars. The people of Greensboro and the surrounding towns lined up to purchase tickets in advance, ordered them by mail, and, if they could, called a phone that had been installed at the theater just to meet the demand for the twice-a-day screenings of D. W. Griffith's *The Birth of a Nation* at the Grand Opera House.[16]

The "story of the South's Reconstruction," like the message delivered at the unveiling of the Nathanael Greene statue, was "the final welding of this nation in bonds of unity," as the errors of the Civil War and Reconstruction were corrected. Little mention was made in Greensboro of the NAACP's campaign to damn the film as "improper, immoral, and unjust" or the rabbi who called it a "loathsome libel on a race of human beings."[17] More typical was one southern woman's response: "[The Ku Klux Klan] was a band of knights sent to make things work out." When faced with the "carpetbaggers' excesses, and the famous rides of the Ku Klux Klan," the excitement inside the theaters inspired more than a few old Confederate veterans in the audience to let loose "the old war shouts . . . momentarily forget[ing] that it [was] only in the play."[18]

The hoots and hollers echoed far beyond the theater, as the film inspired a new era of Ku Klux Klan activity. The architects of white supremacy worked diligently, wielding the full force of their political, commercial, and media enterprises to bind a narrative of racial superiority to America's most resilient mythologies. When, in 1919, Eddie

Dawson entered the world in Fort Lee, New Jersey, hundreds of thousands of white, Protestant Americans paid yearly for the privilege of membership in the Klan and the chance to help protect the country from Catholics, Jews, Native Americans, immigrants, and Negroes. Klan membership, which included senators, congressmen, judges, and governors, peaked at about five million in the 1920s, then collapsed under the weight of scandal and the corrupt misuse of the mountains of dues money. The nativist, "100 percent American" ideas the Klan supported, however, remained vital.[19]

In 1935, the writer and historian W. E. B. Du Bois countered the version of history articulated during the 1915 installation of the Nathanael Greene memorial in Greensboro. In *Black Reconstruction in America, 1860–1880*, Du Bois argued that without the efforts of some two hundred thousand Negro soldiers and the courage of the enslaved people who abandoned the Southern plantations on which the Confederacy depended for food—Du Bois framed this labor walk-off in economic and strategic terms, calling it a "General Strike"—the North could not have prevailed in the Civil War. More controversial still, Du Bois argued that Negroes were active and effective participants in the postwar Reconstruction; it wasn't Black incompetence, but rather the reassertion of old powers and economic interests in the South and the North that buried a dream of political and economic equality under Black Codes and Jim Crow segregation, or "slavery by another name."

To replace the culture and economics of enslavement would have required, Du Bois argued, at least two generations of martial law or dictatorship in the South and, critically, the will of the North to enforce it.

As a Black man grappling with the peculiar intersection of race and class in the United States, Du Bois found the historical and economic analysis of Karl Marx to be a lucid guide to the dynamics of history and power, and a sharp tool for slicing away at America's creed of exceptionalism. Du Bois equated what he called the

"American Assumption" not only with the little questioned doctrine of unfettered capitalism but also with the country's notion of its essential innocence and goodness. Following Marx's logic, Du Bois believed that the United States faced a destiny-determining choice between "freedom . . . for all men" and "industry . . . directed by an autocracy."[20]

Like most Black people drawn to communism's promise of equality, however, Du Bois stumbled over the riddle posed by the relationship between race and class; lured by the leveling and illuminating red flame, Blacks often felt burned when Marxists explained race merely as an outcome of class dynamics. Experience told Black people that this pat answer was too facile. Du Bois, in his work, aimed to carve out space to think about the "color line" as something related to but not wholly dependent on class distinctions and conflicts.

Du Bois ended *Black Reconstruction* with a searing essay, "The Propaganda of History," which attacked the unscientific attempt to confirm white supremacy in the history of Reconstruction. Historians, he wrote, "change the facts of history that the story will make pleasant reading for Americans. . . . Nations reel and stagger on their way; they make hideous mistakes; they commit frightful wrongs; they do great and beautiful things. And shall we not best guide humanity by telling the truth about all this, so far as the truth is ascertainable?"[21]

As an example of the truth distorted boldly, Du Bois referenced the legend on a Confederate monument in North Carolina that read "They died fighting for liberty!"

❖

In the 1950s, as the civil rights movement gained momentum, Klan affiliation and membership surged again throughout the South and in North Carolina in particular. Beside the white supremacists in Greensboro lived an educated and ambitious Black population that had spent centuries chipping away at segregation and inequality. As the 1960s roiled forward, a wave of young activists around the country grew tired of waiting for the courts to enforce equal treatment. They stood ready to seize the freedoms withheld since their people had been brought to US shores. When Nelson Johnson arrived in Greensboro in the mid-1960s, this impatient energy intoxicated him as much as the intransigent resistance to equality infuriated him. A racial narrative different from the one that gathered around Nathanael Greene and *The Birth of a Nation* propelled Nelson forward—a narrative that was also anchored in deep, accumulating layers of personal and collective, local and national history.

SECTION II

DREAMS: 1966-1979

THORNE

After Zelma Thorne married James Ransom Johnson in 1933, she would say, "When you married me there was mules in the barn, wheat in the field."[1] Though he didn't inherit property as his wife had, James had some education, having attended the North Carolina Agricultural and Technical State high school in Greensboro. He proved to be an astute businessman and skilled entrepreneur. Through careful planning, tireless work, and a genius for multitasking, he enlarged the farm, buying land from the white Thornes, his wife's unacknowledged blood relatives, who, seventy years after the Civil War, still lived and farmed nearby. He started a logging business, running two teams of lumberjacks who cut pulpwood and hauled the logs on James's trucks to the paper mill in Roanoke Rapids. Eventually, tenant farmers worked sections of the land, splitting their take with the family. In his dealings with the men who worked for him, James had a reputation for fairness, for treating them as equals.[2]

Zelma and James would have nine children. Artistic, talkative, with a flair for the dramatic, Zelma gave her children names that reminded her of the enormity and possibility she discovered in the history she'd studied at the state college in Elizabeth City. She named her fourth child Ivan after the first czar of Russia. Her fifth son, born April 25, 1943, she named Nelson for her father, bestowing on him the middle name Napoleon. Zelma possessed a gift for music and a love of theater. She played piano at the church her father founded and liked to direct plays at the Negro high school in Littleton. If James instilled in his children the ethics of hard work and fairness, Zelma endowed them with an origin story.

❖

In the 1840s, two white brothers, Samuel Thomas Thorne and John Davis Thorne, had made a journey south from North Carolina and "entered into family ventures," presumably to grow sugarcane or cotton on land they'd purchased in the fertile, swampy lowlands of St. Martin Parish, Louisiana, in the heart of the French-speaking Creoles' Arcadia. During the Civil War, in 1864, with the Union Army holding much of Louisiana, a new state constitution was adopted. The document ended slavery in the state but did not proffer Negroes the vote. The new constitution and the Union occupation threw the local planter society into chaos. In the face of changing circumstances, the Thorne brothers decided to leave Louisiana, organizing themselves for a thousand-mile trek along the perilous roads and tracks of a country at war with itself, back to where they'd come, the hamlet of Airlie in eastern North Carolina's Halifax County.[3]

Joining them on the journey were several Black Thornes, related not only by name but almost certainly, given their various shades of skin, by blood to the white Thornes. The men and women who worked the plantation owners' land and tended to their household and personal needs—the people the landowners claimed as property and on whom they depended economically—also faced an uncertain future and difficult choices. Since Lincoln's Emancipation Proclamation of January 1, 1863, many Negroes had fled Louisiana plantations and the bondage under which they toiled, seeking the protection of Union soldiers. But these Black Thornes, part of the original venture into the Deep South years earlier, missed the relatives they'd left behind in North Carolina. One way or another, they wished to be reunited with them. Lifting family and community above the glint of personal freedom, they didn't light out.

Horses and mules were hitched to wagons and filled with people and their belongings. The party set out on an arduous and risky journey, the white Thornes riding in the wagons, the Black Thornes walking along beside and behind, accompanied by a faithful bulldog. One of the Black Thornes making the trip was an infant, the son of Wilbur and Matilda, whose given name was Nelson.[4]

Months later, when the bedraggled caravan of Black Thornes, white Thornes, horses, mules, and the bulldog arrived in Airlie for an improbable family reunion, North Carolina was still a slave-owning state. That would change on December 4, 1865, with the state's ratification of the Thirteenth Amendment to the US Constitution, which read, "Neither slavery nor involuntary servitude, except as a punishment for crime whereof the party shall have been duly convicted, shall exist within the United States, or any place subject to their jurisdiction."

Born into slavery, Nelson T. Thorne had been freed by the 1864 Louisiana constitution. Swaddled in his mother's arms, he'd traveled back into Confederate territory that had not yet succumbed to Union forces. Within months of arriving in Airlie, federal law freed him a second time. All of this took place before the baby turned two years old, perhaps before the child could speak and when he barely walked, a turbulent forecasting of future racial history in the United States and the constant, elusive, and repetitive quest for liberation. Freedom, this history suggested with its peculiar complexity, is not a permanent state.

❖

Nelson T. Thorne Sr. grew up, married, and fathered twelve children. He became a preacher and founded Lee's Chapel Baptist Church in Airlie. Once considered property himself, he came to own property. When he died in 1930, he passed to his youngest daughter,

Zelma Blanche Thorne, his mules and horses, chickens and pigs, some forty acres of farmland, a rambling home the family referred to as "the plantation," and a legacy of service to the Black community. Zelma made sure that his achievements would be passed down through the generations with pride, imprinted as they were with the country's racial history, like a watermark always visible on a fine sheet of cotton paper. Given the way that her father's courage and fortitude mingled with the vagaries of history, it's little wonder that Nelson T. Thorne's daughter would hear echoes of her family stories in the books she loved to read that narrated the world's dramatic and epic histories.

On Sundays, Zelma took her children to Lee's Chapel Baptist Church. Scripture, however, blended with the everyday burble of life in a working household, the country music they enjoyed warbling through the radio and the sound of the cotton baler booming like thunder from a mile away as it slammed the fiber harvest into bricks destined for North Carolina's great textile mills, including those in Greensboro.

During the school year, young Nelson and the other Johnson children walked two miles south along the dusty road to the Terrapin School in nearby Hollister, where a single teacher instructed all six grades. No seesaw or swing graced the schoolyard. Each day at recess, the boys challenged each other to wrestling matches on the dirt playground. When the students, representing every shade of "colored" possible, from "dark, to tan, to high yellow," walked the two miles home in the slow afternoons, ambling along the country road rain or shine, they'd continue sparring and throwing rocks, watching for the farm trucks that rumbled by.[5]

One of five thousand schools built for Negroes throughout the South with assistance from the president of Sears, Roebuck & Company, Julius Rosenwald, the Terrapin School had been constructed by an enterprising young man named Cary Pittman in 1925. Neighborhoods, villages, and hamlets such as Airlie raised more than half the budget for the schools themselves. Church elders, like Reverend Nelson T. Thorne Sr., usually led the fundraising efforts, collecting pennies at a time from parents who dreamed of better lives for their children. Pittman led the construction of as many as 33 of Halifax County's 46 Rosenwald Schools, the most of any North Carolina county, in a state with 836 of them, more than any other state in the South.[6]

As soon as Nelson and his brothers were old enough, James put them to work. Before school, on weekends, and during school holidays, they'd feed and water the livestock, tend the truck garden that provided most of the family's food, and work the tobacco, cotton, and peanut cash crops. Each morning at dawn, James issued his sons the day's tasks, checked on his tenant farmers, and then drove off into the surrounding woodlots to harvest pulpwood with his teams of lumberjacks.

❖

"You can't trust the white man, he will cheat you, beat you, kill you," Zelma warned her children, marking the boundaries of the racial geography, as real as the air they breathed and the earth they worked, with fear. Mother Zelma would also say, "We need to learn to act decent like the white folk." Between these contradictory ideas of whites as cheaters and killers on the one hand, and civilizing models to emulate for their intelligence and manners on the other, lay a complex social and psychological wilderness.[7]

When the midday summer heat shimmered over the tobacco fields, the Johnson boys headed across the road to the swimming hole in Little Fishing Creek. They'd check to be sure the local white kids weren't there before stripping down and jumping naked into the refreshing water. If the white boys beat them to the pool, the Johnsons would head back to the fields with morning sweat still clinging to their skin. Once, when they'd finished swimming, they saw a group of white youths approaching. Nelson and his brothers hid in the bushes and watched through the foliage and the gauze of myth. They were surprised to see the boys strip and swim and splash just as they did, the only difference the color of their skin.

Contact with whites, even the Thornes who lived nearby, was incidental and rare in the rural Jim Crow South. The all-Black world protected Nelson and his siblings, a "shelter in the storm" of segregation.[8] When contact did occur, for safety's sake one hoped that it hewed to the enforced, racial perimeters: At the movie theater on Saturdays, the Johnson kids knew where to sit—the balcony—to watch Gene Autry sing and ride. They knew not to sit at any of the marble-topped tables at the Three Fountains Drug Store and how to say *sir* and *ma'am* with the right degree of deference at Airlie's crossroads store.

❖

For the white Thornes and other members of the Halifax County planter and banking class, the "big town" wasn't Littleton, but Richmond, Virginia. A first-class train ticket took them to extended stays at the luxurious Jefferson Hotel, shopping sprees in the opulently stocked department stores along Broad Street, and renewal in the shadow of the towering monuments to the Lost Cause of the Confederacy. Class distinctions among Airlie's Blacks, meanwhile, were measured, not by suits and dresses from the stores in Richmond, but by whether a family owned the land necessary to achieve a degree of independence and self-sufficiency.

Color and shade, as well as land, marked divisions within the Black community. Most of Zelma's children inherited her husband's light skin. But their eldest son and Nelson were born with a deep chocolate hue that resembled hers. While Nelson's parents frowned on judging color at home, the judgment seeped in from every direction, a pervasive gradation of color and value from white, to light, to dark. "I was never free from the stigma of color," Nelson would remember years later.[9] Nelson watched his "high yellow" brother Ivan move through life like "flowing water," quick-tongued, never without a girlfriend. By comparison, Nelson felt slow of speech, reticent, and insecure around girls, to whom he felt invisible due to his dark skin.

Nelson's siblings saw their brother differently from the way he saw himself. They were all raised to be tough, scrappy farm kids who worked from dark to dark. But from a young age, Nelson's brothers and sisters identified him as the toughest and smartest among them, quick to fight and the first to take the initiative to improve their lives on the farm. His brothers would never forget watching him save their youngest brother from drowning in the swimming hole, diving in the split second he sensed trouble, while they remained planted to the bank, slower to act. And they'd tell the story about nine-year-old Nelson who tired of the smelly dishwater that spilled from the outdoor sink onto the muddy ground below. Everyone complained about the mess, but no one did anything about it. Then one morning, Nelson arose, grabbed a shovel, and dug a trench from where the sink drained down to the cornfields. He gathered all the tin cans he could find, cut off the bottoms, and placed them, top to bottom, one in front of the next, jury-rigging a pipe to carry the refuse away.

Zelma passed down a story about Nelson's grandfather Nelson T. Thorne Sr. One day Grandfather Thorne waited in line with a full wagon at the only cotton gin in Airlie. His mules inched forward as each farmer's load was processed, when a white farmer exercised an accepted privilege: he skipped ahead of the Black farmer. Perhaps Grandfather Thorne had somewhere to be that afternoon, or maybe he'd awakened tired of the racial hierarchy that permitted so many daily indignities. Whatever the case, he held his mules firmly in place, refusing to give up his spot to the white man. The other Black people nearby scattered and hid, expecting violent trouble. But Nelson Thorne Sr. got his cotton ginned before the white man and escaped reprisals. Perhaps the last name he shared with a prominent white family saved him, or maybe it was the fact that he had earned a degree of status in the community as a preacher and landowner. Maybe his courage and dignity had acted as a shield.[10]

Nelson attended McIver High School on the Black side of Littleton, down the street from the house where Ella Baker, who would found the Student Nonviolent Coordinating Committee in 1960, grew up. Wiry and quick on the baseball field and the basketball court, Nelson was called Eyes by his classmates for his most electric feature.

In 1958, Nelson and two friends bought soft drinks at the Three Fountains Drug Store in Littleton and sat down in the forbidden wicker chairs beside the marble-topped tables, staging an impromptu sit-in. In an instant, a white man charged around the lunch counter, screaming, "You n——s get out!" The "starch" drained out of the fifteen-year-old boys and, terrified, they fled before they could be beaten or worse.

The experience didn't stop Nelson from attempting another act of civil disobedience. Like his grandfather, Nelson found it impossible to resist testing the edges of Jim Crow apartheid. During a station stop in Charlotte on the way to a high school speech and rhetoric competition in Gastonia, Nelson and a friend decided to move up into the "Whites Only" section at the front of the bus. An ominous fog of discomfort filled the vehicle. The boys stared straight ahead as people threw refuse at them and talked about Negroes "getting out of their place." A man approached and suddenly the slight teenager's head exploded in pain from a vicious punch. Nelson flopped into his friend's lap. His head ringing and overwhelmed by the fear of what might happen next, Nelson whispered to his friend, "Let's move back."[11]

Like so many rural kids all around the country, Nelson began to chafe at the grueling subsistence life of the farmer, the painful sting of horseflies, and the bloody, fly-bitten ears of the mules that required constant care. His uncles and older brothers enlisted in the military to get out of Airlie and see the world. When they returned home to visit, they wore their uniforms proudly, bringing stories from beyond the farm.

Nelson's father asked him to put off joining the Air Force for a year after he graduated from high school to stay and tend the farm. The pulpwood business had collapsed, and government assistance to white farmers did not extend to their Black counterparts, so James Johnson spent his weeks on the road, working as a long-haul truck driver far from the demands of the animals and crops. Nelson pleaded with his brother Ivan to take his place, but Ivan planned to start college that fall at North Carolina A&T in Greensboro.[12]

The day after his graduation from high school in 1961, desperate to escape the only world he knew, the eighteen-year-old Nelson jumped on a bus to Raleigh and enlisted in the military. A few days later, he contacted his family and a furious Ivan from boot camp in Texas, one more eager, young American riding his patriotism toward a bright future.

Over the ensuing four years, Nelson, the rural Jim Crow–isolated adolescent, tasted beer, learned to box, and discovered that white people weren't omnipotent. To his amazement, he realized that his white bunkmate wasn't a particularly sharp thinker and that he, Nelson, believed himself to be smarter than many of the white men he encountered. Daily interactions with white people began to loosen the insidious grip of white supremacy on his mind.

After a time guarding nuclear warheads at the Stony Brook Air Force Station outside of Springfield, Massachusetts, Nelson shipped off to Germany. In Europe, he fell in with a racially conscious group of Black soldiers from New York, Detroit, and Norfolk, Virginia. Even so, and despite the problems back home, he kept his faith in America's exceptionalism, sure that he, a military policeman in the US Air Force, stood on the right side of the Cold War.

Late on February 21, 1965, the day Malcolm X was shot and killed, Black soldiers passed the word, and one by one several of them trudged to the far end of the barracks to talk, beyond the gaze of white observers. As some of the enlisted men perched on the edges of the bunk beds or hunkered on the floor, Nelson rested the butt of his automatic rifle with its thirty-round magazine on the ground and leaned his back against the wall. Still in duty uniform, a sidearm hitched to his belt, he looked every bit the soldier he'd hoped to become when he ran away from the family farm at eighteen.

That night, as the soldiers mourned the death of Brother Malcolm, Nelson articulated a contrarian point of view. "You live by violence, you die by violence," he told the men around him. "I'm for nonviolence," he announced, aligning himself, he believed, with the moral philosophy and strategy of Martin Luther King Jr.

Two soldiers from Norfolk became incensed. "Brother, you out of your mind," they yelled, getting up in his face. Nelson readied himself to fight. "What if somebody just walked up and slapped you in the face, and all you could do is turn the other cheek and stand there until you're swimming in the head?" As this sank in, they continued, "Look at you!" Nelson, stunned, watched as they pointed out the weapons bristling on and around Nelson's person. "You're brainwashed. You've been listening to too much King." Nelson felt more than humiliation. The brothers from Norfolk had lifted a veil from his eyes. In that moment of epiphany, he began to see more clearly the contradiction between the nonviolent beliefs he claimed and his role, however small, in the global reach of the US war machine.

The United States that Nelson came back to had changed since he'd left his rural hamlet in 1961. In the classic fable, Rip van Winkle falls asleep under a portrait of King George, only to wake up and find he's slept through a revolution. Above him now hangs the proud image of George Washington. Nelson, brimming with youthful idealism and eager to protect America's "democracy, freedom, and justice," lit out from the family farm and a land shackled by Jim Crow. He returned to a nation where white supremacy was under attack "by any means necessary" and where the militant voices of a "new breed of cats," as Adam Clayton Powell Jr. referred to the likes of Stokely Carmichael and H. Rap Brown, were ascendant. Nelson had left when Martin Luther King Jr. grounded his right to protest in an integrated vision of the "great glory of American democracy." Nelson would return from his military service unsettled by Malcolm X's insistence that he shouldn't even "consider [himself] an American."[13]

Before he was shipped to Europe and prior to the 1964 Gulf of Tonkin incident, Nelson had volunteered to be part of an Air Force special ops mission to Vietnam. "What have those folks ever done to you?" his aunt challenged him when she learned of his request. Now as the United States scrambled to send the first ground troops to Asia, the words of his aunt and the "brothers from Norfolk" rattled around in his head. Months from completing his four-year commitment, he changed his mind about reenlisting. He'd turn down the big re-up bonus and return to civilian life.[14]

One sultry summer night, shortly after he'd left the Air Force, Nelson put on a sport coat and headed for a juke joint near Hollister. Welterweight-trim, strong, and confident after his tour in the Air Force, he approached a beautiful light-skinned woman and asked her to dance. Blacks from the nearby hamlets and towns called Hollister's straight-haired, light-skinned, and light-eyed residents "issues." Some said they were Native Americans. Others insisted they were descended from white loggers who set up camp in the nearby pine forests after the Civil War and "socialized" with local Black women. Whatever the racial roots of these particular people in Halifax County, the term *issue* historically referred to free Blacks who'd been "issued" papers that verified their status in the antebellum South. The blood of the enslaved and their masters mingled in these free Blacks, who gripped a precarious and incomplete serving of privilege. By the mid-twentieth century, on the outskirts of Airlie, the term merely indicated skin tone and eye color, the deeper origins obscured by a fog of complex—often painful—racial histories.

In the loud, close space of the bar, the young woman's boyfriend watched the dark-skinned man push up on his girl. He and three friends jumped the GI. In the scuffle, knives came out, slashing Nelson's jacket. Blood spurted from Nelson's neck. Unable to take Nelson to the hospital in Littleton, his father, James, raced through the night over dirt roads, carrying his unconscious son to find a nimble-fingered country doctor. The man saved Nelson's life. The offended beau, an "issue" whom Nelson had known as a teenager, hadn't recognized his former friend in the barroom haze. But as court proceedings got underway, he consented to pay for Nelson's medical bills and the clothes that had been stained and ruined by the spilled blood. In return, Nelson agreed to drop the charges.[15]

It wouldn't be the last time Nelson survived a stabbing. And it would be just one of many times when it seemed to him as though an angel protected him. But, more practically, the stabbing was another sign that Nelson belonged not at the trailing, rural edge of change, but at its urban vanguard.

In 1965, by way of his upbringing in the rural Jim Crow South, a coming-of-age in an uncomfortably integrated arm of American power, and a stint exploring Europe's more relaxed racial attitudes, Nelson packed his bags and went to Greensboro to earn an education.

ALL-AMERICA

The week before Thanksgiving 1966, a delegation of city leaders jetted from Greensboro, North Carolina, to Boston to pitch the judges of the National Civic League's All-America City Award contest. The seven emissaries, all of them white men, included the mayor, the city manager, the president of the Junior Chamber of Commerce—better known as the Jaycees—and the managing editor of the *Greensboro Daily News*. To deliver the presentation on that chilly autumn day in New England, they'd tapped Thomas Irwin Storrs, a bespectacled Harvard man, who was executive vice president at the North Carolina National Bank and past president of the Greensboro Chamber of Commerce.[1]

The primary author of the official entry, also present, was the city's most tireless young booster and future mayor, Jim Melvin.[2] Greensboro-born, the son of an East Side gas station owner, Edwin Samuel "Jim" Melvin had received a degree in business from the University of North Carolina's flagship campus in Chapel Hill before hurrying home to immerse himself in the affairs of the city he loved. In truth, Melvin's personal ambitions could not be detached from his hopes and dreams for Greensboro. Under his dogged leadership, the Jaycee chapter and its 450 budding civic leaders propelled hundreds of community development projects forward, work that won them recognition as the best Jaycee chapter in the country and, in a first for a US chapter, the most accomplished in the world. Like Storrs,

Melvin made a living as a banker and worked for the North Carolina National Bank. "I decided," Melvin would say, "that I wasn't going to outdo anybody with sheer native intelligence, or any special talents, because I don't have them. The only way I was getting ahead was hard work."[3] If the angular thirty-two-year-old did possess a gift, it might have been that he rarely looked over his shoulder to the past or second-guessed himself. He fixed his gaze on Greensboro's future and swept others up in the wake of his kinetic pursuit of progress and efficiency.

When his turn came to address the panel, Thomas Storrs projected a vision of a midsize city with major-league aspirations. Over the course of the twentieth century, the "somnolent little southern town," in the words of local boy William Sydney Porter (better known as the short story writer O. Henry), had grown into the booming hub of America's textile industry. A 1924 commentator opined that the "only story" worth telling about Greensboro "must be a story of aspiration."[4] Though its population had doubled since 1950, passing 140,000 residents as rural farmworkers streamed into the city in search of industrial jobs, Greensboro had surrendered its quest to become North Carolina's largest city when Storrs's and Melvin's employer, the North Carolina National Bank—the product of a recent merger between a Greensboro bank and a Charlotte bank—planted its headquarters in Charlotte.[5] Now Greensboro aspired to be the state's "finest" city and one that, Storrs announced to the panel, "responds to challenge with accomplishment." "We are," Storrs continued, "the headquarters of three of the largest industrial concerns in the nation, a major divisional headquarters of a fourth. . . . We are home of one of the nation's largest life insurance companies, and of several smaller but important ones. We have four colleges and a major campus of the Consolidated University of North Carolina. The understandably tremendous talents of the people who staff these institutions are available to our community and make unending and major contributions in all areas."[6]

Founded in 1894 by Teddy Roosevelt, Louis Brandeis, and

Frederick Law Olmsted, among others, the National Municipal League promoted best practices to city governments, encouraging citizen participation in local affairs, efficiency of municipal operations, and intolerance of patronage and political corruption. Since 1949, the organization, by then renamed the National Civic League, had selected ten cities each year to promote for the "outstanding" accomplishments of "concerned citizens" who act "resolutely" in favor of "orderly growth and progress" and against "distress and decay."[7] The Greensboro group, aware of the panel's interest in the adversity they'd overcome, enumerated several examples: After a wild (white) high school party at a downtown motel stumbled into drunken disorder, citizens created a Greensboro Youth Council to direct "youth activities into constructive channels." Failing to meet its United Fund donation goals for a number of years, the city's businessmen spurred one another to give generously, resulting in the "highest per-capita contribution . . . of any city in North Carolina." In addition, they'd raised money for the arts and to modernize distressed local hospitals, to support its universities, and to make the Greater Greensboro Open "the richest tournament on the Professional Golfers' Association's winter tour."[8]

Faced, as were so many cities around the country, with the crisis of a "dying downtown," a "Task Force of hundreds of workers from a dozen civic organizations" marshaled by Melvin's Jaycees swarmed across Greensboro, gathering the votes necessary to pass a $19 million bond issue to repair streets and extend water and sewer systems in hopes of luring businesses and shoppers back to the newly integrated center of Greensboro and away from the capacious malls sprouting up in the outlying residential districts.

Greensboro's presentation left the panelists, among them the pioneering pollster Dr. George Gallup, convinced that citizens in the leafy "Gate City," nestled halfway between the mountains and the sea in North Carolina's rolling foothills and situated at the "juncture of two major highways" and beside the Southern Railway line that tethered the city to a steady flow of northern investment, faced their challenges head-on. Four months later, a banner headline in the *Greensboro Daily News* announced, "Greensboro Becomes All-America City," joining Presque Isle, Maine, and Richmond, Virginia, among the ten winners selected from 138 applicants.[9]

Jim Melvin and his fellow Jaycees deserved the lion's share of credit for capturing the honor and for the way their précis breezed by the issue of race in Greensboro. In passing, Storrs mentioned the "mass demonstrations in 1963 which brought paralysis to our downtown night after night" before "the city opened *nearly* [emphasis added] all public accommodations and job opportunities prior to the Civil Rights Act of 1964." In the text of his entry application to the National Civic League, Melvin diagnosed the city's "racial climate" as "healthy."

❖

Despite the Jaycees' much-publicized effort to invite a Black golfer to play the Greater Greensboro Open in 1961, in a first for the PGA's southern tour, Melvin's prognosis would have been news to many in Greensboro's Black community.[10] "The struggle is nothing new," Greensboro businessman A. S. Webb would say, invoking the various strategies local Black people had employed to preserve life and dignity since slavery times, from the Underground Railroad in the early 1800s to the sit-in movement in the 1960s.[11]

Black Greensboro ran north-to-southeast of Murrow Boulevard before hooking west south of Lee Street. Drawing a line on a map that follows this racial geography, the contours of the city suddenly appear to resemble a face with its chin propped in the palm of a hand, the fingers extending up the cheek, to the northeast. Slavery and then legal segregation created the imagined shape of that supporting left hand, the real neighborhoods it outlined, and the city's reliance on the free-then-cheap labor—the working hands, in fact—that Black residents of Greensboro provided.

Traveling east along Washington Street from Elm Street and the heart of downtown, one dipped under the Southern Railway line, through a narrow, two-lane pass, and then gently up into a world quite apart from Melvin's Jaycees, the Greensboro Youth Council, and the Greater Greensboro Open. Some out-of-town visitors, who identified this Black society with its various institutions, businesses, neighborhoods, and accumulated history as "A&T," were surprised to discover that it had anything at all to do with the "white" City of Greensboro.[12] That moment of realization might best be described, in the words of W. E. B. Du Bois, as a "peculiar sensation," an awakening pinch to the "double consciousness" that made the neighborhoods and neighbors economically and physically inseparable from Greensboro and yet, at the same time, imaginatively, psychologically, and geographically "a small nation of people" separate from the white city.[13]

Though isolated in many ways from white Greensboro, Black Greensboro was neither incomplete nor a monolith. A&T and Bennett College for women anchored the community. Due to the presence of these institutions, Greensboro claimed, on a per capita basis, the best educated Black population in the country and, with that, a talented group of groundbreaking doctors, bankers, lawyers, and entrepreneurs, many of whom lived south of A&T in and around the comfortable Benbow Park neighborhood, adjacent to the oak-shaded, brick ranches occupied by the teachers, preachers, college professors, and mailmen who made up the community's middle class.[14]

Between A&T and Benbow Park and a few blocks to the east, one found the large working-class neighborhood of Lincoln Grove. The Grove, as those who lived there called it, consisted of block after block of wood-frame homes and dilapidated rentals (generally white-owned) lining the unpaved streets that surrounded the 380-unit Morningside Homes public housing development. To the west of Benbow Park, near the intersection of Ashe Street, Randleman Road, and South Florida Street, stood Hampton Homes, another public housing project for Greensboro's Negro residents. The people who lived at these addresses and in other similar neighborhoods took the few jobs they could get in the city's vast textile mills and tobacco factory. They worked as laborers, janitors, and cleaning staff in the city's businesses and as domestics and gardeners in the homes of whites on the other side of the railroad tracks.

In 1966, twelve years after the Supreme Court ruled separate education to be unequal in its landmark *Brown v. Board of Education* decision, Greensboro's Black residents, from the maid residing in Morningside Homes to the lawyer ensconced in a swank spread off South Benbow, sent their children to Dudley High School. Only a token number of Black students—enough for white politicians to say integration had taken place—attended the city's white schools.[15] But Dudley, whose teams sported the same deep-blue and gold colors as A&T, distilled community identity and pride. Even as its ill-equipped laboratories and decrepit tennis courts provided unequivocal evidence that the city's resources were distributed unevenly between white and Black schools, Dudley reminded everyone who lived east of Murrow Boulevard and south of Lee Street that, rich or poor, well-educated or barely literate, they still resided together on the same side of the color line.[16] When the sun set the final time for any of Greensboro's Black residents, whether they had lived in Benbow Park or The Grove, they went together to their eternal rest in Maplewood Cemetery, just a few blocks north of Morningside Homes.

And yet, despite the continued presence of the race line in education, employment, health care, and housing, changes were happening in Greensboro. In most ways, the transformations had less to do with the landmark federal legislation expressed in the Civil Rights Act of 1964 and the Voting Rights Act of 1965 than with housing policy and local agitation.

From the late 1950s, spurred by the 1949 American Housing Act, urban redevelopment roared through southeast Greensboro like a tidal wave. Greensboro's business and government leaders embraced the government's "slum clearance" incentives with zeal, instigating a voracious process of acquiring and seizing large swaths of property through eminent domain. Swept from 1,800 repurposed neighborhood properties were 2,200 buildings, 362 businesses, and

2,100 families, mostly Black. These would be replaced by parks and government buildings, malls, a new headquarters for the Greensboro daily newspapers, office buildings, and a parking deck.[17]

Redevelopment, or "Negro removal" as Black residents acerbically referred to it, created indoor and outdoor spaces useful to numerous Greensboro residents but "destroyed old patterns," fraying the community's historical bonds. Where the white city leaders marked urban blight and development opportunities on the map, residents in the shacks that lined the untended streets saw more than poverty and neglect: they saw individual lives tethered together by shared experience and history. The homes along those streets sheltered love as well as simmering resentment, and the businesses provided spaces for both legal and illegal commerce that pushed up slivers of opportunity like weeds through cracked pavement. Laughter and bubbling pots of rich food nourished the children who, buoyed by a community's discipline and hope, would make futures for themselves. However humble were many of the homes and shops, beauty parlors and funeral parlors, storefront churches, and corner groceries, they mapped a social fabric, stitched together during generations of segregation. Not just slums were being cleared, but working- and middle-class lives and their networks and traditions built to enable survival in an unequal world. By the early 1960s, nearly a hundred Black businesses had disappeared from East Greensboro due to redevelopment.

On February 2, 1960, four North Carolina A&T students sat down at the Woolworth's counter on Elm Street and asked to be served. Students throughout the South followed their example, building a movement to integrate restaurants, theaters, department stores, and other commercial establishments. Change didn't happen overnight. In Greensboro, years of persistence, endurance, and unity on the part of the Black community were required to achieve lasting results. The effort crested during 1963 in the massive demonstrations that paralyzed the city's downtown and received a fleeting mention in Thomas

Storrs's presentation to the National Civic League. Jesse Jackson, the quarterback of the A&T football team, emerged as a skillful leader in the movement, supported and coached by pillars of the East Side community, including Dr. George Simkins Jr., a dentist and head of the local NAACP chapter. In the decade prior to the sit-ins, Simkins had challenged Greensboro to integrate its golf course, tennis courts, and hospitals. The courage of these student and community demonstrators and those they inspired around the South forced the end to legal segregation with the passage of the Civil Rights Act. As Black businesses were swept away on one side of town, Black people began patronizing downtown white businesses.

To many in Greensboro's white community, the change represented, quite literally, the cost of doing business in a country where overt expressions of racism were less tolerated, even as they were replaced by a new language that bemoaned those who lacked the self-discipline to take advantage of America's cornucopia of opportunities. Even so, as Black activism increased, membership surged in as many as five Klan Klaverns around the city. Working-class whites stood ready to torch crosses on the yards of Black families who dared to move into white neighborhoods, providing a visible and menacing resistance to integration.[18] After 1954, Greensboro's business elite organized the "North Carolina Citizens League," working through political and institutional channels to "maintain Racial Segregation" and "preserve State Sovereignty."[19] If Greensboro's power brokers were proud of anything after 1963, it was that, in meetings and presentations such as the one before the All-America City Award committee in Boston, they didn't have to answer tough questions about the kind of racial violence that had exploded in places like Birmingham, Alabama, which might have hindered their recruitment of northern capital and businesses to the city. The doors to Gate City remained open.

As the city council and Jaycees sought a new status quo, one that would make their striving management of the city as smooth and predictable as possible, the residents on the A&T side of town were puzzling over how to convert their newly secured civil rights into a more equal share of the city's power and wealth. The federal laws did little to end the intimidation, humiliation, and unease people experienced when, for example, a Black woman could spend two weeks in jail for fishing without a license while police authorities made no effort to inform her terrified family or a known Klansman found work on the construction crew building a prominent Black lawyer's dream home. The NAACP leader, Dr. George Simkins, wishing to see more than the occasional Black face on the city council, pushed for district voting as he decried the current at-large system: "In order for any Negro to sit on the city council of Greensboro, he must now be subjected to the will of the double-standard people in other sections of the city. If it were not so tragic, it would be laughable to hear those who are now in power say that they represent the Negro ghettos as faithfully and well as they do the section of the city where they live."[20]

In 1965, one hundred years after the Thirteenth Amendment freed Nelson Johnson's grandfather for the second time, the grandson set out for Greensboro. Nelson had little idea that he was heading into the eye of an activist hurricane, a place where, as the call for Black Power carried across the land, the struggle to liberate lives circumscribed by skin color, poverty, or both was once again testing America's commitment to its ideals and would soon reach the pitch of, in the words of Frederick Douglass, an "awful roar."

FUND

Nelson Johnson enrolled as a political science student at A&T in 1965. The Black community beyond the campus's stately brick buildings and verdant lawns drew him in and made him feel at home. Growing up, he'd been nurtured in a small, rural community. Now he embraced the reality of the "right and wrong, vengeance and love . . . Beauty and Truth" of the bigger, more complex society that lay to the east of the Gate City railroad tracks.[1]

A thick sulfur smell filled his nose when breezes passing by from the South Buffalo Creek Treatment Facility carried the stench of sewage through Black neighborhoods. Walking the muddy streets, he'd seen the rats, the garbage, the privies out back, the old refrigerators rusting in dirt yards, and the ubiquitous leaky roofs in The Grove.[2] Everyone knew there were few Black city police officers and no resident Black FBI agents or federal judges. No Black politician had won a state election in the twentieth century, and Greensboro voters rejected a proposal to move city council elections to a district system. Fewer than 5 percent of jobs in most of the local factories or industries—including the newspapers—went to Blacks. The well-educated students sent proudly into the world with A&T and Bennett degrees, even when topped off with advanced study at the University of North Carolina, could expect to earn 25 percent less than their white counterparts, if they were lucky enough to get a job in a white-owned company.[3]

On a clear day, looking from southeast Greensboro north-northwest toward downtown, the rose-hued terra-cotta and granite Jefferson Standard skyscraper dominated the view. The New York–born architect Charles C. Hartmann completed the Jefferson Standard Life Insurance Company building in 1923, when it became, at eighteen stories and 374 feet, the tallest building in the state, a symbol of the sleepy town's awakening and its promise as a future center of financial power. Thomas Jefferson's bust welcomed employees and visitors into a building that looked as if it had been transported through some miracle of technology and commerce from Wall Street in New York City to the corner of Elm and Market, the slaps of their leather soles echoing down the marble halls.

Thomas Jefferson's words, Nelson, the political science student, felt, were the most beautiful ever written: "We hold these truths to be self-evident, that all men are created equal, that they are endowed by their Creator with certain unalienable Rights, that among these are Life, Liberty and the pursuit of Happiness."[4] The problem was that the words had never yet been true for *all men and women*. The beauty of the ideals reminded Nelson, as the lonely corporate skyscraper in downtown Greensboro surely prodded the banker and city booster Jim Melvin, of the work each hoped to accomplish.

The spark that compelled the young boy in Airlie to build a tin can pipe to sluice dirty water away from the family sink drove the twenty-two-year-old Nelson to think about how precisely to engage the injustices he saw in Greensboro. "Power concedes nothing without a demand. It never did and it never will," students shouted across A&T's grassy central lawn, the "Bowl," tossing around Frederick Douglass's bold words like a football in a game of catch. What amalgam of words, ideas, and actions, Nelson wondered, would pry greater freedom and equality from the clutches of American power? Hope had arrived when President Lyndon Baines Johnson signed the Civil Rights Act in 1964 and the Voting Rights Acts in 1965, a few months before Nelson enrolled at A&T. Between these pieces of landmark legislations, the president also signed the Law Enforcement

Assistance Act. Johnson's War on Crime unfurled federal law enforcement's tentacles into local police departments, cementing the tension between America's ideals—including the president's own desire to lift the nation's poor and marginalized from poverty—and its fears.

❖

In late 1962, three years before Nelson arrived in Greensboro, North Carolina's governor, Terry Sanford, flew to New York and strode through the glass-and-steel Madison Avenue doors of the world's largest philanthropic organization. "I'm not really coming here for your money. What we need is your ideas. We've got a lot of problems in North Carolina, and we've got to start thinking of the future," he announced to the leaders of the Ford Foundation. Ford's executives quickly succumbed to Sanford's unusual and charming pitch.[5] His vision provided them a unique opportunity to test strategies that might, as the governor hoped, "break the cycle of poverty" in North Carolina, home to some of the nation's most desperate circumstances.[6]

Less than a year later, on September 30, 1963, with a seven-million-dollar commitment from the Ford Foundation and large contributions from the North Carolina–based Z. Smith Reynolds and Mary Reynolds Babcock Foundations in hand, Governor Sanford announced the creation of the North Carolina Fund (NCF). Sanford cannily circumvented the ayes or nays of the state's conservative General Assembly, increasingly uncomfortable with the civil rights movement and integration, by sourcing private funding for a nongovernmental organization. Internally, the NCF's architects began to refer to their mission as a "war on poverty."[7] Governor Sanford gave the NCF staff five years to wrest some control of the New South economy from entrenched tobacco, cotton, and textile interests and to reimagine it in favor of a better-paid workforce.[8]

President Kennedy was murdered in Dallas two months after Sanford made his announcement, and a stunned nation mourned. Six weeks after the assassination, Lyndon Johnson stood to deliver the chief executive's State of the Union address before a joint session of Congress. "Let us carry forward the plans and programs of John Fitzgerald Kennedy," said Johnson, paying homage to the dead president, "not because of our sorrow or sympathy, but because they are right." Dressed in a dark suit and a black tie, the big Texan peered over two-toned glasses at a room full of white men in dark suits and glasses. He didn't show up merely to enact Kennedy's platform; that night he laid out his own ambitious vision, rallying Americans to the cause of their fellow citizens who "live on the outskirts of hope—some because of their poverty, and some because of their color, and all too many because of both. . . . The administration today, here, and now, declares unconditional war on poverty in America."[9] In August 1964, Congress passed the Economic Opportunity Act, from which sprung the Office of Economic Opportunity (OEO), entrusted with the task of "eliminat[ing] the paradox of poverty" in a prosperous country and creating "the opportunity to live in decency and dignity." The primary tool in this fight would be "community action," defined as the "maximum feasible participation of residents of the areas and members of the groups served."[10] In simpler terms, the president's War on Poverty intended to put political power into the hands of the poor, both white and Black, shifting the field of the battle against oppression "from the streets to the Courtroom."[11]

With Ford Foundation money securely in the bank, Terry Sanford had anticipated the president by a matter of months, launching what would be viewed by supporters and detractors as a "laboratory for Lyndon Johnson's great society" in North Carolina.[12]

Governor Sanford couldn't foresee, however, where the spark of his idea would lead when he staffed the North Carolina Fund with talented and committed people. Among them was George Esser, a Harvard Law graduate and University of North Carolina professor, who became the NCF's executive director. A public relations man named Billy Barnes joined him. Barnes's unflinching documentary promotion of the Fund's work would evoke Walker Evans and James Agee's Depression-era masterpiece, *Let Us Now Praise Famous Men*, as well as other great photojournalists of Franklin Delano Roosevelt's

Farm Security Administration. In 1964, a thirty-three-year-old, buttoned-up accounting whiz named Nathan Garrett joined the team. Garrett had grown up in Durham and was among the handful of Black students admitted to Yale in the early 1950s. Together, the small team "had the radical notion," Esser would say, "that the poor can create their own destinies." The NCF identified eleven projects to address white and Black poverty from the state's western mountains to its eastern lowlands. Almost immediately accused of "destroying the Southern way of life," Esser and his team dug in; if by the "Southern way of life," the NCF's detractors meant a caste system designed to keep Blacks at the bottom, just below the poor whites whose grip on a meager half-measure of social privilege kept them, too, mired in poverty, then the NCF team intended to do exactly that.[13]

Esser's most important—and controversial—hire was a twenty-four-year-old social worker from the Midwest. Howard Fuller arrived in Durham to start work at the NCF ready to use the Office of Economic Opportunity's goal of "maximum feasible participation" as a way to lead a "poor people's revolution." On his very first night in the Tar Heel State, Fuller flicked on the local WRAL-TV station and watched as a young radio and TV personality named Jesse Helms railed against the civil rights movement. When Helms's sidekick on the show made passing reference to "Martin Luther Coon," Fuller "froze," unaccustomed to casual, public racism of this sort.[14]

A year earlier, Fuller had counted himself part of an overflow audience jammed into the Cory United Methodist Church in Cleveland, Ohio. That evening, Malcolm X pondered whether the "ballot or the bullet" would set Africans in America on the path to freedom. Malcolm reminded people in the audience to stand up for their rights and their safety: "A segregationist is a criminal. . . . I'm nonviolent with those who are nonviolent with me. But when you drop that violence on me, then you've made me go insane, and I'm not responsible for what I do. And that's the way every Negro should get. You let the white man know, if this is a country of freedom, let it be a country of freedom; and if it is not a country of freedom, change it."[15] Along with the rest of the crowd, Fuller found himself transported by Malcolm's provocative truth-telling to the edge of the valley that lay between his people and the mountaintop of Black liberation. A year later, Malcolm was dead, and Fuller arrived among the segregationists.

Controller Garrett sized up the new arrival, "striking in both appearance and rhetoric," standing "over six feet tall . . . dark and athletic." Though the two were different in temperament, they shared the belief that "poor Black people, who had long been dictated to even by well-meaning whites, should play a major role in determining what they need and how they should get it"—with "it" being a set of basic demands that made revolution seem rather pedestrian: adequate housing, jobs that paid a living wage, access to health care and transportation, and decent education for their children.[16]

It took only a few months for the direct-action protests Fuller organized to unnerve Durham's business and political leaders, white and Black. Many had voiced support for Governor Sanford's Fund, imagining job training programs for North Carolina's poor, not pickets in posh neighborhoods wielding embarrassing signs that read "Your neighbor is a slumlord."[17] In the wake of the 1965 Voting Rights Act, extensive get-out-the-vote efforts, funded in part by taxpayer dollars in the form of Office of Economic Opportunity grants, threatened to disrupt the political status quo, as newly empowered poor Black people suddenly filled the chairs at once-sleepy city council meetings, demanding jobs, food, health care, and schooling to help lift their children from poverty.

❖

Fifty miles down the road, in Greensboro, Nelson joined Youth Educational Services (YES), an NCF program that marshaled volunteers to help poor children with their schoolwork. Three years after the massive demonstrations that had pushed Greensboro to desegregate most public establishments along Elm Street, the volunteers, recruited from white and Black colleges and joined by a wholesome mission, were provided something unusual at the time: an opportunity to socialize across the race line. Nelson, who'd often felt overlooked by young Black women, soon found himself with a white girlfriend. Zelma, his mother, was terrified and sent Ivan to try to convince his brother to end the relationship.[18] Despite passage of the Civil Rights Act, interracial relationships weren't just socially taboo around the South in 1966, they were limited by the law: state miscegenation statutes still made it illegal for Blacks and whites to marry in North Carolina.

Instead of breaking up with the woman, Nelson, his white girlfriend, and a handful of other mixed-race couples from YES decided to challenge the prohibition of interracial mingling at a popular college bar.

At the edge of the University of North Carolina Greensboro campus west of downtown, along a bustling stretch of Tate Street, the Apple Cellar filled a "windowless maze" of basement rooms.[19] Late one steamy August night in 1966, Nelson and his friends descended the establishment's stairs in pairs. It took only about twenty minutes to realize that being served meant having beer spilled in their laps. Soaked through, the protesters retreated, only to discover the police waiting as they emerged back onto the sidewalk. Nelson and another young Black man settled onto the hood of a police car to distract the cops from the retreat of their fellow protesters and were quickly arrested for trespassing and interfering with a police officer. Two nights later, on a Saturday, Nelson and his friends returned. This time, when they left the Apple Cellar, thirty robed men met them on the sidewalk. Policemen stood by as Greensboro's most famous Klansman, George Dorsett, the state's Klan preacher, or Klud, heckled the students. A lean, leather-faced man from New Jersey, who was rising quickly through the secret society's hierarchy and ubiquitous at Klan events, almost certainly joined the "Klan security guards" and Dorsett at the protest; his name was Eddie Dawson.[20]

Nelson's first encounter with robed Klansmen troubled him less, however, than the words of a Black girl he'd been assigned to tutor.

During a study session, she told Nelson she'd prefer a white instructor. This casual comment shook his faith in the prospects of interracial collaboration. How were Black people ever going to get ahead if they thought the "white man's ice [was] a little colder"?[21] Why, he began to wonder, were they tutoring these children instead of fighting so they could live in good houses with lights that worked and shelves full of books?[22] Nelson quit YES. Tuned to the energy beginning to course through the Black Freedom Movement in 1966, some of it crackling down the road from Durham, he began to think of Black self-esteem and self-determination as his guiding stars. He helped found an all-Black tutoring group and then an advocacy organization for residents of Black public housing developments, including Morningside Homes.

As Nelson deepened his engagement with Greensboro, resistance to Fuller and the North Carolina Fund exploded beyond Durham. At the end of July 1966, Fuller had traveled to eastern North Carolina's agricultural Black Belt, the region where Nelson had grown up, to celebrate a half-million-dollar Office of Economic Opportunity grant to a Fund-supported organization. The white director of the local development program announced the grant to a thousand mostly Black "sharecroppers, domestic workers, schoolteachers, preachers, and students" gathered in the region's National Guard Armory. Instead of gratitude, the audience expressed frustration that they'd been excluded from deciding how the funds were to be used.[23]

The director dismissed the complaints. "I think I just gave you some good news. . . . I think we should make some noise over this fact." From his seat on the stage, Fuller watched as the man drew a handkerchief from his pocket. The director instructed the crowd to "shout" when he tossed the square of white cotton over his head and to "stop" when he snatched it from the air. The audience did as they were told. When the director returned to his seat, Fuller stalked to the lectern.

"I'm sitting here in a meeting in the year 1966 and see a white man take a handkerchief and throw it in the air and tell us to yell . . . and what I don't understand about this is the fact that you yelled when he thew it up. . . . I think it's time . . . that we had a little soul talk," said Fuller.[24]

Six weeks earlier, Black leaders had descended on Mississippi to complete James Meredith's March Against Fear after a white supremacist shot the young man who'd integrated the University of Mississippi.[25] From a makeshift stage in Greenwood, Mississippi, Stokely Carmichael, the dynamic young leader who'd recently replaced John Lewis as chairman of the Student Nonviolent Coordinating Committee, issued "a call for Black people in this country to unite, to recognize their heritage, to build a sense of community . . . to define their own goals, to lead their own organizations."[26] To Martin Luther King Jr.'s consternation, Carmichael named this closing of the ranks "Black Power!"[27] His pronouncement arrived like a clarion call to Howard Fuller and other Black activists around the country, as well as to wary politicians and to J. Edgar Hoover, perched in his roost at FBI headquarters.

Now addressing eastern North Carolina's working poor, Fuller echoed the militant message and tone of the SNCC leader's speech in Mississippi and the silenced voice of Malcolm X. Like Carmichael, Fuller extolled the self-reliance and empowerment of the Black Power message, challenging the people before him to move beyond "yes suh" and "no suh." "Let me show you an example," he continued, improvising language that ambitious politicians intent on shutting down the North Carolina Fund as well as the federal War on Poverty would use to full effect: "If I got a baseball bat, and you got one of them little skinny sticks, I'm gon' beat you to death . . . *that's what our society is all about* [emphasis added]. . . . We got to get a baseball bat in our hands to fight the baseball bat in their hands."[28]

White North Carolinians hadn't been this unnerved by a Black activist since the head of the local NAACP chapter in Monroe faced down Klan attacks on integration efforts with guns. Robert Williams had been forced to flee trumped-up kidnapping charges in 1961 for political asylum in Cuba.[29]

If North Carolina began as the War on Poverty's laboratory, it now also represented the front line in the resistance to Terry Sanford's and Lyndon Johnson's efforts to call America's poorest citizens in from the "outskirts of hope." A newly minted congressman from Rocky Mount, North Carolina, led the counterrevolution. Handsome, young, rich, and as conservative as he was charismatic, James C. Gardner, the cofounder of the Hardee's hamburger chain, set his sights on the North Carolina Fund. Gardner trotted out the time-tested strategy: resist civil rights progress by preserving the economic, political, and social order; stoke racial fears; and dangle the "go slow" solution on equality—which generally meant "go nowhere fast."[30] The Fund, together with President Johnson, the Office of Economic Opportunity, and the Ford Foundation, said Gardner, was "spen[ding] taxpayer dollars" to achieve "Negro rule." Targeting the philanthropy's tax-free status, Gardner accused the Ford Foundation of "meddling in the affairs of local communities" for partisan ends. He identified the point of the outsiders' spear as "Howard Fuller," who, Gardner claimed, was "being paid by the federal government" to foment revolution.[31]

After the handkerchief speech, Nathan Garrett worried that Howard Fuller's job had become the most dangerous in North Carolina. As Gardner and other leaders called for his dismissal, Durham's police opened betting pools on how long it would be before someone killed Fuller.[32]

Watching Fuller work, however, had taught George Esser and Nathan Garrett that militant disruption of the status quo gave progressive change a chance. "Harassers," led by Fuller, caused political and business leaders' discomfort and created the conditions for compromise. "Howard made me realize," said Esser, "we could push harder for social change and still be consistent with my ideas of democracy." Echoing a lesson articulated by Frederick Douglass one hundred years earlier, Esser said, "If you don't pose a threat, they won't respond. . . . We adopted that as fund policy."[33] At organizing events and rallies, Fuller would close his eyes and quote Douglass, channeling the great man's famous words as if they were at once his strategy, his justification, and his battle cry: "If there is no struggle, there is no progress. Those who profess to favor freedom, and yet depreciate agitation, are men who want crops without plowing up the ground. They want rain without thunder and lightning. They want the ocean without the awful roar of its many waters. This struggle may be a moral one; or it may be a physical one; or it may be both moral and physical; but it must be a struggle."[34]

In early 1967, despite political pressure to fire Fuller, Esser instead promoted him to director of community development for the NCF, entrusting him with statewide organizing strategy. As urban rebellions rattled cities throughout the country that summer, Howard Fuller led a training program for college students interested in helping "poor people form organizations through which they could effectively bring pressure on those in power to improve the quality of services and to eliminate discriminatory treatment."[35]

Nelson Johnson gained acceptance to the program and, under the mentorship of Howard Fuller, found himself shipped off to organize among the sand hills and pine forests of the southeastern part of the state. In Fayetteville, where Fort Bragg, a military base named for a defeated Confederate leader, powered the economy of that city, Nelson signed up "4,000 members into a poor people's organization in Fayetteville, convened a Black unity conference, [and] secured water service for a rundown neighborhood."[36]

Stressing Black unity, Fuller forbade the Black students in the program from diluting their racial bonds by dating interracially. Nelson's mother hadn't been successful in ending her son's relationship with a white woman, but Fuller's stipulation succeeded.

People, including Fuller, began to make note of Nelson's "imagination and intelligence and commitment and skills."[37] By that fall, back in Greensboro, the young organizer caught the attention of the NAACP head, Dr. Simkins, and other influential figures on the East Side of Greensboro. In the brilliant GI, returned from a foreign tour, they identified one of Greensboro's next important "Negro" citizens, perhaps the future head of the NAACP or a candidate for the "Black seat" on city council. If they continued to advance integration, they could imagine him running for statewide office one day.[38]

In the meantime, Nelson, Howard Fuller, and their collaborators were intent on testing the liberal commitment to the antipoverty movement and grassroots empowerment, or, as they saw it, the freedom and equality of everyone.

LOVE

A shocking event accelerated Nelson Johnson's growth as an activist. On February 8, 1968, at the edge of South Carolina State University, a historically Black institution in Orangeburg, police and National Guardsmen opened fire on students who'd been protesting a segregated bowling alley in the city. A brief torrent of bullets lashed the night, killing three teenagers and wounding dozens, including Cleveland Sellers, a South Carolina native and former leader in SNCC.[1]

In response, Nelson, his new mentor and collaborator Howard Fuller, and others planned demonstrations in cities around North Carolina. Nelson borrowed three coffin boxes from a Black funeral home, filled them with donated flowers, and fashioned a crude effigy of South Carolina's governor. On the Saturday after the Orangeburg Massacre, from a balcony at A&T, Nelson invited students to join him in protesting the shooting of their peers. He, together with other pallbearers, hoisted the coffins and began marching slowly west along Market Street toward downtown. While he embraced the role of organizer, the old self-doubts that he'd known growing up in Airlie lingered. Despite his successes in Fayetteville and his growing passion for organizing and agitating, Nelson didn't yet trust his leadership and rhetorical skills. There were, he insisted, more charismatic and articulate student activists at A&T.[2]

Before he and his student comrades crossed the train tracks, Nelson looked over his shoulder. To his astonishment, hundreds of A&T and Bennett students had streamed from the campus to follow him downtown. In that moment, as if hovering outside his body, he felt a transcendent connection "to people in a way that [he'd] never experienced before."[3]

When they reached Courthouse Square, the students hung the effigy from a post and lighted it on fire. Fire trucks and police cars wailed to the scene, and the students, without any real plan, scampered back to campus. Nelson now knew people would follow him but didn't yet know how to gather the human energy he catalyzed into strategic focus.

After the demonstration, Captain William Jackson, a white detective in the Criminal Investigations Division, called Nelson in for a conversation. Jackson, who'd worked closely with Jesse Jackson during the sit-in movement, explained to the young leader that the police didn't like surprises. He asked Nelson to call him in advance of future demonstrations. Nelson left the meeting conflicted. Despite Captain Jackson's measured tone and reputation for fairness, Nelson didn't consider the police to be allies in his efforts to root out social injustice.

A few weeks later, Dr. Simkins, head of the local NAACP, honored Nelson's rising star in the Black community by assigning him the task of organizing A&T students to welcome Dr. Martin Luther King Jr. at the Greensboro airport on April 4. King's whirlwind tour of North Carolina would promote the "Poor People's Campaign" he planned to bring to Washington, DC, that summer, as well as the candidacy of Dr. Reginald Hawkins, a Black dentist from Charlotte who had the gumption to run for governor of North Carolina.

In the company of his network of activist friends, Nelson's evolution from the patriotic youth who deserted the family farm accelerated. He began to understand the problems he witnessed in The Grove to be due less to racist attitudes than to entrenched racist policies enforced by public and private institutions. Three weeks after the Orangeburg shooting, the National Advisory Commission on Civil Disorders, known as the Kerner Commission for its chairman, Otto Kerner, validated this point of view as it analyzed the cause of the urban rebellions during the summer of 1967. In language as bracing as words penned by James Baldwin, the Kerner Commission observed that "what white Americans have never fully understood—but what the Negro can never forget—is that white society is deeply implicated in the ghetto. White institutions created it, white institutions maintain it, and white society condones it."[4]

Nelson admired King's courage and his stunning gift of oratory. Since Nelson's dressing-down by his Air Force "brothers from Norfolk," however, he, along with Stokely Carmichael, Howard Fuller, and other advocates of Black Power (not to mention white, New Left radicals around the country), began to question the efficacy of nonviolent tactics. Why, Nelson wanted to ask Reverend King, should those seeking freedom limit the tools at their disposal when those who opposed them didn't? Innately curious, he planned to listen carefully to King's answer. King had said that "in the long run of history, destructive means cannot bring about constructive ends."[5] Why were the means paramount when the goal remained elusive?

The questions Nelson hoped to pose to Dr. King weren't only about the conflict he saw between the moral suasion of nonviolent tactics and the declaration of a willingness to defend one's personal safety with weapons. Nelson's questions were fraught with the dilemma of what to attempt to save in the face of change. While Jim Melvin rallied his peers to invigorate downtown and recruit new businesses to Greensboro, people on the A&T side of town, confronted with redevelopment and the uncertain relationship between integration and advancement, wondered how to preserve a close-knit community—Dudley High School, the universities that made them proud, and the surrounding neighborhoods—even as they struggled to gain access to better jobs, equal pay, political power, and the right to make a home in any house on any street in the city. Despite decades of struggles against segregation, the question of whether to push for deeper integration into a resistant American mainstream or instead to circle the wagons of racial solidarity remained vital for many young Black activists, including Nelson and Howard Fuller.

At the last moment, King canceled his trip to North Carolina. The striking sanitation workers in Memphis, Tennessee, demanded his immediate attention as violence threatened to derail their demands for a union, safer working conditions, and a living wage.[6] "We've got to give ourselves to this struggle until the end," King confided to the strikers the night of April 3. "Nothing would be more tragic than to stop at this point. . . . We've got to see it through."[7]

Instead of meeting King at the airport on April 4, 1968, Nelson Napoleon Johnson found himself behind the wheel of his blue Volkswagen Beetle, chirping and rattling south through Greensboro. An early drizzle subsided, the sky brightened, and the temperature of the sticky air rose into the midseventies, unusually warm for an early April afternoon. Nelson accelerated up the on-ramp to I-40, merging with traffic and Dwight Eisenhower's midcentury dream of a country connected by forty thousand miles of roads to move raw materials to factories, manufactured products to market, soldiers and weapons to key military bases and ports, and people to jobs—or to safety "in case of atomic attack on our key cities" from the Soviet Union.[8]

In Granville County, just north of Durham, he turned off I-85 onto rural state roads edged by farmland. For the young activist, it felt like moving back in time, from *Black* to *Negro*, from the leading edge of the struggle for freedom to the lightly frayed but resilient fabric of Jim Crow, from the heady three years since he'd returned from overseas and joined the war against poverty and racism to a childhood on the farm governed by seasonal cycles of life and death.

Settling in for the nearly three-hour journey, the young man had nothing to do but drive and think as he traversed the rolling North Carolina Piedmont, headed for the region's eastern extreme. There the land, shaped by geology and scarred by human history, falls to the flat, fertile coastal plain. One hundred seventy-five million years ago, the shifting tectonic plates tore the earth's giant landmass, Pangaea, into the seven continents that shape the planet we know. North Carolina's Piedmont region marks a vestige of the geologic scar where North America ripped apart from Africa. An ocean rose between the continents, and rich sediment—good for growing tobacco, peanuts, and cotton—filled in and smoothed the edges of the gap, preparing the ground for an unlikely future convergence of geologic and human history.

Little more than a hundred years earlier, the fields along these roads had been tended by enslaved Africans. Four or five generations after the Civil War, the old slave-owning families still held much of the land in eastern North Carolina, having passed down their wealth and outmaneuvered any proposals for radical redistribution. That lost cause, memorialized with a mix of nostalgia and resentment by African Americans as "forty acres and a mule," would have granted freedmen in South Carolina and Georgia independence and a base of political power. Instead, throughout the South, the Ku Klux Klan, Black Codes, and Jim Crow laws followed the Civil War into a twentieth-century America perpetually struggling with its commitment to democracy. The road carried Nelson through Franklin County and Louisburg, where only recently the Klan had been terrorizing residents who advocated for integrated education.[9]

In the fields beyond Nelson's car window, Black and white farmers set tobacco seedlings as they'd been doing in early April for nearly three hundred years. A couple of weeks later, they'd plant cotton to feed the voracious mills in Greensboro. By late May, they'd be pushing peanuts into warmer soil. Having grown up on a farm, Nelson knew the sensations of the fields: the exhaustion of physical labor; the way, as the summer deepens, tobacco leaves turn from deep green toward yellow; how the pungent sap sticks to your hands when you prime the leaves and carry them into the barn to cure. Whatever the color of the hands digging into that dirt, they shared the sun's calendar and exerted equal effort.

Three weeks from his twenty-fifth birthday, Nelson was in no hurry. He kept his eyes on the highway and pointed his Beetle toward the family homestead, where he planned to stay through Palm Sunday, enjoying his mother's home cooking, the family stories, and, likely, a service at the church of his grandfather Nelson Thorne Sr.

By coming up from the south he'd avoided the perfectly proportioned antebellum plantation houses looming in the twilight on the outskirts of Littleton, some still inhabited by white Thorne relatives, and the complicated memories contained in the big town's tall-transomed brick buildings, such as the one that housed the dime store that proffered interactions often cryptic and uncomfortable, like the brush of a white shopgirl's hand against his when she made change.

The afternoon shadows lengthened, the hour ticked past six o'clock, and Nelson entered the home stretch, passing yeoman farmers and sharecroppers emerging tired out of fields from which they would coax one more cycle of life: a living for themselves and their families, and income, in the case of the sharecroppers, for the landowners.

Then a voice came over the radio with the news: Martin Luther King Jr. had been shot in Memphis.

Nelson turned right onto a packed dirt road and a quarter mile later pulled up and parked outside the sprawling family "plantation." In the near dark, he stepped up to the doorway, filled suddenly by his oldest sister, tears streaking her red face. Mute grief filled the house. Then his sister broke through the inarticulate pain.

"We should burn it all down," she said.

Was it the end of something or the beginning? Nelson understood that he could multiply his sister's hot rage across the nation by hamlets and villages, towns and city neighborhoods, and he imagined the dry tinder of dashed dreams bursting into flame. He hugged his mother, hugged his sister, and went back out the door to his car. His future lay in Black Greensboro. He didn't want it to burn.

Nelson Johnson raced back toward Greensboro on roads that, all too often, seemed to turn back against the main thoroughfare of America's bright narrative of progress toward a peculiar and tragic past. Nelson would never get to ask King the questions that burned inside his head and heart.

Across the state and the country, people reacted to the news. At the University of North Carolina in Chapel Hill, a Black student studying in his dorm room heard running footsteps in the hallway, laughter and cheering outside the door. When he emerged to investigate, he learned of the civil rights leader's murder from his gleeful white peers.[10]

At 7 p.m. in Raleigh, students at the historically Black Shaw University poured out of buildings to express their "overpowering emotional reaction" to the assassination. They marched and chanted. Some threw rocks at cars parked along the street. National Guardsmen called up by the governor and city police in riot gear met the students, intent on confining their rage to the campus. Asked to comment on the student anger by the reporter for the North Carolina State University newspaper, the Reverend Willie B. Lewis observed that it burst from the "realization that non-violence had failed. Dr. King was the champion of non-violence, and they see his death as proof that the other side is not moved by non-violent methods." Before the reporter left, the preacher added, "I don't think this will end tonight."[11]

The turmoil in North Carolina mirrored what was happening in cities around the country. Passengers flying in late to National Airport in Washington, DC, witnessed a scene of urban rebellion, chaos, and destruction that could only be compared to war. Below them, hundreds of bright orange fires raged throughout the city, and clouds of glowing smoke rose into the night air, cooled, and turned milky. Down on the ground, activist Stokely Carmichael quickly realized the crowds were beyond his control. Mobs began burning cars and buildings and looting stores in defiance of any authority, Black or white. "We'll just light it again!" one rioter yelled at a group of firemen struggling to put out a small conflagration. By the next day, seven hundred buildings were reduced to smoking heaps, nine people were dead—at least two killed by the police—and nearly eight thousand had been arrested. Troops arriving in the city reached numbers not seen in the metropolis since the Civil War.[12] In all, more than a hundred cities, including Baltimore, Kansas City, and Chicago, experienced rebellious explosions detonated by grief, anger, and hopelessness.

❖

Nelson saw smoke and could hear gunshots as his Beetle homed in on the North Carolina A&T campus. Outside the simple redbrick dorms, a vortex of angry men and women swirled toward action. As tumult broke out around the country, Nelson knew that those most likely to be hurt or injured were the demonstrators themselves. The only way to prevent the same chaos churning through DC and Baltimore would be to channel the angry energy.

Six weeks earlier, when he set out to protest the Orangeburg Massacre, he'd been surprised when a thousand A&T and Bennett students followed him downtown. This time, he couldn't afford serendipity; he was prepared to lead. At around 10 p.m., a column of more than three hundred students formed behind Nelson, moving toward downtown Greensboro, where police were deployed to every street corner in anticipation of rioting. Nelson led chants of "Black Power" and "We shall change the white society, we shall march, and we shall move on!," shifting the emotion away from retaliatory destruction. The rawness couldn't be controlled entirely. Some marchers smashed car windows at the Friendly Ford dealership and hurled rocks at storefronts. Nelson led a silent prayer from the steps of the Guilford County Courthouse, steps that he would have reason to climb and descend hundreds of times over the coming years and decades. The next day, the *Greensboro Daily News* admitted that the students "did not break into uncontrolled mob violence," crediting the relative tranquility to the presence of law enforcement. Nelson Johnson's decision to rush back to Greensboro went unreported. It likely reduced the violence in Greensboro.[13]

The next day, Nelson led another march, this one setting out from the campus of Bennett College and larger than the previous night's demonstration. More than five hundred students walked quietly through the streets, closely observed by an equal or greater number of National Guardsmen called in by Mayor Carson Bain, local police, and FBI agents.

That night, however, a station wagon jammed with white passengers sped by the A&T campus. Someone in the car fired a gun into a crowd of Black students. When GI Bill students at A&T returned fire, the police, firemen, and National Guard surrounded the college campus but allowed the white instigators to flee. Taking aim from darkened dorm windows, the student vets kept the authorities at bay, preventing them from penetrating the campus perimeter. The mayor issued a curfew, students fled the A&T campus, and the threat of more violence gradually dissipated. Thirteen arrests were made in Raleigh, five in Charlotte, and eleven in New Bern, North Carolina. In Greensboro, no one was arrested, though several members of law enforcement suffered minor injuries. The white shooters who pushed the city to the edge of chaos were never identified.

❖

As the FBI began its highly publicized, international manhunt for King's assassin, it also intensified counterintelligence operations against Black leaders around the country. On the morning of April 6, a teletype report originating from the Greensboro Resident Agency and routed through the Charlotte Field Office to Hoover at Bureau Headquarters described "Black militants" who were "shooting up the city" in Greensboro.[14] As Nelson began to grow into his potential as a leader, the white world took note. One city leader warily referred to Nelson as a "master organizer," while the FBI, at the recommendation of its agents in Greensboro, flagged him for the Security Index, a closely held list of agitators to be arrested at the outset of a national emergency.[15]

12

SMOKE

The afternoon of April 4, in Raleigh, Joyce Hobson boarded an airplane for the first flight of her life. An hour later she disembarked in Wilmington, Delaware, and climbed into a waiting car. In a month she'd become a Duke University graduate. The girl from the Southside of Richmond, Virginia, had been invited to interview at DuPont Headquarters the following morning. On the way to a comfortable hotel, the suffocating news of Martin Luther King Jr.'s assassination filled the car like smoke.[1]

She'd met the civil rights leader twice. The last time was in Atlanta, just five months earlier, when she'd traveled to interview the new Georgia state representative, Julian Bond, for the Duke University newspaper. Blocked from taking his seat in the legislature for his views on the Vietnam War, Bond worked in exile from an unheated office, typing away with fingerless gloves. Word came to Bond's office that King had returned to Atlanta from Birmingham after serving out the remaining eight days of his 1963 jail sentence for "parading without a permit" in protest of the city's segregated private businesses and public services. During his first stint in the Alabama prison, King had scratched what came to be known as the "Letter from the Birmingham Jail" on scraps of paper, a text some called the Magna Carta of the civil rights movement.[2] In it, he responded to the charge of being an "outsider" when he arrived in communities beyond Atlanta to organize protests. "I am in Birmingham because injustice is here," he wrote. "I cannot sit idly by in Atlanta and not be concerned about what happens in Birmingham. Injustice anywhere is a threat to justice everywhere. We are caught in an inescapable network of mutuality, tied in a single garment of destiny. Whatever affects one directly affects all indirectly. Never again can we afford to live with the narrow, provincial 'outside agitator' idea. Anyone who lives inside the United States can never be considered an outsider anywhere within its bounds."[3]

Joyce and her friends rushed to the basement of Ebenezer Baptist Church to scoop an interview with King. His wife, Coretta, was there. Ralph Abernathy was there. King's colleagues and advisers Hosea Williams and C. T. Vivian were there. Joyce noticed how King's children clung to their father, seeming to miss him even in his presence. His frequent absences surely frightened them. King would look up every few minutes to ask after someone. They're away or busy, Coretta or one of his friends would respond. The immensity of his loneliness overwhelmed Joyce. Maybe it was the loneliness of a public figure who could never have a truly private moment. But King was also growing more isolated, challenged by the rising voices of Black Power, and losing ground with other allies since he'd spoken out against the Vietnam War. King believed he'd had no choice but to take a stand against the war if he were going to put his body and faith in the service of nonviolence. From the pulpit of Riverside Church in Manhattan he'd said, "I knew that I could never again raise my voice against the violence of the oppressed in the ghettoes without having first spoken clearly to the greatest purveyor of violence in the world today: my own government. For the sake of those boys, for the sake of this government, for the sake of the hundreds of thousands trembling under our violence, I cannot be silent."[4]

Joyce couldn't bring herself to interview the Reverend. It felt invasive to ask him too many questions in such an intimate setting. When she looked back on that moment, she'd recall only the question he'd asked her, a young Black woman poised to graduate from an elite white college: "What are you going to do?"

The next morning Joyce was whisked into a plush, carpeted office at DuPont for her interview. The interview went well. They offered her a job that would pay eight dollars an hour. Her stepfather made about a dollar an hour working in the steel plant in Richmond, Virginia. Her mother made less money working at the Reynolds Tobacco plant. The Duke degree had tendered the chance to step from the laboring class into the middle class.

Joyce remembered the two most vivid smells that pervaded the city air while she was growing up in industrial Richmond. One was the earthy, sharp smell of tobacco; the other, the acrid, synthetic smell of nylon being manufactured. Now, during the interview, she couldn't stop thinking about the harsh odor wafting from DuPont's nylon factory. And when she thought of nylon, she thought of parachutes. And when she thought of parachutes, she thought of young American men plummeting into the jungles of Vietnam to fight a war she didn't believe in. Thoughts of King's death mingled with the memory of that smell. "What are you going to do?" the great, now dead, leader of her people had asked.

A recent *Sports Illustrated* article called Duke's student body a "Timid Generation" and mocked graduates headed for "some post-college cubbyhole—like Daddy's baling wire factory."[5] Joyce's step-daddy didn't own a factory, and she and her friends hadn't earned the right to start an Afro-American Association at Duke by being timid. In fact, Joyce took more pride in the armband she wore in solidarity with the quest of Duke's maids and janitors for better wages and working conditions than she did in her diploma.[6]

She knew, before she left the DuPont interview, that she couldn't accept the job. No, she thought, she'd take the scholarship offer at the University of North Carolina to study medical anthropology.

She'd continue to be part of the movement.

But how could she tell her parents she'd turned down eight dollars an hour?

❖

On April 7, as tension subsided in Greensboro, a woman from the tiny Appalachian town of Tryon, North Carolina, sat down at a piano at a music festival on Long Island. The people in the audience wept as Nina Simone sang, "Everybody knows we're on the brink. What will happen, now that the King of love is dead?"

13

FUSION

As if in answer to Nina Simone's question, Nelson accelerated his organizing work in Greensboro after King's assassination. He joined the NAACP voter registration drives, inching a borrowed pickup through The Grove, blasting Martin Luther King Jr. speeches from a battery-powered turntable anchored to the truck bed. Nothing inspired people to stake their claim to the American system more than the martyred reverend's profound poetry.

The dentist from Charlotte, Dr. Hawkins, wasn't the only Black candidate on the ballot in North Carolina in 1968. Energized East Siders stumped for an A&T graduate, with a law degree from the University of North Carolina at Chapel Hill, named Henry Frye, who, that fall, would become the first Black person elected to the North Carolina state legislature in the twentieth century.

Like a hinge in history, 1968 cracked open the door to a decade of Black gains in electoral politics. Even so, Nelson held few illusions that Black politicians could suddenly and dramatically improve the complicated lives of the poor people living around A&T.

Realizing that the five years Terry Sanford gave the North Carolina Fund in 1963 would not be sufficient to shift North Carolina's political, economic, and social culture, George Esser and Nathan Garrett flipped the remaining funds into a new organization. The Foundation for Community Development (FCD) would be led by Garrett and operate without a sunset. Hurrying to keep a step ahead of local, state, and federal detractors intent on shutting down their work, Esser, Garrett, and Fuller charged Nelson with organizing a force for "community control" that could harass and disrupt the status quo in Greensboro. In late 1968, the FCD funded a small slate of projects, including the Greensboro Association of Poor People (GAPP), set up in late 1968 by a team led by Nelson Johnson under the guidance of Fuller.[1]

GAPP took a spot in a corner of the NAACP office, and Nelson, who'd stepped away from college to focus on community organizing, began reaching out to the thousands of families living in dilapidated housing who bore the brunt of a 30 percent unemployment rate among Greensboro's Black working-age population. In the tradition of Ella Baker's grassroots, bottoms-up methods, which he'd been learning from Howard Fuller, Nelson invited senior citizens, workers, students, and single mothers to set GAPP's agenda on housing, tenants' rights, working conditions, education, disputes at the welfare office, and police brutality. As these community members came together to become, as James Baldwin put it, "an energy . . . which [white business and political leaders do] . . . not really know how to control," GAPP provided support, strategy, and communications expertise.[2]

"It is the opinion of GAPP," read the organization's purpose statement, "that most poor people are poor because of laws, policies, structures and traditions which operate in the interest of property owners and the wealthy. The institutional structures and processes created dependency (both physical and psychological) and a sense of apathy and powerlessness and is reinforced by the operation of these institutions among poor Black people." The words offered a glimpse of the evolution and deepening of Nelson's thinking and affirmed the mission of the sophisticated alliance of private and public funds supporting GAPP, one of the "first independent anti-poverty organizations in the country."[3]

Following the assassination of King, the hard news continued in 1968. Under pressure from the anti–Vietnam War movement, LBJ announced he would not run for a second term. On June 6, less than two months after announcing his candidacy for president, Robert Kennedy was assassinated in California. Outside the Democratic National Convention in Chicago that August, police rioted, brutally attacking mostly white antiwar demonstrators whom they feared and hated. And in November, white voters sick of the disruptions of the civil rights and antiwar movements elevated their backlash to the Oval Office, electing Richard Nixon as the next US president.

❖

In Greensboro, skirmishes between A&T students and the police began in early 1969, during a cafeteria workers' strike that Nelson and GAPP organized at A&T and the University of North Carolina Greensboro. In solidarity with the underpaid and overworked Black workers, students boycotted the meal service for several days, replacing it with an impromptu "bologna line," where they slapped together nearly two thousand sandwiches with groceries provided by local supermarkets and purchased with donations. On the evening of Thursday, March 13, 2,500 students held a rally in support of the workers. A phalanx of Greensboro policemen met the students when they made their way to the edge of campus at the corner of Market and Laurel Streets.[4]

The students and police would never agree on what happened next. Students said the rally had been peaceful until police discharged a fog of tear gas over them and opened fire, shooting "randomly." They said they "didn't know how or why all the violence broke out." One student complained that the Greensboro Police Department used A&T as a training ground for young, inexperienced—in other words, scared and trigger-happy—rookie officers. The police claimed that they returned fire only after students shot at them. However the violence started, the cops—empowered by Mayor Carson Bain's statement in the wake of the King assassination that "the police don't carry guns for nothing. I would think an officer would tell a looter or Molotov-cocktail thrower to halt, and if he didn't do so immediately, the officer would have every right to shoot him"[5]—fired their guns and injured two students.

❖

The next day the catering company settled the strike in the workers' favor. The city's Black elite, though measured in their words, supported Nelson and the courageous stand he'd organized. "I'm extremely pleased," said A&T President Lewis C. Dowdy, "that the settlement has been made . . . for the benefit of our students and in the interest of our cafeteria workers." It was Nelson's first victory as a labor leader.[6]

After the confrontation and the settlement, the police began riding around Black neighborhoods with shotguns lying visibly on the seats of their cars.[7] Many of the student activists, including Nelson Johnson and the other GAPP workers, responded in kind, the barrels of long guns bristling from their car windows.[8]

❖

A month earlier, in February, a friend had introduced Nelson Johnson to a young graduate student at UNC Chapel Hill. Just before Joyce Hobson met Nelson, she'd been part of protests at her alma mater aimed at pushing Duke to establish an Afro-American studies department. The police deluged the student agitators with tear gas cannons.

On their first date, sitting in the stands at the Central Intercollegiate Athletic Association basketball tournament in Greensboro, the "love bug struck."[9] She saw a handsome man with chiseled features and big eyes that looked square on the hard world around them. He saw a beautiful dark-skinned young woman whose hooded eyes emerged from beneath the cloud of a full Afro to shine their trusting light on him. They shared personal details both trivial and profound, quickly absorbing the particulars of each other's young lives. Born prematurely, Joyce was called Juice by her neighbors in Richmond, who early on recognized her intellectual gifts. Joyce attributed her "life, health, and prosperity" to her nurturing village upbringing. She set out for Duke from Richmond's Southside "with the blessing and the responsibility of the whole community."[10] She'd chosen Duke and the role of being an integrator over attending Hampton Institute down the road in Virginia. Her education and personal achievements were "linked with the advancement of my entire race," she'd say. "It makes you serious about your work, but it is an awesome thing."[11] He, though four years older and having grown up with a relative degree of landowning privilege, worked sporadically toward his degree from a historically Black college. Though he'd fast become a dynamic leader in Greensboro's Black community, Nelson confided that he still felt unsure of his speaking ability, an insecurity that he attributed to being darker-skinned than some of his older, smooth-talking siblings. A&T lay fifty miles and a world away from Duke's imposing, well-groomed campus, but Nelson's and Joyce's activism around the Piedmont overlapped; the two were surprised they hadn't met sooner. Their surprise, however, gave way to the uncanny sensation that, despite just meeting, they'd known each other forever.

Soon Joyce was spending more time in Greensboro than she was attending graduate school at UNC, immersing herself not only in new love but also in the work of the Greensboro Association of Poor People. She took over running the office and hit the pavement to talk to women about how an organized community could negotiate with landlords, claim rights at the welfare office, and raise petitions for streetlights and city services at council meetings. She explained GAPP's goal of developing the community rather than allowing redevelopment. The women Joyce met on the porches and in the front rooms reminded her of the kind but eagle-eyed "aunties" who kept watch from the neighborhood stoops in Richmond. They were the matriarchs who glued families together and served as neighborhood protectors and connectors. In the lives of these women who held the community together, Joyce saw not only remarkable resilience but also the legacy of slavery. Public housing such as Morningside Homes had been intended as a stepping stone. But for the Black women and families she knew in The Grove, substandard housing had become a "staying place," a form of economic and physical entrapment, complicated by the fear of displacement caused by redevelopment.

Thanks to GAPP, no one from The Grove went to the welfare office alone. When the housing authority met to talk about the lives of the city's poor residents, Nelson and his colleagues would call on two dozen serious-looking Black men from the A&T campus to ring the room, standing silently, their faces impassive masks, turning white fear into a tool. Unnerved by the direct action, the white people reviewing housing policy often treated Black petitioners less dismissively than they would have if the petitioners had come alone. Nelson cultivated a dual personality as a way to undercut "the very foundations of white power."[12] While he was stoic, assertive, and tactically late for meetings with whites, the Nelson who greeted Black residents in The Grove was quick to smile and ready to listen to whatever they had to say.

❖

Advocacy wasn't a one-way street.

When neighborhood residents Lula Mae Pennix and Miss Mary Oliver emerged from their rented homes, structures with collapsing floors and leaking roofs, they'd say to Nelson, "You need to marry [Joyce], not these other girls."[13] That's how community worked; you received what was offered and you gave what you could from the bubbling pot on the stove or your well of experience in survival and love.

As spring burst around them, Nelson and Joyce became inseparable, bound to each other, Greensboro's Black communities, and GAPP's meaningful work. Though uncertain exactly how, they both believed their work would soon help relegate racism to the past.

❖

Late in 1968, an imposing man arrived on the A&T campus, intent, he announced, on setting up a chapter of the Black Panther Party in the city. Harold "Nunding" Avent stood more than six feet tall, weighed well over two hundred pounds, and wore a big beard and flowing dashikis, from which he would produce sticks of dynamite as a magician might pull a rabbit from a hat.[14] He'd arrived from a New York City life as a jazz drummer. When John Coltrane—who hailed from High Point, just down the road from Greensboro—died in 1967, Avent rode to the funeral with jazz legends Ornette Coleman and Billy Higgins. The next day he recorded an album, *Freedom & Unity*, with a free-form horn player named Clifford Thornton. Nunding wrote two of the songs on the album, including "Free Huey," for Black Panther founder Huey Newton. In New York, Nunding and Thornton planned to "revolutionize . . . the [music] business . . . [and] free the music to evolve naturally." "I'm a drummer," Avent told *The Village Voice*, "but the scene is so bad now that I can't get a real chance to play."[15] Avent soon shifted focus from the business of jazz to guerrilla insurrection in Greensboro.

He "looked like what people thought Black Panthers should look like" and "put people in awe" with his physical presence and revolutionary talk, thought Nelson Johnson, who didn't intend to join the Panthers. Even so, he invited Nunding to stay with him at Nelson's Camel Street apartment in The Grove, Greensboro's informal hub of Black Power organizing. Nelson allowed no drugs or drinking in his apartment or around the GAPP work—nothing that would distract activists from movement work or make them more vulnerable to the police and FBI. What began to make Nelson uncomfortable, however, wasn't Nunding's more uninhibited lifestyle but his talk about killing cops and blowing up white-owned businesses in Greensboro.[16]

The FBI's man in the Greensboro Resident Agency assigned to monitor "Black Hate" for Bureau Director J. Edgar Hoover noticed Nunding the minute he arrived in Greensboro. In reports to the Charlotte Field Office, Special Agent Dag Frierson described Nunding's "full Afro-bush" and noted that the Black Panther assumed the role of "teacher," instructing A&T students in "guerrilla tactics." At a

February 22, 1969, memorial for Malcolm X, Frierson reported that Nunding referred to police officers assigned to the event as "pigs" and advised the several hundred attendees to get a "piece" and to "use it when necessary."[17]

Frierson funneled his reports to the Greensboro Police Department, and, in them, he identified Nelson Johnson as a member of the Black Panther Party. He claimed that Nelson and his comrades were caching arms for a possible insurrection. Neither assertion was true. Nunding's rhetoric supported the most extreme, and false, interpretation of activist activity in Greensboro—and of Nelson. As there were distinct Greensboros, there arose two wildly different understandings of Nelson Johnson's character and intentions—one in the Black community, another in the white. Nelson's own actions had helped cultivate this "double consciousness," though he little understood just how dangerous it would be.

One day in late April, Nelson and Joyce squeezed into a car with Nunding behind the wheel. There were no license plates on the car, and as he drove, Nunding announced that the car's trunk was full of dynamite they could use to blow up white-owned businesses. Without license plates, Nunding said, they'd be untraceable.[18]

Nunding is crazy, Nelson thought. He's going to get us killed or sent to prison for decades. Something was off about the tough-talking man from New York. Nelson became suspicious that Nunding might be trying to set them up. Maybe he'd gone undercover for the Feds.

Conspiracy talk swirled through the movement: Had James Earl Ray really pulled the trigger that killed King? Even if he had, had he acted alone? Did the FBI set up Malcolm? In time, there would be documented reasons to believe that the official narratives around these assassinations might be intricate fictions. In early 1969, activists weren't quite certain how far the FBI would go to suppress dissent. From rumors and anecdotes, they suspected but couldn't yet see the powerful, well-funded, subterranean world of American intelligence, so skilled at covering its tracks.

❖

Nelson got out of the car in an agitated state.

"Joyce," he said, "if Nunding does what he's talking about I might have to go to Canada."

"I'll go with you," she said.

❖

And in that moment, they knew they were ready to heed the aunties' advice. A short time later, Nunding disappeared from Greensboro without blowing up any buildings. Perhaps he'd done his job; the tension between the activists and law enforcement continued to escalate as Nelson and Joyce resolved to march together into a life guided by love, community, and struggle.[19]

TRUE BLUE

During the first weekend in April 1969, golf fans arrived to walk beside the perfect emerald fairways of the Sedgefield Country Club and take in the competition at the Greater Greensboro Open. They witnessed Gene Littler ride a "spectacular hole-in-one at the seventh" to the $32,000 PGA championship winner's purse.[1] It was the Greensboro the Chamber of Commerce advertised in its brochures, the All-America City the bankers and the mayor touted to the investors and business leaders who'd fly in to consider moving their operations—and families—to town.

When the dogwoods and cherry trees bloom along Greensboro's gently undulating streets, it's as if a fine lace has settled over the city, the delicate white and pink colors set off by the electric green of new leaves. It's a beautiful city then, warm as April points toward May but not yet hot, busy, as many college towns tend to be, but not hectic. The city moves at its own pace, enticing visitors to linger over the real estate pages, to consider the schools their children might attend, to check job listings, the hour of a worship service, and daydream about how nice it might be to live in a city that proposes such a comfortable marriage between rural and urban life.

From the vantage point of the country club or the acres of manicured lawns shimmering uniformly beside Irving Park's great mansions, however, a great deal remained invisible.

A month after the PGA contest, a very different event brought people to Greensboro. Students from Cornell, Harvard, and Black colleges up and down the East Coast arrived at the A&T campus to inaugurate a new organization: the Student Organization for Black Unity (SOBU). "Welcome to the Revolution" announced the printed banner staked to the A&T lawn. Attendees were intent on forming a national organization to fill the void left by the Student Nonviolent Coordinating Committee, which had collapsed after the FBI's efforts pushed SNCC's charismatic leader Stokely Carmichael to flee the United States and seek refuge in Africa. Nelson, Howard Fuller, and other Triad-based activists began to imagine a new national network, independent of donations from institutions and individuals uncomfortable with calls for "Black Power" and intimidating self-determination. Scapegoated by South Carolina authorities as the "outside agitator" responsible for the Orangeburg Massacre and bracing for a long grind through the justice system, former SNCC director Cleveland Sellers rolled into town to confer with the group.[2]

It had been barely a year since Nelson had led the local protest of the Orangeburg Massacre. Now, with Fuller as a mentor, support from the Foundation for Community Development, and the groundbreaking work of the Greensboro Association of Poor People, Nelson's national reputation among Black activists bloomed like the trees lining Greensboro's thoroughfares.

"North Carolina was what was going on," believed Milton Coleman, an aspiring journalist who made the trip to Greensboro from Milwaukee, where he'd known Howard Fuller. "Everything and everyone" involved in the Black liberation movement seemed to pass through Greensboro in 1969. They were drawn to the energetic experiments in "community control" and to Nelson Johnson, known in the movement as "Mr. Greensboro." His reputation as a uniquely talented organizer, a "grassroots guy," "concerned about people and not himself," spread through the Black Power grapevine. For Coleman, who'd come to Greensboro from the urban North, Nelson "was the first real southern organizer [he'd] ever met" and "the most atypical leader" who "didn't care about the limelight." No one "had any doubts about where his heart was. He was true blue. If you were in a foxhole you wanted to be in it with Nelson."[3]

❖

From May 7 to 9, the sixty attendees worked to define SOBU's mission and platform. They rejected President Nixon's push for "Black capitalism," stating that "it was simply white capitalism in reverse exploiting the masses for economic gains." They vowed to work in collaboration with other Black organizations, building unity across differences in ideology and strategy. To circumvent the white press, they resolved to publish a newsletter and assigned Milton Coleman the role of editor. They outlined a plan for a speaker's bureau that would send Nelson Johnson around the country to share his organizing experience and strategies and to spark interest in SOBU on any college campus with a population of Black students. In addition, the attendees agreed to form what they called a Black Defense Alliance, a wing of SOBU charged with protecting members and their communities from police brutality.[4]

Nine years after the downtown sit-ins and the concurrent founding of SNCC, a new organization with national aspirations took shape in Greensboro. The goal was now "liberation," not "integration." The ever-vigilant FBI took note of the conference's "basic aim to initiate, coordinate, and lead a black student movement in the United States," observing that the "convention was . . . attended by well-known black militants."[5]

On the final day of the convention, May 9, the attendees selected officers to lead the new organization, voting Nelson Johnson, already a director of GAPP and the vice president elect of A&T's student body, to be SOBU's first national chairman.

Shortly after the vote, a hundred distraught Dudley High School students appeared in the A&T Memorial Student Union.

WAR

Months earlier, when Nelson and his colleagues founded GAPP, they'd turned their attention not only to the plight of poor Black adults but to engaging the community's disaffected youths. One smart teenager drawn to GAPP's community work was Claude Barnes, a wiry, intense junior at Dudley High School, who cofounded two Black nationalist groups for The Grove's young activists: Youth for the Unity of Black Society (YUBS) and Black Students United for Liberation.[1]

Persistent inequities at Dudley High School troubled Barnes. Dress codes were more formal and stricter at the Black schools. Teenagers at white high schools were permitted to leave campus during lunch, while Dudley's students were denied this freedom. Sports facilities at Dudley, allowed to deteriorate over the years, were deemed unsafe. Barnes ran for student body president to address these problems and others.

At an all-school meeting on May 1, a school administrator referred to Barnes as a "subversive" and announced that the young man's name would not appear on the ballot. The next day, student voters defied the school powers, writing in Barnes's name on 600 of the 800 ballots cast. The school's Black administration, afraid that validating the new generation of outspoken Black Power activists would unleash more discrimination from white authorities, refused to seat Barnes.

A student election might have seemed trivial to many in white Greensboro, but Nelson knew that on the Dudley side of town the issue of Barnes's candidacy would be linked to the process of "Negro removal," the unequal unemployment rate, the lack of representation on city council, and the myriad daily injustices of being Black in a city where white business leaders were reluctant to share power. Nelson and his GAPP colleague Walter Brame encouraged Dudley's principal, Franklin Brown, to meet with parents and students to hash out a way forward. Did Brown answer to the Black community that sent him their children or to the white school board who signed his checks? The principal did not take Nelson and Brame's advice.[2]

For the next week, the issue festered, unresolved. Students who'd walked out of school in protest on May 2 were suspended. The superintendent, sensing that a firmer hand would be needed to quash the discontent at Dudley, sent a white colleague to take over the administration of the high school. The temporary principal, Owen Lewis, "had a way of rubbing people the wrong way," and his presence pushed the delicate situation toward chaos.[3] Police cars carrying officers in riot gear began to patrol the area around the high school, the now ubiquitous shotguns in full, threatening view.[4]

In consultation "with lawyers, community leaders and parents" students had tried to ensure that their "protest activities were legal and properly organized." Frustrated by the intimidating police presence and the school administration's continued intransigence, the high schoolers decided they had "no recourse" but to reach out beyond the school for advice and support. On May 9, they walked the mile and a half to the A&T ballroom to appeal to Claude Barnes's mentor at A&T, Nelson Johnson, for help. The high school and college students decided to march together back to Dudley.

The Greensboro police were waiting when the protesters, now numbering close to two hundred, arrived back at the high school. The group entered the gymnasium to meet, but when Nelson Johnson leaped onto a table to address the gathering, the police arrested him for "disturbing a public school." Seventeen high schoolers and two more college students were also arrested, including a young man named Robert Evans charged with "laughing loudly and clapping his hands." As the visiting SOBU founders departed Greensboro, their organization's new national chairman was embroiled in an escalating local crisis.[5] City and state officials would use this arrest of Nelson to try to control his activism for another two years.

❖

On May 11, parents, preachers, business leaders, and teachers held a mass meeting at the Trinity AME Zion Church under a blanket surveillance of the police and, likely, the FBI. Discouraged by city leaders from engaging with "radicals" and "outside agitators," neither Dudley's principal, Franklin Brown, nor the superintendent's man, Owen Lewis, attended the meeting.[6] In a tone-deaf attempt to diffuse the growing crisis, the white chairman of the school board offered to send Black football players, cherry-picked to desegregate Greensboro's white high schools, back to Dudley.[7]

Five days later, on May 16, nine students were protesting peacefully when Owen Lewis called the riot police to Dudley. Lewis told the teenagers to stop or they'd be arrested. As the students faced a row of armed cops, one of them called Lewis a "white pig." Lewis turned to the police and snarled, "Get the n——s." The officers attacked the protesters, beating them and arresting them in front of hundreds of student and parent witnesses.[8]

One A&T coed wrote, "People are just sick and darn tired of [the police] overreacting every time we start to speak our piece. . . . When authority respects us, we will respect it!" Failure to extend this respect, the young woman declared, would result in law enforcement getting their "chops fried."[9]

"The May 16 arrests," Claude Barnes would later say, "convinced everyone that future protests would have to include some plan for organized self-defense."[10]

❖

On May 19, the student picket line at Dudley reassembled. Again, the police were called, arriving armed with "pepper fog" machines and billy clubs. This time, as a young woman was "beaten, thrown to the ground and dragged in the mud" by the police, the students fought back. One police officer was injured. Among the injured were parents attempting to protect their children.[11]

The student body boycotted classes the next day. Tuned to the stream of paranoid intelligence reports issuing from the police and FBI, the newly elected Mayor Jack Elam called the protesters "radicals not interested in the good of the community," even as local clergy, students, teachers, factory workers, and his own Chamber of Commerce urged negotiation.[12]

"I try not to lose my temper, but this really makes me mad," said John Marshall Stevenson, the owner of the Black weekly *Carolina Peacemaker*, as protests resumed on May 21. "We want to do things our way in our own community, and like it or not, this is a separate community."[13] A few short months earlier, Stevenson (who would soon change his last name to Kilimanjaro) had implored Greensboro's citizens to "join hands and . . . see to it that public servants become just that—servants of the people—rather than mere lackeys of big business and industrial giants."[14] Now, as he watched the city simmer toward open conflict, he insisted that equitable representation on the city council would have prevented the school board from acting in such an oblivious and heavy-handed manner.

Around A&T, frustrated youths who'd watched the police criminalize attempts at peaceful protest hurled rocks at cars driven by white people as darkness settled over the city on May 21. Police exchanged gunfire with Black residents in other southeast neighborhoods and pumped tear gas at their assailants. Sensing the gathering chaos, military veterans in the A&T student body secreted weapons into the dormitories to defend the campus and their schoolmates.[15]

North of the A&T campus, a group of angry white men tossed bricks at Black motorists. When it appeared that the police were ignoring this provocation, a group of unarmed Black students headed the few blocks north toward Bessemer Avenue to see whether they could interrupt the violence. They spread out, keeping to the shadows, fearful that the police would shoot them on sight.

At the edge of campus, a student shouted out, warning of an approaching police car. The students scattered, searching for places to hide. One witness would say the car was unmarked. Two others claimed to have heard the siren, seen the flashing lights and a uniformed policeman open the back car door, hop out, and begin firing a rifle or shotgun toward the campus. As the students sprinted away—still on campus—one young man appeared to trip and fall beside a greenhouse. When the shooting stopped and the other students emerged from their hiding places, they discovered that Willie Grimes hadn't tripped. He'd been shot in the back of the head.[16]

The students commandeered a car and sped frantically toward Moses Cone Memorial Hospital, carrying their injured friend. From behind them, gunshots pierced the night air. Three bullets hit the car. The students believed the police were pursuing them as they attempted to save Willie Grimes's life.

When they pulled in at the hospital the police were, indeed, right behind them. Doctors pronounced Grimes dead, and the four young men who'd risked their lives rushing him to the hospital were taken into custody.

The hail of bullets that felled Grimes had struck another student, George Lima, in the leg and abdomen. Lima survived the wounds but refused to talk about what he'd seen.[17]

❖

When Willie Grimes died, Nelson and Joyce were inside their Camel Street apartment, being surveilled by the police.

A short time later, in the wee hours of Thursday morning, May 22, the mayor called Nelson to meet with city authorities. A cop car whisked him from his apartment through the dark to the police department command center. The officers escorted Nelson into a war room buzzing with communications equipment and law enforcement leaders, including the head of the State Bureau of Investigation; the head of the National Guard; the state attorney general, Robert

Morgan (who would later become a senator and sit on the Church Committee); the chief of the Greensboro Police Department, Paul Calhoun; Dag Frierson from the FBI; and the mayor, Jack Elam. Also present was the newest member of the Greensboro city council, Jim Melvin. To Nelson, Melvin likely represented one more white man in a room full of white men standing between him and his quest for freedom and equality. To Melvin and the others, Nelson arrived as the face of a singular problem.[18]

"We want you to call this off," the men ordered the twenty-six-year-old activist. Over the course of a year, Nelson's reputation as a powerful figure in the Black Power movement had inflated so quickly that the assembled officials seemed to think the young leader could snap his fingers and extinguish the rebellious emotions swirling through the city.[19]

A sense of disbelief and anger rose in Nelson. The men around him had wasted weeks. They'd ignored his voice and others in Greensboro, when they could have encouraged a community solution to the problem at Dudley High School. Instead, city leaders sent in the police, pushing the conflict toward violence. They'd had generations to provide jobs, housing, and equal schools. Now as discontent exploded on their watch, they wanted Nelson to make it go away, as if he, not a history of poverty, violence, and inequality, were responsible for the rebellion—as if the problems were new.[20]

Nelson noted something else: the men seemed scared. From what he could tell, they truly believed themselves to be the victims of manipulative radicals and "outside agitators" rather than perpetrators of injustice.

Nelson told the men in the room the truth: "I can't call this off." But he didn't stop there, unable to resist jabbing at the insecurities that united the assembled officials: "And I wouldn't, even if I could." If they didn't want to negotiate with Nelson and the Dudley students, they would have to deal with the enraged community members and the student GIs set on protecting North Carolina A&T State University with guns.

❖

After the meeting with Nelson, the mayor set a curfew. To protect the students, A&T President Lewis Dowdy hastily announced that the school year would end that Thursday afternoon and ordered students to leave the campus by the evening of Friday, May 23.[21]

That Thursday, a white man on his round of daily pickups and deliveries from a linen service contracted by the college made the mistake of driving his van onto the besieged campus. Students overwhelmed by frustration, anger, and perhaps grief attacked him and turned his truck on its side.[22]

That evening the Army National Guard surrounded the A&T campus, exchanging gunfire with the veterans hunkered in the dorms. During the predawn hours on Friday morning, four Black police officers and one white officer were shot and injured, one seriously. As in the case of Willie Grimes, this shooting would never be solved, though the caliber of bullet that caused at least one of the injuries suggested it may have issued from a National Guardsman's weapon.[23] In the collective mind of the police department, however, the person most responsible for the wounded cops was Nelson Johnson.[24]

When news of the injured officers reached the men in the command center at police headquarters, Mayor Elam, with the backing of state and federal officials, ordered a military strike on the A&T campus.

At 6:45 a.m., on Friday, May 23, under the cover of helicopters and airplanes roaring low to dump tear gas over the campus, 650 Guardsmen made their move. President Dowdy had not received warning of the offensive, and his students, oblivious to what was coming, believed they still had twelve hours to vacate the campus.[25] Now the students stumbled from the dorms, sick from fear and inhaled gas. The Guardsmen stormed the buildings, shooting off locks, smashing doors, flipping mattresses, and knocking over bookshelves. A student "saw one guardsman take the butt of his gun and smash the tube of a television set in someone's room." Others claimed that the

Guardsmen stole radios, money, and other valuables from their rooms. "I cannot and will not forget," said the student who witnessed the Guardsman destroy the TV, "being made to crawl in the wet grass that Friday morning and looking up above Scott Hall to see tear gas being dispensed into the crowds of young men."[26]

Despite the sudden raid and intelligence reports the men in the command center received from informants who'd slipped in and out of the dorms, Guardsmen discovered only ten weapons, of which only three were functional. They arrested, booked, and interrogated three hundred students, and yet the authorities couldn't identify a single person who had fired a shot at them. The story circulated that the Guard and police had been held off by just a couple of shooters wielding ancient weapons. In fact, a coordinated, community effort had secreted the men and their weapons through the dorms' air ducts and steam tunnels and away from Greensboro. What Mayor Elam referred to as a "group of not-too-bright Black students . . . led astray by 'outsiders' and 'radicals'" had outmaneuvered every local, state, and federal law enforcement entity present.[27]

By responding to the police and National Guard with armed self-defense, the students now believed they'd prevented state forces from killing more people. Perhaps they'd demonstrated a way to "control their own destinies," a model for SOBU's Defense Alliance, and the answer to the question about nonviolence Nelson had hoped to pose to Martin Luther King Jr. during the Greensboro visit that never happened. Claude Barnes, the unseated Dudley student council president, would reflect that "[the rebellion] left us a respect from the white establishment we never felt before. They knew we'd fight back."[28]

❖

After the violence and grief of May 1969, several Black Greensboro police officers uncomfortable with the raid executed against the state's flagship Black campus resigned. But in Greensboro's Black community there were many who were uncomfortable with the militant activists and the police dissenters. One young Black patrol officer who was on duty the night of May 22 believed the Black officers who quit just weren't cut out to be police. Sylvester Daughtry was patient, disciplined, quietly ambitious, and capable of withstanding the discomfort of being Black in a department ambivalent about integration. Though he'd come to Greensboro from rural North Carolina, like Nelson Johnson, Daughtry disagreed with Nelson's confrontational tactics. Real change, Daughtry believed, would come from the inside, not the outside.[29]

The bitter stench of tear gas lingered over the A&T campus on Saturday morning, as Nelson and Joyce prepared for a future that could wait no longer. The linen truck still lay on its side, an afterthought. Bullet holes riddled the now-deserted Scott Hall. Tanks rumbled over the streets surrounding the campus, as the women Nelson and Joyce worked with at GAPP took charge of the wedding preparations. After a whirlwind three-month courtship, the two activists, in love, tied the knot.

HEARINGS

When school reconvened in the late summer of 1969, hundreds of A&T students jammed into the Memorial Union Ballroom to listen to what Nelson Johnson had to say about the invasion of their campus three months earlier. Dressed in jeans and a short-sleeve collared shirt, Nelson stood at a lectern, a notebook jammed halfway into his back pocket. The confident community organizer surveyed the faces of the students before him. Not one for niceties or a preamble, he said, "We must, as responsible students, first understand . . . [that] what happened last May was more than a battle between police, the National Guard and A&T students, but a representation of the exact situation that exists between blacks and whites."

Narrating the sequence of events that led to violence, he told the students, "After peaceful negotiations had been crushed, there was nothing to do but either submit to these indecencies or stand up and fight . . . and we did engage the enemy in battle and did put a whipping on the white man, simply because we had no choice. . . . We are taught that Thomas Jefferson wrote in the Declaration of Independence to free all men. But he was in fact morally contradictory when he wrote life, liberty and the pursuit of happiness for all. . . . We as black people stand by Stokely Carmichael, Rap Brown, Howard Fuller . . . and all blacks who are ready to speak out in the name of the black man. Long live black people all over the world; long live blacks who will withstand oppression all over the world."[1]

Nelson left the podium, and the mass of students rose to offer the vice president of the student body a thunderous ovation. If the Vietnam War opened the eyes of young white protesters to government lies and betrayals, to many Black revolutionaries in the United States it was just one more unexceptional example of America's racism and the imperial abuses of white power that had carried their ancestors across the Atlantic Ocean in chains. To them, the proxy war wasn't against communism as much as the self-determining power of all the people of color around the globe. The helicopters churning over Vietnam were, therefore, inseparable from the helicopters that had poured tear gas over the heads of A&T's students. "The damage done to 1,300 students who were housed in [the Scott and Cooper] dormitories, and their personal, individual confidence in the respect and dignity of man will be hard to repair, immeasurable and incalculable," President Dowdy had said, reflecting on the long-term effects of the military operation on the campus he oversaw.[2]

Nelson's words that evening offered a glimpse of what had been ruptured: he and his fellow Black students were losing faith that white America had any intention of extending its beautiful ideals to people who looked like them.

Earlier that summer, after the unrest at A&T resulted in the largest military operation on a college campus in American history, the Senate subcommittee investigating "Riots, Civil and Criminal Disorders" in cities and on campuses around the United States summoned the A&T president, Dr. Lewis Dowdy, and Chief Paul Calhoun of the Greensboro Police Department to Washington.[3]

The visitors from Greensboro were received in the wood-paneled Senate Office Building room 1202 on the morning of July 10 by the committee chairman, John McClellan, a conservative Democrat from Arkansas who'd built a career on his opposition to corruption, communism, and integration. McClellan was joined by Robert P.

Griffin, a Republican from Michigan, and the voluble Karl E. Mundt, a Republican from South Dakota, who supported civil rights legislation but was an avowed anticommunist loyal to the disgraced communist hunter and former senator Joe McCarthy. If the three senators in the room found it difficult to understand student rage against the Vietnam War—the takeovers, rebellions, and demonstrations paralyzing scores of predominantly white institutions and universities, including Harvard, Berkeley, and Columbia—Senator Mundt sounded utterly bewildered by the young people embracing Black Power. "Why," he wondered out loud, "the black student body who, in my opinion, rightfully were desirous of having integrated schools and all these things, now suddenly want to go back to having all-black status again. How do you explain that? They want to have black studies, black professors. What we were trying to do, I thought, was eliminate this, so that you had blacks and white commingling as we have Norwegians and Irishmen commingled in South Dakota."

President Lewis Dowdy addressed the senators first. Immaculately attired in a pressed suit and respectable tie, Dowdy had to walk a fine line between his white, politically motivated bosses in the North Carolina university system and his responsibility to his students. Born in 1917, Dowdy had grown up in the small farming town of Eastover, South Carolina, surrounded by vast cotton fields that stretched to the horizon and dated to the antebellum period.[4] He'd picked his way, step by step, between the local plantation culture and Jim Crow laws to become an educated man and, now, a college president; he knew exactly how to present himself to the white men before him.[5] Facing the public officials seated at a high, curved table, he spoke calmly and methodically, describing the institution he ran, telling the senators about A&T's four thousand students and 247 faculty, its six schools and two divisions, and the unprecedented accomplishments of the class of 1969. Graduates, he informed the senators, would soon be heading off for further study at Harvard, Rutgers, the University of

Wisconsin, Columbia, and the University of Michigan, among other elite schools.

President Dowdy recounted the brief occupation of an administration building in December 1968 and the reasonable demands students had brought to his attention then, many of which the university had decided to adopt, including the establishment of an Afro-American center, greater student participation in university decision-making, less restrictive rules for visiting hours at women's dorms, expanded library schedules, and additional outdoor basketball and volleyball courts. He told the senators about the cafeteria workers' strike, focusing not on the clash with police on the night of March 13, but on the outcome of the settlement, which favored the workers: a pay raise and the right to overtime pay and sick leave. "I want to point out very clearly," he told the committee, "the grievances that were presented to us did not carry with them any violence against the university whatsoever. We were able to meet with students and to work out agreements through our channels of communication." He continued carefully and tactfully diagnosing the volatile situation in Greensboro: "I think one of the reasons for some of the unrest is that setting up machinery to actually go through the grievances of students and get them into operative order is a little slower than what students would like to see." He didn't define who or what entity had been slow to listen to the student complaints, though he might have named not only his own administration but also Greensboro's school board, city council, and police department.

President Dowdy never criticized the police department directly, nor did he identify by name a single A&T student. Under the committee's patronizing probing, he maneuvered the labyrinth of explicit and implicit hierarchies masterfully, demonstrating that he maintained authority over the students even as he tried to protect them from misunderstanding, prejudice, and the contagion of paranoia. As the session drew to a close, the committee counsel, Jerry Adlerman, suddenly intervened in the conversation. "Can you tell me whether you know a Lieutenant Avent?" he asked, referring to Harold "Nunding" Avent, the man whose violent rhetoric had caused Nelson and Joyce to consider exile. Yes, responded President Dowdy's colleague, Dr. Marshall, the dean of student affairs: a "bushy haired" man by that name and dressed in a "dashiki [and] black boots" had come to see him as a representative of the Black Panthers. However, Dr. Marshall emphasized, "I want to be certain it is understood, we do not have a [Black Panther] chapter on our campus."

When President Dowdy and Dr. Marshall stepped away from the table, Adlerman swore in Chief Paul Calhoun.[6] Calhoun joined the Greensboro police force in 1940, four years before the department hired its first Black officer. In 1956, Calhoun made chief, and in 1960, when the manager of the downtown Woolworth rushed to the station to insist that he do something about the A&T students sitting in at his lunch counter, Chief Calhoun refused. That quick decision set Greensboro apart from Birmingham, Alabama, where civil rights protesters were attacked by angry policemen and their trained dogs. A planner by nature, Calhoun had tried to get ahead of the recent trouble in Greensboro, reaching out to the local colleges to establish procedures and plans for dealing with student protests.[7] Generally calm and methodical himself, averse to rash decisions, he now found himself, in 1969, nearing retirement and over his head, caught between an old guard intent on preserving power and determined students willing to risk everything to topple hierarchies buttressed by custom and force. His officers were at war with the young radicals in Greensboro's Black community.

As he sat in the hearings room, Calhoun, with the help of the eager panel before him, spun a tale of incomprehensible revolutionary violence disrupting Greensboro and America. He began by quoting from a speech Stokely Carmichael had given at A&T in December 1968 shortly before he went into exile: "If you're walking down the street and you have undying love for your brother and a policeman shoots him and you try to kill that policeman with a brick, bottle, stick, anything you have in your hand, that is undying love. . . . In the [Black Panther] Party, we say before you start talking about killing an Uncle Tom, kill five white cops."

With information gathered from "confidential [FBI and police] source(s) whose identity(s) cannot be revealed at this time," Calhoun drew a line from Stokely Carmichael's visit through Harold Avent's arrival in Greensboro, the rapidly expanding influence of the Black Panthers in Greensboro's high schools and colleges, and the organizing instigated at GAPP by Nelson Johnson, "one of the most militant Negroes in Greensboro for the past 2 or 3 years." That line—Carmichael, Avent, Black Panthers, Nelson—led directly, he said, to the explosion of violence at A&T. He recounted how Black students "ran down the American flag" at Bennett College, only to run up, for a few hours, "the black flag of anarchy," fixing the threat he'd been dealing with in the senators' minds.

"That is living under a reign of terror, is it not . . . ?" asked Chairman McClellan. "That doesn't measure up to law and order in a civilized society in my book."

Senator Griffin then observed that he noticed "the name of Nelson Johnson keeps coming up over and over again. . . . In 1968 [he was] employed by the Association of Poor People, which is funded by the Foundation for Community Development. I understand from a staff member that that actually is funded by the Ford Foundation. Do you happen to know whether that is true?"

It was the moment the senators had been waiting for. Ready to pounce, Senator Mundt piped in, "We are getting into something pretty important, Mr. Chairman. We are getting down to the meat in the coconut. Somebody is financing [student uprisings in high schools and colleges], apparently from outside the State of North Carolina. . . . This affects the whole tax structure of this country. Are we to have these foundations with tax-exempt features or not? The question has been raised, is the Federal Government involved in this? If the Office of Economic Opportunity wants to testify, if the Ford Foundation wishes to testify, if they think they can justify the matter, they have an invitation to come in tomorrow morning or any time they want to come. . . . You have opened up a Pandora's box which probably isn't limited to Greensboro, N.C. . . . . I think it is one of the most important puzzles that must be unraveled that we have come across thus far."

As dangerous as they believed Nelson Johnson to be, the senators were enraged that his organizing and activism had been funded by the Ford Foundation and the Office of Economic Opportunity. Chief Calhoun had attempted to keep Nelson from meddling in Greensboro's affairs by locking him in jail for disturbing Dudley High School. The senators intended something more consequential. They could screw shut the spigots opened by Governor Sanford and President Johnson, cutting off the funding to projects promoting "maximum feasible participation," as the grassroots efforts supported by Ford and the Office of Economic Opportunity were designed to do.

❖

President Richard Nixon had taken the oath of office on January 20, 1969, prepared to dismantle his predecessor's War on Poverty, which had been shaped in significant ways by the poverty work in North Carolina initiated by the Foundation for Community Development. The backlash of Nixon's Silent Majority against LBJ's Great Society–supported apertures had been fierce, not only in North Carolina but also in Cleveland, where voters had elected a Black mayor, and in New York City, where Black residents had fought to control schools in Black-majority parts of the city, particularly in Brooklyn's Bedford-Stuyvesant neighborhood.

The president placed Donald Rumsfeld, "a ruthless little bastard," as Nixon called his deputy, in charge of the OEO. Rumsfeld brought along another ambitious young conservative, Richard "Dick" Cheney, as an assistant. While proclaiming his desire to expand the OEO, Rumsfeld turned his focus to controlling it through tax law, circumscribing the power of foundations, especially the Ford Foundation, and the recipients of their largesse, such as the Foundation for Community Development. Multiracial democracy spreading to an organized base of poor and marginalized people threatened conservatives' political prospects, which depended on the solidarity of a white majority. If Nixon and other conservatives could hamstring the OEO and secure votes while doing so, all the better. The activists who, Nixon reported, were "driving the governors and other people crazy" needed to be stopped.[8]

❖

A short time before the Senate hearing in Washington, inspectors from Rumsfeld's Office of Economic Opportunity had hurried to North Carolina to investigate evidence that taxpayer dollars had been used to support radical activity. They discovered that Howard Fuller, still on the FCD payroll, had legally purchased a gun and bullets in late April and early May. "Howard Fuller has likely the most dangerous job in North Carolina. He [regularly] receives death threats," protested Nathan Garrett. The weapons, he said, were for personal protection from the "Ku Klux Klan and other groups." Garrett's explanations fell on deaf ears. Those opposing the activism funded by the OEO and the Ford Foundation seized the public relations ammunition they needed, linking the purchase of guns by Black men to the violence at A&T. This information had been funneled to the senators investigating "Riots, Civil and Criminal Disorders."[9] The senators then certified it for the American public in their hearing and provided Nixon, Rumsfeld, and Cheney the cover they needed to dismantle the War on Poverty. "It's a reprehensible matter," declared Senator Mundt, "if the Ford Foundation is deliberately and knowingly financing lawbreakers in North Carolina."[10]

Nixon's allies, meanwhile, got busy drafting a tax reform act to, they said, prevent wealthy individuals from setting up phony foundations to dodge taxes. Writing in the *New York Times*, Roy Wilkins, the director of the NAACP, pointed out that the populist talking point of the reforms masked the legislation's underlying motivation to cut funding to voter registration drives and get-out-the-vote efforts. "Negro citizens," he wrote, "are not deceived by the 'tax reform' label. They view the move (and rightly so) as an attempt to halt the increase of Negro voting strength."[11]

❖

When North Carolina's National Guard stormed into Greensboro and laid waste to A&T's Scott Hall, a dormitory named for one North Carolina governor, they were also attacking the legacy of another governor. Terry Sanford's dream that the North Carolina Fund might end poverty in the state had, in the wake of a contested student council election at Dudley High School, been turned into a nightmare.

After he'd left office, Lyndon Johnson described in words that shimmered with anger and regret the impossible choice he believed he'd faced: "If I left the woman I really loved—the Great Society—in order to get involved with that bitch of [the Vietnam] war on the other side of the world, then I would lose everything at home. All my programs. All my hopes to feed the hungry and shelter the homeless. All my dreams to provide education and medical care to the browns and the blacks and the lame and the poor. But if I left that war and let the communists take over South Vietnam, then I would be seen as a coward and my nation would be seen as an appeaser, and we would both find it impossible to accomplish anything for anybody anywhere on the entire globe."[12]

Now, with Lyndon Johnson gone from the executive office and Martin Luther King Jr. dead, the cause of the poor slipped off the agenda of America's top leaders.

In the wake of the A&T rebellion, the North Carolina State Advisory Committee to the United States Commission on Civil Rights located concerns that had been expressed in the Kerner Commission report on the local map: "The incidents in Greensboro provided an opportunity for those persons who are interested in consolidating the Black people in the community, to show that the 'system' is unsympathetic to Blacks and their problems, no matter how valid or severe. Greensboro proved them correct, again."[13]

❖

Accused, along with Nelson Johnson, of instigating the rebellion at Dudley and A&T and of arming the shooters in the dorms, Howard Fuller left the Foundation for Community Development. Liberated from the FCD, the tether that held the activists to liberal foundations and government agencies had been severed; they were freer than ever to deploy their most radical ideas in combat with their enemies.

Fuller and a group of Joyce's Duke student friends started a "counter institution" where Afro-American and African studies would lie beyond the control of white people. On October 25, 1969, hundreds, including Nelson and Joyce, attended the opening of Malcolm X Liberation University (MXLU) in Durham. Arrayed in bright and bold African prints, the gatherers waved red, black, and green Pan-African flags and clapped and sang along with Bernice Johnson Reagon and the Harambee singers (who would later become Sweet Honey in the Rock) up from Atlanta.

The building sat beside the train tracks, and when white train operators rang a bell to interrupt the remarks of Sister Betty Shabazz, Malcolm X's widow, a Black professor climbed onto the locomotive and hugged the bell to muffle it. Fists and cheers shot into the air, and Betty Shabazz continued, audible now, with what she had to say: "A lot of people nowadays are saying this is a class struggle. It perhaps might have been some years back. But because of the treatment of Blacks we can say . . . that we are treated the way we are treated because of the color of our skin."[14]

❖

As 1969 ended, President Nixon signed the Tax Reform Act of 1969, which forbade foundations from funding work that would influence legislation or aid state and local voter registration drives. The law made granting foundations liable for the actions of a grantee. The Ford Foundation, for example, could now lose its tax-exempt status by funding the political work of Nelson Johnson and GAPP. Under Nixon's direction and Donald Rumsfeld's execution, the OEO shifted its strategic direction from "community control" to "community capitalism."[15]

❖

Three weeks before President Nixon signed the Tax Reform Act, news of another murder shot through the Black activist world. The charismatic and visionary young socialist Fred Hampton, chairman of the Chicago Black Panther Party, had been shot to death in the middle of the night. Mark Clark, another Panther, was also killed in the police raid. Official law enforcement reports claimed that when police knocked at the door of the apartment, they'd been met with a barrage of gunfire. They'd had no choice but to respond with force. A team of young lawyers from Northwestern University Law School arrived on the scene and quickly realized that the evidence told a different story. Contrary to the reports hitting the newsstands, all the bullet holes, save one, had been fired at the apartment door from the outside. A blood-soaked mattress indicated that Chairman Fred had been assassinated in his bed, likely while asleep.

The shooting didn't appear to be what officials said it was any more than the Tax Reform Act had been. The mysteries of Willie Grimes's murder and the wounded policemen in Greensboro would remain unsolved. The lawyers in Chicago, however, set out to prove that the government used not only laws such as Nixon's tax reform but also illegal, murderous operations to curb the Black liberation movement.[16]

❖

Joyce Johnson turned twenty-two just three days after Chairman Fred was assassinated. Despite the shocking news from Chicago, the challenges the new tax laws posed to her and Nelson's foundation-supported livelihood, and the pending legal case against her husband, Joyce was optimistic. There were exceptions, such as the young police officer Daughtry, but most people on the East Side appreciated Nelson's efforts to find a peaceful solution to the crisis at Dudley and felt horrified by the unsolved death of Willie Grimes and insulted by the invasion of A&T. They closed ranks to fight the criminal charges leveled against Nelson for "disturbing a public school." "We will need money to pay bail and appeal bonds. And we will need other support to make it clear to these men and the world that the Black community clearly supports their actions and views them as 'not guilty,'" read a public missive signed by, among others, A. S. Webb, one of Greensboro's leading Black businessmen, and Dr. George Simkins, the head of the local NAACP.[17]

Perhaps Nelson and Joyce could identify with the nuanced lines from Nikki Giovanni's 1968 poem "Adulthood," each feeling, as they waded deeper into the waters of struggle, like a "for real Black person who must feel and inflict pain."[18]

DEMANDS

Neither Nelson's legal battles nor President Nixon's maneuvers to kneecap grassroots political organizing could suppress the revolutionary energy flowing through Greensboro. An elegant, Tudor-style house—formerly the capacious abode of an accomplished Black physician, Dr. S. P. Sebastian, who, in the 1920s, helped found a Black hospital across the street—became known as the GAPP House.[1] Just a short march to A&T and Bennett College, Morningside Homes, and a mile from the middle-class Black residences at Benbow Park, the Sebastian home provided an ideal location for GAPP and SOBU to attend to Greensboro's and America's social body.[2] "The whole world was in motion," one SOBU member would recall. Behind all the activity was the nimble coalition-building talent of Nelson Johnson.[3] Black leaders and students from around the United States, the Caribbean, and Africa passed through the doors of the GAPP House for Sunday-morning discussions that took the place of church. Instead of hymns, participants sang freedom songs and recited poetry. A favorite was Langston Hughes's uplifting verse "Good Morning Revolution!," which imagined workers taking over "everything . . . [until] no one will be hungry, cold, oppressed, / Anywhere in the world again."[4]

❖

The 1960s sit-ins at the local Woolworth had sparked a widespread rebellion against segregation. Now, as the calendar flipped to the

1970s, the Dudley and A&T conflict moved many in Greensboro and beyond to embrace Black nationalism, self-determination, and armed self-defense. To the chagrin of local white officials, the city had become the most significant laboratory for Black Power on the East Coast. Also perplexing to Greensboro's business and political powers was the larger Black community's continued embrace of Nelson Johnson.

In the aftermath of the rebellion, a wave of visible changes rippled through the city. Blacks were appointed to assistant superintendent positions in the school department. The city hired a Black assistant city manager for the first time, and, despite continued resistance to district voting, Greensboro's citizens elected a new Black city council member. Soon nearly all major city agencies counted a Black person among their board members. Black Greensboro celebrated these advances and believed that the events in May had forced the city's white leaders to view the status quo and its links to Jim Crow segregation as a "direct threat to their own wellbeing." Even Mayor Jack Elam had to concede, albeit in his own language, what people on the East Side knew: the "riots speeded things up."[5]

Unity was the word on everybody's lips. And for the next couple of years, the pastors and businesspeople, the sorority and fraternity brothers, the newspaper editors, the educators, and the NAACP supported the local work of the Greensboro Association of Poor People and the national and international work of a constellation of radical organizations, including the Student Organization for Black Unity, that had planted their roots in the city's fertile soil.

The network of local organizations founded with the support of the North Carolina Fund and the Foundation for Community Development didn't disappear when President Nixon scratched his signature on the new tax law. Unable to fund GAPP directly, for example, Nathan Garrett at the FCD, per Nixon's directives, awarded grants to support community capitalism. Joyce, together with Lewis Brandon, founded the Uhuru Bookstore, which quickly became not only a community hub but also an oasis for travelers between Washington, DC, and Atlanta and a place where locals cultivated pride in their history, discussed strategies of resistance, and imagined a more equal world. Profits from sales of books by Toni Morrison, Maya Angelou, James Baldwin, and Richard Wright and art prints by Jacob Lawrence and Charles White put bread on the activists' tables and allowed them to continue developing "projects to help poor neighborhoods." Earnings were supplemented by donations and support from Black professionals in Greensboro as well as other cities along the East Coast, from Cambridge, Massachusetts, to Atlanta. Nelson brought in extra income giving paid speeches to the ninety-three campus chapters of SOBU around the country, sharing successful strategies for gaining a measure of community control of Black neighborhoods. Drawn to this vibrant energy, Howard Fuller relocated Malcolm X Liberation University and its mission of developing a "Black Revolutionary ideology" to meet the "physical, social, psychological, economic, and cultural needs of Black people" from Durham to the Greensboro ecosystem.

The energy and ideas emanated less, however, from a specific and coherent ideology than from the practical needs of the community and the relentless, organic, and opportunistic street-level organizing the activists called Black Power. In early 1970, when a rat crawled through a gaping hole in the floor of a rented home and bit a four-year-old girl on the neck, GAPP catalyzed community distress to confront the city's largest landlord. The AAA Realty Company controlled more than a thousand decrepit shacks where people lived not only with rats but also with leaky roofs, rotting floors, and faulty plumbing. At least one rent collector for an East Side slumlord appeared on tenants' stoops with a pistol strapped to his belt, demanding payment as he deflected appeals for repairs.[6]

GAPP activists discovered that the derelict conditions were a breach of the term *substandard* in the city's housing code. Joyce saw this "ghetto housing [as] violence," which affected the material, emotional, and social health of the inhabitants confined, some hundred years after emancipation, by greedy slumlords, limited job opportunities, and a fear of homelessness.[7]

Under GAPP's guidance, the Black women tenants in AAA Realty Company housing formed a strike committee to lead demonstrations and file a class action lawsuit against the company. Nearly three hundred of them agreed to take the perilous step of withholding rent until the houses were brought up to code. Kay Agapion and other AAA Realty Company principals hurried to the negotiating table. But as the conversations dragged on, the company began filing evictions against the tenants withholding rent. Flyers were circulated accusing Agapion of "TERRORISM IN THE BLACK COMMUNITY." Then the houses from which people had been evicted were discovered to have suffered "significant damage." Saboteurs, evading police surveillance, poured sand down drainpipes, cut electric wires, and busted holes in walls and windows, rendering at least fifty houses completely uninhabitable.[8] "We destroyed the houses," Nelson Johnson said years later.[9] Despite these aggressive tactics, the city's Black community kept faith with the tenants. Worried about an escalation of the GAPP activists' tactics, the city pressured Agapion to settle.

"All parties negotiated in good faith," announced Jim Melvin at the settlement between AAA and the tenants in April 1970, four months after the rent strike began. The tenants paid their back rent, and the company committed to making repairs and paving the dirt streets in front of the homes. Melvin claimed a victory, receiving credit for skillfully bringing a close to the strike. Even so he decried the "malicious damage inflicted upon the propert[ies]. . . . Such actions," he said, "cannot and will not be tolerated or condoned." The very tactic Melvin condemned, however, had led to the quick settlement and delivered some hope to the tenants. Melvin said that he hoped "personal animosities will be forgotten." But they wouldn't be.[10]

Next, Nelson and his collaborators set their sights on the National Institute for the Blind's local Skilcraft plant, which employed blind laborers to assemble pens, brooms, and other simple products to sell to the federal government. GAPP activists invited a delegation of local Black leaders to tour the plant. Visitors were shocked by the circumstances under which the 150 workers, more than half of them Black, toiled. Clouds of dust choked the room, and piles of garbage impeded their path through the factory. "Little short of slavery" was how the visitors described what they'd witnessed. Greensboro's local papers demonstrated only passing interest in the story, but when it was fired out through the SOBU News Service, Black newspapers and *Jet Magazine* picked it up and transmitted the scandal to a national audience.[11]

The Greensboro Police Department shuttled scabs to the Skilcraft plant across the GAPP-organized picket line. By early 1971, after just a few months, the company accepted terms of a settlement that included better working conditions and increased wages. A spokesperson for the blind workers provided the moral to the story: "unless Black people act in their own behalf no one else will."[12]

Each victory reinforced Nelson and his comrades' belief that the city's business and government leaders compromised only when they felt threatened, proving the wisdom in Frederick Douglass's words that "power concedes nothing without a demand."

The city and state, however, could exert pressure of their own to isolate the engine of the organizing campaigns, Nelson Johnson. County lawyers quickly won indictments and convictions against Nelson Johnson and Robert Evans "in District Court and Superior Court on a charge of disrupting Dudley High School."[13]

In East Side churches and social clubs, Greensboro's prominent Black citizens passed the hat to raise the money to hire a lawyer to appeal Nelson's and Robert Evans's convictions. A fundraising letter circulating through southeast Greensboro stated that it was "crystal clear that these two Black men have committed no crime. Rather there has been a crime committed against them, because they are being punished for innocent behavior." "Blame" assigned to Nelson and Evans was a diversion to "cover up the murder of Willie Grimes." James Ferguson, a young, ambitious Black attorney from Asheville with a law degree from Columbia University, signed on for the job.[14]

While city officials argued that the courts had been fair and impartial, no one on the East Side believed that. The report on the Dudley/A&T rebellion released by the North Carolina Advisory Committee to the United States Commission on Civil Rights supported the Black community's hunch that Nelson Johnson was a scapegoat. The commission placed blame for the episode squarely on the school board and the Greensboro Police Department, stating bluntly that "the main issue [causing the disturbance] was the unequal treatment of citizens of Greensboro because of their race: discrimination in housing, employment, education, and the delivery of services, coupled with institutional racism and the unresponsiveness of the official system. Calls for law and order in the absence of justice," the report continued, "will not be heeded by those persons who have been led to believe, by the inaction and over-reaction of persons in authority, *that disruption and militant advocacy on their part are their only weapons in their fight for full citizenship* [emphasis added]."[15]

While city officials dismissed the report as the work of outsiders, calling it "shallow, biased, erroneous . . . and potentially divisive in its threats," local and national law enforcement increased their scrutiny of Nelson Johnson.[16]

NATION TIME

Greensboro Police Department officers hovered nearby wherever Nelson happened to be in the city, hoping to catch him for any petty transgression, such as parking illegally. The FBI tracked his activity. Meanwhile, Guilford County prosecutors moved to stymie the appeals process and lock him away from the streets and neighborhoods he aimed to organize. Though the maximum sentence for disrupting a school was six months, they asked that Nelson be sentenced to two years.

On August 12, 1970, Nelson and Evans were sent to a state prison to begin serving a six-month term. Even as he found himself gritting out dark-to-dark days on a chain gang, Nelson took time to pen a letter to supporters. "I point to my involvement [in the May rebellion] with pride," he wrote. "I can honestly say from this jail cell that if circumstances dictated, I would do the same thing again. . . . Who are the criminals," he asked, "those that fight for freedom, or those who deny freedom to our people?" Everything that had happened, argued Nelson, emanated from a coordinated effort to "stop the development of Black consciousness," to "develop chaos and confusion in our community," and to "blame someone Black for the situation they created."

As he closed the letter, Nelson applauded the fact that the Black community had "maintained a united front; maybe a weak front, but a 'united' front. Struggle and sacrifice should bring us closer together. . . . The jails are filled with Black men and the courts are 'white' with hate. . . . We shall overcome."[1]

Lawyer Ferguson convinced the state Supreme Court to issue a temporary stay. After only a week in prison, the two men were to be released on a "recognizance bond" secured by Nelson's family's farm in Airlie. On the evening of August 19, 1970, Nelson entered the auditorium at Greensboro's Hayes-Taylor YMCA, the "Black Y," at the edge of A&T. The overflow crowd stood to welcome him home.[2]

Joyce sat anxiously in her seat, guarding a secret; three months pregnant with the couple's first child, she was terrified that the baby might be born to a father behind bars.[3] Exhausted, the returning young man spoke only briefly, offering a thankful message to the people whose trust had helped free him from prison: "The essence of our struggle is a very, very high ideal that addresses itself to the best in all Black people—the best of what is right for you, the best of what is right for me, the best of what is right for our brothers and sisters and the generations to come."[4]

Home for the birth of his first daughter, Akua, in February 1971, Nelson found himself back in prison a month later, when the courts lifted the stay. Henry Frye, whom Nelson had helped become the first Black person elected to North Carolina's state legislature in the twentieth century, spearheaded an effort to convince Governor Robert Scott to commute the remainder of Nelson's six-month sentence. Diplomatic as always, Frye didn't complain that Nelson had been scapegoated or was being used as an example to deter Black activism. Instead, he argued that whatever justice was deserved had been served. If Nelson were to remain in jail, he continued, it would only further fray Greensboro's fragile social fabric. The governor accepted the arguments and commuted the sentence.[5] He did not, however, vacate the conviction, a fact that would justify continued surveillance of Nelson's activity and, years later in 1979, be used to smear his reputation. While his release marked a victory for Nelson and his supporters, in the minds of Jim Melvin, elected to his first term as mayor in 1971, Greensboro's business elite, its police force, and the local FBI agents, the lingering conviction certified Nelson as a troublemaker.

After a month as a single parent, Joyce welcomed her husband home. Like his grandfather, who'd been freed twice from slavery within a year, Nelson had been released from prison twice for the same charge.

❖

Each week at the GAPP House, the GAPP and SOBU activists would choose a topic to analyze, such as the war in Vietnam, the anticolonial struggles in Africa, or, closer to home, the idea being floated by the North Carolina state government to merge historically Black state colleges into white institutions. Should a vision for the future be built around integration into the American economic and political machine or around Langston Hughes's revolutionary dream of replacing the country's economic system with something fundamentally different? Visiting African students tutored the Americans on their continent's anticolonial struggles and pushed them to work not only for Black unity but also toward class solidarity. Unconstrained by American Cold War paranoia, the smart foreign visitors justified their arguments using Marxist and Leninist theory, impressing their hosts with their incisive arguments and breadth of historical knowledge.[6] "You cannot conceivably frighten an African by talking about the Kremlin," James Baldwin had observed.[7]

In early 1971, Howard Fuller took the African name Owusu Sadaukai, which meant "one who clears the way for others" and "one who gathers strength from his ancestors to lead his people." Several months later, Owusu traveled to Africa. Bedazzled by glamorous Nairobi, he set out into the Mathare Valley, where the poverty and destitution he witnessed stunned him. It wasn't what he had hoped to see in a country that had tossed off the yoke of British colonialism eight years earlier. How, he wondered, could this misery still exist in a country run by Black people? In Dar es Salaam, he signed up to visit territory held by the Mozambique Liberation Front in their fight for independence from the Portuguese. Owusu set out on what would be a grueling monthlong, four-hundred-mile trek, for which he was ill prepared. Deep in the bush, his city shoes gave out and had to be taped together. He survived on lizard and gazelle, ducked attacks from Portuguese troops firing American-made weapons, and witnessed his tireless and committed revolutionary hosts—men, women, and children, too—build a national identity through struggle.

He returned to the United States changed. The African freedom fighters, to whom he felt devoted, had troubled his Black-against-white view of the world. His hosts described their struggle as one for local power against ravenous global capitalism, not white people. The next stage of the Black freedom struggle, he and Nelson soon agreed, would require a more sophisticated understanding of class dynamics and economics.[8]

❖

Even as GAPP built support for North Carolina's Black colleges and kept organizing at Morningside Homes and around The Grove, Nelson's focus began to shift from carving out a local space for Black self-determination to confronting US imperial power, particularly in Africa and Vietnam. In short order, the Student Organization for Black Unity was renamed the Youth Organization for Black Unity (YOBU), in an attempt to expand the organization's base beyond the campus to working-class Black people. The *SOBU Newsletter* became the *African World*, a bimonthly newspaper that, under the direction of Nelson and the editorial guidance of Milton Coleman, would reach a national and international readership of more than ten thousand and would be banned from many US prisons for its radical views. The paper recruited Black students into a Pan-African Work Program that placed them in internships with Black-run community organizations, businesses, and farms around the country. "Black and beautiful is not enough," proclaimed one promotion: "OUR PEOPLE MUST BE FREE!"[9]

❖

The political unity among Black people across the country likely crested during the late winter and spring of 1972. Nelson Johnson and Howard Fuller led 110 delegates to the "smoke filled little [industrial] city called Gary" in Indiana, joining some 4,000 representatives from "almost every state of this former Indian territory."[10] Those making the trip included elected officials, Black Power activists, Pan-Africanists, Black nationalists, integrationists, and Black socialists and communists. They were celebrities and poets, grassroots organizers and businessmen, women and men, young and old, rich people and poor. Luminaries on the ticket included the famous widows Coretta Scott King and Betty Shabazz, Harry Belafonte, Dick Gregory, Barbara Jordan, Vernon Jordan, Julian Bond, Bobby Seale, the Jackson 5, and A&T's own Jesse Jackson. All had heeded the urgent call put out by Gary's mayor, Richard Hatcher; the poet and Black nationalist Amiri Baraka; and Charles Diggs Jr., a congressman from Detroit. The trio, representing both the "power of the ballot box" and the "power of protest," hoped to emerge from the convention with a national Black political platform. Those in attendance believed the country to be at an inflection point. The problem to solve was how to move from the new legal protections for civil rights to the positive guarantees of human rights that might somehow begin to account for centuries of stolen labor.

"Black is our common denominator," Jackson declared in his riveting keynote address. "As a result of 1964, and Dr. King and others, we got our civil rights. As a result of the Selma movement, we are beginning to get our Civil Power [voting rights]. But now we find ourselves with the right to move in any neighborhood in this country and we can't pay the note. We got the right to go to any school in the nation, we can't pay the tuition. We got the right to buy any car in America, but we can't stop it from being repossessed. We're not arguing about our constitutionality, we're raising a basic question: When will we get paid for the work we have already done! . . . Economics is the issue."

What time is it? Jackson asked the crowd. "It's Nation Time," came the full-throated response, answering Jackson's call with the title of Amiri Baraka's famous poem. The question, Mayor Hatcher warned in his closing remarks, was whether "we [will] walk in unity or disperse in a thousand different directions."[11]

Only Black America, announced the "Gary Declaration" hammered out at the conference, could pull the country back from the "abyss created by its own racist arrogance, misplaced priorities, rampant materialism, and ethical bankruptcy." "Will we believe the truth that history pushes in our face," the declaration asked, "or will we, too, try to hide?" Black people, it stated, must take responsibility for creating "fundamental, far-reaching change in America."[12]

"Will you put your body where your ideals are?" Jesse Jackson wanted to know.[13]

❖

Two months after the March 1972 conference in Gary, still riding the electric wave of Black unity, Owusu, Nelson, Joyce, Amiri Baraka, and others called for simultaneous marches in Washington, DC, and San Francisco to bring attention to African struggles against European colonial rule. Drawn to the exhilarating energy rippling out from the Gary conference, Black politicians joined civil rights leaders, revolutionaries, intellectuals, performers, and pastors in support of what Owusu called African Liberation Day. In all, some thirty thousand people flocked to Washington, DC, and an equal number gathered in San Francisco and other cities, making it the largest demonstration of Black American support for Africa since Marcus Garvey's Pan-African movement of the 1920s.[14]

While marchers denounced colonialism, imperialism, and US support for racist settler regimes in Rhodesia and South Africa, the joyous drumming and dancing, the array of "yellow, tan, and ebony faces," the proximity of the powerful and the poor, the young and the old, the militant and the middle class, the revolutionaries and the functionaries, made a powerful impression. Representing the Black

Panther Party, the dynamic and elegant Elaine Brown looked out over the variegated sea of Black faces and proclaimed it the "most beautiful sight I've ever seen in my life."[15]

Owusu brought the perfectly sunny, late spring afternoon to a close: "The road ahead will be difficult. We will not be free simply because one day we came to Washington DC. We will no longer engage in discussions about violence and nonviolence. We ARE an African people! We will win because we are going to struggle." And, closing his eyes, he channeled Frederick Douglass, as he'd been doing since he began organizing for the North Carolina Fund in Durham: "Find out just what any people will quietly submit to and you have found out the exact measure of injustice and wrong which will be imposed upon them, and these will continue till they are resisted with either words or blows, or with both."[16]

Amazed by the event's success and hoping to bottle its fugitive energy, Owusu, Nelson, Joyce, and others formed the African Liberation Support Committee (ALSC) to plan a 1973 march and to continue their effort to tie the struggle for freedom in the United States to the African fight against colonialism.

Several months after the African Liberation Day march, one of Nelson and Joyce's African heroes, Amílcar Cabral, the leader of independence movements in Guinea-Bissau and Cape Verde, arrived at Lincoln College in Pennsylvania before traveling to New York City to address the United Nations on October 16.

Nelson and Joyce handed Cabral a check for $2,200 raised from ALSC and YOBU members to support the struggle against Portuguese colonizers. Even as he accepted their gift, the serious and bespectacled Cabral, three months from being assassinated, gently guided their attention back toward the United States. "All you can do here to develop . . . the total realization of your aspirations as human beings is a contribution for us," he said, explaining that he did not conceive of his struggle in racial terms: "We are not fighting against the Portuguese people or whites. We are fighting for the freedom of our people—to free our people and allow them to be able to love any kind of human being." You must "combat the causes of racism," not the racists, advised Cabral. Do not, he'd written, "make sacrifices combating shadows."[17] Indeed, the very concept of race, he seemed to be saying, was not only about color prejudice but also about politics, class economics, and power.

One of Cabral's gestures that day affected Nelson and Joyce even more than his words. After he spoke, Cabral embraced a white man on the stage. The Black Power–Pan-Africanist activists from Greensboro, who had long defined themselves in opposition to white people, white power, and white cultural dominance, were startled.[18]

TABOO

The Foundation for Community Development's support of GAPP, Malcolm X Liberation University, and the Uhuru Bookstore had provided Nelson and Joyce with a degree of economic stability since Nixon passed his tax reform bill in 1969. By 1973, however, as the country's—and North Carolina's—march to the right accelerated, the FCD was winding down. Jesse Helms, who'd shocked Howard Fuller with his unapologetically racist opinions in 1965 and had rallied voters in opposition to Fuller and Nelson's activism, became the first Republican in the twentieth century to win a North Carolina Senate seat. As he knew it would, Lyndon Johnson's civil rights legislation caused white voters in the South to abandon the Democratic Party for a Republican Party quickly being reinvented by Helms and others to accommodate their reactionary views.

Now with two young daughters to raise, Nelson and Joyce adapted to their changing circumstances. Joyce found a steady paycheck as a research associate at North Carolina A&T's Transportation Institute, working to make essential services more accessible to poor and rural people.

Nelson and his comrades, meanwhile, untethered from foundation and government support, were freer than ever to embrace radical ideas. Through YOBU and the ALSC, Nelson had developed a working friendship with an intellectual professor at Fisk University named Abdul Alkalimat (Gerald McWorter). Inspired by African leaders and the well-read African students he'd met in Greensboro, Nelson would rap with Alkalimat over the phone and late into the night analyzing history, capitalism, imperialism, economics, the Black experience, and Marxist revolution.[1]

New language began to echo through the GAPP House: *means of production, dialectical materialism, heightening the contradictions, one divides into two, dictatorship of the proletariat, democratic centralism.* The lingo and international vision baffled some of the GAPP and YOBU grassroots organizers. "What about our problems right now in Greensboro?" asked one GAPP member, debating Nelson and others over steaming bowls of collard greens and pinto beans and platters of fried chicken. "Going to Africa or waiting for African Revolution ain't no solution for us everyday folks."[2]

When Nelson traveled around the country speaking on behalf of YOBU and the ALSC, he began encouraging allies to set up Marxist-Leninist study groups. He advised that the study groups be circumspect about the theory they were teaching so as not to spook people in the community or to give law enforcement another reason to monitor and disrupt their activities. He knew that they were playing with fire.[3]

Since the 1917 Russian Revolution, association with Reds, pinkos, or Bolsheviks ruined careers in America, destroyed lives, launched sudden journeys into exile, and, if one hesitated too long, could lead to jail or deportation. Created in 1938, the House Un-American Activities Committee (HUAC) joined forces with J. Edgar Hoover and the FBI to police America's political ideas and root out those they labeled as likely to subvert the country's way of life. The committee publicly interrogated intellectuals, politicians, writers, journalists, activists, and artists suspected of communist sympathies, including the folk singer Pete Seeger, the playwright Arthur Miller, and the Black performers Lena Horne and Paul Robeson. Fear drove some dissidents underground and others to Mexico or Africa. In 1951, the Justice Department arrested the eighty-three-year-old W. E. B. Du Bois as a Soviet agent. The government provided as evidence a pamphlet Du Bois had disseminated decrying the nuclear arms race. Du Bois beat the charges in court, and yet the State Department still revoked his passport to prevent him from carrying antiwar and civil rights messages abroad.[4]

The State Department had already withdrawn the renowned actor and singer Paul Robeson's right to travel beyond US borders when HUAC called him in for questioning in 1956. Robeson, the child of a slave, prepared a blistering rebuke of the government efforts to undermine his freedom of speech, saying that the "Constitution is a scrap of paper" to the men who would prevent him from continuing his "struggle at home and abroad for peace and friendship with all the world's people, for an end to colonialism, for full citizenship for Negro Americans, for a world in which art and culture may abound . . . for the American Negro, our workers, our farmers, and our artists."[5] The committee refused to allow Robeson to read into the record his statement, which included a particularly pertinent question: "How can [Senator James] Eastland [of Mississippi] pretend concern over the internal security of our country while he supports the most brutal assaults on fifteen million [Black] Americans by the White Citizens' Councils and the Ku Klux Klan?"[6]

Despite the perils to one's freedom of speech, movement, and ability to earn a living, Black Americans continued to be drawn to the "converted church"—Ralph Ellison's apt metaphorical location of the Communist Party headquarters in his novel *Invisible Man*—and its promise to mandate equality. In the early 1920s, Harry Haywood, the most prominent Black Communist Party USA member, argued that an autonomous Black Belt Republic—a nation within a nation—should be carved from the Deep South's plantation territories. The Soviet general secretary, Joseph Stalin, supported Haywood's idea, and American communists got to work on the "Negro Question." CPUSA members courageously helped build sharecropper unions in the Jim Crow South and defended nine Black teenagers in Tennessee, known as the Scottsboro Boys, against accusations of raping two white women, helping to fuse civil rights to communism in white supremacists' minds.[7]

In addition to Du Bois and Robeson, the head of the Brotherhood of Sleeping Car Porters, A. Philip Randolph, for a time advocated socialism. In the 1930s, Langston Hughes, whose political sympathies led him to be called "a red devil in a Black skin," joined a delegation of Black Americans on a tour to witness firsthand the Soviet Union's worker-led society.[8] Black artists traveled to Mexico to explore the nexus of art and politics with the radical painters there. Organizers Bayard Rustin, a lifelong pacifist, and Ella Baker, who grew up in Littleton, North Carolina, where Nelson attended high school, took up socialist ideas as tools to pry freedom for their people loose from the bedrock of American culture and tilted economics. By the mid-1960s, the Black Panther Party built its organization on a ten-point, essentially socialist plan. Every one of them sought a way to make America's founding ideals real for Black people and also for the poor.

After a time, however, many Black Americans found communism to be an uncomfortable fit. Before the communist hunter Senator Joseph McCarthy hounded the author Richard Wright out of the country, the author of *Native Son* had already defected from the Communist Party. He didn't appreciate the pressure to have politics define his art. "I wanted to be a communist," wrote Wright, "but my kind of communist." Others struggled not only to hold open a space for individual voices but also to articulate, within a system of thought constructed around the idea of class struggle, the distinct yet simultaneous reality of race. Wright called this "double vision," and Du Bois's famous conception of "double consciousness," if taken broadly, can capture, perhaps, not only the complex negotiation between the white and Black worlds but also between identities circumscribed by both race and class.[9]

Nelson and Alkalimat tried to formulate a way out of the dilemma of a minority experience within a majority-white Communist Party striving for ideological unity. Layering elements of Black nationalism and Pan-Africanism into their Marxist analysis, the two imagined Black industrial workers coming together in an all-Black communist organization to buttress African independence by striking at the roots of global capitalism nurtured in American soil.

❖

On May 2, 1973, journalist Tony Brown, dapper as always in a gray suit and pink-and-white striped shirt, introduced a special episode of the *Black Journal* TV program.[10] He invited the program's national public-television audience to participate in a conversation about the "diversity of positions and philosophies held together by the concern for all Black people." To this end, Brown assembled twelve "Black spokesmen," ranging from the legendary Mississippian and grassroots organizer Fannie Lou Hamer to Berkeley Burrell, president of the National Business League. The panel included the "lawyer for the Black revolution," Haywood Burns; William Lucy, who'd organized the 1968 sanitation workers' strike in Memphis, where Martin Luther King Jr. was assassinated; Manhattan borough president Percy Sutton; Ohio congressman Louis Stokes, who also chaired the newly formed Black Caucus; the New York State Supreme Court judge and activist William Booth; and James Williams, spokesman for the National Urban League. Stokely Carmichael, spruce in a guerrilla-green suit, his eyes hidden behind impenetrable, wraparound sunglasses, sat next to Angela Davis, dressed in a stylish red-and-white blouse, her Afro floating above the gathering like an exclamation point.

Nelson Johnson, representing YOBU, fidgeted in his seat, the only man not wearing a suit to the set. The TV lights ricocheted off the shiny, light-green shirt he'd pulled over a lime-green turtleneck.

Judge Booth introduced "the question of the hour": "Some folks believe you can work within the system . . . and others believe you can't work within the system." In the middle of 1973, "the system" made up of public and private institutions appeared to be breaking down. President Nixon's illegal surveillance of his Democrat rivals, known as the Watergate scandal, threatened to upset the political order; the unpopular Vietnam War approached its twenty-year anniversary; and leaks of unlawful FBI domestic counterintelligence tactics were beginning to percolate in the press.

Burrell, the business advocate, said, "The problem with [capitalism] is that we don't have any Blacks operating in it. I wonder if we'd have the same feeling about the capitalist system if we were the capitalists and somebody else were sitting outside."

"I would be against it," muttered Stokely.

"Well, Stokely says he'd be against it," chuckled Burrell.

Angela Davis jumped in. "If somebody is exploiting me, I don't care if he's white or Black or red or yellow. As long as he's doing the exploiting there's something wrong."

Burrell backtracked. "It's difficult to say that people haven't been damaged by the free enterprise system in this country. The failure of our cities is probably a direct result of the failure of the free enterprise system to do something about it. When big business begins to move out and leave the poor people to solve the problems of poor people."

"I'm sorry," Davis continued, her words flying like well-aimed knives, "but . . . there is no such thing as free enterprise. Capitalism in this day and age is monopoly capitalism. It's controlled by multi-billion-dollar firms, multinational firms, it's controlled by people like Rockefeller and Hughes and DuPont. Now there's a real difference between those folks and the Black man or woman who decides to open up a grocery store on the corner. That is not capitalism. Richard Nixon has been trying to convince us that all we have to do is get a little grocery store on the corner and then all of a sudden, we are Black capitalists."

Through their ideological differences, the panelists expressed universal dismay at President Nixon's rollback of the federal poverty programs that had supported Nelson's work in North Carolina; the Urban League spokesman, James Williams, observed that the immediate cost of eliminating the programs had been some 200,000 to 300,000 jobs. All agreed that after the social and legal advances of the 1960s, the challenges facing Black people in America were economic. The question, as Booth had said, was how to address them.

Representative Stokes picked up this thread of the conversation, turning back to Burrell's point. "What . . . do you do when you are the oppressed and the repressed under the capitalistic form of government? You examine the system and you see how you can make changes in that system. . . . The only thing that this country responds to is power. Economic power and political power."

Stokely quipped in response, "If we went to President Nixon and said, all you gotta do is give us the fruits of our labor from slavery and we'll forget the score, we would be the richest people in the country."

Nelson, who'd turned thirty a week earlier, shifted in his chair.

While the others appeared to enjoy a moment to debate, reflect, and expound, Nelson seemed nervous and impatient with all the theoretical talk. He leaned forward and rested his chest against the edge of the table.

"We have to talk about the merits of capitalism," he interjected. "But . . . very importantly . . . [we must] get down to the nitty-gritty of the . . . day-to-day work on real problems that affect us as a people. We could hem and haw all day about capitalism and how bad it is. Obviously, it's bad. . . ." Always the organizer, Nelson continued, "But . . . we haven't done anything to denounce capitalism unless we are able to devise some sensible way . . . to organize ourselves to resist it."

Picking up the implication of Nelson's comment, Congressman Stokes countered, "I think we have to be pragmatic about what we are talking about. . . . A system that's committed to capitalism [is] not going to change to communism or socialism or any other form of government."

The camera moved on, but the microphones picked up Nelson's voice. "That's not true," he said.

FROGMORE

Shortly after the *Black Journal* interview and for the second consecutive year, in 1973 African Liberation Day supporters marched against "racist exploitation and domination of African people throughout the world."[1] The number of cities in the United States, Canada, and the Caribbean hosting marches increased to thirty, but the event in Washington, DC, drew only about half the number it had the previous year. Tony Brown's diverse panel notwithstanding, the roster of African Liberation Day supporters had changed significantly. The politicians, many of the clergy, and the more traditional civil rights activists who'd supported the 1972 march, in the wake of the Gary, Indiana, conference, now stepped away, wary of Owusu's and Nelson's increasingly radical language.

At the end of June, more than sixty members of the African Liberation Support Committee's leadership from around the country and Canada convened at the Penn Center in Frogmore, South Carolina, to discuss strategy and tactics for the coming years. At the small campus nestled under the moss-garnished branches of ancient live oaks, the activists leaned into a distinguished history. The Union Army controlled St. Helena Island and its swampy lowlands when, the year before President Lincoln signed the Emancipation Proclamation, a Quaker from Pennsylvania founded the Penn Center as a school for free Blacks. A hundred years later, Martin Luther King Jr. held his Southern Christian Leadership Conference (SCLC) retreats at the Penn Center. In that remote country where land, water, and sky converged and traces of African language and culture were still vital in the voices and ways of the local people, King found a place to relax, remove his tie, and contemplate "where we go from here."

When King and his staff arrived at Frogmore in May 1967, they knew that the movement had reached an inflection point. Less than two months earlier, at Riverside Church in New York, King stepped beyond a disciplined focus on civil rights to call for a general "revolution of values" to confront the "giant triplets of racism, extreme materialism, and militarism" that made the United States, he said, the "greatest purveyor of violence in the world today." Silence on the issue of the "tragedy of Vietnam"—a war that King believed had "broken and eviscerated" the federal poverty program—would be a betrayal of his movement's values.[2] The backlash from the media, the Johnson administration, and even the NAACP was swift, and their message clear: don't mix civil rights with calls for global peace; don't challenge America's might abroad.[3]

In Frogmore, King expressed his opinion that "we have moved from the era of civil rights to the era of human rights." He explained the need for a "radical re-distribution of economic and political power" and the shift from a reform movement to an "era of revolution." King defined "power" as the "ability to affect change" but emphasized that love and power form an essential tandem. "Power without love is reckless," he said, but "love without power is sentimental." Together, however, he believed they could be used as nonviolent tools for justice and to "restore the broken community." Even as he called out the deep flaws of capitalism and the need for economic and social revolution, King worried that communism's elevation of the goals of revolution over the means of achieving them could lead to unethical and, ultimately, harmful acts. Even so, he understood the lure of Marxist revolution in America as "a judgment against our failure to make democracy real and follow through on the revolutions we initiated."[4]

Six years after King's 1967 visit to the Penn Center—his final retreat in Frogmore—Nelson and his comrades in the African Liberation Support Committee arrived to advance the "era of revolution."[5] After hours, they got up to bits of mischief and tippled some potent moonshine distilled by the local Gullah Geechee people. Inside the simple, wood-frame conference center, however, the participants were all business, discussing the strategy and tactics they believed would enable them to make progress in the freedom struggle.

They agreed to lobby American politicians to revoke the Byrd Amendment, which allowed chrome mined in colonial Rhodesia to be imported into the United States. They vowed to organize boycotts of petroleum extracted from Angola, where revolutionaries were waging war against their Portuguese colonizers. They made plans to distribute literature and films to inform Black Americans about the hundreds of US-based companies whose investments supported the system of apartheid in South Africa. And they resolved that their own tactics as members of ALSC would avoid "violence, force, or intimidation," even as they raised thousands of dollars to support freedom fighters in Africa.[6]

Not yet ready to heed the advice of Amílcar Cabral, a consensus formed to eschew alliances with white progressive groups, which they deemed "divisive, and disruptive." This prohibition extended to "so-called Blacks who are married to, or who sleep with Hunkeys [sic]"; the "bedroom" could not be "separated from the battlefield." Members from Oakland who disagreed with this rule were purged from the group and sent home.

Building on their late-night phone conversations, Nelson and Abdul Alkalimat presented a paper in Frogmore that, though it made no direct mention of Marxism, included the phrase "Black workers take the lead." They were ready to assert what they'd come to believe: working-class Black people employed in the nation's factories, schools, restaurants, hospitals, and homes were the group nearest the levers of capitalist power and, therefore, if organized, the ones who were best able to force changes to the nation's economy.

Black nationalists, including the writer and publisher Don Lee from Chicago, pushed back, arguing that all Black people shared the same interests and should not be divided by class. Nelson and Alkalimat responded that all capitalists—white or Black—profited from the labor of the poor.

For reasons both practical and philosophical, King had kept his distance from communism. But he well understood Nelson and his comrade's weariness with the intransigence of American political and economic power and the tempting allure of Marxism's revolutionary prescriptions. An old debate in the activist Black community was heating up again.

❖

On February 1, 1974, eighty ALSC members, including Amiri Baraka, arrived in Greensboro for a three-day meeting at the Forest Lake Country Club to continue the "ideological struggle" that began at Frogmore. Despite the tony name, the "country club" had formerly served as a recreational retreat for Greensboro's Black mill workers, making it an appropriate venue for a debate about the centrality of the Black working class to the movement. As the conference attendees assembled in the down-at-the-heels space, a chill enveloped the gathering that derived as much from the hardening ideological positions as the winter breeze seeping into the room. One whole day had been reserved to debate a "Statement of Principles" authored by Nelson and Abdul Alkalimat. "Now is the time," Alkalimat exhorted the gathering, "for a Black united front . . . against monopoly capitalism, imperialism, and racism. Now is the time to rally the progressive forces to throw Nixon out of office, fight against wage freezes and inflated prices, fight against police repression, and match the ruling class blow for blow until the people win out in a victorious manner." Don't, implored Alkalimat, become another "jive-ass organization that lets Black people down!"

The people Nelson called "Narrow Nationalists," who emphasized Black unity in the face of white racism, continued to resist joining a class-based struggle. Don Lee—who would soon change his name to Haki Madhubuti—now argued that between capitalism and communism existed little difference. Both, he said, "belong to the white boy. . . . It is past time," he continued, "for the 'so-called' black right, left, middle, and otherwise to recognize one undeniable fact: the major enemy of the black race is the white race whether they be Communist, Socialist, or Capitalist."

After an exhausting debate, Nelson and Alkalimat's "Statement of Principles" passed by a vote of 64–10.

A more public confrontation over the way forward for the Black movement took place just four months later. Two thousand energized people packed into the auditorium at Howard College in Washington, DC, on May 22, 1974, to attend a debate between Howard alum Stokely Carmichael, representing the Black nationalist point of view, and Nelson and Owusu, promoting the Marxist position of working-class unity against a capitalist system that harmed poor people of every background around the world. Carmichael disagreed with the men from Greensboro, arguing that all Black people—not primarily the working class—should fight capitalism, which he described as a tool invented by white supremacists to justify racial exploitation.

Based on the cheers and jeers heard in the raucous heat of the public moment, it appeared that the Marxists won the room. Some would identify this moment as the end of the Black Power movement in the United States, as Owusu and Nelson pushed working-class solidarity over racial and cultural unity.[7]

At the end of the *Black Journal* discussion with Tony Brown, the lawyer Haywood Burns made a prescient observation. "What [Watergate] is," he'd said, referring to the scandal that would end President Nixon's second term in office on August 9, 1974, "is an indication of the lawlessness of law officials and the abuses of state power at the highest levels." Burns, who had successfully defended Angela Davis against murder and kidnapping charges, represented the inmates in the 1971 Attica prison uprising, and would later marry Jennifer

Dohrn, sister of the Weather Underground activist Bernardine Dohrn, continued, "If they're doing this against the established opposition, what are they doing against Black people, what are they doing against activists? . . . What we see in Watergate is just the top of the iceberg."

❖

In August 1973, one month after being sworn in as the new director of the FBI, Clarence Kelley signed off on an investigation of the ALSC, checking the box that defined them as "potentially dangerous because of background, emotional instability, or activity in groups engaged in activities inimical to the United States." The FBI suspected the group of "rebellion or insurrection," "seditious conspiracy," "advocating overthrow of the government," and "illegal exportation of war materials." The FBI observed, not incorrectly, that Howard Fuller believed "black people of the whole world must destroy . . . the capitalist beast . . . not by mere rhetoric alone but by any means necessary . . . [in a] struggle to merge the Black Liberation Struggle with the process of World Revolution." The FBI defined Malcolm X Liberation University as an institution established to "produce Black militants with the capability of extremist acts with their loyalty primarily to black people regardless of the nation in which they live."[8]

Unbeknownst to Nelson, the FBI had two informants at the 1973 Frogmore conference. Now, with Kelley's blessing, the Bureau declared that all attendees of the Frogmore conference "should be considered leaders or activists . . . and should therefore be subjects of investigation."[9]

Though Nelson and Alkalimat had been careful not to mention communism or Marxism in their position papers, the FBI agents reviewing the files knew what to look for. Noting the phrase "Black workers take the lead," the agents reported that "this development has been expected, with regard to the revolutionary Marxist-Leninist concept of Pan-Africanism as interpreted by Black extremists. . . . They have formerly linked their struggle with the continent of Africa but have recently turned part of their attention to the defeat of capitalism at home."[10]

Teletyped FBI reports zipped around the country, to and from Greensboro, Boston, New York, Los Angeles, Cincinnati, Houston, Baltimore, Buffalo, Atlanta, Chicago, Cleveland, Denver, Detroit, Indianapolis, and Newark, New Jersey, where LeRoi Jones—the FBI refused to use Amiri Baraka's chosen name—held up the banner of African Liberation Day. Agents scoured the campuses of Columbia, Brown, and Harvard, looking for ALSC collaborators. They monitored "travel plans, meetings with other extremist leaders, writings or publications . . . , fundraising activities and public appearances or speeches" of those in the leadership.[11]

The collaboration and communication between federal, state, and local law enforcement agencies—including the Greensboro Police Department—ensured that the reputations of the activists under investigation preceded them wherever they went. A subject of FBI reports in the wake of both the King assassination and the 1969 uprising at A&T, Nelson had now been identified not only as a "subversive" but also as a leader in an "extremist" and "communist" organization "inimical to the United States." The labels covered up the journey that had carried Nelson to this point, and the way, since the late 1960s, the reactions of local and federal institutions had pushed him toward the very radicalism they feared.

BUREAU

Special Agent Cecil Moses was working out of the Jackson Field Office in Mississippi when J. Edgar Hoover died on May 2, 1972. Over the course of forty-eight years, the Bureau's patriarch had built the government agency into the most powerful law enforcement operation in the world and perhaps, some suggested, the most powerful institution in America. While some called Hoover a "feudal baron" who controlled American political thought through fear, manipulation, and a relentless drive for good publicity, to Moses he would always be "the Director," the only head of the Bureau who'd ever merit a capital D.[1] On a personal level, the Bureau had lifted Moses, along with thousands of other young white men, from a farming life to one that engaged each day with what Hoover believed to be the nation's most pressing crises. "To my mind," J. Edgar Hoover told *Newsweek* magazine in 1970, "the big question for every American is whether he wants to support and defend our free society or let it be overrun by visionary agitators."[2]

The troubles at the Bureau began the year before the Director's death when a small, dedicated group of Vietnam War dissenters calling themselves the Commission to Investigate the FBI broke into a Resident Agency, or FBI office, a short drive from Philadelphia. They walked out with a trove of files and proof that the FBI covertly surveilled and harassed Vietnam War protesters. But the documents revealed more than the dissenters had imagined. As J. Edgar Hoover launched a massive—and unsuccessful—manhunt to track down the citizen spies, journalists at major newspapers began receiving packets of the stolen files. President Nixon's attorney general, John Mitchell, demanded that the journalists return the classified documents. Most did. But Betty Medsger at the *Washington Post*, with the blessing of her editor Ben Bradlee, read through the pages and began to publish what she found in them.

Combing through the FBI internal memos and field reports, Medsger learned of a secret FBI program called COINTELPRO, short for *counterintelligence program*. Generally believed by the public and most lawmakers to be a set of tactics designed to disrupt foreign threats, such as Soviet spies attempting to steal nuclear secrets, this particular use of counterintelligence had been deployed to surveil, disrupt, and actively sow paranoia among US citizens whom Hoover and the FBI deemed "un-American."[3]

The domestic program got its formal start in 1956, when President Dwight Eisenhower approved Hoover's plan to disrupt and discredit homegrown communists while disregarding their constitutional rights. In short order, COINTELPRO targets came to include antiwar activists, feminist organizations, advocates of Puerto Rican independence, environmentalists, agitators for Native American sovereignty, gay rights advocates, and, beginning in 1965, the Ku Klux Klan. But two specific operations outranked all others in expense and effort: the communist infiltration operation and the one called "Black Hate," designed to "neutralize" Black activists from Martin Luther King Jr. to the Black Panthers. Even as President Johnson signed the Civil Rights Act, Hoover disregarded the civil liberties of any Black American he deemed a threat to the way the country ran its business. The secret program depended not only on Hoover's power but also on the complicity of presidents and congressmen from both political parties, as well as a long string of federal attorneys general. It also relied on the loyalty of the special agents who, like Cecil Moses, stood at the front lines of Hoover's directives to protect the "American way of life."[4]

In 1957, when an FBI recruiter showed up at Pleasant View High

School, set in a remote stretch of Appalachia in Kentucky, just across the state line from Tennessee, forty-one of forty-two graduating seniors—boys and girls—lined up for an interview. The only student who didn't was one of that year's two valedictorians. Cecil Moses had a plan. He'd attend the Baptist Cumberland College in nearby Williamsburg, Kentucky, and as soon as he turned twenty-one, whether he had his degree or not, he'd sign up with the Kentucky State Police. Pleasant View's principal, a distant cousin who gave Cecil a lift to school each morning in the bed of his pickup truck, convinced the boy to take the interview. The FBI recruiter assured Cecil that with some experience in the Bureau, he'd have a leg up on the competition when he was ready to join the state police.[5]

After the background checks and other preliminaries were completed, the FBI offered Cecil Moses a job as a clerk in the Cleveland Field Office. He fit the Bureau's ideal profile: smart, young, and white.[6] At nineteen, he left for the first time his remote Appalachian "holler" and the cash-poor but self-sufficient life on his family's hardscrabble farm. He set out with a headful of country know-how expressed in a twang as thick as the morning fog over the Cuyahoga River where it empties into Lake Erie. At the downtown Cleveland FBI office, the young man got the lonely feeling that he'd gone from being Cecil Moses, valedictorian with a promising future, to just another hillbilly four hundred–some miles from home, adrift in the big city.

He thought about quitting and returning to live with his loving, religious mother and his hardworking father, who traveled between the farm and his coal-mining job in "Bloody Harlan County," Kentucky, so-called for the brutal battles between the coal bosses and the miners. An organizer for the United Mine Workers of America and devoted to the union's leader, John L. Lewis, Cecil's father carried a revolver in his dinner pail for protection against the company's hired strike busters and communist infiltrators. The daily farm chores he left to his young son, as Nelson Johnson's father had charged his children with keeping their subsistence operation running. Before he turned ten, Cecil would be up before dawn to build a fire in the fireplace. Then, a coal oil lamp swinging from his hand, he'd head for the barn to milk the cows, feed the hogs, and collect eggs from the hens. On Sundays he went to church with his mother in Williamsburg. No Black people lived in his isolated holler, but Cecil looked forward to the music that the white and Black Pentecostals made together at revivals in the county seat. If he'd slaughtered a hog, his mother brought some of the meat to share with her Black acquaintances. As a teenager, he noticed something that seemed strange to him: the county newspaper didn't publish the obituaries of Black people.

When he turned thirteen, Moses wired the barn for electricity, stringing a coil of old electric wire tree by tree from the house, until raw bulbs illuminated his predawn work. When his father returned from the mines one night, Cecil "had the place lit up like Times Square." "Cecil's always fiddling with something," his mother said. Not long after that, Cecil rigged an old refrigerator motor he'd salvaged, turning it into a corn sheller, freeing his grandfather and himself from the arm-numbing work of removing kernels from the cobs by hand. Cecil thought of himself as an accomplished mule skinner, only half joking when he'd say that his mules got paid more than he did for twitching logs out of the forest to the lumberyard. Back in the holler he'd felt useful and appreciated.

Oscar Hawkins, the special agent in charge of the Cleveland Field Office and a "big old former Texas Ranger," noticed Cecil's "hangdog look" and called the young clerk into his office.

"Close my door," Hawkins said, scaring the hell out of Cecil. "You're going to quit, aren't you?" Hawkins asked.

"Yes, sir, I am," admitted Cecil. "I'm homesick, I don't fit in. I've heard *pardon* so much, I feel like I'm in prison," said the young man, referring to the fact that his co-workers made him repeat everything he said until they could make some sense of his accent.

"At least you have a sense of humor," said Special Agent in Charge Hawkins. "I've pulled your file. I know you grew up down there in that holler. I know you followed broom tails."

When he used the down-home nickname for a mule, Cecil knew then that the SAC was a country boy, too.

The SAC continued, "Now you put any of these kids from the city down in that holler and they wouldn't last a month. But you're going to make it on their turf. Get that chin off your chest, hold your head up, and get out there. I don't want to hear any more of this business about quitting. It wouldn't surprise me if you didn't go on to get your [college] degree. I think you have the wherewithal to be an FBI agent."

As a young FBI clerk, Moses learned that Hoover possessed a genius for collecting and organizing information and institutionalizing his vision at the agency. Young Hoover had worked at the Library of Congress, and once he joined what would become the FBI, he created categories and codes for some two hundred types of criminal violations that were indexed on cards in the organization's vast filing system. His information management systems kept tabs not only on the people he and his colleagues knew had committed crimes but also on those who they believed might do so in the future. Wielded shrewdly, the information could be deployed to isolate people with "subversive" ideas. The information, together with the ability to quickly retrieve, share, or hide it, was power.[7]

It took twelve years, but Moses strung together enough night classes at Kent State University—where he switched his major from political science to personnel relations and labor law to avoid left-wing professors that ticked him off—and at Cleveland State to finally earn a college degree.

The day after he received his diploma in 1969, the FBI promoted Cecil Moses to special agent. He'd spent more than a decade internalizing the values and processes that made J. Edgar Hoover's bureaucracy run. He'd sat for hours listening to the phone calls of communists and union bosses. In addition to catching bank robbers, kidnappers, and fugitives, he accepted his charge—Hoover's FBI mission—to protect America from anyone who might diminish the country's extraordinary power. The FBI, in return, pulled him from a remote corner of rural America, paid for his education, and handed him not just a good job but a spot in an institution that eight in ten Americans held in high esteem. America and the Director, that single conjoined entity inside the FBI, depended on Cecil Moses and the phalanx of men like him.

One moment from his time as a clerk would stick with Moses always. From gathered intelligence, he'd been asked to write a comprehensive analysis of John L. Lewis's leadership of the United Mine Workers of America. He concluded that the man his father idolized had sold the miners out for personal gain. Cecil's father dismissed his son's theories, keeping faith with Lewis. Cecil wouldn't buttress his arguments with the classified details he believed to be facts. He never again brought the subject up with his father. And over the years, as the FBI became a new family to Cecil, any flaws were softened by loyalty, friendship, and the faith that he and his colleagues were doing the right thing.[8]

❖

In September 1969, the Bureau assigned Special Agent Moses to Des Moines, Iowa, where a smart, fearless law school dropout named Charles Knox co-led an active chapter of the Black Panther Party, inspired by the Oakland Black Panther Party's Ten-Point Plan calling for "land, bread, housing, education, clothing, justice and peace" and an "end to police brutality."

Two months before SA Moses arrived in Des Moines, J. Edgar Hoover publicly called the Blank Panthers "the greatest threat to the internal security of the United States."[9] A 1967 teletype to the Field Offices called for "imaginative Special Agent[s]" to "expose, disrupt, misdirect, discredit, or otherwise neutralize the activities of Black nationalists, hate-type organizations and groupings, their leadership, spokesmen, membership, and supporters." "No opportunity," Hoover continued in that 1967 memo, "should be missed to exploit through counterintelligence techniques the organizational and personal conflicts of the leadership of the groups."[10]

When SA Moses arrived in Des Moines, Knox was busy organizing resistance to urban renewal ("Negro removal") and police

violence against Black youths, as well as working on improving education in the city's predominantly Black schools. The Des Moines
Panthers helped people struggling with addiction and, as chapters all
around the country were doing, instituted a breakfast program. Each
morning they fed nearly two hundred schoolchildren. As the kids
ate, members rapped to them about the dangers of imperialism, capitalism, and racism.[11] SA Moses would soon learn that Knox led dozens of local Black Panther Party members and an even larger number
of white sympathizers in discussions about readings from Chairman
Mao's little red book of quotations.[12]

❖

A lumber company burned to the ground the year before Moses arrived in Des Moines. Charles Knox was among those arrested for
arson, but the charges didn't stick. Then in April 1969, the Black
Panther Party headquarters in Des Moines exploded. Other detona-
tions followed, and the rookie special agent kept being roused from
sleep in the wee hours to investigate. On May 13, 1970, a bomb blew
up the Des Moines Police Department. The Chamber of Commerce
was hit on June 13.[13] Nine days before that, dynamite rocked the
Ames City Hall, thirty-five miles away. A building on the campus of
Drake University exploded on June 29. One night, Moses and his law
enforcement colleagues discovered and disarmed a bomb before it
could detonate and collapse a bridge.[14]

Authorities blamed the Panthers for the bombings and for many
of the hundreds of explosions rocking communities around the country. The Panthers claimed they were being set up. In response to the
situation, Black Panther headquarters in Oakland expelled the Des
Moines chapter, believing they'd been infiltrated by state agents and
provocateurs.[15] When a young man who had been an occasional
member of the Des Moines Panthers died in a blast in Minneapolis,
the bombings ceased. Had he been responsible for the other bombs?
Had he been a true Panther member or an agent provocateur planted
and then discarded by law enforcement? Could he have been part of

a COINTELPRO operation, like those described in Betty Medsger's files? These questions would never be answered.

This much was true: by the time Cecil Moses left Iowa in the fall of 1970 for a new post in Jackson, Mississippi, the Des Moines Black Panthers had been disrupted and neutralized. The FBI closed its case against them.

The demise of the Des Moines Panthers would barely register in the national consciousness. Before he left Iowa, however, Moses participated in another operation that, eventually, caused an international scandal. The Los Angeles Field Office of the FBI wanted to know why calls from a Black Panther in California had been traced to a pharmacy in small-town Iowa. Moses agreed to help, driving an hour northeast to Marshalltown, a leafy municipality on the banks of the Iowa River. There he discovered that the father of Hollywood star Jean Seberg owned the pharmacy in question. The information Moses passed along to an agent in Los Angeles likely confirmed what they already suspected. The FBI knew Seberg had donated more than $10,000 to the Panther Party and had thrown a star-studded fundraiser for the organization. Now Hoover wanted the "sex-perverted white actress," as the FBI termed her, "neutralized." Following Hoover's counterintelligence directive, the agents aimed to "cause her embarrassment and . . . to cheapen her image." In his 1967 memo initiating the "Black Hate" COINTELPRO program, Hoover urged agents to enlist "news media contacts" in the effort to discredit Black leaders.[16]

So the FBI sent an anonymous tip to a journalist, hinting that the married and pregnant Seberg carried the child not of her husband but of a Black Panther. The Los Angeles Times ran the story first. Newsweek published it a few weeks later. Two months after that, Seberg went into premature labor and lost her child. Ten years later, when she committed suicide in Paris, Seberg's ex-husband blamed the actress's deep depressions, the loss of her baby, and her suicide on the trauma caused by the FBI stunt to harm her reputation.[17] Actions like the one against Seberg and likely the one that destroyed the Des Moines Black Panther Party were part of COINTELPRO.[18]

❖

In Jackson, Mississippi, "White Hate" also became a focus of Moses's job. He cultivated informants in the Klan and, as did hundreds of agents, performed "black bag" jobs, slipping without a warrant into homes and offices to steal membership lists of white supremacist organizations in the state.[19] The members and their wives would then be surprised to receive embarrassing postcards and letters in the mail mocking their "secret" Klan membership, hinting at extramarital affairs, embezzlement, or other un-Christian activities. After his experience with Charles Knox, Moses came to believe that Black Power radicals were a lot better educated and smarter than the Kluxers, which also meant to him that the Black activists were more dangerous and more likely to be imprisoned or killed in FBI plots than Klansmen.

When the FBI began to come under scrutiny for its COINTELPRO operations, agents such as Moses circled the wagons, surely believing that if they protected the institution, their colleagues—and Hoover—would protect them.[20]

The month after Hoover died, police arrested several men for breaking into the Democratic campaign headquarters at the tony Watergate building in Washington, DC, located just a mile from the White House. Among those apprehended were ex-FBI and ex-CIA agents and contractors. The attempted burglary would eventually implicate President Nixon and top officials at the FBI.[21]

When the embattled President Nixon swore in former agent Clarence Kelley as the Bureau's new director in the summer of 1973, "nerves were raw" at the FBI. Kelley had left the Bureau twelve years earlier to run the Kansas City Police Department. Now he returned, a trusted member of Hoover's Bureau family, to right the FBI's foundering ship.[22]

If Kelley had a choice between saving the FBI or helping to preserve Nixon's presidency, he chose his Bureau family over the commander in chief. As the president stonewalled and lied to cover up his scandals, the official FBI investigation, involving nearly every one of the Bureau's fifty-nine Field Offices, and leaks about their findings, attributed to an FBI source called "Deep Throat," would lead to the president's undoing.[23] Kelley maneuvered expertly to distance the FBI from the "moral permissiveness" and "nefarious activities" issuing from the White House, hoping to shield the Bureau from accountability for its own abuses of power.[24]

Nixon resigned a year later. On August 9, 1974, the disgraced chief executive flashed his wide grin and the iconic double victory sign, ducked into a helicopter with his wife, Pat, and flew away to postpresidential life. In his farewell address, Nixon made no mention of the articles of impeachment drawn up by Congress that outlined his "high crimes and misdemeanors," which included evidence of his lying, bribery, obstruction of justice, and use of "unlawful covert activities." He'd been accused of impeding the FBI investigation of Watergate and of misusing the Bureau "by directing or authorizing such [Bureau] personnel to conduct . . . electronic surveillance or other investigations unrelated to national security."[25] Over the course of the investigation, it was revealed that the FBI ran illegal wiretaps on journalists and government employees at Nixon's request and searched desperately, illegally, and futilely to link antiwar activists to international communist influences. Unlike Kelley, L. Patrick Gray, who served briefly as the acting director immediately following Hoover's death, had acted to protect the president, even destroying evidence that linked the White House to the Watergate burglary.

❖

Headquarters summoned Cecil Moses from Mississippi to Washington, DC, in 1974 to supervise the FBI's Civil Rights Section's Criminal Investigative Division for the Northeast region. At Civil Rights, he was assigned the job of supporting the Department of Justice lawyers prosecuting the National Guardsmen indicted for using excessive force when they shot and killed four Vietnam War protesters on the Kent State University campus, the same college where left-wing professors caused Moses to change his major. The Kent State Massacre of

May 4, 1970, echoed the 1969 military strike on the A&T campus, though the latter, likely because it had occurred on a Black campus, had not garnered the same national attention.[26] Now in the room with the federal prosecutors, Moses made no attempt to hide his contempt for their case against the American soldiers. "This is one case I hope we lose," he said, taking note of the stunned faces looking back at him. "I don't mind telling you. These kids [the protesters] were out of control. The Guardsmen had no intent. They were scared."[27]

By the time a US District Court judge, to Moses's gratification, dismissed the charges against the Guardsmen in November 1974, Moses, now in his midthirties and the father of three young children, was on the move again. During his shameful year as acting director, L. Patrick Gray created a new division inside the FBI called the Office of Planning and Evaluation (OPE), a name that conjured up the image of a roomful of men dressed in gray flannel suits, analyzing data tables as half-smoked cigarettes smoldered in ashtrays. When Kelley took the reins of the Bureau, he saw an opportunity in the new division and kept it. The OPE, he imagined, could serve as an internal think tank where a cohort of bright agents could help him review FBI operations. As it performed this function, Kelley hoped the OPE might act like a gyroscope at the heart of the behemoth, holding the Bureau steady against the torrent of criticism gathering around the revelations stemming from Watergate and Betty Medsger's reporting.

In bland bureaucratic language, Kelley laid out what he expected of the OPE. The division should be "an effective instrument for providing a continuing review of the Bureau's operations, administrative and investigative, to objectively evaluate the same, and to make frank and unvarnished recommendations along these lines . . . providing immeasurable assistance in long range planning and establishing measurable goals." If this sounded vague, Kelley crafted another, clearer message for the FBI employees frustrated by the escalating calls for more oversight of their intelligence-gathering operations. The FBI, Kelley assured the Bureau family, had "the talent within itself to *overcome any obstacle in the path of maintaining procedures which are sound* [emphasis added], and making improvements where needed." As much as Kelley would talk about "raising the windows and letting in fresh air," his regard for the Bureau's traditions and public claims that the FBI did nothing illegal during COINTELPRO operations were what won him the respect of veteran agents. He defended his Bureau family's means by promoting the results: the Communist Party USA, the Black Panthers, and other radical groups had been marginalized.[28]

For this delicate project of both changing and not changing, Kelley recruited people to the OPE with various levels of tenure at the Bureau and expertise in security, science, administration, and computers, financial crimes, inspections, field management, and racial matters. New and small, the OPE bore an air of mystery only enhanced by its nickname: "the Group of 12." The moniker emphasized the division's small size—actual staff numbers would vary from less than twelve to a couple dozen—and lent it a mystical, even biblical, air. Once accepted by the director, any recommendations from the Group of 12 would be handed down by Kelley himself to a field staff "accustomed to rigid adherence to a chain of command."[29]

The internal document recommending him as a member of the "Group of 12" describes Moses as "a conscientious and enthusiastic career employee who exercises good judgment," in possession of "thorough knowledge of Bureau policies and procedures." The plum posting offered direct and frequent access to Director Kelley. Asked to study the FBI's use of computers, Moses found himself reporting bad news to the top man. "Boss," he concluded, "we're like a lapped horse. We're so far behind, we think we're ahead." Kelley, apparently, appreciated both the candid assessment and the rural charm.[30]

Not long after Moses arrived at the OPE, Lee Colwell, the man who would go to bat for Moses in 1979 so he could continue to lead the investigation in Greensboro, joined the Group of 12 from the Inspections Division. Colwell's reputation as an operations and administrative genius preceded him. Moses and Colwell became fast friends. Colwell, Moses learned, could parachute into any FBI division or Field Office experiencing problems to set things right and ensure that administrators and special agents followed protocols. This responsibility, though real, wasn't his only function. Colwell never talked about the rumor that he belonged to an elite Cold War counterintelligence team recruited from various US intelligence agencies and military forces. To establish his deep cover, Colwell had, during his travels to FBI Field Offices around the country, visited cemeteries, searching for the graves of infants. When he found one, he'd read the town papers and study the local history. He'd pore over the yearbooks of schools the child would have attended had he lived, memorizing the names and faces of classmates, team records, constructing imagined memberships in pertinent clubs and societies. Eventually, he possessed six of these identities and a passport for each. The Inspections Division had offered Colwell the perfect cover. Not only was he, by all accounts, exceptional at his public job, but that job gave him a reason to travel and to "fix" other problems. Both an operations expert and a trained executioner, Colwell became known to his ultimate bosses as "the Prince of Darkness." President Lyndon Johnson once called Colwell "the luckiest man alive." Lee understood that President Johnson meant he was lucky *to be* alive. In a division intent on both "making improvements" and "maintaining procedures," some of which were secret, the man who married operational management with covert missions made a smart addition.[31]

In early 1975, the Senate appointed Frank Church, a Democrat from Idaho, to lead a Select Committee to Study Governmental Operations with Respect to Intelligence Activities that would investigate wrongdoing at the CIA and FBI. Publicly, Kelley agreed to cooperate with the committee as he pointed the world outside the Bureau to the work of the OPE, building a wall between the present and the past. Kelley gave Watergate files and twenty thousand pages of COINTELPRO documents to the Church Committee, terrain that the senators and later scholars, journalists, and activists could mine for illegal operations. In the present, however, existed reform and a publicly humbled Bureau. Academics from Princeton and Harvard camped out in the Group of 12 conference rooms, lending the division a patina of think-tank objectivity. While lawmakers and journalists fought the Bureau for greater access to its past, Kelley and his agents stepped toward the future.

The Church Committee interviewed agents, informants, and the targets of FBI operations. The sampling of FBI files, though a fraction of what the FBI possessed, gave them plenty to shock the American public when they published their report in April 1976.

Their research revealed careers ended and lives destroyed by COINTELPRO activities, including the Bureau's surveillance, disruption, exposure, and interference in the personal life of Martin Luther King Jr. Fascinated by the tawdry details of his intelligence targets' sex lives, Hoover, with the approval of Presidents Kennedy and Johnson, had discovered that King had affairs with multiple women. Hoover's men shared their lewd recordings from surreptitious electronic surveillance with lawmakers, the press, President Johnson, and King's wife, Coretta. The FBI sent King an anonymous letter, intimating that he should kill himself. The possibility that King could be influenced by what Hoover called the "perverted idealism" of communism gave unquestioned cover for this unlawful peeping. Black equality elided with communism in Hoover's mind, making the two threats nearly indistinguishable for him and, through him and his accomplices, for a majority of white Americans around the country. James Baldwin, also a target of FBI surveillance, made this connection, noting that "the people who are running around throwing people in jail and ruining reputations and screaming about Communists wouldn't know one if he fell from the ceiling. And wouldn't care! What they are concerned about is propping up somehow the doctrine of white supremacy, so that they can seem to have given it up, but really still hold the power."[32]

The Bureau's use of informants particularly interested the Church Committee. On December 2, 1975, a figure wearing what appeared to be a white pillowcase with eyeholes cut into it took a seat at the witness table facing the members of the committee. Gary Thomas Rowe Jr. had been whisked to Washington from Savannah, Georgia, where he lived in the Witness Protection Program under a new name. For five years during the 1960s, he'd worked as an FBI informant in the Ku Klux Klan. And as an FBI informant, he'd participated in some of the most notorious and horrific Klan violence perpetrated during the civil rights movement.

A former Marine and Klan sympathizer, Rowe joined the Kluxers at the behest of an FBI agent in Birmingham, Alabama, in about 1960. In 1961, a multiracial group of student activists and Black journalists set out to ride buses from Washington, DC, through the South in defiance of Jim Crow laws mandating segregated seating. Three weeks before the buses crossed the Alabama state line, Rowe let the FBI know that the Klan planned to teach the group a lesson. White supremacists firebombed the first bus in Anniston, Alabama. During his testimony, the hooded Rowe told the committee that in Birmingham, the Klan had been "promised 15 minutes with absolutely no intervention from any police officer whatsoever." The Klansmen took full advantage of their time, viciously beating the Black and white Freedom Riders. Rowe admitted that he, as a paid FBI informant, had beaten one of the Freedom Riders. In each case, the police hung back, permitting the violence. The FBI, meanwhile, took notes and gathered information for their voluminous files. Rowe's work with the FBI had just begun.[33]

One couldn't help but wonder what other terrible secrets lay beyond the reach of the Church Committee. An even more troubling question emerged from the revelations: How much of the twentieth century's shocking political violence had been caused by the FBI's repressive tactics, the fear it fanned, and its cultivation of domestic terrorism by secret informants and provocateurs?

Over the years, one Church Committee member, Senator Philip Hart of Michigan, had pushed Hoover to get informants in the Klan to "report planned violence, and as a result, prevent the violence which was occurring." Now it seemed to him that prevention wasn't the FBI's objective. "I was too dumb to realize," an agonized Hart continued, "that [Rowe's] presence there did not prevent violence, and indeed, maybe contributed to it."[34]

When the Senate committee released its report in April 1976, one member, Senator Robert Morgan from North Carolina, delivered a speech at Wake Forest University defending the findings. Eschewing the formal language of the committee report, Senator Morgan called the FBI intelligence work "morally reprehensible," saying that it showed a "lack of respect for the law." The FBI, Morgan said, had even set up "Klaverns of the Ku Klux Klan." "National security," Morgan told his audience, was just a "catchall for [the FBI's] illegal activity." What he did next made him one of the most hated men inside the FBI: he revealed that George Dorsett, one of the most powerful Klansmen and white supremacist preachers in the state of North Carolina, the man who'd led the Klan rally when Nelson Johnson attempted to integrate a Greensboro bar in 1966, had been in the employ of the FBI from 1959 until 1970.[35] Cecil Moses, for one, wouldn't forget Morgan's breach of trust—he'd revealed the name of an informant—or his judgments.

The Church Committee's findings demanded an official response; on April 6, 1976, Attorney General Edward Levi issued a set of guidelines, on which he'd collaborated with the FBI through the OPE, designed to curtail the unconstrained and reckless surveillance of people holding controversial political views.[36]

Along with the release of hundreds of informants, including Eddie Dawson in Greensboro, from their FBI work, the number of open FBI investigations dropped from over 20,000 to about 4,000. "Quality over quantity," Kelley announced: the FBI would focus on big cases and leave the rest to local law enforcement.[37] The Bureau stopped using the politically charged term *subversives* and adopted the word *terrorists* to emphasize violence rather than ideology. Opening a full FBI investigation, the new Levi Guidelines stated, would require "specific and articulable facts giving reason to believe that an individual or a group is or may be engaged in activities which involve the use of force or violence."[38]

If these changes helped appease some lawmakers and the majority of the public, other small changes amounted to something more than a simple set of bureaucratic efficiencies. Later in 1976, the president signed new Freedom of Information Act (FOIA) rules intended to make federal intelligence gathering more transparent. Now with more public scrutiny and limitations imposed on the FBI director's tenure, secrecy would require a more impersonal system, one that could no longer rely on Hoover's iron-fisted control. With guidance from the OPE think tank, the FBI's information gathering and filing system, the language used, the flow of information, and the format in which the information was presented appeared to better conform with the legal requirements. It would have been no surprise to either Senator Hart or Senator Morgan, however, that the FBI paperwork became both more banal and more opaque, more difficult for outsiders to decipher. Cecil Moses might have called the changes "simple things to fool the wise man."[39]

When the attorney general and FOIA guidelines were issued, police forces in cities and towns all around the country destroyed (or moved off-site) reams of intelligence files. In Greensboro, officers spent days shredding "civil intelligence" files, including what they'd collected on Nelson Johnson, Joyce Johnson, and Sandi Smith.[40]

Despite the flurry of regulatory activity, Church Committee members harbored little hope that their exposures would immediately or permanently change the way the FBI operated. "If COINTELPRO had been a short-lived aberration," they warned, "the thorny problems of motivation, techniques, and control presented might be safely relegated to history. However, COINTELPRO existed for years on an 'ad-hoc' basis before the formal programs were instituted, and more significantly, COINTELPRO-type activities may continue today under the rubric of 'investigation.'"[41] To put it another way, *COINTELPRO* was just a made-up word that had made a political and social point of view operational. The FBI could stop using the word and continue to operate from that same point of view.

At the end of the long days, Director Kelley would call Lee

Colwell up to his spacious office in the new J. Edgar Hoover Building. "What happened in the FBI today?" the director always asked. There were no secrets between the two men. As darkness fell and the lights of Washington, DC, twinkled to life, the men sat in the twilight, gently swirling cocktail glasses that held a finger or two of Johnnie Walker Black. Both had lost their wives to cancer. They'd bonded over personal tragedy and a common worldview. Taking a sip of whiskey in the near dark, Kelley would return again and again to a familiar theme: the American public just didn't understand what the Bureau did or how the FBI had to fight the "unfortunately secret battle with those who would promote anarchy and violence."[42] And Colwell, the cold warrior, would nod in ascent. As they battled through the Bureau's time of crisis, Kelley had learned the same lesson that had kept Colwell alive during his most risky operations: don't get caught.[43]

The rules constraining their intelligence gathering would loosen over time, they believed. And, when that happened, the public trust in the Bureau would rise again.[44]

By October 1977, the OPE disappeared as a stand-alone division, and Cecil Moses moved on to the Memphis Field Office. The FBI, however, hadn't finished paying for its past sins. A federal grand jury considered evidence of the FBI's illegal break-ins, wiretaps, and bugs. In 1978, shortly after Clarence Kelley retired under pressure from President Carter, Moses received a breathless call from a friend who'd just been interviewed by the grand jury, giving Moses a heads-up that he might be subpoenaed. Moses passed a few anxious months, but the call never came. He would never have to answer any difficult questions about his activity in Des Moines or Jackson, Mississippi.[45]

In the end, only two FBI agents were indicted for conspiring to deny American citizens their civil rights.[46] A third agent, Horace Beckwith, who had led the FBI's pursuit of the Weather Underground, escaped indictment by cooperating with prosecutors.

Beckwith had personally attempted to recruit Malcolm X to inform on the Nation of Islam for the FBI and, when that effort failed, may have been involved in the joint FBI and New York Police Department operation that would eventually be linked to Malcolm's 1965 assassination.[47] As the FBI lost significant repositories of institutional memory—people and documents—Lee Colwell argued that Beckwith, despite his taint, was too valuable to fire. Headquarters sent him back to the field.[48]

The frustration and bitterness at how his Bureau family had been criticized lingered for Moses. Given his unique set of experiences, there were few people in the FBI who understood better than Cecil Moses how it worked, its rules and regulations, its language, culture, and secrets. He'd learned it from the ground up, using every bit of country charm, grit, and smarts to climb a steep institutional ladder. His accent had softened, and he'd done everything asked of him until he'd made it on the city kids' turf. And in return, the FBI had given him a career, a road from the Kentucky hills to high-level management at what he still considered to be the greatest law enforcement operation in the greatest country in the world.

A couple of years later, when Cecil Moses arrived in North Carolina—Senator Robert Morgan's home turf—as the new assistant special agent in charge assigned to the Charlotte Field Office, he discovered Horace Beckwith sitting idly in a corner, riding out his time until retirement.

Not long after Assistant Special Agent in Charge Moses arrived in Charlotte in September 1979, Beckwith appeared in the ASAC's office with a file on a communist group engaged in organizing work, primarily in Greensboro and Durham. Moses authorized Beckwith to open a preliminary investigation and find out whether the Communist Workers Party might be involved in any violent or illegal activities. Beckwith, in turn, reached out to the special agents in Greensboro to inquire what they might know or be able to turn up about their communist neighbors.

ELECTRIC

In May 1976, the year of the US bicentennial, Nelson and Joyce, along with a contingent of Greensboro activists, drove to Durham to attend a debate about revolutionary strategy. Since the ideological fights and fractures that had taken place in Frogmore, in Greensboro, and at Howard University in 1973 and 1974, the couple had struggled to consolidate a local or national base of support to continue their push for economic and racial advancement. The heady days of the AAA Realty and Skilcraft strikes—back when the two were receiving Reynolds family, Ford Foundation, and OEO funding—had receded. In the mid-1970s, several Black leaders founded communist organizations, or "pre-parties," as they called them, including Amiri Baraka, whose interactions with Owusu and Nelson had drawn him deeper into Marxism. After the ideological debate at Howard, Nelson and Owusu participated in founding a communist organization they named the Revolutionary Workers League (RWL), activating the African Liberation Support Committee and YOBU networks to organize Black workers in factories or, as they said, using the Marxist term, "at the point of production."

But the RWL faltered, plagued by infighting and a lack of direction. Something was off about the organization, Nelson thought. Too often the leaders subjected other members to demeaning and humiliating hazing that crossed a line into psychological and physical violence. A toxic blend of power, competitiveness, and insecurity might be causing the chaos, he thought. But after the COINTELPRO revelations, one always worried about informants and provocateurs. How many moments in Nelson's activist life had been complicated by them, he wondered. He'd suspected Nunding back in 1969, and now as the RWL foundered, the suspicion that agent provocateurs were sowing seeds of discord seemed reasonable. For the first time in their activist lives, Joyce and Nelson felt their organizing momentum stall. Ideological disagreements and cynicism had corroded close relationships. Their embrace of Marxism-Leninism-Maoism made some old Black allies in Greensboro uneasy. Nelson drifted apart from Owusu, who remained in the RWL. Even Joyce's friendship with her beloved sister Sandi Neely Smith, who remained committed to the RWL, suffered in the face of uncertainty about how to address persistent economic inequality.[1]

Joyce and Nelson needed to figure out the strategy and tactics that would work in an ever more fragmented world, where political, economic, social, and activist norms were shifting. The Vietnam War had ended, a corrupt president had tumbled from power, and some of the FBI's dirty tricks had been exposed. The women's, environmental, gay rights, and Native American movements were gaining force and momentum. Schools were being integrated, and Black politicians were now winning public office all across the South. And yet, despite this progress, so many people still suffered. When Nelson and Joyce pulled back from the RWL to regroup, they initiated the Bolshevik Organizing Collective to delve deeply into the study of political and revolutionary theory. Indeed, it seemed then that anyone involved in leftist politics around the country had joined a "study group," applying themselves as if they were enrolled in a graduate school seminar, poring over Marxist theory for hours at night and gathering weekly to discuss and debate what they'd read and learned. On the bookshelf in Nelson and Joyce's rented home at the edge of southeast Greensboro sat a complete, dog-eared set of the works of

Vladimir Lenin. Perched beside these tomes were Ralph Ellison's *Invisible Man*, Richard Wright's *Native Son*, and the first book by Joyce's new favorite author of escapist novels, Danielle Steel.[2]

❖

Now, on a warm May evening, the two walked into a Durham auditorium packed with a couple hundred curious people armed with their accumulated theoretical models. In addition to the several carloads of attendees from Greensboro, including Signe Goldstein, there were dozens in the crowd from various study groups and collectives in Durham, including Jim Waller, Paul and Sally Bermanzohn, and Cesar Cauce. Most of the people arriving from Greensboro were Black. Many in the Durham contingent were white. They didn't yet know one another, at least not well. They sat in folding chairs, their energy bright and expectant, like stars in a constellation that had yet to be imagined and named. They scanned the room full of the men and women who would become their comrades and, in some cases, husbands and wives.

The common bond that brought most of them there that evening was Owusu Sadaukai, formerly Howard Fuller, whose presence had shaped a decade of organizing work in both Greensboro and Durham. A short time before this event, Owusu had kicked white organizers, including Sally Bermanzohn, out of the union drive at Duke Hospital. The drive failed, and bitterness and resentment followed. His Black Power mystique, built up during the heady years of poverty work with the North Carolina Fund and the Foundation for Community Development, was losing its luster and falling out of fashion. That evening Owusu had been selected to debate a man from out of town: Jerry Tung led a group based in New York called the Workers Viewpoint Organization. The RWL had nearly merged with the WVO six months earlier, but at the last minute retreated to its Black-only organizing stance.[3]

As he took a seat, Nelson reflected on the near merger. It took courage, he thought, for Jerry Tung and the two African American

Harvard students Phil Thompson and Dwight Hopkins to venture into Owusu's territory and engage him in a "line struggle," a debate about revolutionary strategy. Even so, despite the rivalries and the grudges, few in the crowd expected Jerry Tung, a muscular but diminutive Chinese American man who spoke with a thick foreign accent, to rival the towering, charismatic orator they knew in Owusu.

From the start, however, Tung's fiery presentation kept the crowd on the edge of their seats. Immediately, he criticized the strategy of the RWL, which advocated building a Communist Party by recruiting only people ready to accept strict adherence to the group's ideological line. The way forward, Tung argued passionately, was to engage in union building, "anti-racist" community activism, and anti-imperialist demonstrations. They would bring workers into the struggle over time, but first they'd establish a provocative presence in the world. Nelson and Joyce listened closely. Theory mattered, but, to them, the application of the theory in the hard work of community organizing was critical. From what he said, Tung seemed to agree.[4]

Signe Goldstein tried to interpret the arguments in the swirl of barely comprehensible communist jargon and acronyms: *Menshevik. Bolshevik. Dialectic. Contradiction. Treacherous opportunists. Voluntarism. Right errors. Left errors. Revisionist. Anti-revisionist. Divide one into two. Chauvinism. Subjectivism. Neo-Trotskyite. General line. Political line. Correct line. Gangsterism. Fascist gangsterism. Pre-Party. Racist dogs.* The PL, OL, AIM, BLA, LRBW, MAYO, OWS, RUP, and WFHC. It felt hard and disorienting, more like listening to a boxing match on the radio than witnessing a debate. Yet the compelling energy told her something was happening.[5]

Tung's theory of organizing became clearer when he presented the WVO's analysis of the violent crisis that arose from the effort to desegregate the Boston public schools by busing students to unfamiliar parts of the city. The busing, Tung argued, wasn't about integration; it was about keeping working-class white people and Black people divided by "whip[ing] up racist hysteria," which distracted everyone from a generally "deteriorating educational system." Integration by itself, Tung argued, didn't improve the quality of education. In fact, he continued, the Black and, particularly, the white working classes weren't yet prepared for school integration. A bridge of trust that rested on a foundation of common interests had to be built first. America's working poor, whatever their race, needed to understand that the government had failed to improve the "dilapidated, overcrowded, and underfunded" schools in all their communities. Building that bridge would be the work of the WVO and would take time. In the meantime, said Tung, good education applied equally should be the goal whether the school is in a Black neighborhood or a white neighborhood. "As communists," he said, "we must fight for the rights of the oppressed minorities, to go to the schools of their choice . . . and for more fundings to improve the conditions in the schools, for better programs, better curriculum, better facilities, better staffing."[6]

He had Nelson and Joyce's attention now.

A key moment in Nelson's political awakening had occurred when the young Black girl he mentored requested a white tutor. His belief in the importance of strong Black institutions, beginning with schools, like Dudley High School, that fostered community pride, had brought him into conflict with people wedded to the idea that integration would be the answer to all the problems of segregated education. Tung's vision offered something that Owusu's had not—a way to organize across race while still allowing space for people to embrace their own ethnic and cultural identities.

Tung's magnetic confidence and intelligence were winning over the racially mixed audience, giving hope to everyone there—white, Black, Asian, Latino, and Native American. In 1976, Tung's vision of multinational organizing made sense to the people in the audience. After Tung spoke, they looked around the room and believed that despite racial and class differences, it might be possible to align their stars. When he finished, Tung invited Owusu, sitting in the front row, to run his "raggedy line." Tung didn't know that his ideological adversary had lost his will to fight.[7]

Owusu knew he was on the ropes as he stood and glumly read

an uninspiring defense of the Revolutionary Workers League. Howard Fuller had come to North Carolina in 1965 for a job with the North Carolina Fund and galvanized the state's Black liberation movement with his bold rhetoric and fearless organizing. He'd mentored Nelson Johnson and changed the lives of hundreds of students and activists, Black and white. Now, more than a decade later, he'd lost his way, horrified by what he was seeing in the RWL and unable to comfortably or authentically embrace working across the race line.

For the next several hours, the audience conversed and debated with the WVO's Jerry Tung, Phil Thompson, and Dwight Hopkins. By 1 a.m., as the event wound down, the Black people from Greensboro and the white people from Durham shared an inchoate vision of how they might work together.

Out in the parking lot, after the event, Nelson told Owusu that he and Joyce planned to join the WVO. The decade-long collaboration between the two men had come to an end.

Violence and psychological abuse increased in the RWL. Owusu, now worried other members might kill him, packed his car and fled, driving to the city where he'd grown up. In Milwaukee, he began again as Howard Fuller.[8]

After the debate, Paul and Sally Bermanzohn invited Nelson and Joyce for dinner, so the two couples—all respected leaders in their communities—could get to know one another. Sally nervously ran the vacuum cleaner around the apartment, worried the hair of their two cats and dog would make Nelson and Joyce uncomfortable, as Paul fretted over how he might find common ground with a fierce Black nationalist.[9]

Joyce knew Sally from their undergraduate years at Duke but hadn't seen her in nearly a decade. Nelson, since the late 1960s and with Owusu's mentoring, had trained himself not to smile at white people, internalizing the disdain he projected.[10] Despite their attraction to Tung's vision, Nelson and Joyce were skeptical about the prospects of working with whites, who tended to dominate interracial organizations and then walk away when they grew tired of the struggle. Over the previous few years, Nelson had come to believe intellectually in multiracial organizing, even if his emotions kept him from working across the line. Now an emphasis on class-based organizing carried forward by the multiracial WVO, which emerged from the New York–based Asian Study Group and was led by a Chinese American, made interracial collaboration seem possible.

When Paul opened the door, Nelson greeted him with a broad, warm smile. Nelson struck Paul as not only friendly but also gentle, hardly the intimidating person he'd been hearing about. To Sally's surprise, Joyce remembered her from their years together at Duke. To Nelson and Joyce, Paul and Sally came across as serious, smart, and committed organizers.[11]

By the end of the evening, as Paul and Sally walked Nelson and Joyce to their car, Paul asked Nelson a question that had been nagging him: Sally wanted children, but Paul wasn't sure how kids would fit into a life of revolutionary politics. What was it like to be a revolutionary and a parent? Nelson draped an arm tenderly over Paul's shoulders. "You know how when you are doing a lot of things, there's always something you can put on the back burner? Well," Nelson said, "kids aren't like that."[12]

After visiting Nelson and Joyce's house and seeing the beat-up carpet on the floor and the half-finished carpentry projects, Sally realized she could relax about the cat hair. Paul, negotiating for the Durham-based Communist Workers Committee (CWC), with Nelson representing the Bolshevik Organizing Collective (BOC), spent countless hours at Alamance Church Road talking deep into the night about how to work together. During those endless conversations, Paul witnessed how children fit into Nelson and Joyce's revolutionary politics. If one of Nelson's daughters suffered from nightmares, Nelson would move to a rocking chair and comfort the young girl as she returned to sleep and he continued to discuss organizing strategy until dawn.[13]

The merger between the white communists from Durham and the Black communists from Greensboro to form a new chapter of the Workers Viewpoint Organization rippled like electricity through North

Carolina activist circles. It had been a decade since the Student Nonviolent Coordinating Committee had kicked out white members and nearly as long since Nelson stopped collaborating with white people to focus on strengthening Greensboro's Black community. Beside the Black activists' belief that even well-intentioned whites would try to hijack their ventures lay a concern for security. The Ku Klux Klan wasn't the only institution that bristled at race mixing. J. Edgar Hoover had feared a merger between white and Black leftist organizations, especially one between the white-led Students for a Democratic Society and the Black Panthers. He'd directed COINTELPRO operations to neutralize that possibility. His successor, Clarence Kelley, shared this concern and the objective of keeping white and Black revolutionaries apart.[14]

History confirmed that interracial collaborations in the fight for racial and economic equality were perilous. The interracial Freedom Riders were brutally beaten by the Klan with explicit permission of the Alabama police and the implicit permission of the FBI. Viola Liuzzo, a white civil rights worker from Detroit, died on the last night of the 1965 march in Selma while riding in a car with Black men. Not only Martin Luther King Jr.'s public opposition to the Vietnam War, but also his 1968 campaign to bring impoverished people of every race and from every overlooked holler, reservation, and urban ghetto in the country to camp out in Washington, DC, raised the hackles of government officials from the president on down. The FBI shamed Jean Seberg, a white woman, for helping the Panthers. Even Malcolm X had been shifting his views toward a class-based, multiracial analysis of social history when a New York City Police Department detail failed to protect him from assassins during a speech in Harlem. Fred Hampton had been building alliances with Puerto Rican and white organizations when he was murdered. With the help of the Church Committee revelations, the lawyers at the People's Law Office in Chicago, through years of work, were getting closer to proving that the Chicago police and the FBI, using a paid informant, had assassinated Hampton.

Now these Piedmont activists, having surmounted personal fears and biases to come together, faced a bigger question: How could they bring white and Black workers together in common cause? The roots of these tensions, as for so many ingrained reflexes of the American social and economic reality, reached back to slavery and the Civil War. Frederick Douglass noted the distrust between enslaved Blacks and poor whites who'd earned a meager living as overseers and slave catchers. In America's Civil War, Karl Marx envisioned a global victory for both the enslaved and working white people, who would no longer have to compete with slave labor. Writing to President Lincoln on his second inauguration, Marx announced that the "American Antislavery War" would usher in a "new era of ascendancy" for the "working classes" around the world.[15] It didn't happen. Looking back at the Reconstruction period, W. E. B. Du Bois lamented that the post–Civil War "dictatorship backed by the military men of the United States" over the "Southern states" had not lasted long enough to shift the "balance of power" to the "the freedmen and poor whites." The "organized wealthy," Du Bois argued, reasserted their interests, and the racial hierarchies snapped back into place, enforced by Black Codes, Jim Crow laws, and the terror of the Ku Klux Klan.[16] The final vestige of Reconstruction had been stomped out in Wilmington, North Carolina, in 1898, when Southern Democrats staged a bloody coup, interrupting the growth of a "fusionist" party that included both Blacks and whites.

After 1898, Southern Democrats established a system of one-party, white rule in North Carolina that would last inviolate for seventy years, until Henry Frye's election in 1968 as a Black man and Jesse Helms's in 1972 as a Republican. Both Greensboro's Mayor Jim Melvin and North Carolina's Governor Jim Hunt descended from this line of Southern Democrats.[17] It wasn't only Blacks who learned a lesson. Poor whites understood the danger of mixing politics and race and tried to guard the scraps of privilege and low-paying industrial jobs kept open to them at the expense of their Black neighbors. In these divisions, Du Bois identified the failure of the "whole theory of American government." While abolitionists and northerners bemoaned the plight of the Negro, Du Bois noted, the "white work-ers in the South" constituted a "forgotten mass of men."[18]

One could see these dynamics at play in nearly any town around North Carolina. There were the haves and the have-nots, the busi-nessmen and the laborers. The farmers who grew the tobacco didn't trust the buyers. The lintheads working in the mills chafed at the mill owners' paternalism, which might provide them a place to live but left them in hock to the company store, just like sharecroppers. The owners hired just enough people to keep the social order clack-ing along the rails. Burley Mitchell, Governor Hunt's secretary of crime control and public safety, remembered during his youth how "whenever people got hot" the powerful men in any North Carolina town would play the poor whites against the Blacks. The people with the money didn't want things to change in Kannapolis or Burlington or Greensboro. They didn't want to have to pay their maids, the to-bacco farmers, or the lintheads any more than they had to.[19]

These were dynamics that the North Carolina Fund and the Foundation for Community Development had been founded to ad-dress, before unleashing an overwhelming backlash. The members of the WVO's new North Carolina chapter understood the politics. They would focus their efforts both on building interracial unions in the textile mills and on community organizing around racial justice issues. And as they did the grassroots work, they planned to teach communist ideas.

With the steady stream of revelations about the country's intelli-gence agencies, Nelson and his comrades assumed that the FBI and police would haunt them and hunt them. They kept their local WVO chapter membership small, never more than about fifty trusted indi-viduals. They discussed sensitive issues on pay phones. The work would be supported, not by foundation or government grants, but by what they could earn in factory jobs, as moonlighting doctors, or in the white-collar jobs some members kept. Joyce's steady position at the Transportation Institute at A&T, for example, would continue to be critical. Word crackled through the ALSC/YOBU grapevine about

Nelson's new campaign, and people in cities around the country joined up.

Indeed, the FBI had been tracking Nelson's movements for a long time, having years earlier placed him in the Administrative Index (ADEX, formerly the Security Index) of subversives the Feds marked for arrest at the outset of any national security crisis. When agents attempted to interview Nelson in 1971, ostensibly to recruit him as an informant, he'd been, in Bureau language, "uncooperative." In 1976, Clarence Kelley renewed the authority to continue monitoring Nelson's movements in the community and at his job at the Cone Mills Proximity plant in Greensboro, where his presence put mill management on edge. The updated FBI file tagged him as "potentially dangerous because of background, emotional instability or activity in groups inimical to the U.S." The report justified the surveillance by labeling Nelson "ARMED AND DANGEROUS" and "in possession of multiple weapons."[20]

Nelson and Joyce's abode again became a hub of activity, as it had been in the late 1960s and early 1970s. Joyce learned not to stock too many groceries; comrades could devour a week's worth of groceries in a single evening. Even so, cheese toast greeted visitors in the morning—courtesy of Nelson—and vats of Joyce's famous pasta warmed their bellies at night. This was collard greens and pork chops communism, informed by the ideals of the Declaration of Independence and the songs of Sam Cooke, Otis Redding, Pete Seeger, and Sweet Honey in the Rock. It was, Nelson thought, the beginning of a beautiful period in his life, as he and his new allies agreed to take up the "smallest daily work with a sense of urgency, with a strong determination to cast aside all that stands in the way." Nelson and Joyce's daughters, Ayo and Akua, had an ever-expanding, extended roster of aunties and uncles who were Black, white, Jewish, Asian, Native American, and Latino.[21]

LABOR

It drove Joyce crazy that Nelson would fork over cash to any comrade or worker going through a tough spot.

It wasn't as if they had money to burn, with two growing girls and what they invested in the organizing work: the gas to drive all around the Piedmont, the supplies for marches and picket lines, the meals for the insatiable people strategizing and theorizing at their home.[1]

As she guarded the family bank account and insisted that Nelson share domestic duties, Joyce protected her marriage fiercely, holding open space to raise a family amid the busy, public life they'd chosen. Given the risks associated with being a militant Black activist in the United States, close friends doubted that Nelson would have been alive if it weren't for the love and tempering pragmatism Joyce brought to their relationship and their shared struggle in the world. She did what she could to protect her husband both from the forces arrayed against their political work and his own willingness to risk his safety for the struggle.[2]

The energized WVO activists seemed to be everywhere at once in North Carolina. "Things are heating up," Nelson liked to say, feeling the organizing energy and focus of 1969 and 1970 returning. They faced off against Governor Hunt's effort to introduce standardized testing into the school system, arguing that it would relegate Black and poor kids to a menial existence, locked too early in their lives beyond reach of a ladder to better jobs and the middle class. They led a rally of 3,500 marchers through Raleigh in support of the Wilmington Ten, who, when they came to the aid of bullied and abused Black students desegregating the coastal city's schools, had been railroaded through the North Carolina courts and into prison on manufactured evidence. Meanwhile, the white supremacists who instigated and escalated the violence in Wilmington had still never been arrested. In an attempt at compromise between brazen judicial corruption and the racial attitudes of his white constituents, Governor Hunt reduced the activists' prison sentences. "A slap in the face," Joyce Johnson called it in a public letter, "to all the freedom loving people, especially Black people who are the main victims of the North Carolina 'justice' system."[3]

In 1977, the WVO descended on the tiny eastern North Carolina town of Whitakers, less than thirty miles from where Nelson had grown up. They were there to seek justice in the case of Charlie Lee, a Black man who'd been shot dead by a white store owner for demanding correct change. Nelson sent Paul Bermanzohn to organize the community around Lee's murder. Paul slept on the floor at the home of Lee's widow, Leola, for months, relishing her country cooking and adapting to the backyard outhouse. His stories about growing up as the only son of Holocaust survivors helped build trust in the Black community, but it took a disco rally and other creative tactics to build a movement. Soon Black Whitakers residents were marching with Leola and Paul around the county courthouse chanting "Socialist revolution is the only solution," a scene nearly as foreign to the agricultural Black Belt as the landing of an alien spaceship. The effort culminated in an elaborate community theater performance. Joyce Johnson presided over a people's court. Appointed citizen-prosecutors presented evidence. Others prepared the defense of the store owner, Joe Judge. The community solemnly and unanimously convicted Joe Judge, law enforcement officials, and others for murder and conspiracy to avoid justice.[4]

The theater worked.

Shamed by the public attention, the state bent to the community's demands and charged the racist store owner with second-degree murder. After a plea bargain, Joe Judge agreed to ten years' probation and was forced to pay $25,000 in restitution to Charlie Lee's widow, though he never served a day in jail.[5]

When it was all over, Paul and Sally named their first daughter after Leola: *loyal and faithful as a lion*. Marriage and parenthood were becoming part of the revolution.

While all the campaigns to disrupt the social and political status quo were important, the work to organize the Piedmont mill workers who fueled the region's economic order became the central project of the WVO.

Two Jewish brothers, Moses and Caesar Cone, had arrived in Greensboro from Baltimore and built their first cotton mill on the outskirts of the city in 1895, calling it Proximity because it stood close to the cotton fields. Ten thousand people lived in Greensboro in 1900. In 1905, the Cones opened the White Oak plant to produce denim. Ten years later, White Oak became Levi Strauss & Company's primary supplier, a collaboration that produced sturdy blue jeans for more than a century. The mills boomed. A local pharmacist invented Vicks VapoRub, for which demand exploded during the 1918 Spanish influenza outbreak. The Jefferson Standard Life Insurance Company built its impressive headquarters downtown, and banks formed to support the burgeoning businesses.[6]

By 1930, nearly a third of the city's more than fifty thousand residents lived in mill villages built by the Cones. These communities had their own grocery stores, schools, a dairy, and a butcher. The mill owners sold tenants coal and wood to heat their houses and helped build churches and lay out ball fields. The Negro "mill laborers" lived in East White Oak, the smallest of the Cones' five mill villages. The houses were a bit smaller, a bit closer together. And the men who left those houses to work in the mills were the industry's lowest-paid laborers, performing the most backbreaking, dirty, outdoor work.[7]

The Cone family, like other mill owners around the South, had created their own private city where every inhabitant lived in houses owned by Cone, ate Cone-supplied food, shopped in Cone stores, and accepted Cone discipline. Until the 1940s, the Cone Mills Corporation maintained its own police force, separate from Greensboro's. If the workers had elected the mill owners to operate the community and had shared equally in the company profits, the mills and villages might have looked like an advanced form of socialism. Instead, they constituted a vast industrial plantation, with the big houses located in opulent Irving Park a couple of miles away.

The mills—and the cheap labor that operated them—were the engine of the city's revenue and explosive growth; for the next thirty years, Greensboro's city leaders, its resident titans of industry, believed that theirs could be the most powerful metropolis in the state. Predictability and stability are the friends of businessmen who work to control the operating variables and make accurate predictions based on inputs and outputs, wages and sales. But social disruption began with the 1954 Supreme Court decision in *Brown v. Board of Education of Topeka*, which held that segregation in public schools was unconstitutional. In response, leading Greensboro bankers and executives formed a group they named the White Patriots of North Carolina. The Cones, being Jewish, were not invited to be members of the White Patriots, but statewide membership surged into the tens of thousands and included politicians, judges, and eugenicists. The White Patriots didn't wear hoods or burn crosses, but they were dead set against school integration and the "mongrelization" of the races, both of which might trouble the caste labor system that kept wages low and profits high.[8]

For nearly two decades, the White Patriots led the resistance that prevented meaningful integration in North Carolina. But by 1960, city leaders were forced to adjust their business aspirations and social expectations. In 1959, Research Triangle Park, situated between Raleigh and Durham to the east of Greensboro, began attracting innovative businesses in an effort to help the state evolve away from its economic reliance on textiles, tobacco, and furniture manufacturing. In 1960, as the sit-in movement paralyzed downtown Greensboro, the Charlotte-based American Commercial Bank merged with Greensboro's Security National Bank. The newly named North Carolina National Bank moved its operations to Charlotte, leaving Greensboro without a prominent banking business headquarters. (NCNB would become Bank of America in 1998.)

The textile industry was transforming, too. Apparel brands such as Levi Strauss were siphoning power away from the manufacturers. And when retail brands such as Gap entered the market in the late 1960s and early 1970s, Cone Mills felt the squeeze. While the Civil Rights Acts and subsequent lawsuits challenging unequal hiring practices (including one against Cone Mills in 1969) cracked open employment opportunities for Black people at the mills, the economics of the business were changing. Shirts could be assembled in Asia for a fraction of the cost of making them in North Carolina. Jeans were stitched together in northern Mexico by workers earning 10 percent of what it cost to employ an underpaid American worker. Greensboro, home to four Fortune 500 companies in the late 1960s, wouldn't have a single one twenty years later.[9]

When the WVO began sending organizers into the textile factories in 1977, however, Cone Mills—number 350 on the Fortune 500 list—still employed more than fourteen thousand workers. Despite the uncertainty looming just over the horizon, Cone Mills' power hadn't ebbed at home; the mills churned out fabric and netted impressive profits. The influence the Cones and other industry bosses exercised from their Irving Park redoubt included major philanthropic projects; they built hospitals and funded various social programs. And when they needed help from the city, they communicated their wishes through informal channels. Greensboro's titans of business weren't going to be found lining up at the microphone during the public comments slot at the city council meeting. Most days, business and city leaders would cross paths at a country club cocktail party, a Jaycees meeting, or on the links. The clean smell of gin and fresh-cut grass lay little more than a chip shot from the lint-filled air and sweltering industrial cacophony of the mills. And in these exclusive rooms there was always an opportunity to drop a gripe, express a wish, or compare notes on a problem the city leaders and mill owners were dealing with.[10]

A strong union presence in the mills would shift the balance of power from what had existed since the Cones began to build their empire in the North Carolina foothills. There'd been little union-building success among the Piedmont mills in the past. Throughout the country, only workers in South Carolina were less likely than those in North Carolina to be members of unions.[11] Sandi Smith, who'd renewed her friendship with Joyce and joined the WVO, took a job at Revolution Mill, which had never hosted a union. At the White Oak plant, a subdued Amalgamated Clothing and Textile Workers Union (ACTWU) counted about thirty dues-paying members among the two thousand employees when Bill Sampson started working in the dye shop. And about twenty miles east of Greensboro in Haw River, at the Cones' corduroy-producing Granite Finishing plant, another weak local of the ACTWU counted a dozen members among six hundred employees. As with the local at White Oak, no effort had been made to grow the membership of the Granite Finishing's local or to increase its power in years.

The WVO activists remained undaunted. When Jim Waller showed up at the Granite Finishing plant with his big beard, strange accent, and lunch box packed with fresh fruit and tofu sandwiches, he knew he wouldn't earn the trust of the other workers overnight. When she was growing up, Sandi Smith's father had worked in a textile mill in South Carolina, and despite her Bennett education, Sandi hadn't forgotten her roots. She sounded like one of the workers and could talk directly with the female workers about the challenges of balancing work and family. And Bill Sampson, despite his lofty Sorbonne, Harvard, and University of Virginia education, had southern roots and an easygoing manner that drew other workers to him.[12]

For the next two years, working side by side with the doffers, cutters, beamers, carders, pickers, combers, rovers, forklift operators, and dyehouse workers, the WVO members put constant pressure on the mill management. At White Oak and Granite Finishing, where a union contract between Cone Mills and the ACTWU existed, the WVO members filed a steady flow of grievances on behalf of workers unjustly fired, for sick workers, and against pressure from supervisors to work at an unsafe pace. They won these grievances, forcing the mills to rein in aggressive supervisors and rehire dismissed workers with back pay. The small victories added up to a big lesson that the workers understood: unity equaled strength, and the bigger the union got, the more strength the workers would have.

By the end of 1977, Cone Mills owners and management knew that they were up against a smart, energetic, and increasingly organized force intent on changing the dynamics of their business. They cut jobs, eliminating whole union-infiltrated divisions at some of their mills, and sent a letter to every employee at the White Oak plant warning them that a "small group of radical employees is threatening your job security."[13] They wanted workers to know that joining the union fight came with risk. The mills hired private investigators and off-duty cops to photograph the agitators, take down license plate numbers, and pass this information along to the Greensboro Police Department.[14]

Cone Mills may have given up operating its own police force in the 1940s, but the company carefully cultivated relationships at the GPD and in city government and expected special treatment.[15] At their request, the GPD's Criminal Investigations Division stepped up its surveillance of the WVO, assigning Detective Jerry "Rooster" Cooper to keep an eye on communists in the mills. When a mill supervisor ordered Bill Sampson to leave a meeting and Bill refused, Greensboro police arrested Bill for trespassing. A judge threw the case out. The union filed a grievance, and Bill went right back to work at the mill. The goal, Bill told the workers, was to renegotiate a contract that included better pay, pensions, and safer worker conditions, which meant, among other things, filtering the cotton dust from the factory air, which afflicted the workers with brown lung disease, or byssinosis.

With no existing union contract to buttress her work at Revolution Mill, Sandi did everything she could to build support for a union within the plant. She and fellow organizers worked tirelessly, passing out flyers, holding rallies, and calling out rampant and crude sexual harassment inside the plant. For most of 1977 and into 1978, momentum grew. Once she had the numbers to support a union vote, she would still have to convince the ACTWU to join the organized workers. But the ACTWU refused to support Sandi's Revolutionary Organizing Committee. When five critical union organizers were fired, the movement stalled. "The major criticism of the organizing group from *both Cone and the union* [emphasis added] centers around the ideology of the organizing group," the *Greensboro Daily News* reported. "A number of its members admit freely they are communists, others are socialists, and others say they just want to organize a union."[16]

The specter of communism obscured the progress the organizers had made. Seeing the workers acting together and sticking up for one another scared the mill owners. The warnings of a red menace were convenient and compelling in a culture shaped by Cold War fears and molded by the House Un-American Activities Committee, J. Edgar Hoover, Senator Joe McCarthy, Jesse Helms, and other conservative politicians in North Carolina and around the country.

Twenty miles from Greensboro, out at the Granite Finishing plant in Haw River, Jim Waller slowly overcame the suspicion of his fellow workers. When Jim passed out flyers outlining the plight of the Wilmington Ten, a white union member called him a "n—— lover" and told him he'd better watch his back. White and Black workers ate lunch separately at the plant and didn't socialize. Jim suspected that there were Klansmen working at Haw River, patrolling the race line. But to whomever would listen, he calmly and relentlessly repeated what he believed: in a plant whose workers were 60 percent white and 40 percent Black, they couldn't win important concessions from Cone if they remained divided. As Jim stepped in to offer assistance with their problems, workers started to bypass the union president and come to him with their grievances. They'd called him Wolfman when he first arrived but soon, out of respect, changed his nickname to Blackbeard.[17]

By the summer of 1978, when the company announced another wage reduction at Haw River, the results of Jim's steady advocacy led a hundred workers, Black and white, to crowd into the musty union hall across the street from the mill. Their paychecks plummeted as inflation moved above 12 percent. As it was, the mill job didn't pay enough to support a family. They were sliding backward. After a long discussion, the workers decided to walk off the job. It would be a wildcat strike, one unauthorized by the national ACTWU. They would be out on their own.[18]

That night, the second shift workers ran out of the plant, hollering "Shut her down!" to the third shift workers arriving in their cars. For a few remarkable days, the plant sat idle. Tractor trailers carrying cloth to be cut into corduroy were turned away, and no finished corduroy left the plant. Black and white workers picketed together. Sally Bermanzohn and others organized day care for children at the union hall. People brought food and water to the picketers. Longshoremen, sanitation workers, and other union laborers rolled in from around the state, donated to the strike fund, and spent a few hours walking the picket line in solidarity with the mill hands.[19]

The company fought back. An injunction limited the number of strikers who could stand by the gate to the mill and where they could walk or park. When a strike breaker nearly drove his car into the picket line, the local sheriff stood by unconcerned.[20]

After a few days, the prospect of losing a paycheck or, worse, their jobs caused commitment to the strike to wobble. Jim called a meeting, and after a long and heated discussion, the strikers decided to retreat rather than lose. During the strike, the union had grown to two hundred Black and white dues-paying members, nearly a third of the entire mill. They could go back to their jobs now, keep building the union, and prepare for the next fight.

Then the Granite Finishing plant fired Jim for omitting his medical degree from his job application. A few months later, the ACTWU placed the White Oak and Granite Finishing locals under administratorship, which meant that they'd be run from headquarters. The powers of the locally elected union leaders were stripped, in what seemed to be a coordinated effort between the ACTWU and the mills to reduce the influence of the WVO. The mill owners, rattled by global economics and paranoid about the prospect of strong unions, couldn't control workers by bolting machine guns to the roofs of the mills, as they'd done in the 1930s. It had taken a year and a half and collaborations with national union leadership and local police, but they'd finally managed to interrupt the WVO's union drives.[21]

During the wildcat strike at the Granite Finishing plant, Sally had paused to talk with a young white mill worker. He'd told her a bit about his life and the fact that he had a four-year-old son. "Why don't you bring him to the strike?" Sally asked. "I can't do that," the man replied, looking around to see whether any of his Black colleagues were listening. "Every other word out of his mouth is *n——*." The changes taking place inside this man and others had not yet made their way home and were a stark reminder of the ongoing tension between class interests and racial attitudes. Even so, some said that after the strike had ended and Jim had been fired, Black and white workers now sat together in the mess hall. They'd learned something on the picket line.[22]

But the Granite Finishing plant was just one small mill and, as Nelson and Joyce and their comrades knew, the race problem in North Carolina ran deeper than the shallow Haw River. Powerful forces kept stirring it up. With the union organizing efforts stalled in 1978, Sandi Smith wondered, with a combination of bitterness and despair, "How can we organize a revolution, if we can't even organize one textile mill?"

The WVO members faced a critical choice. They could keep organizing around issues of health and safety, wages, work hours, and the right to strike, or they could use the respect they'd earned in the mills to call for communist revolution.

Jim Waller believed that the WVO should build a union and replace the ACTWU. Nelson's instinct told him to stay focused on the organizing, to build a base of power between the community and the workers, the strategy that had been so effective during the cafeteria workers' struggle in 1969 and the AAA Realty and Skilcraft fights in 1970.

As the WVO members in Greensboro studied how they might get back into the mills, the direction came down from Jerry Tung in New York to seize every opportunity to instruct the mill workers on the benefits of communism and the need for revolution. Democratic centralism, a core tenet of communist organizing, meant once the line was set, every member would cast aside individual opinions and doubts and throw in with the collective will—as it had been defined by leadership. Though Nelson would have given priority to organizing over ideology, as a committed WVO member, he would follow Tung's direction.[23]

❖

After the groundbreaking but incomplete work of 1977 and 1978, a series of strange events occurred as the North Carolina WVO entered this period of recalibration. A man from a different communist organization berated Signe Waller and punched her in the eye while she passed out literature in front of the White Oak plant. Over the coming months, the Revolutionary Communist Party (RCP) instigated other fights with the WVO, apparently to recruit workers to their group by demonstrating superior toughness.[24]

Members of a fringe group led by Lyndon LaRouche called the National Caucus of Labor Committees passed out flyers at Cone's

White Oak Mill accusing Nelson Johnson of working undercover for the CIA.[25]

During the early summer of 1979, Nelson and a WVO comrade attended the biweekly Greensboro City Council meeting. When the councilors finished with the business on their agenda—the impact of zoning issues on city neighborhoods, noise ordinances, the need for water and sewer improvements along various streets—a white WVO member named Ed Butler stood to complain about an interaction with the Greensboro Police Department on the night of June 7. He'd been home with his family when a man he didn't know knocked on the door and then left. A short time later, the police burst into Butler's house with their guns drawn and proceeded to ransack the home, claiming they were searching for a fugitive. Did they have a warrant? Butler asked. No. Were they going to search his neighbor's house, too? That wouldn't be necessary. It was harassment, plain and simple, Butler told the city council, retaliation for the union drive at Cone Mills. Nelson then spoke in support of Butler, advising that people doing organizing work could expect to be "politically harassed" by the police.

These are serious charges, responded Mayor Jim Melvin. Take them up, he recommended, with the city manager, the public safety director, and the chief of police, Ed Swing.[26]

Jim Melvin lingered in the room near Martha Woodall, a young journalist who'd come south from Northampton, Massachusetts, the previous fall to take a job at the *Greensboro Record*, as she sat writing up her notes.

"You know who that is," Melvin said, gesturing toward a now-empty seat in the galley. "That's Nelson Johnson. He's a dangerous man." He was, the mayor confided, "the most dangerous man in Greensboro."[27] Perhaps Melvin recalled the middle-of-the-night meeting in May 1969 as Greensboro teetered toward violence—or the 1970 AAA Realty rent strike. Likely he thought about the organizing in the mills, the frequent accusations of police brutality, and Nelson's interference with the smooth and efficient city operation in which Melvin took great pride.

Woodall, a newcomer to the city, hadn't known who Nelson was. The man she'd seen speak that afternoon had impressed her as smart, passionate, and very political. Melvin, meanwhile, casually offered her a little insider context for the brief exchange she'd just witnessed and, perhaps, for any future events she might cover involving Nelson. Political repression, some would say of the exchange, telegraphs its punches.[28]

"Be bold, comrade, be bold," WVO members encouraged one another, embracing their right to self-defense. They practiced martial arts moves and, every week or two, would drive to remote sandlots to blast away at cans and bottles with a haphazard assortment of firearms.[29]

CHINA GROVE

In early 1979, the Winston-Salem public library allowed local Klansmen to mount an exhibit featuring Klan-robed mannequins, Confederate flags, and photographs of prominent Klansmen, including the
rising Louisiana politician David Duke and nineteenth-century Klan
founder Nathan Bedford Forrest. What happened next would make
the national news. One hundred and fifty people packed into the library basement for the opening of the exhibit. A Black attendee asked
Klansman Gorrell Pierce what he thought of Black people. The Klansman replied, "I have no animosity towards Black people, as long as
they're on their side of the street and I'm on my side of the street."

"Rip this stuff off the walls!" someone yelled.

"White power!" came the shouted reply.

The giant Roland Wayne Wood, who'd left the Klan to become a
Nazi, announced he would "kill all n——s and Jews if they interfere
with the Klan."[1] A moment later, a half dozen uniformed Nazis,
swastikas on full display, burst into the room, jacked their arms into
a salute, and shouted "Sieg heil!" Policemen rushed in behind the
Nazis, and in the officers' wake appeared picketers from the local
NAACP branch chanting, "Nazis and Klan are the scum of the land."
A few punches landed before the police restored order. The next day,
the library "discovered" a fire hazard that forced it to close the exhibit
indefinitely.[2]

For those who studied the ebbs and flows of white supremacy, what happened at the library seemed less like a Mel Brooks comedy skit and more like evidence of increasing racial violence around the South and of a growing public Klan presence.

The Anti-Defamation League reported that Klan membership around the South surged 25 percent between 1978 and 1979. Klansmen in Kentucky had been arrested for plotting to murder public officials. Demonstrators leaving a civil rights march in Tupelo, Mississippi, were pulled from their cars and beaten by Klansmen in December 1978. And in Decatur, Alabama, when a preacher spoke out against the wrongful conviction of Tommy Lee Hines, a mentally disabled Black man, Klansmen dragged him into the woods and beat him.[3]

Joseph Lowery, who'd succeeded Ralph Abernathy as the leader of the Southern Christian Leadership Conference and grew up in Huntsville across the Tennessee River from Decatur, organized a march to protest Tommy Lee Hines's thirty-year prison sentence for raping three white women, a crime experts deemed him incapable of committing.[4] On May 26, 1979, seventy-five marchers followed Dr. Lowery through Decatur toward a wall of more than one hundred robed Klansmen ready to "defend the justice system" with axe handles, clubs, and chains. As the two sides approached, a Klansman shouted, "N——, that's as far as you go." The marchers announced that they would keep going and asked the Klan to "please" clear the way. When one marcher tried to move around the line of Klansmen, the white supremacists grabbed him. A Black man fired a gun, and a Klansman fell. Suddenly bullets thrashed the air, felling two Klansmen and two Black protesters. Perhaps a dozen more were bloodied and bashed in the panicked brawl.[5]

❖

When Lowery prepared to march again, two weeks later, Nelson and Sally and Paul Bermanzohn drove nine hours from the North Carolina Piedmont, arriving at 3 a.m. in a Black Decatur neighborhood locked down by armed guards. Five hundred law enforcement officers stood ready to keep the 150 Klansmen and 1,500 civil rights demonstrators apart. At a church meeting prior to the march, WVO members argued that marchers should arm themselves. The SCLC leadership remained unyielding in its commitment to nonviolence, explaining that carrying guns on a route lined with rooftop snipers and state police would only increase the danger. As the leaders of the march sang "We Shall Overcome," the WVO led provocative chants of a different tenor: "We're fired up, we're gonna smash the Klan." Even so, the event ended without violence.[6]

Tommy Lee Hines's conviction would eventually be overturned by the Alabama Court of Criminal Appeals, releasing him to live out his days in a residential home, where he died in 2020. However, an all-white jury rejected the claim of self-defense by the Black man who'd shot the Klansman on May 26, convicting him of "assault with intent to murder."[7] No Klansmen were held responsible for the wounded Black protesters.

❖

Three weeks after the Decatur march, Sally, Paul, and Nelson were meeting in Signe and Jim's Cypress Street backyard when Signe emerged from the house carrying a pitcher of lemonade and the newspaper. She pointed out a small notice she'd happened upon, announcing that the Klan planned to screen *Birth of a Nation* in the China Grove community center on July 8.[8]

Sixty miles to the southwest of Greensboro, China Grove sat next door to Kannapolis, home to the JP Stevens mill where Sandi Smith hoped to get a job and restart a union drive. As they sipped their cool drinks in the summer heat, the four activists talked about the Klan and the covert role they believed the white supremacists played in impeding their organizing in the textile mills. They suspected, too, that mill management had encouraged the working-class white supremacists to undermine their organizing.[9] Sally, Paul, and Nelson had witnessed the Klan in action in Decatur, and they'd all read the news about the uproar at the library in nearby Winston-Salem. Confronting the Klan in China Grove, they now agreed, offered an opportunity to prepare the ground for Sandi's organizing in Kannapolis and to set the WVO apart from rival groups such as the RCP, while asserting the bold, communist leadership that Jerry Tung called for.

❖

On a scouting trip to China Grove, Nelson found an anxious Black community divided between an older generation afraid of stirring up trouble and young militants. The younger group, led by a local man named Paul Luckey, threatened to blow up the community center during the film screening. Nelson listened and, attempting to focus the raw energy, instead suggested a march to interrupt the Klan's recruiting event. Most community members readily agreed to Nelson's plan. Something about Luckey's violent talk made Nelson uncomfortable, perhaps reminding him of the possible FBI provocateur Nunding ten years earlier. Little did he know that his suspicions were well founded.[10]

Luckey secretly met with China Grove's mayor and police chief to complain that communists were organizing the response to the Klan meeting. He accused Nelson of advocating bank robberies and promising riches to the people in the community. The chief made urgent calls to the North Carolina Highway Patrol and the State Bureau of Investigation, putting them on alert. And someone in the tiny China Grove police force called the Klan to warn them of the gathering protest, agreeing to "look the other way" if the Klan had to defend themselves.[11]

On July 8, Nelson and Joyce dropped their girls at the home of friends and drove with fifty adrenaline-filled WVO members from the Piedmont to China Grove. Earlier that day, in a quiet moment before they left, Signe had confided her fears to Jim. We could end up in jail, she'd said, "or in the hospital, or worse." Jim agreed, making no attempt to soothe her anxiety, saying only that their boldness would serve to protect others from Klan "horrors."[12]

❖

Beside the deep fear of the Klan lay a parallel and persistent popular image of cowards hiding under sheets who committed their crimes in the dark and avoided open confrontation. One particular story burnished the belief in Klan cowardice. In early 1958, near North Carolina's border with South Carolina, the Robeson County Klan planned a late-night rally. They'd been terrorizing the local Lumbee Native American tribe as well as the area's Black residents and, despite the local mayor's opposition to them, were flexing resistance to school integration in the wake of the *Brown v. Board of Education* decision. The January 18 rally would "put the Indians in their place" and "end race mixing," announced the local Klan leader, Jim "Catfish" Cole. About one hundred Klansmen gathered in a field, under a single electric bulb running off a generator. In the darkness beyond, invisible to the tight gathering of Klansmen, hundreds of Lumbee men waited for the right moment. Then they charged, whooping, shooting out the single bulb, sending the white supremacists scurrying to their cars and hightailing away, raising dust as they fled down the dirt roads they'd rode in on. No one was killed, but the message traveled. For a *Life* magazine account of the event, one Lumbee participant, who'd been a flight engineer on a World War II bomber, posed wrapped in a Klan flag, his wide grin a relief to readers who wished to relegate the Klan to the past, a nightmare reduced to a bad joke.[13] In the 1940s, the historian V. O. Key had called the Klan a "dying movement in which southerners take no pride."[14] The Lumbee victory appeared to support Key's analysis. The Klan, by most accounts, never held another public meeting in Robeson County. Even so, membership surged throughout North Carolina during the 1960s and again in the late 1970s.[15] As Cecil Moses and the FBI well knew and despite their efforts, violent white supremacy in America could not be shamed out of existence.

Twenty-one years after the rout by the Lumbees, Nelson stepped forward to lead one hundred marchers east from China Grove's Westside Black neighborhood. More than half the marchers were local; the rest had arrived that morning from out of town. Across town, Klan members, together with their wives and children and a few potential recruits, were gathering to watch *Birth of a Nation*. As the Lumbee had done in Robeson County, Nelson, his comrades, and

China Grove's Black residents hoped to bury the Klan in public humiliation. Many carried bats and clubs. Some held broken bottles. A
few wore old football helmets, and various hard hats, and wrapped
their forearms in towels to cushion blows if they had to fight. Nelson
had insisted that the march be nonviolent but that people be prepared
to defend themselves. Long guns were left locked in cars, but a small
number of marchers tucked pistols into their pockets should the need
for them arise. "Decease, decease, decease the rotten beast," they
chanted as they walked through downtown China Grove, deserted
but for a few policemen. "Death to the Klan," they hollered, a chant
becoming popular around the South and that they'd first heard at
the march in Decatur, Alabama.[16]

The group passed the center of town and came upon a police car
parked at a fork in the road. It was hot, and as the noonday sun beat
down, they paused, teetering for a moment between their identities as
individual, everyday citizens who would stop when a policeman tells
them to stop, and the militant, outraged group, ready to blow down an
empty one-way street like a tornado, intent on reducing an unjust past
to rubble. "A fucking one-way sign is going to stop the revolution?"
Paul Bermanzohn hollered from the rear of the group. They started up
again, came around the edge of a copse of trees, and suddenly saw, fifty
feet away, a little brick community building squatting in a field.[17]

A dozen men stood on the porch below the Confederate flag
they'd hung that morning. They'd heard the swell of chants moving
toward them before they could see the mass of people. When the
raucous voices reached their ears, "Decease, Decease . . ." and "Death
to the Klan," a few of them ran to their cars, pulled out weapons, and
hurried back to the porch. It's like, thought the Klansman Gorrell
Pierce, "you're in the Alamo and you look out and see all of Santa
Anna's army coming." "Hitler was right, Hitler was right," the men
on the porch screamed back at the approaching throng. "White
power!" they hollered, quoting the shirt that Roland Wayne Wood
wore as he waved a .357 Magnum in the air. Others clutched shotguns or pistols, and one held an automatic rifle.[18]

The protesters rushed to the edge of the porch. Three terrified young policemen and a flimsy row of wooden balusters separated the Klansmen and the demonstrators, who banged sticks on the porch rail and hurled raging shouts at the armed men.

We are lined up, Gorrell Pierce thought, like the Confederate and Union Armies. He could feel the breath of the protesters on his face. On the other side of the porch, men and women imagined beating back the Redeemers after Reconstruction to prevent Jim Crow from ever sinking its roots into southern soil, killing Nazis before they could murder their Jewish relatives, and stepping in front of every Black man the Klan ever came for. Above the tumult, Willena Cannon could hear the lynching she'd witnessed as a girl, the dying man's screams mingling with the smoke of the burning barn as the local sheriff turned his back and walked away.[19]

Nelson sprinted back and forth through the crowd, checking on people, steeling their nerves, leading the chants. The frenzy mounted. The Klansmen cocked their guns. Hands clutched clubs and bottles and sticks. Under a hot blue sky, in a dry field, surrounded by pine trees, at the edge of a rickety porch, "time was hammered flat," Signe felt, as history converged on a present moment.

A policeman whispered in Gorrell Pierce's ear. Pierce nodded, turned, and suddenly ushered Jerry Paul Smith, Raeford Milano Caudle, and the other men back into the community center. Roland Wayne Wood tried to push himself out the door again, but someone grabbed him by the belt and yanked him back. They were a firecracker away from a bloodbath, Pierce thought.[20]

The demonstrators hooted victory. They'd backed the Klan down. To mark the victory, they ripped down the Confederate flag from the community center and burned it, marched around the building, and then headed back to the Westside. They'd faced down their fears. The white supremacists on the porch may have been the objects of their fear, but their own bodies were its vessels, carrying trauma encoded in cells and synapses and passed along through the generations. One Black woman, exhilarated by the cathartic energy flowing through her body, said simply: "I wish my grandmother was here."[21]

After they'd left and the Klansmen and Nazis stepped back onto the quiet porch, Klan leader Joe Grady said, "I'll get revenge for this."[22]

As evening fell in Westside, someone handed Joyce a rifle and told her to stand guard at one of the roads entering the Black neighborhood. For the next few nights, no one unknown or white was allowed in.[23]

❖

While Nelson believed nothing terrible could have happened while the policemen were present, others felt they'd barely escaped death. "I don't regret none of that," one marcher would say later, "but we could have been killed right there. If you are going to die, die doing something the best you can do."[24]

❖

A few days after China Grove, Nelson and Sally Bermanzohn, then the regional secretary for the WVO, drove to New York to debrief with Jerry Tung. As the group discussed how to follow up the China Grove demonstration, Sally demurred, telling Jerry that confronting the Klan again would be a mistake. Jerry berated her, calling China Grove a "shining example" of bold, revolutionary leadership. No one in the room said a word, not even Nelson. After the meeting in New York, Sally kept her worries to herself, and the CWP exclaimed how the "force of militant, armed and organized fighters, fighting in the people's interest" had affirmed "THE CORRECTNESS OF HOW TO FIGHT THE KLAN AS SHOWN BY CHINA GROVE!!!"[25]

❖

Nelson suggested that the next step in the anti-Klan campaign should be a march and a conference for mill hands in Greensboro to discuss how, for more than a hundred years, the Klan had been used by industrialists to keep Black and white workers apart.

The new direction, however, might have been seen to contradict the compelling argument Jerry Tung had made about the Boston bus boycott three years earlier during his debate with Howard Fuller. If the Klan weren't the root but rather a symptom of pervasive racism, and the goal was to unite the working class across race, what could be gained by emphasizing racial discord between its white and Black members? If the poor Klansmen were mere pawns of the capitalists, as the WVO propaganda claimed, perhaps they represented a diversion. "This is crazy. This is really off the wall," said the doctor and WVO ally Mike Nathan when he learned of the proposed anti-Klan march.[26] Mike Nathan and Sally Bermanzohn and a few others believed the focus should remain on the powerful forces arrayed against them: the mill owners, the politicians, and law enforcement. Amílcar Cabral, the African leader who'd been assassinated shortly after his visit to the United States in 1972, when Nelson and Joyce handed him a check, likely would have agreed that they were beginning to chase shadows.

On October 4, three months after China Grove, the WVO, soon to become the CWP, publicly announced its Anti-Klan March and Conference. An internal CWP document captured the excitement Nelson and most of his comrades felt: "On November 3rd we should have a red-hot, really fired-up demonstration. We will use everything we have learned. We will march through the streets, banners high and voices booming. We will plan creative measures to draw out the full might of the enraged masses. This will be followed by a short conference."[27]

The legal investigation after November 3 would eventually reveal that, by then, the Klan and Nazis, too, in secret meetings and at rallies, had begun planning their revenge for the humiliation they experienced at China Grove.

SECTION III

BACKLASH: 1979-1985

BANNERS

In the hours after the shooting on November 3, 1979, dozens of East Coast journalists rushed to Greensboro, jamming into a makeshift interview room at the police department to glean what information they could from the Greensboro police chief, William "Ed" Swing, and Mayor Melvin.

"We had no indications that there were guns in the Klansmen's car; there's no way we could have known," Chief Swing told the reporters, before noting that officers had arrived on the scene of the shooting in "under a minute."[1] Mayor Melvin called the shooting an "isolated, senseless, barbaric act of violence" that "would be dealt with as such."[2] A few days later, Cecil Moses, in charge of the FBI investigation of the shooting, added his voice to the official narrative: "[The FBI] had no evidence that the Klan was actively engaged, or any other organization for that matter, was actively engaged in any violent activities. . . . We have not tried to penetrate or to direct any informant to the group *because that's not within the guidelines to do so* [emphasis added]. And so we had no advance knowledge at all that we could pass on to local authorities that there might be that kind of situation brewing."[3] Moses said more in his statement than that the FBI had no advance warning of the violence; he'd taken a swipe at the restrictive 1976 guidelines that had resulted from the Church Committee investigation and, in a clever flourish of circular logic, claimed the FBI couldn't know anything they weren't permitted to know. The guidelines, which he resented, would function in this case as a shield—official cover for FBI denials about what they knew. At the same time, the shooting presented an opportunity to demonstrate the urgent need to loosen the legal restraints on FBI methods, which had been championed energetically by Senator Robert Morgan of North Carolina.

On November 4, Jerry Tung, the Communist Workers Party's general secretary in New York, announced, "We will start [to avenge our comrades] by holding a militant funeral march next Sunday [November 11]. We will bury them [in Greensboro] and build a monument there that people can come to years from now." The press wanted to know whether the marchers would be armed. The CWP, believing they were still assassination targets, affirmed that they intended to carry guns when they laid their dead to rest.[4]

❖

In Greensboro, as CWP members grieved and officials burnished narratives of their innocence, an act of revolutionary anger more than 6,500 miles away snatched the country's full attention. In Tehran, on November 4, hours after the shooting at Morningside Homes, Iranian students overwhelmed the US Embassy, taking scores of Americans hostage. "An accident of history," one journalist would call the confluence of events that buried the Greensboro story; no major news outlet would ever mount an independent investigation of the Greensboro shooting.[5]

The foreign crisis proved easier to talk about than the one at home. From the chair of his ABC news program, later called *Nightline*, Ted Koppel dispatched daily updates on the status of the fifty-two American hostages.[6] In response to geopolitical shock waves rippling from Tehran, Governor Jim Hunt, who remained mostly mum about the CWP murders, implored North Carolinians to cut their oil and gas consumption, peg their thermostats at sixty-five degrees, and drive no faster than fifty-five miles an hour. By reducing a "dangerous addiction on foreign oil," he said, Americans would keep "an unstable nation" from having the power to place a "stranglehold on our economy."[7]

A presumption of innocence guided the US coverage of the hostage crisis. Few in the media dared suggest that the anger in Iran erupted from the complicated history between the two nations or that the crisis might be reason to reflect on how the United States exercised its power in the world. As W. E. B. Du Bois wrote in his searing essay "The Propaganda of History," historians "have too often [made] a deliberate attempt so to change the facts of history that the story will make pleasant reading for Americans."[8]

Indeed, the Iranian hostage takers nursed an uncomfortable grudge. In the early 1950s, the Iranian people had elected Dr. Mohammad Mossadegh as prime minister to lead them from the grip of colonialism to a more independent future. He acted quickly, nationalizing the British-held oil industry. In 1951, *TIME* magazine named Mossadegh its "man of the year." Yet no accolades could protect him when the British, regretting the loss of Iranian oil riches, enlisted the aid of the Americans to reclaim their juice. In the black-and-white world of Cold War geopolitics, the American and British allies labeled Mossadegh a "communist," and President Eisenhower signed off on Operation Ajax. The CIA shipped Teddy Roosevelt's grandson Kermit to Iran in 1953. He organized a coup, forced Mossadegh into exile, and replaced him with an Iranian dictator, Mohammad Reza Shah Pahlavi, ushering in an age of US-backed, covert operations to topple foreign leaders who didn't acquiesce to American interests.[9]

The Shah's ubiquitous secret police force, skilled in the violent repression of dissent, had kept him in power until a rebellious network of liberals, communists, and Islamic fundamentalists banded together in 1979. They kicked out the Shah, breached the small piece of territory held by the United States in Tehran, and made a demand: in exchange for the hostages, the Iranians wanted the Shah returned from his refuge among the "world predator imperialists" to face justice at home for abusing his people's human rights.[10]

❖

Back in Greensboro, city officials intended to refuse the CWP a parade permit for a funeral march but were chagrined to realized that local law did not require one for a cortege. Once the procession was announced, the *Greensboro Daily News* urged people to "stay away" and "let it pass," remarking that the previous Saturday's shooting had been "imposed on the city by tiny fringe elements seeking confrontation."[11] Spooked by FBI visits and the CWP's radical politics, local employers heeded Senator Jesse Helms's call to fire all CWP members.[12] Agents from a little-known Justice Department agency charged with building trust between law enforcement and victimized communities in the wake of racial tensions and crimes arrived in Greensboro from Washington, DC. The first thing the Community Relations Service agents did, however, was to go door-to-door in Greensboro's Black community to warn people of potential violence during the funeral march. They convinced North Carolina A&T's administrators to send students home for the weekend. Rather than acting on their stated mission of bringing people together, the federal agents seemed intent on isolating the CWP.[13]

If the march couldn't be prevented, city, state, and federal officials could still prescribe routes and deny the mourners the right to carry guns. But after the massacre on November 3, the CWP refused to be disarmed. At a meeting to discuss the march with city officials, representatives of the FBI, the State Bureau of Investigation (SBI), the Greensboro Police Department, and the Justice Department, a CWP lawyer did what Jerry Tung had ordered him to do. He looked the officials in the eye and said with righteous fury, "We're Maoists, we'll attack wave upon wave like the Chinese Red Army."[14]

The official response to this speech was to declare a state of emergency, install a National Guard command center at a local high school, close the city's liquor stores, and place medical personnel on standby. The state police, FBI, and sheriff's department began to monitor traffic into the city. "We seek no confrontation," Nelson Johnson told the press, attempting to turn the conversation from swarming Chinese soldiers back to the funeral of his American comrades. However, he continued, "if we are attacked, we will be prepared to defend ourselves and we will defend ourselves." As the tension built, Mayor Melvin disappeared for a couple of days. Rumors spread that he'd suffered a nervous breakdown, although it's more likely that, worried for his family's safety, he was busy moving them out of the city.[15]

❖

As Saturday, November 10, gave way to Sunday, and Sunday morning ticked over to Sunday afternoon, Burley Mitchell, Governor Hunt's man in Greensboro, didn't have a clue what to do. The longer it took to find a solution, the more dangerous the situation became. Deal or no deal, the CWP intended to march and, late in the fall as it was, sunset arrived just after 5 p.m. After dark, law enforcement's ability to control the situation would plummet, especially, Mitchell believed, if the CWP were carrying guns. If someone got spooked, they might set off a firefight in downtown Greensboro.[16]

The phone rang in the command center at the police department. When Mitchell got on the line, he recognized the voice of a defense attorney he'd known from his time as a state prosecutor. "Listen," the man said, "I think we can work something out," letting Burley know that he had the ear and trust of the CWP. "Can you meet?" he asked.

Mitchell slipped out the door and into a ready car, directing the driver to a Greensboro street corner. The lawyer who'd called waited there with his proposal, offering a ray of murky light on a miserable day. The CWP, he confided, might be willing to carry guns that weren't loaded.[17]

Mitchell hurried back to the command center and presented the compromise. "They get to save face," he explained. "In reality," he continued, "it's more risky for them. If someone shoots at them because they have guns, they won't be able to shoot back. But this way," he said, going into pitch mode, "we can get them down to the cemetery and then the hell out."

No one in the room liked the idea.

"Open carry is legal in this state," Burley reminded the men.

After they'd groused for a few minutes, Mitchell's law enforcement colleagues realized they didn't have much choice. An honor guard of twenty CWP members would carry long guns, inspected for bullets at the start of the march by the National Guard.

Burley called his contact back. "You've got a deal," he said.[18]

Cecil Moses fidgeted in the police command center, sweating bullets, terrified that all hell would break loose. In his two decades at the FBI, he'd never witnessed anything like the scene unfolding on Greensboro's streets. At his direction and under the legal cover of Mayor Melvin's emergency proclamation, the FBI and the state police set up checkpoints to search every car entering Greensboro. Finding guns tucked above visors and hidden under car seats, they arrested some thirty-five CWP members and supporters and packed them off to the county jail to wait out the funeral.[19] Despite the blanket police coverage, the nasty weather, and the intimidation tactics of the Community Relations Service, hundreds of CWP members, allies, and sympathizers from up and down the East Coast made it into Greensboro.

Overwhelmed by crises near and far, everyone in Greensboro anticipated the November 11 funeral march with anxiety and fear. At about 3 p.m. that Sunday, eight days after the Morningside shooting and in the wake of the negotiated deal on carrying weapons, about five hundred CWP members and supporters donned boots, hats, and warm jackets to shield themselves from the icy rain. Around their necks or pinned to their jackets they wore laminated photographs of the dead: Jim Waller, Sandi Smith, Bill Sampson, Cesar Cauce, and Michael Nathan. The weapons that delayed the march for hours were clutched in the hands of a select twenty-person honor guard, barrels pointed skyward. In defiance of the agreement reached with the state negotiators, loaded guns secreted behind the

Cosmos Club's ceiling tiles in the days leading up to the march were tucked inside some marchers' foul-weather gear. The bodies of Jim, Bill, Cesar, and Mike lay in coffins resting on wheeled carts. They'd be wheeled one and a half miles to Maplewood Cemetery, likely the first white men to be interred in the cemetery. Everyone knew, however, where their civil and human rights allegiances lay. Sandra Neely Smith, the only Black person killed on November 3, would be buried elsewhere, her body delivered in the coming days to her family in Piedmont, South Carolina.

As Nelson and Joyce, together with Signe, Dale, Floris, Marty, and Sally, spilled out of the club onto East Market Street they looked like a motley band of guerrilla soldiers. Nobody had to ask where the police were now. For every marcher, there were two law enforcement officers or soldiers mustered to duty: 175 Greensboro policemen, nearly half the city's force; 250 Highway Patrol officers; and 500 National Guardsmen lined the route. An unknown number of FBI agents and SBI agents in plain clothes slipped among the marchers. Snipers, silhouetted like gargoyles against the slate sky, decorated the tops of buildings. Two helicopters beat the freezing air above the route. As the procession moved, the National Guardsmen tilted their bayonet-tipped rifles toward the marchers, who'd accepted that they might die that day. No one wanted this, but as one CWP member said, "Any other choice meant denying what these people had died for."[20]

❖

Nelson and Joyce had witnessed the same National Guard unit surround and then invade North Carolina A&T State University in May 1969. Now, ten years later, Nelson Johnson pulled a dark beanie down over his ears and clutched a poster bearing an image of Michael Nathan, who'd succumbed to his injuries on November 5, two days after being shot. Only Joyce knew the depth of another conflict inside Nelson Johnson's broken heart. Since he'd arrived at A&T in 1965, his commitment to the city's Black community had motivated his activism. Earlier in the week, a troop of police officers escorted Nelson from the premises of his job at Rockwell Industries. After that, the national NAACP office told the local branch to keep its distance from Nelson and the CWP. When Nelson went to visit a longtime pastor friend, the police blocked his entrance into the church. The night before, church offices had been vandalized; the cops claimed to suspect the CWP. "The United Front crumbled around us," Nelson would say. "The weight of anti-communist propaganda knocked out our initiative."[21]

"Nelson Johnson is an enigma," read the first line of a profile in the *Carolina Peacemaker*, Greensboro's Black weekly. The journalist wondered, Was he a skilled community advocate or an agitator who led people into harm's way? One local businessman who'd known Nelson since the mid-1960s extended the activist an opportunity to clarify his politics. "I don't believe Nelson is a communist," he said. "I believe any of his tendencies toward communism are more of a devil's advocate point of view."[22]

Nelson refused the opportunity to distance himself from his political allegiance. "When people think of communists," a wary Nelson told the interviewer, "they think of men in gray suits, holding babies by their feet and smashing their heads against trees." "He denies fitting into that category," the writer noted earnestly. For Nelson, quite simply, the writings and theories of Marx and Lenin offered sensible solutions to the problems of the day.[23]

If Nelson had stepped away from the CWP prior to the funeral march, he likely could have slipped easily back into East Greensboro's protective embrace. But he refused to abandon his political comrades in their—and his—most vulnerable moment. "I was loyal to the Black community, but that pulled against my party loyalty," Nelson would say. "I lived between two worlds, those of 'my people' in the community and 'my people' in the organization. The main thing that bothered me was that I couldn't bring [them] together. . . . People in the Black community were suspicious of my communist friends. 'Someone else is calling the shots,' they said. They called on me to break ranks."[24]

Nelson's ideologic and strategic quest had carried him out past where his country was willing to go and then, beyond that, his community. In the week since the shooting, relationships Nelson had cultivated for more than a decade broke down under the fear and stress.[25]

Freezing rain and a lonely, frightening walk lay ahead. Indeed, Nelson felt like a marked man. Rumors flew that the Klan and Nazis regretted having missed the opportunity to kill Nelson. Far more alienating and painful to Nelson than Klan threats, however, was the suggestion by the host of a program on a local Black radio station that Greensboro might be better off if Nelson had died on November 3.[26]

❖

Pushing the caskets through a perilous gauntlet, the mourners raised their placards—"Avenge the CWP 5" and "Unite the Working Class"—thrust their fists into the air, and started to sing:

We are soldiers in the army.
We've got to fight through though some fall at our side.
We've got to hold up the blood-stained banner.
New fighters joining us to seize the time.

On seeing the coffins, one CWP member lost her composure. "This is no time to cry," another woman comrade chided her.[27] The marchers passed a pickup truck with a hand-painted sign bolted above the cab: "Greensboro People Don't Want You Communist Bastards in Our Town."[28]

❖

At Maplewood Cemetery the mourners stood in the rain and strained to hear the eulogies above the percussive pounding of the helicopter rotors. "This is the single largest assassination of communists in this nation's history," proclaimed Phil Thompson, the young Black Harvard graduate and member of the CWP Central Committee, standing in for Jerry Tung. These are, he said, "the first communist martyrs [in the United States] since Sacco and Vanzetti and the Rosenbergs."[29]

After the marching and the speaking, the funeral ended, the dead were laid to rest, night fell, and the rain persisted. More scared than cold, however, the mourners refused to board the city buses idling at the edge of the cemetery ready to carry them back to the center of town. Instead, for a second time, they set out on foot through the rain. They peered into the darkness, moving step by step toward futures transformed and unknowable.

❖

While photos of the funeral march dominated the front pages of Greensboro's daily newspapers on November 12, another item barely caused a ripple. Three short paragraphs buried in Monday's edition of the *Greensboro Daily News* reported that Virgil Griffin, the Grand Dragon of the Knights of the Ku Klux Klan, had emerged from a South Carolina swamp and turned himself in to the FBI during the funeral march. If he'd been looking to avoid front-page headlines, it was a canny move. Cecil Moses and his team spent a couple of hours questioning Virgil. Though he'd been a primary organizer of the caravan to Morningside on November 3 and had scouted the parade route, the FBI let him walk. After the interrogation, Virgil told the press that he'd survived a conspiracy "to get the Klan killed. . . . We figured there would be so many police that all we could do was heckle them, but there was no police." The article made no mention whatsoever of Eddie Dawson, the man Virgil had enlisted to convince the Klansmen to come to Greensboro.[30]

Many more people read a column published on November 11 in the *New York Times* titled "Klan Killings Last Weekend Were Not the Only Examples of Violence." In it, Anthony Lewis, the *Times*'s well-regarded legal columnist, who would go on to win Pulitzer Prizes and publish bestselling legal histories championing freedom of speech, worried about the "politics of provocation." Had the CWP's calls for revolution and their challenges to the Klan represented a form of violence? Lewis wondered. Had their taunt-ing posters, letters, and statements directed at the Klan crossed an "established limit" to free speech? Were they, in other words, the party most responsible for the "hostile reaction" that left five of their own dead? Quoting the Supreme Court Justice Hugo Black, an un-wavering champion of the First Amendment, Lewis wrote: "When groups with diametrically opposed, deep-seated views are permitted to air their emotional grievances, side-by-side on city streets, tran-quility and order cannot be maintained even by . . . the finest and best [police] officers."[31]

Staring into the abyss of judgment, the CWP members had to figure out how to survive without jobs, health insurance, or savings. They'd celebrate Christmas in 1979 with food stamps and welfare cheese. Joyce, Nelson, and their daughters moved in with Willena Cannon for safety and to cut costs, where they all shared responsibil-ity for cooking and taking care of five children. "Why did the mean people kill Aunt Sandi?" the kids wanted to know.[32] Nelson and Joyce's girls, and others who'd been herded to safety by Sandi Smith, were terrified to be alone, overcome by the memory of Sandi getting a "bullet between her eyes." Joyce removed a photograph of Aunt Sandi from the wall. Riot charges still hung over both Nelson and Willena.[33]

At school, teachers were nervous about having the Johnson girls in the classroom. Joyce, whose boss at A&T courageously protected her, was one of the few North Carolina CWP members who managed to hold on to her job. As the tragedy headed for the courts, Joyce's pay-check would help allow Nelson and their CWP comrades to focus on pursuing justice for their murdered friends.

POLITICS

Ahandsome, diminutive Greensboro native with a penchant for colorful quotes, Michael Schlosser insisted that the "band of marauders . . . that descended on Greensboro, cutting a path of destruction that left dead and bloody bodies" be denied bail.[1] This description of the Klansmen and Nazis would be one of the few things the Guilford County district attorney said that Nelson and Joyce Johnson agreed with.

DA Schlosser might well have considered himself one of the most fortunate men in Greensboro. His 1978 campaign for the job as the county's top prosecutor had lurched from scandal to scandal. His wife left and accused him of abuse, though Schlosser would deny the charges, calling his wife a "pathological liar," and schemed with his lawyer to keep court documents out of the hands of the press until after the election. Rumors of heavy drinking dogged his trail.[2] Rivals told the press that the former assistant DA possessed a special talent for removing Blacks from jury pools, a rare public admission of a common practice among county litigators.[3] He'd also received some questionable—and substantial—campaign donations that nudged up to, if not just over, the legal line.[4]

Schlosser didn't allow the steady stream of controversy to slow him down. Running as a Democrat, he presented himself as an up-right graduate of the Virginia Military Institute, a Vietnam veteran, and—contrary to the spousal allegations—a tenacious defender of victims of domestic violence. He pushed an aggressive law-and-order platform, handed out hundreds of yard signs, and outspent his primary opponent, who happened to be his boss, four to one. Schlosser promised to cut through the "justice maze" and make criminals pay for their crimes. "Cases," he assured voters during his political campaign, "shouldn't be looked at politically."[5]

Schlosser received an endorsement with "reservations" from the *Greensboro Daily News*. But it was the paper's subtle put-down of his general election opponent, a Black Republican with an impeccable public reputation, that may have helped Schlosser most. Could Leon Stanback, the editorial writer wondered, "see his way clearly through the battle?"—a lightly coded critique, it seemed, of the Black man's intelligence.[6]

Schlosser and Stanback both represented the quickly receding pasts of their respective parties, allegiances linked more closely to Abraham Lincoln (Republican) and Jefferson Davis (Democrat) than to Jesse Helms's project to reengineer the Republican and Democratic Parties in the wake of Lyndon Johnson's civil rights legislation. For the time being, white Greensboro voters still recognized Schlosser to be a Southern Democrat, just as they did Mayor Jim Melvin and Governor Jim Hunt. That fact trumped Schlosser's flaws, and he eked out a victory against an opponent who could never win the local nostalgia vote.

When Schlosser took office in January 1979, a journalist noted that after the newly installed DA replaced two Black attorneys, the remaining prosecutors were all white men. "I tried to find the 12 most qualified people I could," Schlosser retorted. His staff would "serve the needs of all citizens," he said, echoing Mayor Melvin's defense of a Greensboro City Council culled from one geographic and demographic sector.[7]

Schlosser had held the elected office for less than a year when the most complicated case in the county's two-hundred-year history landed on his desk.

Schlosser assigned two of his prosecutors to the case, too big for any single lawyer: Rick Greeson, who'd tried dozens of grisly murder cases since he'd joined the DA's office in 1971, and one of the new hires, Jim Coman. A smart, outspoken northerner, Coman had spent the previous six years as the attorney for the Greensboro Police Department.[8] The three Vietnam War veterans, Greeson, Coman, and Schlosser, had all earned their law degrees from Wake Forest University in nearby Winston-Salem. DA Schlosser and his prosecutors would have the first chance to sight the shooting through the limited scope of the law.

With Schlosser's blessing, Greeson and Coman did something atypical: they set up a satellite office in the finished basement of Greeson's stately colonial home, about eighteen miles from downtown Greensboro in High Point.[9] Away from the cramped DA's offices in the Guilford County Courthouse, they spread out all the material—the reports, interviews, and evidential records pouring in thanks to the efforts of Cecil Moses and the FBI—from which they would construct a case. Though beyond the consciousness of most Americans, the Greensboro shooting quickly became one of the most scrutinized murders in American history, surpassing the JFK assassination investigation in terms of the volume and weight of new documents generated.[10]

Greeson's basement offered an additional advantage: the police officers the prosecutors invited in to clarify details could relax, a world away from the DA's Government Plaza office and the CWP demonstrators who frequented the courthouse steps. Coman, the former police department lawyer, set the cops at ease with his collegial manner, New Jersey accent, and artful cussing. Two weeks after the shooting, Chief Swing had issued an administrative report on the November 3 shooting. The GPD's actions on November 3, the report concluded, had been "adequate and proper." As Cecil Moses and his FBI colleagues had done, Coman and Greeson accepted Chief Swing's conclusions, dismissing the CWP's accusations that police were complicit in the shooting.[11] They also took seriously another observation made in the police report, which suggested that

Nelson Johnson intentionally misled the department by naming two different starting points for the march, Windsor Community Center on posters and Morningside Homes in the parade permit filed with the GPD.[12] As Jim Coman saw it, the police could be accused of "misfeasance" at worst, not "malfeasance." Questions about strategy, tactics, and operations—about misfeasance—generally were "administrative" and better taken up by the city council or some other civic body, according to the lawyers.[13]

Compressing the vast quantities of information into a compelling narrative for a jury would be the challenge of Coman's and Greeson's lives. Even so, when a grand jury returned hasty indictments against fourteen of the Klansmen and Nazis for murder and felonious rioting barely a month after the shooting, the prosecutors believed they'd been handed a slam-dunk case. They dismissed the claims by lawyers appointed to represent the indigent Klansmen and Nazis that their clients intended only to heckle the communists and toss a few eggs; that when threatened, the Klansmen and Nazis had acted in self-defense. "Guns and eggs don't mix," quipped Schlosser, calling the caravan that arrived at the corner of Carver and Everitt a "mobile arsenal" driving to "a turkey shoot."[14] Even if the Klansmen and Nazis believed they were defending themselves by shooting into the protesters with high-powered rifles, shotguns, and pistols, said Schlosser, they'd far exceeded what could qualify as self-defense.

Meanwhile, DA Schlosser made it clear in his conversations with reporters that, as he followed the evidence, he wouldn't rule out prosecuting Nelson Johnson or other members of the CWP.

❖

After November 3, letters poured into Governor Hunt's office. A handful expressed worry about the rise of the Klan and the legal system's ability to achieve justice for the November 3 murders. One correspondent noted that "the [Black] Panthers cannot be accused, nor can they boast of a third of the wrong that the Ku Klux Klan has done and gloated in the name of the Lord for their heinous crimes.

The Ku Klux Klan has never received scarcely more than a wrist spanking in its American History; while the Panthers were shot to death by the Police Force of this nation even as some of them slept in their own beds. . . . The question is not whether the people killed in Greensboro were communists, Ku Klux Klansmen, or Baptists, wrong has been committed."[15]

Responses to letters of this sort were referred to the governor's counsel, who, while decrying extremism of any sort, offered the vague assurance that the "tragic event is being thoroughly investigated and that those responsible will be prosecuted to the full extent of the law."

Most of the letters, however, worried about the economy, communism, and the tenuous place of white people in North Carolina and the country. White North Carolinians complained about their children being bused to integrated schools on the "last of the world's oil." They bemoaned the influence of the "Russian Trojan horse— the United Nations." One writer invoked a Christian hymn: "You ought to have sung 'heavenly sunshine' that somebody had the guts to stand up to those Communists. They deserved to die." "Greensboro," proclaimed another constituent, "is the most beautiful city I have ever lived in. . . . However, the tranquility and peace of our community is threatened by the likes of . . . the Communist Workers Party . . . unpatriotic arrogants [who] are demonically clever." "My heart," wrote one man, "goes out to the men who shot the communists [in] Greensboro. . . . If I was Governor of N.C. I would pardon those men before trial and announce it was not a crime in N.C. to shoot a communist."

"It is wrong," opined one Hunt constituent, "for the Government to pay for Black Studies which is Hate Whitey." Another posed a series of rhetorical questions: "How come the Blacks can organize and demonstrate, but when whites do it the wrath of the country is upon them? . . . Why is white supremacy in America so wrong, and communism exalting Mother Russia so right?"

Some of these missives were typed; many were scrawled by hand on letter paper, note cards, and on old Klan handbills, including one proclaiming the "Ugly Truth About Martin Luther Coon, Jr.," which warned that the dead civil rights leader had intended to lead the "Negroes down the crimson path to a Soviet America." While most of the letter writers cloaked their racism in patriotic anticommunism, some were as unvarnished in their views as a splinter on a wooden privy seat: "The KKK is a fine bunch of people. They don't want to see the country to get to be a half breed state, n——s and whites one color. . . . If this keeps going in a few more years the poor white people will have to get down on their knees and beg for survival from the n——s. . . . The march from Selma to Montgomery, Alabama should never [have] happened. It was a disgrace to [the] U.S."

To these letters expressing anger and fear of communists and Black people, the governor offered a short, but cordial personal response:

> *Thank you very much for your letter. Your views are most welcome,*
> *and I appreciate your taking the time to share them with me.*
> *My warmest personal regards,*
> *Sincerely,*
> *(signed) Governor James B. Hunt, Jr.*

With the rise of Jesse Helms and the state's Republican Party, an ambitious Democrat in North Carolina could ill afford to alienate white voters. "My job," the governor would say, "is to make people feel safe."[16] "We weren't afraid of the Klan," said Hunt's colleague and friend Burley Mitchell, noting that any white, rural North Carolinian from a big family would likely have cousins who'd joined the Klan. The word *we*, of course, meant white North Carolinians who believed that even if the secret society had devolved into a terrorist organization populated by, in Mitchell's words, the "ignorant lower classes," the Klan had provided critical protection to southern "natives" during Reconstruction.

In the governor's letters and Mitchell's parsing, one hears echoes of the historian Allen Trelease's words: "Democrats sympathized with the Klan, benefited by it, were intimidated by it, and were ashamed of it, often simultaneously. This is part of the burden of white supremacy."[17]

At a prayer breakfast in Greensboro two months after the shooting, Hunt praised Greensboro's response to the shooting and argued that law enforcement should be granted more leeway to gather intelligence on "the activities of violence-prone organizations" or, as he also liked to call them, "wild and crazy groups."[18] Virgil Griffin didn't feel threatened by Hunt's advocacy for deeper penetration of "potentially violent groups." "We welcome all police in the Klan as long as they are white. We don't hold [the statements] against Hunt. He couldn't single out one organization [the CWP by implication] but had to include all in his remarks," said Griffin, as he endorsed Hunt's reelection campaign.[19]

Hunt's words played like music in Cecil Moses's ears. A sitting governor with presidential aspirations had publicly challenged the 1976 attorney general guidelines limiting the FBI's intelligence gathering.

❖

Taking a break one morning from the grueling twelve-hour days spent preparing the case, attorney Rick Greeson headed for the barbershop. His usual man lathered him up, snapped open the straight razor, and then paused, the razor resting lightly against the prosecutor's throat. "Go easy on those boys," the barber said.[20]

The two men laughed. But Greeson felt the blade and knew the man wasn't joking: Why, his question implied, are you going after these good ol' boys for doing their patriotic duty? As an undergraduate at the University of North Carolina, Greeson told his father that the war in Vietnam was a stupid one. "You got a country," his father responded. "You can join it or not." And so, despite his misgivings, Greeson took a home-front Army intelligence post, choosing patriotic conformity. As America unleashed its vast Cold War arsenal on a small country halfway around the world, Greeson learned "who the communists were. . . . Their beliefs [are] political. They aren't factual. [T]hey believe in violence . . . in revolution."[21]

Jim Coman and Michael Schlosser's personal politics, too, chafed against the task before them. The newspaper quoted DA Schlosser saying he'd "fought in Vietnam and we knew who the enemy was then," implying that the dead American activists for whom his office sought justice were un-American. Schlosser insisted the startling quote had been taken out of context, that he'd told the reporter he "had no good feelings about any of [the participants in the shooting]." His father had fought in World War II, so Schlosser did not look kindly on the Nazis; as a Catholic, he had no good feelings about the Klan; and he'd fought in Vietnam against communists.[22] For the DA in charge of prosecuting the killers of five communists, it seemed an odd thing to say. However, it likely won him points with the white Guilford County barbers, housewives, farmers, laborers, and textile mill administrators who had voted him into office.

The newspapers, too, reflected the prevailing attitudes. Despite the journalists present on November 3 who described what they witnessed as a "complete massacre," news coverage persistently referred to the violence at Morningside Homes as a "shootout." Nelson, according to local scribes, left little but deadly violence in the wake of his agitation. One article concluded that "somewhere, something went wrong" in Bill Sampson's life when the dead labor organizer abandoned a promising career as a minister or a doctor. Jim Waller was "looking for a martyr," and the widows didn't grieve properly.[23]

Sitting there in the barber's chair, Rick Greeson's personal views and professional obligations collided. Convincing a jury that the Klansmen and Nazis had committed a crime, it suddenly occurred to him, might be more difficult than he'd imagined.

❖

While the DA's office built its case against the Klan and Nazi shooters, the FBI's open "GreenKil" investigation allowed Cecil Moses and his team of agents free rein even under the restrictive 1976 guidelines to probe the CWP and its members.

They and the police were everywhere, outside the CWP members' homes, trailing their cars, and stalking the workplaces of those members fortunate enough to still hold jobs. Heading into the city from the airport, Nelson and Signe somehow escaped injury when a truck rammed their car into a ditch. The CWP suspected, but couldn't prove, it was an FBI agent who ran a woman member of the group off the road one night. Police stopped one of the widows, accusing her of hiding guns in the back seat of her car. When they looked inside the bundle of blankets, they found that she'd tucked in two young children against the cold. A woman renting a room in Willena Cannon's house turned out to be a police informant. Nowhere felt safe. Exhausted and frightened, overwhelmed by the surveillance and threats, immersed in a cloud of paranoia, Nelson kept a high-powered rifle at home. Jerry Tung sent down a fierce dog from New York for additional protection.[24]

Frustrated by DA Schlosser's comments about communists, the FBI's apparent lack of interest in investigating the Greensboro Police Department, and the "inciting a riot" misdemeanor charges still hanging over the heads of Nelson, Willena Cannon, and Rand Manzella (the CWP member who was captured in a news photo holding an archaic pistol), the CWP called in vain for William Kunstler, the legendary civil rights attorney from New York, to be named special prosecutor in the case. A Duke historian named Sydney Nathans supported the idea, writing in a *Greensboro Daily News* op-ed that while the CWP's conspiracy talk could sound bizarre to many Americans, he understood "why [the CWP] might be suspicious" of public officials. Nathans warned against persecuting dissenters, as the United States had during Senator Joseph McCarthy's inquisitions and the "reign of J. Edgar Hoover." "All those remotely suspected of involvement should be interrogated," he argued, referring specifically to law enforcement, as he worried that "people in the community [would] find a way to excuse [the Klan's] violence."[25]

The CWP took their message to the public square, believing law enforcement, the prosecutors, the media, and politicians from Mayor Melvin to President Carter to be aligned against them. Despite fundamental political differences, the NAACP, the SCLC, and other civil rights groups joined with the CWP in a fragile front to march against white supremacy.[26] Greensboro's leaders tried desperately to prevent the march, but on February 2, 1980, twenty years after the sit-ins began at the Woolworth store on Elm Street, nearly ten thousand people walked through Greensboro, in solidarity and subfreezing temperatures, against the rising Klan. The National Association of Black Law Enforcement Officers sent off-duty members to protect the demonstrators as they wound their way through the city to the Greensboro Coliseum, which was famous, not for radical political rallies, but for hosting the Atlantic Coast Conference basketball tournament.[27]

The four Morningside widows—Signe Waller, Dale Sampson, Marty Nathan, and Floris Cauce—sat in the Coliseum's front row beside Paul Bermanzohn, who, propped in a wheelchair, had survived brain surgery and three months in the hospital but still had to submerge his left side in ice to move it at all. (When Paul's mother, a Holocaust survivor, rushed to visit her son in the hospital, CWP members pleaded with her not to harangue him about his communist politics. She entered the room, embraced her son, and told him how proud of him she was.) The CWP's Phil Thompson, civil rights legend Anne Braden, and Ben Chavis, the Wilmington Ten leader who'd been released from prison shortly after the November 3 shooting, headlined the event. They all agreed that their goal was not just to solve the Morningside murders but also to promote the need for political revolution in America. In the minds of the CWP members and many of their allies, justice for the CWP Five was inseparable from the fight for political freedom and human rights in the United States. Ben Chavis told those in attendance, "I want to send a message to Jimmy Carter—there ain't going to be no reinstatement of the draft. We're not going to fight no more wars for capitalism; we're not going to fight no more wars for imperialism. We're going to be drafted into the freedom struggle. We're going to march; we're going to march; we're going to tear this system down."[28]

Not long after the unity march, Nelson began a lonely tour of the state in a beat-up van, stumping as a write-in candidate for governor. While pushing a progressive platform that "guaranteed jobs for everyone who wants to work; an end to racism and nationalism; universal education through college; an end to drugs and crime; women's liberation with equal pay for equal work . . . ; and an end to slum housing," he aimed to "demystify communism" and, perhaps, find a way through the wall of negative public opinion he and the CWP faced.[29]

Then on April 30, the US Department of Justice (DoJ) issued a statement signed by Black assistant attorney general Drew Days III, announcing that the DoJ found "no basis for liability under the federal criminal civil rights statutes on the part of any member of the Greensboro Police Department." While Days noted that his office was "not authorized to comment on the wisdom of the actions taken or to make suggestions about alternative courses of action," the DoJ had "cleared the Greensboro police of any criminal wrongdoing in connection with the Nov. 3 shooting." The Justice Department had based its determination on a review of the GPD's own internal report of November 19 and a nod from the FBI.[30]

With the benefit of official cover, Jim Melvin announced plans to hire a private company to assess police performance on November 3 and to determine whether there might be operational improvements to consider.[31]

"Obviously we're pleased with the report. I can't say I'm surprised," said the city manager, Tom Osborne. "This eliminates any question of conspiracy, as has been alleged."[32]

Two days after the Justice Department ruling, on May 2, a special grand jury returned indictments of Nelson Johnson and five other Morningside marchers for felony rioting. Much more serious than the earlier misdemeanor charge, this meant that Nelson and the others could be held legally responsible for the deaths of their comrades.

DA Schlosser quickly announced he would initially try six of the indicted Klan and Nazi defendants, creating what seemed to be an intentional symmetry: six indicted communists and six Klansmen and Nazis going to trial—equal numbers of the opposing "extremist, hate groups," as Mayor Melvin and other city officials had been calling them since the afternoon of November 3.[33]

Feeling hunted by the FBI and police and slandered in the press, Nelson and his comrades now saw DA Schlosser's decision as both political and a "blatant play for the Klan's acquittal."[34] They were outraged by the idea that their small dissident group, which had existed for less than a decade and talked theoretically about violent revolution, could be equated with the Klan and Nazis, with their bloody history and for whom violence had been a "companion and an instrument."[35] In the symmetry, Nelson saw a cynical attempt to shield the Greensboro Police Department and the FBI from being forced to reveal their complicity in the shooting.[36]

CHARGED

Snipers lined the roofs of the Guilford County Courthouse and the surrounding buildings on June 16, 1980, for the first day of jury selection in the trial of the six Klansmen and Nazis for murder and felony riot. Looking up at the rooftops from the ground one could spot Greensboro Police Department ball caps and peeking binoculars silhouetted against the bright sky as the temperature sweltered into the high eighties.

Marching past police officers who'd staked out every downtown corner, hundreds of protesters lifted banners blaming the murders of the five activists—the CWP Five, as they'd become known—on President Carter, the Greensboro Police Department, and the FBI, making no reference, curiously, to the men set to stand trial. On the courthouse steps, surrounded by the widows and joined again by Anne Braden, Nelson declared the trial "part of the cover-up of the single largest political assassination in the history of the United States."[1]

The Klan and Nazi defendants, dressed neatly in simple clothes, looked meek and terrified as they filed into the courthouse past the metal detectors. Behind them, Paul Bermanzohn in his wheelchair led dozens of CWP supporters and nearly as many police officers toward the courtroom. When sheriff's deputies informed the CWP supporters that only a few of them would be allowed to enter the courtroom, the gathering became agitated. "I have a bullet in my head and . . . you are going to keep me out of the courtroom?" said Bermanzohn. When an officer told Nelson to "hush," he bellowed, "Don't you tell me to hush!"[2]

Inside the courtroom, the lawyers, the Klansmen and Nazis, the potential jurors, and Superior Court Judge James Long could hear the chaos. Trial lawyers had nicknamed Judge Long "Blinky" because they'd never seen him bat an eye when staring down a lawyer or a witness. Now, the man known also for his perfectly parted hair and as a strict enforcer of courtroom decorum calmly ordered the hallways cleared so that he could get to the business of jury selection.[3]

Following the judge's orders to clear the courthouse halls and prevent all but a couple of CWP members from entering the courtroom, a policeman put CWP member Tom Clark in a choke hold, and another officer grabbed Bermanzohn's head. As she tended to do, Willena Cannon leaped into the fray and began pummeling the two officers. Other CWP members sprinted from the building, yanking fire alarms as they went.[4]

Eventually, order was restored. Leaving the Klan and Nazi trial to his designees Jim Coman and Rick Greeson, district attorney Michael Schlosser waited down the hall in another courtroom to arraign Nelson and five others for the felony riot charges. When the judge ended his prayer—"Save us from violence, discord and confusion, pride, arrogance and every evil way"—Schlosser accused the six of actions that provoked the deaths of their comrades.[5]

"Do you realize that Bill Sampson was my best friend and the best man at my wedding?" Rand Manzella screamed at the prosecutor.[6]

Feeling the unbearable weight of grief and guilt, Nelson told the judge and prosecutor that their proceeding was a sham. Alienated from Greensboro's Black community, without a job or the prospects of getting one, how could he support his family? Who had he become?

His parents would guarantee his bond, putting up the family farm as collateral, the son's freedom safeguarded by a proud and bitter past.[7]

That first tumultuous day of jury selection for the trial of the Klan and Nazi shooters, the prosecution accepted five of the twenty-four jurors subjected to voir dire interrogations. Even so, the defense attorneys would control the composition of the jury. Each side could dismiss an unlimited number of jurors for cause. In addition, both the prosecution and the defense held eighty-four peremptory, or free, challenges—fourteen for each defendant—allowing them to dismiss a juror without explanation and for any reason, including race. Over the next seven weeks, 2,250 potential jurors were reviewed to find twelve sitting jurors and four alternates. Some days, the prosecutors questioned more than one hundred people. Those who passed muster with the prosecutors were then subjected to the defense attorneys' questions.[8]

Jim Coman and Rick Greeson were frustrated. The better-educated jurors, the ones the prosecutors suspected would be less sympathetic to the Klan, were clever at coming up with reasons to exempt themselves. Many potential Black jurors took a principled stand against the death penalty, a sentence they'd be forced to consider for first-degree murder in North Carolina. Others admitted that being neutral arbiters of evidence against Klansmen would be difficult.[9] "We can't tailor make charges because we are worried about what a jury pool will be," Jim Coman said defensively, bristling at those who wondered whether the DA's office should have removed the specter of the death penalty by charging the defendants with a lesser crime.[10] How would it have looked, Greeson thought, if it appeared prosecutors were going easy on the good ol' boys? However, since nothing prevented the defense from striking every Black person from the jury, the debate may have been moot.[11]

However, the prosecutors' questions to the jury pool troubled at least one journalist observing the selection process. Greeson and Coman asked every potential juror whether "the fact that the alleged victims were communists who held views which are *anti-American and repugnant to all of us* [emphasis added] would make it difficult for you to find the defendants guilty?"[12] The question seemed to play right into the hands of the defense lawyers who planned to put the victims' ideology on trial.

The CWP created the Greensboro Justice Fund to support the legal defense of the members who'd been arrested. The Justice Fund attracted luminaries to its board, including the Catholic priest and peace activist Philip Berrigan and the theoretical physicist and humanist Michio Kaku, who would compare the "murderous terror" against the CWP to the "scapegoat tactics . . . used against Japanese Americans during World War II."[13] The Greensboro Justice Fund also prepared a civil suit against the City of Greensboro and various law enforcement agencies, including the Greensboro Police Department and the FBI, for permitting the attack.

For a time, the CWP members discussed going underground, separating themselves as completely as possible from "the system" they aimed to topple and change. They could choose new names, become itinerant, and cloak their lives and struggle in invisibility. Nelson argued against it. Many of them had children. Most important, he and his comrades were some of the best grassroots organizers in the country, accustomed to the door-knocking, polemic-writing, poster-hanging grind of making something from nothing. They wouldn't abandon their quest for justice.[14]

REVELATIONS

Just before the presses turned out the Saturday edition of *Greensboro Record* on November 3, 1979, the photo editor had charged across the newsroom and tossed a walkie-talkie to Martha Woodall, the young reporter who'd come to Greensboro from a newspaper job in Massachusetts. Get over to Morningside Homes and find out what happened, he said. They'd hold the presses long enough to get a story. Woodall had jumped in her car, managing to find the intersection of Everitt and Carver in a neighborhood she'd never visited. Using the walkie-talkie, she called in the horrible scene to the copy desk.[1]

Over the ensuing months, Woodall stayed on the story. In a series of articles, she detailed the city's underhanded efforts to block the big February 2 march to the Greensboro Coliseum in protest of Klan violence. After that march, Harold Covington, the portly, bespectacled head of the American Nazi Party, announced that the Nazis would march through Greensboro in support of the men who'd been charged in connection with the November 3 killings. Nelson hadn't been the only person associated with November 3 to dip a toe into North Carolina electoral politics that spring. Covington, who hailed from Chapel Hill, entered the Republican primary, seeking the nomination for North Carolina's attorney general. While Nelson's gimpy campaign van sputtered to stops in a few towns, Covington, sporting swastika armbands at his campaign events, would pull in 43 percent of the statewide primary vote, and forty-five of North Carolina's one hundred counties.[2]

Covington told Woodall that he'd canceled the Greensboro march "at the request of the defense attorneys" for the Klan and Nazi defendants, who worried the march might prejudice people in the jury pool. He still planned to march on the birthday of the "greatest anti-communist of all time," Adolf Hitler, he told the reporter, but in Raleigh rather than Greensboro.[3]

❖

During their conversation, Covington suggested that Woodall talk with Roland Wayne Wood, one of the Nazis on trial. Video of the shooting showed Wood casually remove a shotgun from the trunk of the powder-blue Ford Fairlane, raise it to his shoulder, and start firing. Through it all, a lighted cigarette dangled casually from his lower lip. The big man with the shaggy beard appears like an eddy of calm at the center of the violent chaos.

Wood doesn't have a phone, Covington told Woodall. "If you want to talk to him, leave a message with his minister." A few days later, Woodall found herself in Wood's run-down house, set in a "depressed, blue-collar neighborhood" in Winston-Salem. Over the house, a billboard read "Iran: Let our people go!" Cartoons danced on a TV screen as the big man rambled on about how he "got to this place" of hating people enough to kill them.[4]

Wood told her about the poor kid with "deep religious roots" who dropped out of school at fifteen with the equivalent of a fourth- or fifth-grade education. "They failed me when I was 15 mostly because I refused to answer questions according to the theory of evolution— that man evolved from the monkey. I don't believe my God is a monkey," Wood whispered.[5]

As an adult, Wood found the Klan's "idea of protecting the freedoms in this country and the democracy which we have" inspiring. He adopted the CB radio handle "Robert E. Lee" and believed joining the Klan to be a patriotic act. Later, he flipped to the American Nazi Party and threw his considerable energy into distributing pamphlets and "rapping to all the people about Adolf Hitler."

Wood told Woodall that on November 3, he'd planned to confront the communists by singing "My Country 'Tis of Thee" at the top of his lungs. "It wasn't a racial thing" that made him want to go to the CWP rally, but "communism vs. freedom." The fact that his gun ended up in the car at the rally was an accident. But when he arrived at Morningside, "all you saw was danger," he said. When a man with a "black beard and black hair" grabbed a shotgun, Wood said he felt so terrified he "wanted to throw up."

Out on $50,000 bail, Wood told Woodall he spent his time in church and with his ten-year-old son, playing in a bluegrass band, and painting pictures. "The [painting] people are wanting most . . . is the one with the beat-up church. The windows are knocked out. The doors are breaking off the sides. There's a sign out front that says: Closed for Rapture."

"Who died for you?" Wood asked his son, as Woodall prepared to leave.

"Jesus," the boy answered.

"Why'd he die though?" the father continued.

"To save our sins," the son affirmed.

If the defense attorneys for the Klan and Nazi defendants were glad that Harold Covington agreed to cancel his Greensboro march, Wood's pro bono attorney, the crafty, smooth-talking Robert Cahoon, no stranger to defending Klansmen, must have been thrilled when the interview (for which he'd likely provided coaching) with his client appeared in the *Greensboro Record*. Wood came off as a God-fearing, country-loving family man whose life was turned upside down when he defended himself against vicious communists. The article made no mention of Wood's professed hatred of Jews and Blacks; his turn as a pornography salesman (which may have been the real reason he was forced out of the Klan and into the arms of the less squeamish Nazis); a Bureau of Alcohol, Tobacco, and Firearms investigation into the possibility that Wood blew up a car and the woman inside it; the fact that he broke a Black man's leg for dating a white woman; Wood's desire to hurl tear gas rather than lyrics at the communist marchers; or the scars left in the psyche of an insecure, learning-disabled boy by the fight over the integration of his working-class school. Woodall noted the Confederate flag license plate and the Jesse Helms bumper stickers on Wood's old car, but her article made almost no overt mention of race.[6]

After the story ran, Wood called Woodall, whom he'd come to trust. He had something else to tell her. When she returned to Winston-Salem, Wood was with Raeford Milano Caudle, the barrel-chested Nazi who'd been peddling automatic rifles on November 3 and whose Ford Fairlane transported a trunkful of weapons to Everitt and Carver. Something hadn't been right about one of the men in their group, they told the reporter, speculating that he "might have been a federal agent."[7] They showed her a group photograph of twelve Nazis posed like a school sports team pointing out a handsome, clean-cut man. That's Bernard Butkovich, the men said. Present at a November 1 meeting at Wood's house to coordinate their plans for going to Greensboro, Bernie "wanted to make sure I was going," recalled Wood. "But he didn't show up [on November 3]." Calling Bernie "the mystery man in this whole thing," Caudle said that Butkovich "knew [which CWP members] was [supposed] to be shot."[8]

Woodall then called Harold Covington. "He looked like a cop," Covington said about Butkovich. Gorrell Pierce, a gifted raconteur whose affiliation also bounced between the Klan and Nazis, told her that the "guy bugged me more than anything about this whole thing." Like Covington, Pierce had kept clear of the November 3 confrontation, due in part to the presence of Butkovich. Bernie, Pierce elaborated, was "a Northerner and Slavic . . . he was not native," meaning Anglo-Saxon or southern. You want to know who the FBI agent in the Klavern is? Pierce asked the reporter. He's the one with the shiny shoes—like Bernie. It wasn't only Butkovich's lineage or style that bothered the Nazis. Bernie had tried to convince them to commit crimes. He offered to teach them to make bombs and Molotov cocktails, to booby-trap cars and purchase illegal grenades and automatic weapons. He even recommended that they assassinate a Klansman who disapproved of an alliance between the Klan and the Nazis.

When a detective shuttled Wood from the jail to the Greensboro Police Department for questioning on November 4, a police officer told him, "We don't know his name, but there's a man who claims to be with your [Nazi] unit who wants to talk with you." In a break from department procedures, the policeman had ushered Butkovich into the interrogation room and left the two men alone. Wood demurred when Butkovich offered to burn his house down and make it appear to be an act of CWP revenge. Wood's brother was present a short time later when the Greensboro FBI agent Tom Brereton, assigned by Cecil Moses to lead the local investigation, interviewed Wood. According to both Roland Wayne Wood and his brother, Wood picked a photograph of Butkovich out from a set Brereton presented to him during the interrogation, raising the same concerns he now revealed to Woodall. Butkovich's name, however, appeared nowhere in Brereton's transcript of the interrogation.

On a tip, Woodall placed a call to the Bureau of Alcohol, Tobacco, and Firearms office in Cleveland. To her surprise, she found herself speaking directly to Bernie Butkovich. "I wish I could sit down and talk to you," he said. "I'm sure I could enlighten you and you could approach [the story] in a more enlightened manner."

Woodall dialed Micky Michaux, the federal prosecutor for North Carolina's Middle District. She told Michaux what she'd discovered. "I am a little bit disturbed here by what you are telling me," he said. DA Schlosser told her, "I have no comment to make with any specificity about the individual at all. That's my statement."[9]

The bombshell headline of her story, "Nazis Say Federal Agent Infiltrated Unit, Knew of Plans for Nov. 3 Motorcade," filled every inch above the fold in the July 14, 1980, edition of the *Greensboro Record*. Woodall didn't go to lunch. Instead, she sat at her desk to watch the *Greensboro Daily News* reporters walk in and, as was their habit, pick up the freshly printed copies of the sister paper. If she'd had any doubts about the importance of the story, the stunned looks on the faces of her colleagues banished them. It was her biggest scoop, the kind of article that could crack the door to a dream job in Boston, New York, or Philadelphia.

There were details, however, that Woodall left out of the article. After Wood named the policeman who slipped Butkovich in to speak with him, Woodall went to the GPD to track the officer down. She prepared her questions in advance. Did he know that Butkovich was a BATF agent? Why had Bernard Butkovich been let in to talk with Wayne Wood? Why didn't Butkovich's name show up in the logs that tracked everyone who entered and exited the interview rooms?

She never got an answer to her questions. Startled by what the reporter had discovered, Captain Larry Gibson, the policeman who'd told Nelson Johnson he wouldn't issue a parade permit unless the CWP agreed not to carry guns, screamed at Woodall until she fled his office. He was, she'd say later, the angriest person she'd ever encountered. Gibson would later say that if he did get angry, it wasn't directly at Woodall, but at his GPD superiors, who'd left him in the dark about Butkovich and unprepared for the reporter's compromising questions.[10]

Top officials at the Bureau of Alcohol, Tobacco, and Firearms quickly admitted that Butkovich's "deep undercover" infiltration of the Winston-Salem Nazi group had been approved by headquarters, though they wouldn't offer any details about his mission.[11] One official insisted, however, that before any major undercover operation, the BATF "notifies the U.S. Attorney, the FBI, the prosecutor and the police in the area." Mickey Michaux, the FBI, and the GPD all denied that the BATF had provided them any notice.

The BATF had fallen into the Church Committee's blind spot.[12] The full set of orders and directives that governed BATF operations still remained classified. Years later, Cecil Moses would say that if the personal relationships were good, the FBI might get around the 1976 guidelines that limited the Bureau's work by outsourcing projects to the BATF. Not subject to the same scrutiny or restrictions that limited the FBI, the BATF could infiltrate an agent into a group and, in the words of one BATF official, "offer someone the opportunity to violate the law." Neither Woodall nor the Nazi Wood knew that, in the hours after the shooting, Moses's men had met with Butkovich and his BATF handler Robert Fulton Dukes at a motel on the outskirts of Greensboro or that Dukes was no stranger to the agents. Later it would be discovered by the CWP's lawyers that the FBI, as suggested in conceptual terms by Moses, coordinated the Butkovich operation with the BATF.[13]

❖

On July 23, nine days after Woodall's article appeared, CWP members around the country, believing that government agencies were hiding their complicity in the November 3 shooting, demonstrated at BATF offices in twelve cities, including New York, Chicago, Denver, San Francisco, Los Angeles, Baltimore, Charlotte, Detroit, Philadelphia, and Washington, DC. That same day in Raleigh, Nelson Johnson and Dale Sampson, enraged that officials were ignoring the possible involvement of police and others in the shooting, waited for their moment at the back of a briefing room to interrupt Governor Hunt's press conference. They didn't know how else to make their voices heard. Suddenly Nelson stood up and walked toward the governor shouting, "You are nothing but a murderer, you're nothing but a conspirator." As Nelson moved closer, the governor's security force closed in around him. "You're nothing but a sham and a liar," Nelson continued. He saw the governor's face blanch, his lips begin to tremble with fear and anger.

From the back of the room, Dale Sampson shouted, "You have the blood of my husband on your hands."

"We're going to put you out if you don't hush up," the governor said to Nelson.

Moments later, Nelson and Dale left, having made their point in front of the assembled press, trailed by SBI security officers.

After they'd gone, the governor told the journalists, "I so deeply detest what these people stand for that it's hard to keep your temper, but I had to."[14]

Tensions continued to rise. A week later, Nelson, Signe Waller, and Dale Sampson took their "fight-back campaign" to a Greensboro City Council meeting. Nelson and Mayor Melvin each told the other to shut up. Waller and Sampson were arrested. The next day, Nelson delivered a soapbox speech in Government Plaza. The police arrested him for disorderly conduct and resisting arrest, roughing Nelson up in the process. They arrested Marty Nathan for swearing and for carrying a concealed weapon. The charges against Nelson would be summarily dismissed by the no-nonsense African American judge Elreta Alexander-Ralston in September, but the revelations and official denials were just beginning.[15]

It took more than seven weeks and 616 voir dire interviews to seat twelve jurors and four alternates.[16] Most were working-class; some had retired from military careers. A nationalized Cuban who'd participated in CIA-funded excursions to topple the Cuban communist Fidel Castro from power embraced the opportunity to participate in his adopted country's judicial system and became jury foreman. An active Greensboro policeman made it through as an alternate. To no one's surprise, every man and woman on the jury was white. The state prosecutors had accepted thirty-one Blacks. The defense attorneys struck fifteen of these potential jurors for cause and the other sixteen with the attorneys' nearly limitless supply of preemptory challenges.

On August 3, 1980, a day prior to the trial's opening arguments before the newly seated jury, another bombshell story broke, this time in the *Greensboro Daily News*. Sources revealed that in the weeks leading up to November 3, the Greensboro Police Department had hired the Klansman Eddie Dawson as an informant. The GPD had previously acknowledged having an informant in the Klan but had refused to identify him. The GPD also noted that a copy of the CWP's parade permit had ended up in the hands of a Klansman. What the police hadn't said was that the informant and the recipient of the parade permit were the same person. Eddie Dawson had recruited Klansmen to Greensboro, received a copy of Nelson Johnson's parade permit from the police on November 1, driven the march route with Virgil and two of the shooters, Jerry Paul Smith and Coleman Pridmore, rushed the Klansmen and Nazis into their cars at 11 a.m. on that fateful Saturday, and led the caravan to the start of the march at Morningside Homes.[17]

After the article appeared, the head of the GPD's Criminal Investigations Division, Captain Byron Thomas—"Tom" to those who knew him—invited Eddie to a hotel room to talk with the prosecutors, Jim Coman and Rick Greeson. "I might remember events different from what you want me to say," Eddie warned the prosecutors and the detective. Lying about the truth in a newspaper article carried little risk; perjuring himself in a witness box would be different. And he certainly didn't want the other Klansmen to know that he'd been an informant—for years. If he were subpoenaed, he threatened the prosecutors, he could "fix" the department by revealing details that would be uncomfortable. He wasn't specific about what these details might be. Jim Coman finally lost his patience with Eddie's demands and innuendos, shouting, "If you're called to testify you just tell the truth."[18]

A few days later, instead of calling the prosecutors, Eddie phoned Captain Thomas. He'd made up his mind, he said; he'd go to jail for contempt of court rather than testify. "I knew you'd do the right thing, Eddie," said Captain Thomas. Eddie had a good reason for not wanting to cross the police department. Many of his most dependable house-painting and handyman clients were police officers and FBI agents, including Special Agent Thomas Brereton. Captain Thomas would say he was being sarcastic when he applauded Eddie's decision to stay mum. Eddie didn't hear it that way. And he recorded the call, in case anyone doubted him.[19]

PITTS

The CWP began looking for lawyers to help file a federal civil suit against the police and the FBI. A contingent of CWP members drove to Washington, DC, to locate the team that had prosecuted the case against the Kerr-McGee Corporation on behalf of the family of Karen Silkwood. At the unfurnished offices of what would become the Christic Institute law firm, the CWP delegation found a handsome young man sitting on the floor. He wasn't wearing any shoes, and they tried not to notice that he was wearing shorts but no underwear. In a banjo twang of a voice straight from the South Carolina hill country, Lewis Pitts confirmed that he had a law degree and that he'd volunteered on the Silkwood case.

Karen Silkwood had been an employee at the Kerr-McGee factory in Oklahoma that produced plutonium pellets. An active member of the Oil, Chemical and Atomic Workers International Union, she had gathered evidence about dangerously lax safety standards in the Kerr-McGee plant. On the night of November 13, 1974, just before she planned to blow the whistle on problems at the plant, she died in a car crash. Evidence suggested the car had been rammed from behind before it crashed. Plaintiffs' lawyers convinced a federal jury to hold Kerr-McGee liable for "damage to the person and property of Karen Silkwood," and the company eventually settled for $1.38 million.[1]

❖

Lewis Pitts told the Greensboro crew that he wasn't sure practicing law was the best way to effect real change. Instead, he planned to join the underground fight against nuclear power plants, he told them. Even so, he agreed to visit Greensboro and learn more about their case.[2]

Lewis Pitts and his girlfriend rolled into Greensboro during the late summer of 1980, looking like a pair of tumbleweed hippies. Lewis wore his hair long, sported an earring, and still considered shoes an optional accessory. Meeting Pitts for the first time, Nelson wasn't sure what to think of the lawyer, but as they talked, Nelson saw something unusual in Pitts: a white southerner who understood the Dixie snarl of race and class and who, despite his personal style, possessed impeccable manners, an asset in any southern courtroom. The revolution, Nelson argued, addressing Pitts's reservations about the efficacy of the law, needed lawyers "to expose the illusion of democracy and fairness" that too often covered up injustice.[3]

After listening to Nelson, Joyce, and their comrades tell their story, Pitts understood that they were smart, serious, and committed. From what they said, he also believed that, at the very least, officials were covering up elements of what they knew about November 3. While the Silkwood case employed a "national campaign that combined education, organizing, and litigation" to challenge corrupt corporate power, Greensboro presented a chance for the young lawyer to expose the prejudice of local, state, and federal officials.[4]

It didn't take Pitts long to accept a job as chief legal counsel for the Greensboro Justice Fund. He removed his earring, cut his hair, bought a tie, moved to Greensboro, and, at his new clients' insistence and despite the fact that he didn't consider himself a communist, joined the CWP. "Ain't life rich," Lewis would chuckle. You never knew where it might lead.

The clock was ticking; Pitts and the CWP had only until November 3, 1980—the one-year anniversary of the shooting—to file a federal civil case.

❖

Even as they marshaled time and money to support a legal case, the CWP members continued a risky agitprop "fight-back campaign" to bring attention to their plight. Less than two weeks after the Eddie Dawson bombshell, Signe Waller traveled to New York to conduct a secret operation.

Through Democratic Party connections, the CWP had managed to acquire two "honored guest" passes to the 1980 Democratic National Convention at Madison Square Garden. On August 14, as President Jimmy Carter accepted his party's nomination to run for a second term, Signe shouldered her way through the crowd on the Garden floor. Within a few dozen feet of the podium, she lighted a cigarette, slipped a film canister from her pocket, pulled out a string of Black Cat firecrackers, and touched the tobacco ember to the fuse. Carter barely noticed the explosion, but within seconds Secret Service officers tackled Signe and escorted her to the nearest police precinct. From farther back, Dale Sampson, who'd also entered with credentials, yelled, "It's payback time for the murder of my husband. Carter, Reagan—they're all the same!"[5]

Outside the venue, more than one hundred CWP members, mostly from the New York chapter, had gathered. Many wore helmets and carried lead pipes, looking like a makeshift shock force of people for whom the American system of government had lost all legitimacy. For several minutes, they faced off with a large patrol of New York City cops.

One of the CWP members smashed a storefront window, a deliberate provocation to start a riot. Then the police and the CWP members attacked each other. Nineteen policemen were injured, and seventeen CWP members were caught, arrested, and delivered to a precinct basement. "Are these the shits who sent our guys to the hospital?" one policeman asked before exacting his revenge, fracturing hands, wrists, ribs, and heads. Activists lay on the cement floor barely on the breathing side of death before being delivered to a hospital the next morning. The Greensboro CWP members had suffered so much; their comrades in other chapters felt obligated to suffer, too. The national organization of the CWP had crossed the line from violent rhetoric to violence. Not only would that street fight mark the end of the CWP's most extreme tactics, but, said one member, it was "the beginning of the end for the organization."[6]

But the suffering in Greensboro was far from ending. The trial of the Klansmen was finally getting underway.

TRIAL

It began with shouting and a bad smell.

Inside the Greensboro courtroom on August 4, 1980, as Judge Long offered jurors instructions before the lawyers' opening arguments, Dr. Marty Nathan, the widow of Dr. Michael Nathan, stood up and bellowed: "This trial is a sham and a farce. The U.S. government conspired with the Klan and Nazis to kill five members of the Communist Workers Party and to murder my husband."[1] The bailiff taped her mouth shut, but she kept shouting through the gag. The bailiff clapped a meaty hand over her mouth, and the judge ruled her in contempt, packing her off to prison for thirty days. Moments later, Floris Cauce, the widow of Cesar, continued the theater, tipping a vial of skunk oil onto the floor. The judge ruled her in contempt, too, and then cleared the court to allow the stench and the accusations to dissipate.[2]

When Judge "Blinky" Long's gavel banged the court back to order, prosecutors Rick Greeson and Jim Coman readied themselves to present what they believed to be a strong, commonsense case against the Klan and Nazi defendants. They'd have to win, however, without the help of the CWP members who, as Marty and Floris's disruptive antics made clear, didn't trust them. The CWP hadn't liked the prosecutors' anticommunist statements or the tenor of their voir dire questions to the jury. The primary source of the mistrust, however, continued to the charges of felonious rioting against Nelson and the others. Any statements CWP members made from the witness stand during the Klan and Nazi trial could, theoretically, boomerang back against them at their own pending felonious rioting trials. And in light of the Eddie Dawson and Bernard Butkovich revelations, which suggested law enforcement knowledge of and, possibly, complicity in the November 3 tragedy, the DA office's refusal to investigate the police, the BATF, or the FBI seemed, from the CWP's perspective, like a cover-up.

Greeson and Coman didn't intend to call Dawson or Butkovich to the stand. Neither man, they'd say, could have helped their murder case against the six white supremacist shooters. Nor did the prosecutors believe that they needed their help to win a conviction.[3]

In his opening argument, Coman confidently told the jury that the Klansmen and Nazis had driven to Greensboro and killed demonstrators who were "engaged in lawful assembly." "Why," he asked rhetorically, "did they come armed to the teeth if they planned to peaceably demonstrate?" The defendants "were the aggressors," who hurled the first taunts and, instead of hiding or fleeing, fired not only the first shots but the bullets that murdered five people.[4]

The defense, led by the silver-tongued lawyer Robert Cahoon, who had been assigned by the judge to represent Roland Wayne Wood, spun a different story. The true victims, Cahoon argued, were the Klansmen and Nazis who'd been lured into an ambush designed by the CWP. His client had expected the police to be present and to keep order. Only when shots rained down on them from "rooftops and trees" and Black men threatened them with shotguns did the terrified defendants open fire, saving themselves from the communist attack. Even then, Cahoon argued, his client fired his shotgun into the air "to avoid hitting anyone."[5] Another shooter was said to have "pumped" his shells onto the ground without firing them. Jerry Paul Smith, seen in the videotapes firing two pistols at Cesar Cauce, claimed he'd been slugged in the head with a stick and suffered complete amnesia for the seconds in question. As for Wood's Nazi membership? Don't take that too seriously, Cahoon urged in his soothing drawl. Born after World War II ended, Wood, the lawyer claimed, had no idea what Hitler had done to the Jews. These men, Cahoon argued, were motivated not by racial hatred, but by anti-communist patriotism when they drove to Morningside Homes. And don't forget, Cahoon chided the jury, distancing his client even further from responsibility for the shooting, that it was Eddie Dawson, the police informant, who led his client and the others into a "closed area" from which "they couldn't escape."[6]

Cahoon's assertion that the Klan and Nazis had acted in self-defense, a claim bolstered with lies—no shots were ever fired from trees, and no Black people wielded guns that morning—left Coman and Greeson incredulous. But now that the claim had been made, it would be the prosecutors' responsibility to convince the jury beyond a reasonable doubt that the white supremacists had not acted out of fear for their lives. Or that even if they had acted to defend themselves, they'd used excessive force, thereby negating the self-defense plea. Bob Cahoon, one of the state's most skilled defense attorneys, wasn't going to make this easy for his opponents. Neither, it appeared, would the jury. Glancing over at the jury box, Rick Greeson noticed one juror flip him the middle finger, just beyond the judge's line of sight. That juror continued to signal his allegiance every day for the next four months.[7]

Greeson and Coman still weren't that worried. They had time to make their case. They had eyewitnesses, such as the cameraman Ed Boyd, to strengthen their arguments, and technology on their side. The FBI's cutting-edge forensics laboratories, which had worked for months to determine which bullets had been shot from which guns, promised to pinpoint the location of every shot fired by analyzing sound captured on the film and videotapes of the shooting, a technique never before used in a trial.

From the coroner's report and the FBI report on the bullets, Greeson and Coman knew that bird shot from the gun Bob Cahoon claimed Roland Wayne Wood had pointed into the air wounded several demonstrators. Wood's bird shot had burrowed into Jim Waller's body, but Klansman Dave Matthews's buckshot ripped him apart inside and killed him. Matthews's buckshot had also hit Mike Nathan in the face, Sandi Smith in the head above her right eye, and Bill Sampson in the chest. As Cesar Cauce stumbled after being clobbered in the head with a stick, a bullet from Jerry Paul Smith's pistol ended the Cuban's life. Roy Toney, firing a shotgun he'd wrestled away from Jim Waller, shot Paul Bermanzohn in the head.[8]

Rick Greeson called an FBI expert to the stand to explain how the laboratory used a small nuclear reactor to identify the projectiles and assign them to specific guns. As Greeson prepared to lay out additional evidence, the defense lawyers countered with a brilliant tactic. Before Greeson could tell the jury who shot whom, they forced him to present and document the chain of custody of each individual bullet and pellet he brought into evidence: Where had the bullet been collected and by whom? When was it delivered to the FBI lab in Quantico, Virginia? Who had custody of it at each point along its journey? How did the bullet return to Greensboro and arrive in the courtroom? They refused, in the language of the court, to "stipulate to" the laboratory-supported correlations as a general fact.[9]

While Greeson walked the FBI technician through the peregrinations of hundreds of projectiles, the drama of the crime leaked from the courtroom like air from a balloon. "But you're doing such a good job," Cahoon would compliment him, twisting the knife as the prosecutor lost the jury to tedium.[10]

Some of the injuries to the prosecution's case were self-inflicted. In a baffling effort to introduce an objective account of the shooting, Jim Coman played a film of an eyewitness responding to questions under hypnosis. From the depths of a trance, the journalist recalled Paul Bermanzohn saying that the CWP wanted to "physically exterminate the Klan." She referred to Nelson Johnson as "a real mess" and an "asshole." The defense lawyers, primed to declare a mistrial based on the hypno-testimony, were gleeful; they "couldn't have written a better script themselves," one anonymously told a reporter.[11]

Throughout the trial, Coman and Greeson referred to the

murdered activists as "the communists" and the "alleged victims," making little effort to humanize them. No friends or colleagues took the stand to compensate for the impersonal labels and remember the activists as kind and generous people. Sensing the need to gin up more empathy in the jury box, the prosecutors did something every lawyer knows to be risky: they subpoenaed a witness without knowing what he'd say.[12] Tom Clark had been strumming a guitar as the Klan and Nazis rolled up Everitt Street. A shotgun he owned had ended up in the hands of the Klansman Roy Toney, who'd used it to shoot Paul Bermanzohn. Clark had been injured, too, catching Wood's bird shot in his neck and head. On the stand, Greeson asked Clark to identify photos of his dead comrades. He ignored the lawyer's request, saying only, "I have nothing but contempt for this court." Greeson implored him to change his mind. When Clark refused, Greeson, overcome by rage, hurled the photographs at Clark and had to be restrained from attacking his witness.[13]

After nearly one hundred witnesses and six weeks of testimony, a bit of horse-trading gave Greeson and Coman a glimmer of hope. They'd been anxious to show film of the shooting to the jury to refute the self-defense narrative. North Carolina law, however, prohibited playing film or video in the courtroom for any reason other than to corroborate a specific witness statement. But the defense wanted something, too.

In early September, the FBI's pioneering expert in sound analysis, Bruce Koenig, had completed his study of the videotapes for the prosecutors. Like the videotapes, this technical sound analysis could be admitted only as corroboration for witness accounts. For reasons that would soon become obvious, the prosecution had decided not to introduce Koenig's study into the trial. When the defense lawyers studied it, however, they suspected the sound analysis might help their clients. So with the consent of Judge Long to amend the rules, both sides got what they wanted and agreed not to base any objection or appeal on the introduction of the video or the sound analysis as evidence to the jury.

On September 17, the prosecutors ran the tape of the shooting frame by frame for the jury. Despite the fumbles and setbacks, they believed the visual images offered incontrovertible visual evidence of murder. There were no threatening "Blacks" with shotguns, no gunfire raining down from rooftops and trees, as Cahoon claimed in his opening presentation. They pointed out the primary shooters: Matthews, Wood, Smith, Jack Fowler, and Coleman Pridmore. None looked frightened. Wood appeared calm and even slightly bemused as he fired his weapon. There was no visual evidence of anyone hitting Jerry Paul Smith on the head to cause temporary amnesia. Roland Wayne Wood shot into demonstrators, not over their heads, a detail that corroborated what Greeson had already established: that bird shot from Wood's gun had been found in the bodies of multiple victims. This wasn't self-defense, the prosecutors informed the jury. Even if the men had been more fearful than they appeared to be, their response was excessive. The prosecutors' confidence returned. They'd regained the upper hand.

When Greeson and Coman finished their presentation that Wednesday, Judge Long suggested the court reconvene the following Monday.

During those four suddenly empty days, Jerry Paul Smith, Dave Matthews, and Coleman Pridmore donned satin Klan robes to attend a fundraiser for their defense. Away from the strict "anticommunism" narrative crafted by their attorneys, the sudden celebrities of a nascent national white power movement spoke differently. "I have my white race," said Smith as he showed off a scrapbook into which he'd pasted the graphic autopsy photos of the people killed on November 3, "and I'll stand and fight for it even if it means the gas chamber." The Klan, he said, had been on the right side of history in 1865 and would be again. "Greensboro," he declared in his pitch, "is nothing compared to what's to come. We fought for you in the streets of Greensboro; now it's time for you to fight for us." Another man at the rally observed philosophically that "a communist is a n—— turned inside out." Black people and communists were to them—as they had been in many ways to J. Edgar Hoover—like a Möbius strip, two inseparable elements of everything wrong with America; once inside this peculiar geometry, where one began and another ended could be impossible to discern. Perhaps this elision explained Dave Matthews's admission to police in the immediate aftermath of the shooting that he "got two or three of them . . . n——s were falling." Everyone he'd shot, apart from Sandi Smith, was white.[14]

When court resumed on Monday, the defense called Bruce Koenig to map the shots at Morningside based on sound analysis. Koenig came with an impressive résumé. He'd analyzed President Nixon's Watergate tapes, pulling damning coherence from muddled sound. He'd been studying the famous Abraham Zapruder recording of the Kennedy assassination to see whether sound evidence might reveal a second shooter. (He would announce later that, based on his analysis, there'd been only one shooter.) Until Koenig produced his results of the November 3 shooting, no one knew how many shots had been fired. There'd been, he now told the court, thirty-nine separate shots fired over an eighty-eight second period. By interpolating between the explosions and the echoes ricocheting off the surrounding buildings, trees, and cars, Koenig claimed that he could pinpoint each shot to within about three feet of where it was fired. The first two shots, he said confidently, were fired into the air by Mark Sherer and Brent Fletcher, causing the demonstrators to run. Then, there on the stand, Koenig ran into trouble. He could not pinpoint the third, fourth, and fifth shots with the same level of accuracy. On a map, he drew a box, saying that the shots issued from a large general area. Some Klansmen and Nazis had been in that space, but it was big enough to possibly include a few CWP members. After lunch, the defense attorneys asked Koenig to reconsider the area from which those three critical shots had been fired. This time, he outlined a much smaller area that conformed neatly to where some CWP demonstrators had been standing.[15]

Shocked, Greeson and Coman realized a truck blocked the cameraman's view of that very same small area in question and, therefore, the video footage could not resolve the uncertainty.[16]

Bob Cahoon and his colleagues rose to revise their defense. The first two shots fired into the air by Mark Sherer and Brent Fletcher they now called "friendly" warning shots, meant to disperse the crowd and discourage fighting. The CWP, they claimed, fired shots 3, 4, and 5, the first aggressive blasts. Only after that did the Klan and Nazis return fire. If the CWP had fired shots 3, 4, and 5, then the Klan and Nazi shooters hadn't used excessive force to defend themselves.[17]

Greeson and Coman's pillar of visual evidence collapsed behind a parked truck in a cloud of ambiguous sound analysis. The jury suddenly realized there were things that the videotape didn't and couldn't show—such as the area behind that truck. What *else* couldn't they see? Black men with shotguns? Shooters in trees? The film that seemed to the prosecutors to be their greatest asset became a liability, full of blind spots, projecting doubt rather than facts. Of the thirty-nine total shots fired, the most meaningful were no longer those that killed and injured people, but the three that Bruce Koenig could not, with certainty, place. Jim Coman was so angry he fired off a letter to the FBI asserting that when Bruce Koenig altered his analysis on the stand he'd lied.[18]

The DA's case was, therefore, in deep trouble before the defense put Rex Stephenson on the stand. After Jim Waller lost his job at the Haw River Granite Mill, he took a job at Greensboro's South Buffalo Creek Treatment Facility, where Stephenson also worked. In the courtroom, Stephenson claimed that Waller had tried to recruit him into the CWP. Waller, Stephenson said, told him during one of their conversations that the CWP, to grow nationally, needed a martyr. To the delight of the jury, Stephenson said in response he offered to buy Jim a one-way plane ticket to Russia. One of the jurors applauded.[19]

Signe Waller would deny that Jim ever talked of martyrs.[20] But she, like the other CWP members, didn't take the stand to refute Rex Stephenson.

❖

As the November 3, 1980, deadline to file a federal civil case to establish liability for the deaths of their comrades approached, Lewis Pitts raced to complete the complaint. When an office printer malfunctioned, Lewis Pitts worried that he and his colleagues wouldn't make it to the US District Court for the Middle District of North Carolina in Winston-Salem by the deadline. The document they slipped in just under the wire didn't attempt to obscure or soften the politics of plaintiffs: "Plaintiff Nelson Johnson, a Black citizen of the United States and of North Carolina who is a communist, labor organizer and/or advocate of equal rights for Black people."[21]

Trimmed to a neat forty-eight pages, the complaint described a wide-ranging "class-based . . . anti-civil rights" conspiracy designed to provoke the November 3 confrontation and then cover it up. The outlined conspiracy named Klansmen, Nazis, federal agents, local police, government officials, and managers at the mills where the CWP members had worked. In all, the document named more than eighty people as defendants, including Mayor Jim Melvin, Assistant Special Agent in Charge Cecil Moses, Guilford County DA Michael Schlosser, the Greensboro resident FBI agent Tom Brereton, the "informant provocateur" Eddie Dawson, and the BATF "agent provocateur" Bernard Butkovich.[22]

As a legal document that was political and a political document that was also legal, the complaint named not only the people the CWP believed to be conspirators in the specific crime, but the actors who'd created the social, legal, and political conditions that made the murders possible. It included, for example, every US attorney general dating back to 1968. If the CWP won the millions of dollars in damages they requested—the complaint asked for a total of $48 million—it would be the richest left-wing radical group in the country. The CWP hoped to use the court battle to fight for working people and to use the settlement to fund the labor and racial justice activists who advocate for them.

❖

Jury deliberations in the state murder trial began on November 10, 1980, a week after Pitts filed the federal complaint.

After nearly four months, from jury selection to closing arguments—the longest criminal trial in North Carolina history—Robert Lackey and his fellow jurors were tired, frustrated, and ready to get back to their lives. That didn't make the decision about the fate of the men that rested in their hands a simple one. The complicated orders from the judge carefully delineated the differences between first-degree murder, second-degree murder, and voluntary manslaughter. The jurors were instructed to be aware of the concept of excessive force in self-defense, which meant that someone threatened by a stick, for example, cannot automatically claim self-defense after killing the stick-wielding person with a gun. The judge, Lackey thought, did a damn good job under difficult circumstances.[23]

Robert Lackey grew up on a small tobacco farm outside Greensboro and joined the Marines in 1954. Over his twenty-one years in the service, he'd spent time in various countries, including a thirteen-month tour in Vietnam, as a heavy equipment engineer supporting the fight against communism. Either fight to win or don't go, he'd say when asked about what he'd learned in the military, believing US ambivalence had lost the war in Vietnam. He'd been plucked from his current job as a diesel mechanic to sit on the jury. Once, in the late 1950s or early '60s, he'd attended a Klan meeting out of curiosity, and he came away thinking the Klansmen didn't know what they were talking about. While he agreed that underpaid mill workers should be treated better, he didn't like the violent race talk.[24]

Lackey and the other men and women on the jury elected as foreman the only college graduate among them. Octavio Manduley, a naturalized Cuban, never got excited or raised his voice, approaching the whole business like the trained engineer he was. Manduley, who'd known Fidel Castro personally, fled the Cuban Revolution for Miami in 1960. He spent a year helping plan the Bay of Pigs invasion to overthrow Castro and, when that plan went bust, Manduley plotted against the revolutionary regime for another two. He could never understand why, when the CIA gave the Cuban exiles guns and a boat, the Coast Guard would chase them down and confiscate the same boat and guns. Did America intend to fight communism or not? In 1963, he gave up and said to his family, "We've lost our country. Let's go be Americans."[25]

Betty, Octavio's wife, was a Quaker, and sponsored by the New Garden Friends Meeting, the family migrated to Greensboro. Manduley got a job as a janitor. Then he worked in a machine shop. It wasn't long, however, before he was running the lab at the cigarette manufacturer P. Lorillard, a position he held for thirty years. When he made the cut as a juror, Manduley considered it an honor and a duty to take part in the American legal system.[26]

The jurors all agreed that Bob Cahoon was the most talented lawyer in the courtroom. Cahoon had paid special attention to courting the female jurors during his presentations. It worked. "That's got to be the sweetest man on earth," one woman swooned. After the first vote, all six of the women and the middle-finger-flipping juror voted to acquit the Klansmen and Nazis of all charges. Five, among them Lackey and Manduley, held that they should be convicted of some crime.[27]

In the jury box, Lackey sat staring at the tables weighted down with the weapons the Klan and Nazis had carried that day—guns, brass knuckles, nunchucks, knives, lengths of chain, and more guns—and had no doubt that the Klansmen had intended to kill demonstrators that November morning. He wasn't buying the "Klansmen always carry guns" line. But the defendants' intention wasn't the primary question the jurors were wrestling with. The juror who'd given the prosecutors the bird argued relentlessly that the Klan and Nazis had done exactly the right thing. Why should they find them guilty of killing communists when they should be hailed as patriotic heroes?[28]

After a few more votes, the edge for those in favor of acquittal swelled to ten to two. Had the jurors heard the rumor that a group of Nazis were threatening to blow up a local oil refinery if they voted to convict? If so, they didn't discuss it.

Lackey and Manduley were at the bottom of the mountain looking up. There was no way they'd swing ten people around to a guilty vote. As he sat there wondering what to do, Lackey couldn't stop pondering the prosecution's failures. Incompetence on the part of the DA doomed the trial, he believed, and Manduley agreed. They'd let Cahoon and his confederates walk all over them. Instead of murder, Cahoon had the jurors worrying "about the spread of communism."[29]

Finally, Manduley told Lackey that he thought they should switch their vote. It wasn't fair, the Cuban native argued, to put Greensboro and North Carolina, the defendants' lawyers, or even the defendants through another trial. Let's call it off and allow the majority to win, he said. Bob Lackey accepted the foreman's direction reluctantly. Years later he'd say, "It's just a joke, that trial," believing he should've resisted the pressure and hung the jury.[30]

When the verdict came in, Dave Matthews, the shooter who'd admitted killing three or maybe four of the CWP members, put his head in his hands and wept.[31]

The jury's decision stunned Mayor Melvin.

Even those who loathed Nelson Johnson and his communist comrades didn't believe the Klansmen and Nazis were innocent.

"What went wrong?" one woman asked. "I saw a man with two pistols shoot someone. Why isn't he in jail?" The trial dangled and then withdrew hope of closure for a horrific event. In the city's southeast, despair at the fact that the Klan could still murder with impunity overwhelmed people. "Keeping people from losing their mind became an issue," said one pastor. State Senator Henry Frye, the man Nelson campaigned for in 1968 and who, in 1971, convinced the governor to commute Nelson's prison sentence, was shaken by the verdict. "I'm almost speechless," he told a reporter. "A lot of people said they were going to turn them loose and I took the position, no way. I'm wrong. It makes me want to reevaluate ... my approach to things," he said.[32] In Durham, the civil rights activist and politician Julian Bond, whom Joyce had met years earlier, led hundreds of students and faculty out of North Carolina Central University and into the streets to protest the acquittals and to call for the Department of Justice to file civil rights charges against the Klansmen and Nazis. Governor Hunt could not be reached for comment.[33]

Given the prosecution's clumsy mistakes and open prejudices, the CWP would say Greeson and Coman had no intention of winning. After the prosecutors called neither Eddie Dawson nor Bernard Butkovich to testify, Nelson and his comrades became even more convinced that the prosecutors were more concerned with hiding the roles of the police, FBI, and BATF in the murders and cover-up than with convicting the Klansmen and Nazis.[34]

Stung by the verdict, Coman, Greeson, and their boss Michael Schlosser blamed the CWP, rather than their own missteps, for the loss. Michael Schlosser "held [Nelson Johnson] if not legally, then morally responsible for Nov. 3" more than anyone else.[35] The prosecutors decided that the CWP hoped they'd blow the case, just to confirm their belief in the essential corruption of the American system. The public scenes the CWP created inside and outside the courtroom— calling the trial a sham, confronting Jim Hunt, setting off firecrackers at the Democratic National Convention—turned the jury against them, the prosecutors believed. If the Klan and Nazis weren't guilty, to many in Greensboro it meant that the CWP and, particularly, Nelson Johnson must be. They're "scumbags," Coman would say of the CWP, his voice still thick with visceral anger years later.[36]

After more than a year of working long hours, seven days a week, Greeson and Coman were exhausted. At the veterinarian's office one day not long after the trial, Greeson leaned over to pick up his dog and passed out. The fainting spells would continue for several years. The stress triggered a chronic illness in Jim Coman. Neither would ever be part of another case that demanded so much. Their careers, however, were not harmed by the loss. If anything, the trial gave their reputations as tough, top lawyers a boost.[37]

Within days of the acquittal, Schlosser dropped the charges against the other Klansmen and Nazis as well as those against Nelson and his comrades. Neither the DA's office nor the state could afford another bruising trial.

Racked by doubt and guilt over his own mistakes leading up to November 3, but also certain that the responsibility for the murders of his friends had not yet been properly assigned, Nelson hit rock bottom. Struggling to hold his life, family, and marriage together, Nelson began building elegant wooden trunks, hoping to make a business of selling them while Joyce's steady job at A&T kept them from destitution and stark isolation. One day, Nelson approached a Jewish man who ran a junk shop. He asked the man for a job. The man agreed to hire Nelson. Before he accepted the offer, Nelson said, "I have to tell you who I am." The man listened before responding, "As long as you work hard, I don't care." It was a generous gesture, something to hold on to, a small space beyond his existence as a pariah in Greensboro.[38]

KLAN ACTS

If the courts were going to find anyone criminally responsible for the killings on November 3, 1979, it would be up to the Department of Justice, where a changing of the guard and of philosophy loomed. On November 4, 1980, voters joined Ronald Reagan in his invitation, "Let's Make America Great Again." At his inauguration, looking west from the White House, Reagan beckoned the country to embark on "new beginnings" and to leave Jimmy Carter's "old wounds" behind. That same day in Iran, the hostages boarded a plane and began their journey home.[1]

Despite Cecil Moses's quick determination of federal jurisdiction on November 3, the DoJ waffled, uncertain, officials claimed, about whether federal laws applied in the Greensboro case. If the DoJ's delay reinforced the CWP's suspicions of a cover-up, it also caused consternation among legal experts and politicians. Religious and civic leaders, as well as hundreds of civil rights activists and numerous high-profile public figures around the country, including the singer and civil rights activist Harry Belafonte and the actor Michael Douglas, signed petitions and wrote letters pressuring the DoJ to act. The Congressional Black Caucus publicly backed a federal criminal trial against the Klan and Nazi shooters.

Joyce Johnson and other CWP members traveled to Washington to seek an audience with Representative John Conyers of Michigan and his staff. The stories they told troubled the lawmaker.

In December 1980, less than a month after the state trial in Greensboro ended, Representative Conyers convened the first of four hearings to shed light on the rise in racist violence around the country. The Conyers hearings conducted by the House Judiciary's Subcommittee on Crime investigated the Klan rallies in Decatur, Alabama, in early 1979; the brutal killing of a Black man by Miami police officers and the cops' expeditious acquittal of any wrongdoing by an all-white jury; six sadistic and unsolved murders of Black people in Buffalo, New York; the strange child murders in Atlanta, which had reached eleven victims at the time of the first hearing (a number that would more than double over the coming months); the shooting of Vernon Jordan, president of the National Urban League, by a white supremacist in Indiana; and violent racial incidents in Detroit, Salt Lake City, Youngstown, Ohio, and Chattanooga, Tennessee. Witnesses reported white nationalist paramilitary training camps operating openly in several states, including North Carolina. At the heart of the hearings lay the Greensboro shootings, a primary source of the gusts of "hysteria" howling through the nation's Black communities, fanning a belief that "conspiracies exist and that their lives are endangered."[2]

The lawyer and Rutgers University professor Arthur Kinoy, who'd spent his life defending the civil rights of dissenters and activists in America, told the Conyers committee that the violence presented "a problem as grave as the country has faced in many years." In 1871, President Ulysses S. Grant signed into law statutes designed to protect the constitutional rights of Black people from the Ku Klux Klan and their white supremacist allies in positions of power. Enforcement of the new laws was both effective and brief. Kinoy pointed to the 1877 Hayes-Tilden compromise, which ended the hope for permanent Reconstruction in the South and "Federal enforcement of the [Civil War] promise of equality and freedom for the supposedly emancipated Black people." The anti-Klan statutes were buried, Kinoy continued, leading to the Jim Crow period, "which allowed the Klan to lynch, murder, castrate, burn, bomb, and terrorize Black people back into virtual slavery." "Federal governmental inaction," Kinoy warned, could lead to a "new 1877," which would "bury the elementary promises of the freedom and equality set forth in the 13th, 14th, and 15th amendments."

After the "total failure of state and local attempts at the prosecution of the elementary civil rights of citizens," a strong federal response in Greensboro, Kinoy suggested, would demonstrate a renewed commitment to the American dream of freedom and equality.[3]

❖

A mile away from Capitol Hill, Justice Department officials, heeding the Gipper's call to a bright future, denied their responsibility to remedy historical injustices through litigation, turning their backs on more than two decades of DoJ work to level uneven playing fields in education, employment, housing, and voting.[4] As Kinoy feared it might, the Reagan administration replaced a mission to affirm and extend the basic rights of the poor and minorities with a vision of ascendant corporate power rising through a fog of amnesia.[5] The Greensboro shooting presented a conundrum for Reagan's DoJ. On the one hand, the shooting showed what appeared to be a demonstrable and intentional infraction of victims' civil rights. On the other hand, the political intent of the victims and their framing of the event as an example of the country's deep-rooted racism and antilabor tendencies ran counter to Reagan's ideological framing of United States history and the directives he handed down to the DoJ. The applicable law itself, the old Ku Klux Klan Act referenced by Kinoy, raised uncomfortable questions about America's relationship to its past. And then there was the issue of communism. As the Reagan administration stoked the Cold War, increasing support to anticommunist paramilitaries and right-wing death squads in Central America, the defense of communists at home was not going to be undertaken with enthusiasm.

After Ronald Reagan took office, Mickey Michaux, the only Black federal attorney in North Carolina, sat in his office running out the clock on his political appointment. Impatient with the inaction of his bosses on the matter of the Klan and Nazi shooting, the lame-duck attorney asked a former DoJ lawyer and law professor at Duke University named William Van Alstyne to analyze the case. With Van Alstyne's opinions in hand, Michaux fired off a memo to the DoJ's Civil Rights Division, laying out a legal basis for bringing charges against the Klansmen and Nazis. In June 1980, as he cleared out his office, he made his recommendations public: "It would indeed be hypocritical for the [Reagan] Administration to express concern about the rise of violence and its effects on our citizens, or the right to life of the unborn, yet stand idly by when five human beings are gunned down in front of television cameras by fanatical members of hate groups solely because of their ideology."[6] When asked for comment about Michaux's letter, Jerry Paul Smith, the Klansman who'd claimed amnesia during the state trial, said, "You can take . . . [Michaux] and bury him just like they buried Sandy [sic] Smith. Now print that in your lie newspaper."[7]

❖

When the Guilford County prosecutor blamed him for the deaths of his five comrades at the felony riot arraignment in May 1980, Nelson had exploded in rage and anguish. The judge slapped him with a contempt charge. During the summer of 1981, after exhausting his appeals, Nelson entered the Guilford County Jail to serve a twenty-day sentence for contempt. He announced that he would refuse food during his time inside, saying "I've been hauled into court in order to silence me."[8]

Nelson "has a few extra pounds, like most people in their 30s," Joyce joked to reporters, suggesting the hunger strike would help him trim down. Turning serious, she called her husband a political prisoner and said she and "the girls" were "very concerned about his health and safety" in Guilford County's "notorious" and brutal jail.[9]

In a letter from prison, Nelson wrote that he owed his life to the political support of the "thousands of people" around the country who kept the plight of the CWP in the spotlight during a "huge and continuing cover-up." "Step by step," he wrote, "the truth is bursting forth," even as he pointed out the irony of the fact that while he sat in jail, the November 3 killers remained free.[10]

Twenty days later, when he passed back through the gate leading from the high-rise penitentiary, Joyce handed him a cup of strawberry yogurt. It was the first solid food he'd eaten in three weeks. Nine months to the day after the Klan and Nazi shooters were acquitted, Nelson looked more like the wide-eyed activist he'd been in the late 1960s than a revolutionary approaching forty. He'd dropped twenty-six pounds during his fast.

Later that day, at a press conference at the Uhuru Bookstore, which Joyce and Lewis Brandon had founded in the early 1970s, Nelson said, "I want to challenge the Government and the Justice Department to bring charges." Explaining why he believed the Feds were slow to move, he said, "If the Klan and Nazis were convicted, they would squeal on the government and expose its role."[11]

When Representative Conyers called Duke Professor William Van Alstyne to testify at the last of the congressman's four hearings, on November 12, 1981, the DoJ had still not committed to entering the fray in Greensboro. The man who had helped Mickey Michaux write his memo questioned the "integrity and zeal" of his former colleagues in the Justice Department.[12] There was no excuse, Van Alstyne told the committee, for the DoJ's "highly disturbing sense of aloofness and suspect silence, when the very kind of situation which produced these federal statutes over a century ago is not fully explored and dealt with by the Justice Department. This is, after all, the Ku Klux Klan Act. This is part of the South . . . with its history of unequal racial treatment. There is, here, a background of general intimidation linking race, unorganized labor, left leaning ideological groups harassed as such and because they seem 'threatening' to anti-union and anti-Black groups."[13]

According to Van Alstyne, three statutes under Title 18 of the US Code, sections 241, 242, and 245, warranted consideration for a prosecution of the Klan and Nazis. Section 241 targeted conspiracies—agreements between two or more parties—to deprive a person of their constitutional rights. Section 242 introduced the term *color of law*, to charge "federal, state, and local officials" acting "within" or "beyond" their "lawful authority" to "willfully deprive or cause to be deprived from any person those rights, privileges, or immunities secured or protected by the Constitution and laws of the United States." Van Alstyne thought it imperative to explore the possibility that law enforcement officers in Greensboro colluded with the Klan and Nazis. Following the ratification of the 1964 Civil Rights Act, Congress enacted section 245 as a clarification to section 241, removing the requirement of either conspiracy or law enforcement complicity to trigger a federal civil rights case. A successful prosecution under section 245, however, required proof that a defendant was motivated to deprive a victim of his or her constitutional rights due to his or her "race, color, religion or national origin."[14]

Hearing this, Conyers made an astute observation: none of the laws that fell under the Ku Klux Klan Act addressed murder. The right to vote and the freedoms of assembly, of speech, and from bondage were all constitutionally protected. As the laws were written, merely living was not a protected activity. Therefore, an apparently racist murder of a Black person did not automatically trigger federal jurisdiction unless the victim, at the precise time of the murder, had been participating in an activity protected by the Constitution *and* prosecutors could prove race to be the motivating factor in the killing.

During that final hearing in the late fall of 1981, Representative Conyers delivered a message to the assistant attorney general for the Civil Rights Division, William Reynolds: "[Greensboro,] as you know, has attracted worldwide attention, and we are watching it" to see whether your stated principles align with the "reality of your day-to-day operations. . . . It seems to me that some laws very likely were broken somewhere. I don't know how five people can be killed and everybody can say 'Things are OK.' That's a staggering conclusion to come to." If the DoJ didn't see fit to investigate the Greensboro shootings, Conyers gently threatened the federal prosecutor, maybe Congress would have to do so.[15]

COAT

By 1982, the CWP members involved in the legal fight in Greensboro began to climb out of the sectarian corner they'd backed—and been pushed—into. They renamed the Greensboro Justice Fund the Greensboro Civil Rights Fund (GCRF) and hired an American Civil Liberties Union director as their head of the fundraising. Signe Waller took on media outreach. Dale Sampson moved to New York to dedicate herself to raising money to cover the growing legal fees. Marty Nathan traveled the country, often together with Lewis Pitts, drumming up support at both the grassroots level and among high-profile activists. The celebrity pediatrician and antiwar activist Dr. Benjamin Spock joined the board of the GCRF. Father Daniel Berrigan visited Greensboro in support of CWP's quest for justice, as did the folk singers Pete Seeger and Joan Baez.[1]

In combination with this grassroots support, the pressure from Representative Conyers worked. During the late winter of 1982, the DoJ attorney assigned to the case empaneled a grand jury to test probable cause, bring indictments, and seek some justice for the November 3 killings.

As DoJ prosecutor Michael Johnson reviewed the FBI investigation, he doubted he could prove that the Klansmen conspired in advance to kill the demonstrators. From the reports compiled by Horace Beckwith under Cecil Moses's direction, Johnson concluded, as had the state prosecutors, that the accusation of law enforcement collusion with the Klan and Nazis was "baseless." Given these assumptions, he rejected both the "conspiracy" statute, section 241, and the "color of law" statute, section 242. This left him with section 245 and the task of demonstrating that the white supremacists' actions on November 3 had been motivated by race. But Johnson had interviewed Rick Gree-son and Jim Coman when they lost the murder case and knew that the Klan and Nazi defense team would be ready for this charge. The Klan's lawyers had wrapped their defendants in the flag, claiming that communism, not race, impelled the men to Greensboro and that fear for their lives impelled them to fire their guns. It would be the government's task, then, to overcome these arguments and convince a jury that race and race mixing had motivated Klansmen and Nazis to interfere with the marchers' right to assemble, a right guaranteed by the Constitution and certified by the city-issued parade permit.[2]

Michael Johnson assigned the role of lead investigator—the person who would be the "first witness before the grand jury to 'orient' them on the facts" of the case—to Greensboro FBI agent Thomas Brereton. The relief the CWP members and John Conyers had felt when the DoJ snapped into action mutated into outrage.

The CWP's list of problems with Brereton was long and growing longer. Lewis Pitts enumerated them in a letter to US Attorney General William Smith. Over the years, Brereton had hired Eddie Dawson, a likely target of the grand jury investigation, to work on his house. This fact likely qualified as a conflict of interest. Roland Wayne Wood asserted that Brereton had failed to transcribe the parts of his postshooting interrogation in which he talked about Bernard Butkovich. And twenty minutes of Brereton's recorded interview with Jerry Paul Smith had disappeared into thin air. All of this and more had led the CWP to name Brereton in their civil suit as playing a part in the November 3 cover-up, together with Cecil Moses and numerous other FBI agents.[3] But to DoJ attorney Johnson, Brereton, with his bold, Bronx charm, seemed the essence of a straight shooter.[4]

Twenty-one people—one of whom was Black—were seated to

the grand jury, which would grind on with its secret deliberations for thirteen months.

During the longest-running civil rights grand jury in the history of the Justice Department, events relevant to the Greensboro case continued to take place, causing Representative Conyers, the Black Caucus, civil rights leaders, and the CWP to worry about the grand jury's lack of attention to the role law enforcement might have played in the shooting. In San Diego, a BATF agent infiltrated a CWP group that was working and organizing at the National Steel and Shipbuilding Company. The agent taught the group to build bombs and encouraged the activists to blow up ships, though they chose to detonate the bombs in a wild stretch of desert instead. Closer to Greensboro, at a trial in Asheville, North Carolina, evidence surfaced that the threat to blow up an oil refinery in Greensboro and kill a journalist if the Klan and Nazis were convicted of murder in the state trial had originated with an undercover BATF agent who'd tried repeatedly to convince Nazis, including at least one who'd been in the November 3 caravan, to carry out the terrorist mission.[5] Then, during the grand jury, a document from an anonymous sender arrived in the mail for lawyer Pitts. It indicated that the BATF operation involving Bernard Butkovich had, despite Bureau denials, been coordinated directly with the FBI, or "SAC to SAC," with knowledge of each agency's top state official.[6]

Through all this, the CWP remained committed to participating in the federal trial. But working with the FBI and entrusting the quest for justice to Brereton—who, most CWP members suspected, "had known about November 3rd before it happened"—led to awkward moments.[7] In her interview with Brereton, Joyce described being tailed by police cars and other law enforcement personnel in unmarked cars while hanging posters advertising the "Death to the Klan" march. One of the men who'd followed her, she said to Brereton, "looked like you." In his interview with Nelson, Brereton fixated on the activist's ideology, demonstrating little interest in the murders. Nelson called the two days he spent with the agent a "COINTELPRO-style" interrogation. But with no say in the matter, Nelson, Joyce, and the others continued to work with people and institutions they believed to be at least partially responsible for the murder of their friends.[8]

❖

By 1983, everyone connected to the shooting was on edge, expecting the grand jury to reveal its findings any day. Then, in early March, a long letter on pages torn from a yellow legal pad and tucked inside an envelope arrived at the Greensboro Civil Rights Fund office. Addressed to "Mr. Nelson Johnson and Whom It May Concern," the thirteen pages were filled with a tight, neat cursive. The author was a sometime mill worker and habitual criminal named Henry C. Byrd Sr., who'd been arrested for insurance fraud that January and was being held for trial in the Guilford County Jail. "Please," the letter began, "read the attached . . . pages. . . . Make yourself a copy and send it back to my wife so she can take it to my attorney." Then Byrd began his story: "I remember [these] shocking matters as if they all started yesterday . . ."[9]

The young Black man claimed he hadn't acted alone in his insurance fraud scheme, but in partnership with a Greensboro police officer. But it wasn't this crime that caused him to send the letter to Nelson. "For some time over the years since 1977," Byrd wrote, "I have worked for a Greensboro Policeman by the name of Bell, not being I wanted to but because I had to in able to maintain my freedom." Neither Nelson nor Lewis Pitts could believe what they read next as Byrd's "facts" became stranger than fiction—if, that is, the intricate details of police corruption, drug dealing, and murder that he recounted weren't, in fact, fiction. If true, they'd surely, as Byrd wrote, "lay scandal on the Greensboro Police Department."[10]

After a car accident in 1977, Byrd claimed that Officer Raymond Bell shanghaied him into a drug-dealing operation.[11] Byrd acted as the bagman, storing large amounts of cocaine and heroin for Bell and driving three or four street-level dealers, also employed by Bell, to spots around Greensboro and the nearby municipalities of High Point and Burlington. On Saturdays or weekday evenings, according to Byrd, when Bell wanted to collect the cash, he'd meet Byrd, sometimes in the parking lot across from the police department. They'd take off together, and at the appointed stops, Byrd would hop out of the car and pick up the money from the dealers while Bell waited.

One day, Byrd wrote, he went to meet Bell at the police department. One of Bell's dealers, a man Byrd called "Big Head," had turned up dead. Byrd suspected that Bell himself had murdered the man for skimming the drug money. Right there in the police department, Bell asked Byrd to begin selling for him. When Byrd agreed, Bell pulled out a one-pound bag of heroin and handed it over. Byrd put the drugs in a bag and strolled out of the Greensboro Police Department. When Byrd arrived back at the apartment he shared with his wife and two children, neighbors told him that a police detective had been asking after him. Frightened that he'd be discovered in possession of a heroin stash with a street value north of $200,000, Byrd flushed the drugs down the toilet.

Byrd wrote that he lied to Bell, telling him that he'd given the drugs to someone else to sell. Meanwhile, Byrd sold his car and dipped into his and his wife's paychecks to pay Bell a couple hundred bucks every week, maintaining the illusion that he was slinging the heroin. By October 1979, Byrd said he'd paid the cop over $20,000 dollars, but still owed Bell north of $40,000.

Byrd claimed that one October afternoon, about a week before November 3, Bell drove him down to East Market Street and stopped in front of the Uhuru Bookstore. Bell pointed out a man entering the store. That's Nelson Johnson, he told Byrd. Shoot him, Bell said, and I'll forgive your debt. He handed Byrd a loaded .38-caliber pistol.

Shortly after this, according to Byrd, GPD Detective Herb Belvin, asked him to infiltrate a CWP meeting. When Byrd told Bell about Detective Belvin's request, Bell told him to forget about shooting Nelson Johnson.[12]

❖

Lewis Pitts contacted Byrd's lawyer and arranged a time to meet with his client. Was Byrd telling tall tales as revenge against the police officer who'd arrested him for insurance fraud? Or was he relating a twisted, true story of police corruption? The level of detail in Byrd's letter intrigued Pitts and Nelson; Byrd listed addresses, license plate numbers, names, and people's physical characteristics. He even described the way Officer Bell set his briefcase on the floor of his car. In the interview with Pitts, Byrd, a six-footer with a quiet, matter-of-fact voice, repeated the allegations he'd spelled out in the letter.[13]

From his interview notes, Pitts typed out an affidavit. He found Byrd again in a holding pen at the courthouse awaiting a hearing. Byrd skimmed the affidavit quickly and signed it. Pitts then rushed to the grand jury room to deliver the stunning document. It was mid-April 1983. The grand jury was due to wrap up within days.[14]

Michael Johnson read the affidavit and immediately asked Special Agent Brereton to investigate. The FBI agent called Officer Bell, who denied all of Byrd's claims. Brereton called Detective Belvin, who also denied that he'd talked with Byrd in the days before November 3, 1979, though the detective admitted that he had recruited Byrd as a street-level informant in the past. Then Brereton interviewed Byrd, who contradicted some minor details in the written affidavit. On April 15, the grand jury questioned Byrd but not the policemen he'd named. Thomas Brereton then summarized the police rebuttal to Byrd's accusations for the grand jury.[15]

When the grand jury shut down on April 21, 1983, after thirteen months of deliberations, they indicted nine men for violating the civil rights of the marchers on November 3, including, this time, the police and FBI informant Eddie Dawson and the Klan leader Virgil Griffin. The absence of any law enforcement officials among the indictments prompted Nelson to call the process "incomplete," despite the 140 witnesses and thirteen months of deliberation. Former Greensboro mayoral candidate Sol Jacobs also regretted that the grand jury neglected the participation of law enforcement, saying presciently, "This type of thing will hang over us. . . . It won't clear up the lingering questions."[16]

Though they didn't indict any police officers, the grand jury did indict Henry C. Byrd Sr. for perjury. The trial of the Klansmen and Nazis would take place a year later, but Byrd's trip through the justice system traveled at a pace, thought Lewis Pitts, that was possible only if a prosecutor and judge agreed on the urgent need for trial. Byrd was arraigned on May 2, less than two weeks after being indicted, and brought to trial in federal court on June 14. At trial, a simple choice was presented for the jury: Did they believe Byrd or the policemen who contradicted him? In the witness box, Officer Bell, a gung-ho cop with the full support of the GPD, looked to Byrd's lawyer as if he were about to explode with fear.[17] As lawyer Bob Warren attempted—and failed—to force the Greensboro Police Department to turn over its informant payment records, he would say in court that, if what his client said were true, it's likely that Bell's activities weren't meant for personal enrichment, or only personal enrichment. Rather, Warren suspected they may have been part of a police department scheme to create a secret fund, independent of city oversight, with which to pay informants like Byrd or Eddie Dawson.[18] The stocky Brereton who'd presented the case against Byrd to the grand jury sat at the prosecution table throughout Byrd's trial. By the first week of July, the jury declared Byrd guilty of perjury. Lewis Pitts called it an "if there's smoke there's fire conviction," a quick trial, not to find the truth, but to discredit and silence Byrd and keep the reputation of the police department—and possibly the FBI—intact.[19]

Appeals would carry Byrd's case up the legal ladder, until, finally, it died on the doorstep of the Supreme Court when the nation's top justices declined to hear it, and sank back into the deep reservoir of murk and mystery that haunted the November 3 shooting.

❖

The DoJ's Michael Johnson worked hard to build trust with the CWP members, calmly negotiating between the smart and wary activists and his impatient bosses in Washington. Some at the Justice Department suspected Johnson of handing Pitts the document revealing the FBI's knowledge of the Butkovich undercover operation. When the FBI interviewed him about the breach, Johnson offered to take a lie detector test to clear his name. A short time later he resigned, saying that the Reagan administration wasn't fully behind the prosecution. Worried that the DoJ was not committed to the prosecution and that, after all his work during the grand jury proceedings, he'd be sidelined during the trial, he left Washington to work as a federal attorney in Little Rock, Arkansas.[20]

Eight months after the grand jury disbanded, the criminal civil rights trial began in January 1984 with secret jury selection. Despite the judge's apparent care to ensure a diverse jury pool, the defense lawyers again struck all the Black candidates, resulting in a second all-white jury. Five of the nine defendants were the same as in the earlier trial, and several of their lawyers returned to defend their clients a second time.

The nine men weren't facing murder charges this time. Federal prosecutors, arguing for a conviction under the criminal statute section 245, would have to convince the jury that the Klan and Nazis, acting out of racial malice, had interfered with the marchers' civil rights. Despite the federal resources, the media spotlight, and the testimony of the CWP widows, the second trial turned out to be, for the most part, a rerun of the first.

The powerful video imagery worked against the prosecution, as defense lawyers pointed out again what couldn't be seen in the horrific images flickering across the screen. What lay behind that truck? Did the distortions of the video make it impossible to gauge distance? And for a second time, too, the testimony of the FBI ballistics expert Bruce Koenig damaged the prosecution's case. From the witness chair, Koenig implied that the critical three shots—shots 3, 4, and 5—were more likely to have been fired from Klan and Nazi guns. One of the Klan lawyers, a veteran of the state murder trial, leaped to his feet and asked for a five-minute recess. After a quick conference, the ubiquitous Thomas Brereton dashed from the courtroom and returned with the evidentiary map from the state murder trial. It showed where, more than three years earlier, Koenig had reconsidered and reduced the area from which the shots had originated. The credibility of the FBI expert's testimony evaporated again.[21]

During the grand jury proceedings, Mark Sherer, the young man who'd fired the first shot with the powder pistol on November 3, secretly pleaded guilty to conspiracy, telling Brereton and Michael Johnson that the Klan had indeed made plans to start—and finish—a brawl with the communists.[22] On the witness stand, likely terrified of Klan retaliation, he claimed that he'd been "browbeaten" into the agreement with prosecutors, recanting statements he'd made that Virgil Griffin had hoped to provoke a "race war" and that Jerry Paul Smith wanted to bring a pipe bomb to the march to see what it might do if tossed into a "crowd of n——s."[23]

When Jim Cooley, the defense attorney for Klansman David Wayne Matthews, rose to offer a closing statement, he knew he had the prosecution on the ropes. All he had to do was create reasonable doubt in the minds of the jurors, as Bob Cahoon had done so skillfully in the murder trial. Cooley took parts of two days to blanket everything the jurors had heard in a fog that, despite the video and all the technical analysis, made it impossible to truly determine who shot whom. "No burden of proof is on me," he reminded the jurors. That burden rested with the prosecution.[24]

The demonstrators, he argued, had relinquished their constitutionally protected civil rights when they brought guns to the march in violation of the terms of the parade permit. The defendants, on the other hand, had been scared to death and acted out of self-defense. Then he gave his rhetorical knife a twist, shredding the law that formed the basis of the government's case. Even if the shooters didn't act in self-defense, Cooley said, there was no way of saying with any certainty that they acted out of racial hatred. "Are you able to say, ladies and gentlemen, that the substantial motivating factor that caused Dave Matthews . . . to fire in this situation at this time and place was because these people were involved in a racially integrated activity? . . . Or was it fear? Or was it personal anger because these people had jumped on the cars and attacked the cars of his friends? . . . Was it that these people were communists, and is that why he fired?" Given all the doubt, Cooley said audaciously, the shooters could not be convicted, even if the jury believed they'd committed murder. As John Conyers had astutely observed during his hearings, these civil rights statutes didn't protect life.

In a dramatic gesture, Cooley produced a navy-blue wool jacket and draped it over the back of the witness chair. In the sweep of the crime scene, police had picked up the coat that Nelson Johnson removed to lay over the back of his dead friend Jim Waller. They'd added it to the vast store of physical evidence, along with the guns and bullet shells, the knives, nunchucks, brass knuckles, clubs, sticks, and broken spectacles. To Cooley, the empty jacket represented an opportunity. Though many of the widows had testified during the federal trial, Nelson had not. Now, as Cooley finished his remarks, he could define the Black activist however he wished.

"David Matthews," said Cooley of his client, "is a poor man. He's not well educated. He has no facility with words, like some of the people on the other side of this case. He loves his family and his country. He dislikes communism. He is no hero. He is no murderer. He was a pawn, I contend, in a cruel game."[25] Matthews, Cooley asserted, had been manipulated by the communists to come to Greensboro, to engage in a battle that would raise the CWP's profile and help them build the party.

As he came to the end of his closing remarks, Cooley's rhetoric reached its crescendo. "In *Paradise Lost*, the English poet John Milton wrote the basic dramatic formula for inciting crowds to evil behavior, a formula, ladies and gentlemen, which Nelson Johnson learned very well. Milton's description is that of Satan exhorting his fallen angels to rise up as one mighty army and overthrow God by force or trickery. All of the props for that, all of the props for inciting a riot were at Everitt and Carver that bright day in November, four and a half years ago. The banners—remember them?—with the weapons. The weapons themselves. The music. The shouting. The chanting. And the speeches, ladies and gentlemen. The speeches. Here they are, the speeches full of lies. It was a shabby performance, and five people are dead." What chance, he'd asked the jury, could this uneducated white man have against the overeducated, sinister communists? Against Satan? Against Nelson Johnson?

And with a final, brash flourish, before the all-white jury, Cooley marshaled a civil rights song to the defense of his Klan client and to beat a federal law enacted to protect Black people and their allies from the Klan: "'I woke up this morning with my mind stayed on freedom,'" he chanted. "Set them free from this nightmare, ladies and gentlemen, set them free."[26]

On April 15, 1984, the shooters and their coconspirators were acquitted for a second time.

After the Klansmen and Nazis and Eddie Dawson, perhaps no one felt more relief than the Guilford County attorneys Rick Greeson, Jim Coman, and Michael Schlosser. The federal government couldn't convict the Klansmen and Nazis either.[27]

The acquittals sent a powerful message. In 1980 and 1981, Representative Conyers had pushed the federal government to prosecute the Greensboro case and deter the spread of white supremacist violence. As the Klansmen and Nazis again walked free, he called this second round of acquittals a "mockery of justice."[28]

With the results of this second trial, Nelson Johnson's responsibility for the November 3 shooting hardened into an article of legal faith in Greensboro.

❖

While Jim Cooley conjured Satan in his closing remarks, Nelson was stumping around rural Mississippi for Jesse Jackson's 1984 presidential campaign. In the Deep South state—"Mississippi Goddam," in the words of Nina Simone's song—known for its terrifying history of racial violence but far from the hatred of him that was polluting Greensboro, Nelson felt liberated. He enjoyed the camaraderie of his fellow organizers and the political work among ordinary folk.[29] He thought, "Mississippi's a nice place," and his mind caressed the idea of a fresh start.[30]

Joyce had begged Nelson not to go to Mississippi to work on the presidential campaign of his fellow Aggie, Jesse Jackson. She, too, faced challenges in Greensboro. One Saturday morning as she hustled the girls out the door to a dance class, police arrived and arrested Joyce for unpaid parking tickets. After that incident, she carried receipts around in her wallet to prove that the charges were unwarranted. When she traveled to transportation conferences for her job, government officials would say they'd been advised to avoid her. She refused to let her hurt and anger show, instead offering impromptu "seminars about the trials of a race-driven South, a right-to-work South." With the backing of A&T, she worked through the harassment, successfully soliciting and managing multimillion-dollar contracts from the US Department of Transportation.[31]

Nelson had nothing like his wife's professional stability. Consumed by rage during the interminable fight-back campaign, he'd often been inaccessible, not the same man who, in 1976, told Paul Bermanzohn never to put children on the back burner. Nelson and Joyce's bond, forged during the tumult of 1969, now hung by a thread, frayed after years of stress, grief, and isolation. Desperate to find a meaningful place in the world beyond the legal struggles, Nelson departed Greensboro for Mississippi in tears.[32]

The CWP renamed itself the New Democratic Movement, replacing a vision of violent revolution with a new faith in the power of grassroots politics. As the country continued its rightward march under Reagan, CWP members, along with many others in "ultra-left" organizations, set aside their most provocative rhetoric and contributed their organizing expertise to the Jackson campaign, which won 18.2 percent of the Democratic primary votes, enough for a surprising third-place finish.[33]

Nelson returned to Greensboro from Mississippi with his spirits buoyed. He and Joyce, two self-professed communists, knelt and, reaching back to simpler times in their lives, prayed for their marriage. They didn't pack up the family and leave Greensboro; they took the girls to church on Sunday. More than faith, they sought community; and much of Black Greensboro now stood ready to accept a prodigal son and his family back into its healing embrace. When Nelson inquired, A&T, too, quietly opened its doors, allowing him to reenroll.[34]

DISCOVERY

No federal judge in North Carolina would sit for the pending civil trial, which, if it followed the pattern of the state and the federal criminal trials, promised little but embarrassment and uncomfortable conversations about communism and white supremacy with friends, neighbors, and colleagues.

By the time Robert Merhige Jr. volunteered to hear the trial, the LBJ appointee had served on the US District Court for the Eastern District of Virginia in Richmond for fifteen years. There he'd earned the nickname "Rocket Docket" for dispatching cases with alacrity, as well as a polarizing reputation as an activist, liberal judge. He'd ordered the University of Virginia to admit women; ruled that despite the US government's intentional lack of definition, the conflict in Vietnam was, indeed, a war; maintained the convictions of three of the Watergate criminals; and ordered Allied Chemical to clean up the toxic chemical Kepone the company had dumped into Virginia's James River. After a 1972 order to desegregate the schools in Richmond, white supremacists spit in his face, shot his dog, and burned down the guest cottage at his Richmond home. For two years, US marshals shadowed Merhige, guarding the judge against a steady stream of death threats.[1]

Despite the stress of that case, Merhige's love of the law never faltered. Pegged to his desk late into the night, a ball cap flipped backward on his head, surrounded by photos of his beloved generations of law clerks, he'd answer the phone with a signature, gruff bark, "This is Bob Merhige, district judge." He relished traveling to far-flung districts, like a benevolent dictator touring his domain, cleaning up jammed dockets, settling cases and expeditiously trying a few, all the while muttering about the work habits of the resident judge.[2]

Born in Brooklyn, New York, Merhige was familiar with the Piedmont Triad. He'd matriculated at High Point College, where he played point guard on the basketball team, before transferring to the University of Richmond. It didn't take a judge of his experience to know that opposing sides in the case of *James Waller, et al., Plaintiffs, v. Bernard Butkovich, et al., Defendants* would never agree to settle. If the judge determined the case had merit, he'd likely preside for months at the brutalist cement cube of a federal courthouse in Winston-Salem, far from home, applying the nation's law. Around the corner from the federal building, beside the classically columned Forsyth County Courthouse, stood a statue of a Confederate soldier, as if to remind Judge Merhige what he'd be up against.

Though the CWP plaintiffs had submitted their complaint by the November 3, 1980, deadline, Judge Merhige refused to allow discovery to begin until the federal criminal trial ended. Finally, on April 22, 1984, one week after the federal acquittals, lawyers from all sides of the civil suit appeared before Merhige, to discuss the merits of the case and the applicability of the 1871 Klan Act to redress the shooting. Defense attorneys for the FBI, the BATF, and the City of Greensboro argued that the judge should immediately and summarily dismiss the entire case, describing it as nothing but a hot pile of "revolutionary rhetoric."

Since the summer of 1980, when he'd agreed to take the case, Lewis Pitts had been living in Greensboro on a "pinto bean" salary of a couple hundred dollars a month raised by the Greensboro Civil Rights

Fund and supplemented by his wife's wages from teaching.[3] Cops or agents tailed anyone involved in the suit wherever they went. The CWP suspected the FBI or the SBI of listening in on Pitts's activities from the apartment adjacent to the one he shared with his wife.[4] A surveillance team had taken over an attic apartment across from Signe Waller's house.[5] Despite the intimidation and the pittance of a budget, a crackerjack legal team came together to finally eke out some justice for the victims of November 3. Gayle Korotkin, a shy, impossibly hardworking lawyer, relocated to North Carolina from New York to support the cause. Talented CWP lawyers from the West Coast, including Tom Ono and Stuart Kwo, pitched in. Pitts's boss, Danny Sheehan, who'd loaned the scrappy young Pitts to the Greensboro Civil Rights Fund from the newly formed Christic Institute, joined the effort. Carolyn McAllaster, a member of the North Carolina State Bar who'd defended CWP members arrested for spray-painting and postering, provided the team access to the North Carolina courts. CWP lawyer Earl Tockman reached out to his Northwestern Law School classmates at the People's Law Office (PLO) in Chicago. In 1982, the PLO had finally scored a stunning victory on behalf of the families of Fred Hampton and Mark Clark, the Chicago Black Panthers assassinated in 1969. The Chicago lawyers' tenacity in the face of official resistance and judicial bias favoring law enforcement had won the largest civil rights award in American history at the time, paid by the parties behind the COINTELPRO murders: the FBI and the Chicago Police Department. It would be revealed later that J. Edgar Hoover had personally approved the deadly raid. Flint Taylor of the PLO agreed to participate in the CWP civil trial.

The plaintiffs clearly presented their case in the complaint: "Agents of local, state and federal law enforcement agencies," it asserted, "operating under cover as members of the Klan and Nazis, participated in the planning and execution of the attack. In fact," the complaint continued, "the November 3 attack was the culmination of a conspiracy among local, state and federal police and executive officials and members of the Klan and Nazis to deprive plaintiffs of their equal rights, privileges and immunities . . . motivated by the defendants' hostility to communists, labor organizers and advocates of equal rights for Black people." The cops and politicians "took no action to prevent" the shooting and, the CWP and their lawyers asserted, the conspiracy "continues to this day . . . to conceal and cover up their involvement in and responsibility for the November 3 attacks."[6]

The net they'd cast had grown even wider. Among the now nearly one hundred defendants were three dozen Klansmen and Nazis, more than thirty Greensboro Police Department officers, and high officials at state, local, and federal levels. But Merhige warned the plaintiffs to tighten up their case. "You people have done a disservice to your own clients," he chastised Pitts and the others. "You sued everybody. . . . Stop wasting time and costing the government thousands and thousands and thousands of dollars, and everybody else here, needlessly, foolishly. For what? Publicity?" Then he tossed out charges against a number of the defendants for lack of evidence.[7]

Merhige, a pragmatic and patriotic institutionalist, knew also that the country had not fully faced its legacy of slavery.[8] In his opinion on the Greensboro case, he mentioned Gary Thomas Rowe, the "informant provocateur" revealed by the Church Committee to have participated in brutal violence against the 1961 Freedom Riders as the police and FBI stood by. "The fact is," he continued, making reference to the slippery elision of race and politics, "that animus against communists and advocates of equal rights for Black people may be inextricably intertwined." He drew an analogy between the CWP in Greensboro and the "Republicans who 'championed [the] cause' of Black people in the South during Reconstruction." He wrote, "If the evidence supports this view, then the conspiracy alleged herein would clearly be at the heart of the racially discriminatory activity that [the Ku Klux Klan Acts] intended to forbid." Despite his annoyance at aspects of the plaintiffs' complaint, he held the defendants' sweeping motions for dismissal to be "meritless."[9]

With that, and to the shock of the defense lawyers for the FBI and BATF, he allowed the unprecedented suit to proceed, initiating the discovery period. The lawyers representing Nelson, the widows, and all the victims who'd suffered in the aftermath of November 3 could now test whether the Reconstruction-era Ku Klux Klan Acts might exact justice in a late twentieth-century trial. Jurors in the state and federal criminal trials required certainty beyond a reasonable doubt to convict. In this civil trial, the burden of proof would be different; the preponderance of the evidence would be enough for a jury to assign liability for wrongful death or injury.

The two previous trials had failed in the same way. Prosecutors had been unable to persuade juries that the Klan and Nazis were motivated by racial hatred, that they'd intended violence when they set out for Greensboro, or that they had not acted in self-defense. The white supremacists' talented defense lawyers "wrapped them in the flag" and anointed them with holy water, presenting them as God-fearing cold warriors, themselves victims of dangerous, anti-American communists. Coupled with uncertainty over the origin of three of the shots that morning—confusion exacerbated by the FBI expert's contradictory testimony—this patriotic pastiche had been just enough to allow two juries to set the shooters free.

Pitts believed that by including law enforcement and government officials in the events leading to November 3, the plaintiffs' case would be stronger, not weaker. Faced with the expensive threat of legal shaming, the Greensboro Police Department, FBI, BATF, and City of Greensboro "fought discovery tooth and nail."[10] The four months Merhige allowed for discovery turned into eleven. In the face of constant stonewalling, Pitts and his team managed to gather some two hundred depositions and would, eventually, submit more than a hundred thousand pages of documentation to the court. Though many files were never turned over to them, the CWP lawyers exhaustively reviewed deposition transcripts, affidavits, grand jury testimony, police radio transcripts, press clips, and all the FBI investigative files they could get their hands on. A pattern of half-truths, obfuscations, and outright lies emerged—Marty Nathan called it "a pit of snakes"[11]—that pointed in the direction of official knowledge about the possibility of violence on November 3 and the cover-up of that knowledge in the shooting's aftermath.

Indeed, the brazen picture that emerged over the course of discovery would amaze even Lewis Pitts.

❖

Evidence of Klan and Nazi racism was everywhere. On July 8, 1979, from the steps of the community center in China Grove, a Klansman named Joe Grady had vowed revenge after the CWP and local Black citizens interfered with a screening of *Birth of a Nation*.[12] Two months later, in September, several white supremacist groups, including Virgil Griffin's Invisible Empire gang and Harold Covington's National Socialist Party of America, gathered amid a cross-burning pageant of swastikas and white power T-shirts. As Jim Crow segregation receded into the past, they agreed across their ideological differences that "the time [was] right for white revolution." They formed a "United Racist Front" to redeem their embarrassing retreat at China Grove and to call for a white ethnic state inside America. Bernard Butkovich, the undercover BATF agent, was present at the formation of the United Racist Front and voted, along with the Nazis he was supposed to be gathering information on, to ratify it.[13]

A month later, in mid-October, Virgil Griffin invited Eddie Dawson, then a paid Greensboro police informant, to Lincolnton, North Carolina. Dawson urged nearly one hundred Klansmen to do their "patriotic duty" and confront the "communists" and the "big buck n——s" in Greensboro. Jerry Paul Smith, the Klansman who shot Cesar Cauce, and Mark Sherer, the young man who fired the first shot into the air on November 3, practiced making pipe bombs that, Smith said to Wood and Butkovich, among others, "would work good thrown into a crowd of n——s."[14] Eddie Dawson, meanwhile, had kept himself busy hanging his posters around Greensboro threatening "communists, race mixers, and Black rioters" with lynching.

And then there was the detail of Jerry Paul Smith's annotated collection of autopsy photos of the five slain activists. During his white supremacist celebrity tour, he wielded the photos, like scalps, saying, "Sometimes black people stick their heads where they don't belong, and they get some double-aught buck between the eyes."[15]

Pitts didn't believe the plaintiffs would have much trouble proving the Klansmen and Nazis' "racial animus." However, they'd also have to overcome the argument that the Klansmen and Nazis fired their guns only in self-defense. This claim rested on two assertions: first, that the crowd at Morningside initiated the fighting by striking the Klan cars with sticks, and second, the mystery shots 3, 4, and 5. Ed Boyd's video clearly showed Mark Sherer loading his powder pistol before anyone hit a Klan car. Then, relying on testimony rather than dubious FBI sound analysis, the sequence of shots became more certain. Sherer fired the first shot into the air. A drunken Brent Fletcher discharged the second from his shotgun. Then Sherer fired twice more—shots 3 and 4—and shouted his racist challenge.[16] The last shot in question, the fifth, was fired by Klansman Roy Toney after he ripped a shotgun from Jim Waller, who'd run to collect it from a truck when the shooting started.[17]

After Toney's shot, the first seven cars in the caravan, led by Eddie Dawson and his Wisconsin running buddy, James Buck, roared off, leaving only the blue Ford Fairlane and the canary-yellow van.[18] Roland Wayne Wood squeezed off shot 6 from a shotgun. Jerry Paul Smith unloaded shots 7 and 8 into Cesar Cauce. Wood then fired two more times—shots 9 and 10—injuring multiple people. David Matthews then pulled the trigger of his rifle firing shot 11 and killing Jim Waller. It wasn't until shot 12 that the first CWP member to fire, Dori Blitz, discharged an errant bullet from an old derringer. By cross-checking the film and forensics against the depositions taken under oath, the cloud of mystery around the shots parted, and the plea of self-defense evaporated.[19]

As they fled and hid their guns, Virgil Griffin had told Mark Sherer, "You better lie about the fact that you had a gun, and you shot." Virgil also warned his mistress to remember her "Klan oath" of loyalty. "I got three of them," David Matthews openly admitted to police in the immediate aftermath, saying, "There were innocent people shot, but I was shooting at the n——s."[20]

Indeed, as the plaintiffs' lawyers scoured the grand jury testimony and transcripts of their depositions, they found evidence of planned violence beyond Jerry Paul Smith's pipe bomb experiments. "We can't let them march in the streets, the communists and the Blacks, we can't let them," Virgil had exhorted his fellow Klansmen. One Klan insider said that on November 2, Virgil Griffin, Jerry Paul Smith, and Coleman Pridmore had studied pictures from China Grove and selected the people they wanted to beat up at the "Death to the Klan" march and in grand jury testimony stated bluntly, "It was clear that we planned and intended to go and provoke violence, deliberately start a fight."[21] Once the fight started, Mark Sherer told the grand jury, the Klansmen were "prepared to win any confrontation."[22]

Most, if not all, of the above evidence had been available to prosecutors in the two previous trials.

Confident in their case against the white supremacists, the CWP's lawyers turned their attention to the role law enforcement had played in the weeks leading up to the shooting. The Greensboro Police Department had certified its version of events in the November 19, 1979, report released less than three weeks after the shooting. The report concluded that the "planning and preparation for the anti-Klan march and rally were adequate and proper" and that the number of assigned personnel was "sufficient."

Many assertions in the report and in public comments emanating from the police department quickly proved to be misleading or flat wrong. Though police officers would blame the Black captain Trevor Hampton for the decision, Pitts and his team learned that it was actually the assistant chief, Colonel Walter "Sticky" Burch, who, in the days leading up to the march, ordered the police to keep a "low profile," out of sight of the marchers. Nelson Johnson's antagonism toward the GPD (not their antagonism toward him) "justified" this decision, the department argued. The GPD blamed the police absence from Carver and Everitt on "confusion" created by the CWP when the party designated both a starting point for the parade in the permit application (Carver and Everitt) and a staging area on the posters (the Windsor Community Center). However, in meetings leading up to the march, including on the morning of November 3, there was no confusion at all about the fact that the march would begin at Morningside Homes. The GPD also, seeming to contradict their lack of concern for the security of the event, blamed the Klan for "early movement," which brought them to Morningside Homes "forty minutes prior to the scheduled march." Apart from there being no police presence at Morningside Homes, there were several notable gaps in the chain of command that day, beyond, some suspected, the possibility of coincidence. Captain Hampton had delegated oversight of the march to his lieutenant Paul Spoon. Captain Larry Gibson, to whom Lieutenant Daughtry reported, took a day off. The two top people in the Field Services Division, to whom both Captain Gibson and Sylvester Daughtry reported, were also absent on November 3. Detective Jerry "Rooster" Cooper's boss, Lieutenant Talbott, went to the beach. And Talbott's boss, Captain Thomas, head of the CID, left in the midmorning to accompany his son to the barbershop, leaving his police radio at home.[23]

As for the GPD's failure to stop the caravan before it arrived at Morningside, the police claimed they had no probable cause. In his public comments after November 3, Chief Swing reinforced this claim, saying that he'd received "no indication of violence. In our planning we did not talk of violence. We talked of confrontation, bickering back and forth."

When Pitts and the other lawyers deposed police officers and studied department records, they were struck by the incongruity between the intelligence the GPD had access to, which clearly forewarned violence, and the operational plan for the November 3 march coverage.

The CWP lawyers learned that by mid-October 1979, Eddie Dawson had told Rooster Cooper about the Klan's bitterness over China Grove and plans to come to Greensboro. Cooper, in turn, had informed Talbott. Talbott reported what he'd heard to the head of the Criminal Investigations Division, Captain Byron "Tom" Thomas, and Captain Thomas relayed the intelligence to Colonel Burch. Chief Swing would say under oath that he'd been well briefed on all the intelligence. The whole chain of command, in other words, shared the stream of information provided by Eddie Dawson.[24]

As Lewis Pitts and the team of plaintiff lawyers re-created the GPD planning meetings in the days leading up to the march, they learned that Detective Cooper referred to Virgil Griffin as a "hothead" and passed along Eddie's assertion that as many as eighty Klansmen, likely armed, planned to "confront" the communists in Greensboro on November 3. Cooper also knew that the out-of-town Klansmen would gather at Brent Fletcher's house. In these meetings, too, the police continually reminded one another, again contrary to the conclusions in the police report, that the starting point for the march was at Morningside Homes, not at the Windsor Community Center.[25]

Then the CWP team discovered two key facts that appeared nowhere in the November 19 police report. In the days prior to the march, the police received a tip from an informant other than Eddie Dawson that the Nazis planned to bring a machine gun to the march and "shoot up the place."[26] "The information we had about the machine gun," Captain Larry Gibson would say, had contributed to the delay in issuing the parade permit and convinced the police that restricting the CWP's right to bear arms was warranted. Even so, when Nelson came to pick up the parade permit, no one warned him of the machine gun rumors or any other potential violence.[27]

If that evidence of possible violence weren't enough, the next detail exploded the police department's argument that officers had no "probable cause" for stopping the caravan on its way to Morningside Homes. According to Talbott's grand jury testimony, Detective Cooper had watched from an unmarked vehicle as, on the morning of November 3, Jerry Paul Smith and others loaded weapons into the cars parked beside Brent Fletcher's house. Cooper, Talbott reported under oath, knew firsthand that the Klansmen and Nazis were mobilizing an arsenal as they set out to confront the CWP.[28] Cooper, in his testimony and depositions, would deny that he'd seen guns being loaded into cars outside Brent Fletcher's house. Pitts believed Talbott.

There was more. According to Eddie Dawson, Cooper told him to ask Captain Gibson for a copy of the parade permit on November 1. And, said Eddie, Cooper made a point of reminding Dawson that the parade started at Morningside Homes, not the Windsor Community Center as was advertised on the posters Eddie had been covering up with Klan propaganda.[29] Cooper's immediate superior Talbott, present for this conversation, admonished Cooper, telling him that "we obtain information from informants, we don't give information."[30] (In his depositions, Cooper would insist that Eddie, not he, initiated the conversation about the parade permit.)[31]

Meanwhile, under oath, Chief Swing changed the story he'd told in the immediate aftermath of the shooting, saying he'd expected "hundreds" of Klansmen to come to Greensboro and "some encounter or confrontation that would include rock throwing, egg throwing, and as a result, fights and stick fights. . . . Yes, we felt there could be some violence."[32]

And yet, despite all the intelligence—the machine gun rumor, the weapons reported by Dawson and likely seen by Cooper, as well as Virgil Griffin's reputation—that signaled the potential for violence, Colonel Burch had still ordered the department's roaming Tactical Service Units to keep a low profile, blocks away from the marchers gathering at Morningside Homes. In this light, Chief Swing's administrative report, issued three weeks after the shooting and validated by the FBI and Justice Department, looked more and more like a whitewash.

❖

Coverage of the march that day involved three primary police units: the Field Operations Division, the Tactical Service Units, and the Criminal Investigations Division. Captain Trevor Hampton, the highest-ranking Black officer in the GPD, led the District II Field Operations Division, the police unit that would bookend the march. Hampton delegated responsibility for covering the march to Lieutenant Paul Spoon.

Detective Cooper represented the Criminal Investigations Division, led by Captain Thomas (at the barbershop with his son), while Lieutenant Sylvester Daughtry, the second-highest-ranking Black officer in the GPD, who reported to Captain Gibson (who'd taken a day off), would command the roaming Tactical Service Units, or "Tacts," that day.

On the morning of November 3, Detective Cooper briefed Spoon, Daughtry, and a handful of others, informing them that the Klansmen had indeed gathered at Brent Fletcher's house, that his informant said they'd brought guns, and that they possessed the parade permit designating Morningside Homes as the starting point.[33]

The meeting broke at around 10:30 a.m.

There were moments in life, Sylvester Daughtry knew, that came up like a fork in the road when you're driving fast without a map. As he looked back, his mind would return to one particular night in his youth that could have changed everything. The year before he matriculated at A&T, his sister volunteered to desegregate the white high school in Sampson County, just north of Wilmington. Word whipped through the community that the Klan would ride, set on preserving the color line. Daughtry grabbed a gun and ran across the street, crouching in a drainage ditch with a clear view of his home. If night riders tried to burn down his family's house, he'd shoot them. And if he shot them, he knew a white jury would never grant him the plea of self-defense; he'd likely spend the rest of his life in jail. Daughtry waited in the dark for hours, but the Klansmen didn't show.

When William "Ed" Swing replaced longtime chief Paul Calhoun in 1975, he brought swagger to the Greensboro Police Department. He replaced the blue uniforms with solid black.[34] The Los Angeles Police Department, they'd say, provided their model for professionalism, toughness, and style. They were, by the standards of the day, well trained. Chief Swing encouraged officers to attend night school and earn BAs and MAs. For a midsize city, an unusually high number of GPD officers were extended the prestigious invitation to attend the FBI's National Academy in Quantico, Virginia. Others, like Sylvester Daughtry, spent time acquiring skills and information at the Southern Police Institute in Louisville. Officers returned home with their heads full of new information about behavioral and forensic science, insight into the "terrorist mindset," and having forged relationships with FBI agents as well as officers in other cities around the country.

Chief Swing also prioritized hiring minorities and women. Daughtry's career accelerated, and the percentage of minorities in the GPD rose from the low single digits in the 1960s to 17 percent by 1979, despite the less-than-welcoming reception some encountered when they arrived. In 1977, about a third of the training class was made up of women, including several Black women. During a self-defense class, the trainer, Lieutenant Paul Spoon, called on a young Black woman to help demonstrate a defensive combat move. He explained the move to the class and then, as the other trainees looked on, flipped her and slammed her to the floor. Turning onto her back, she gasped to recover her wind before clambering onto her hands and knees. But Spoon wasn't done. He came up behind her and kicked her. She pitched forward onto the floor. As the other recruits gaped in silence, the woman ran from the room, blood streaming from a busted lip onto her khaki uniform. She never returned.[35] Spoon kept his job and was assigned to protect the November 3 march by Captain Trevor Hampton.

One tactical services officer assigned to cover November 3 had been twiddling his thumbs at Fort Bragg when Chief Calhoun showed up on a recruiting trip in 1974. The soldier jumped at a ticket out of the Army and moved to Greensboro. Quickly he accumulated an impressive arrest record which he attributed, in large part, to his knack for telling a "bad" Black man from a "good" Black man just by the way he walked. As a Greensboro police officer, if he spotted a "bad" Black man, he'd just follow along behind until the man did something the officer could pick him up for. Once he made an arrest, he'd establish proper hierarchy by referring to the man as "boy." He didn't need to say "n——" for his collar to understand the predicament he was in. If, despite the verbal cues, a Black man gave any lip during the arrest, the elevator ride from the underground parking garage to the booking room offered a private place to deliver a more physical message.[36]

As Sylvester Daughtry won promotions and ascended the GPD ladder, he became skilled at negotiating the department's complex and often contradictory racial politics. And he learned who to stay away from. One of those was Jerry "Rooster" Cooper, whose casual and frequent use of the N-word signaled to Black officers something beyond shallow ignorance.[37]

Before recruits could earn the badge, when they were still walking around in khaki uniforms without a sidearm, they learned about the "regulars" who could lure them into embarrassing or compromising situations. There was the woman who made a hobby of seducing men in uniform and the tough guy who, after a couple drinks, would pick a fight with the first cop he saw. Legend had it that Connie "The Bull" Tysinger once beat up six cops at the same time. And watch out, they were taught, for Nelson Johnson who'd seize any opportunity to accuse the police of brutality or bias. Some of these warnings elicited a wink and a chuckle, an exaggerated roll of the eyes. Mentions of Nelson Johnson fired up hate in generations of cops who'd never laid eyes on the man, but who'd had it drummed into them that since the 1969 Dudley/A&T uprising Nelson's race-baiting trouble was a threat to the department and to Greensboro.[38]

Now, years later, despite knowing that armed Klansmen and Nazis were nearby, Daughtry did as he'd been ordered to do. He told his men to be in their low-profile positions blocks away from Morning-side Homes by 11:30 a.m. and, with that, sent the seventeen Tact officers to lunch.

At around 11 a.m., Dawson hurried the Klansmen into their cars. A few minutes later, Detective Cooper observed them stopped along an I-85 off-ramp and watched, together with a police photographer, as the blue Ford Fairlane with the trunkful of guns caught up to the stopped cars and took a spot just ahead of the canary-yellow van. Cooper radioed to let Spoon and Daughtry know that nine cars carrying Klansmen were moving. For the next ten minutes, as the caravan wound slowly to Morningside Homes, neither Daughtry nor Spoon tuned in to Cooper's live radio broadcast of his surveillance.[39]

At 11:16, Cooper finally raised Daughtry and told him that the Klan and Nazis were "approaching Florida Street" from Route 29. Daughtry, instead of immediately rushing his men to Morningside, told them they had "fourteen more minutes" to report to their assigned "low-visibility" positions. Just two minutes later, Cooper announced that the caravan had turned onto Willow Road, meaning that the Klansmen and Nazis were heading not to the Windsor Community Center, but toward Morningside.

The Klansmen rolled slowly on toward their destination tailed by Cooper in an unmarked car. The rest of the Greensboro police force still did nothing.

At 11:22 a.m., Cooper, close enough to see the corner of Carver and Everitt, radioed, "They're now at the formation point. . . . It appears as though they're heckling at this time. . . . They're creating attention and some of the parade members are, uh . . . they're scattering, stand by one." Half a minute later, his voice crackled over the line: "We've got a 10–10 down here, you better get some units in here." Where, exactly, was the location of the gunfire he reported? Cooper didn't say. Captain Hampton's designee, Lieutenant Paul Spoon, aware finally of a gunfight in progress, ordered police not to Morningside but to the Windsor Community Center. Neither Cooper nor the photographer riding with him made any attempt to intervene during the eighty-eight seconds of shooting.[40] By the time Daughtry arrived, one police squad had stopped the yellow van. Minutes later, Daughtry ordered the arrest of Nelson Johnson.

❖

Lewis Pitts thought that alone any one of these police failures—the low-profile order, the failure to stop the caravan, the lackadaisical response to the armed Klan caravan, sending police to the wrong location—might have been excused as a bad decision. But as he studied the evidence Pitts became convinced that "there were just too many screw-ups, but [the police] would have you believe it was just coincidence and bad luck." He called it their "doofus defense." "Consider the amount of prior knowledge they had, this is ridiculous," he said as he and his team puzzled together what they'd found. "Low profile? Come on! Their story is unbelievable on its face, unless you really want to believe it."[41] Instead, the evidence gathered in discovery led Pitts to believe, as Nelson and others had presumed in the immediate aftermath of the shooting, that the "preponderance of the evidence" would show the police absences were not mistakes, but criminal examples of "deliberate indifference."

The GPD had a problem the federal agencies did not. Once police finally granted Nelson Johnson a parade permit, they accepted the duty to ensure a safe march. Though he'd deny that the police and the Klan conspired together, Eddie Dawson didn't disagree with the CWP that the police could have prevented the shooting. He and Virgil Griffin had expected "wall-to-wall" cops at Morningside. Dawson didn't trust the official statements coming out of the department any more than Nelson and Lewis did. "Every time Swing stood up and made a statement on TV it was a goddamn lie," Dawson would say, without elaborating.[42]

❖

A great deal about Bernard Butkovich had appeared in the press thanks to Martha Woodall's investigative reporting. But during discovery, Pitts and the CWP documented the extent to which But-kovich and his superiors at the BATF understood the likelihood of violence on November 3 and even appeared to encourage it. Though John Westra, the special agent in charge of the BATF in North Carolina, had denied having any knowledge of potential violence, he forbade Butkovich from attending the march, worrying that the undercover agent would put himself in a position where he might "have to defend himself."[43] According to Roland Wayne Wood and Raeford Milano Caudle, Butkovich told Wood that he "wasn't going [to Greensboro] unless" he had a "little pistol or something stuck in his belt." Butkovich was present when Jerry Paul Smith talked about exploding a pipe bomb in a crowd of Black people.[44] These details appeared nowhere in the BATF's official report of the incident, which they'd readily shared with the CWP lawyers. As much as they did discover, the CWP lawyers didn't know that immediately after the shooting two FBI agents had sent Butkovich and his handler, Robert Fulton Dukes, off to get their official story straight. It wouldn't have surprised Pitts, though, since an anonymous source had sent him the internal BATF memo documenting coordination of the BATF's undercover operation with the FBI.[45]

Pitts also discovered Cecil Moses's order for a preliminary investigation of the CWP two weeks prior to November 3, following his conversation with Horace Beckwith. Even before Moses initiated his investigation, however, Eddie Dawson had reached out to his old FBI case agent in Greensboro, Len Bogaty, to ask whether he could trust Detective Cooper. Cooper, in turn, had contacted Bogaty to assess Dawson's reliability as an informant. Bogaty vouched for the cop and the Klansman. Around this time, Bogaty began offering briefings to the resident Greensboro FBI agents on Nelson Johnson and the communists in Greensboro, presumably as part of the FBI's preliminary investigation of the CWP. Despite evidence of this operation, the FBI would confirm and then deny there'd ever been an investigation of the CWP.[46]

As Eddie Dawson informed the police about his talks with Virgil

Griffin and his attendance at the Klavern meeting in Lincolnton, Dawson kept his FBI friend in the loop as well, contacting him multiple times. As the day of the march grew closer, Eddie got nervous. He reached out to Bogaty. "There could be trouble," he told the FBI man, asking him to do whatever he could to stop the march. Bogaty told Dawson to talk with Detective Cooper and Greensboro City Attorney Jesse "Skip" Warren. When Jesse Warren told Dawson he could do nothing to stop the march, Eddie's temper flared. "Next time I want something from you," he barked at Warren, "I'll bring you a bucket of blood."[47] When this effort failed, Bogaty urged Dawson to stay home on November 3, likely to help keep their communication secret if the situation should blow up.

During his deposition on August 31, 1984, Mickey Michaux, the former US attorney for North Carolina's Middle District, said that, "a few days prior to the incident," FBI agents, "Mr. Pelczar, Mr. Brereton, and somebody else—it could have been Len [Bogaty] . . . came in my office . . . and we talked about the possibility of some trouble occurring on Saturday [November 3]." The FBI agents expressed concern to Michaux that the "Klan would seek some type of retaliation for the China Grove incident." Michaux told the agents to "keep their eye on" it even as they "let the locals [the GPD and the district attorney's office] . . . handle the situation."[48]

Despite US Attorney Michaux's order and what Greensboro's FBI agents knew from Dawson as well as from their own investigation, the Saturday morning of November 3 found them, like many of the GPD's commanding officers, out enjoying the weekend. Tom Brereton and Andy Pelczar stalked the fairways and greens of a local golf course. Agent Len Bogaty took off early for Raleigh to visit his daughter. Others entered a tennis tournament.

❖

Though the CWP was never able to get the FBI to release the results of Moses's preliminary investigation,[49] the plaintiffs and the legal team did find evidence of it. Daisy Crawford, a worker at the

Cannon Mills plant in Kannapolis, swore in an affidavit that around October 30, 1979, two men dressed in suits knocked on her trailer door. They "flashed FBI identification" and proceeded to ask her to identify photographs of different individuals. One she could positively ID was Sandi Smith, who'd just started organizing Cannon Mills workers. The others she didn't know, but in retrospect believed they may have been Paul Bermanzohn, Bill Sampson, Jim Waller, Cesar Cauce, and Mike Nathan. Crawford immediately called Sandi to let her know about the visit. She also called Lyn Wells in Atlanta, a coordinator for the National Anti-Klan Network. Daisy Crawford had planned to attend the November 3 march in Greensboro, but after the visit from federal agents she decided not to go.[50]

Mordechai Levy, who worked for the Jewish Defense League, picked an agent with a "Jewish-sounding last name" in the FBI's Raleigh Field Office and called to deliver an anonymous tip. "I have information that Harold Covington of the National Socialist Party of America is up to heavy illegal activity. . . . He and his group plan to attack and possibly kill people at an anti-Klan gathering this week in North Carolina."[51]

The FBI denied that any agents visited Daisy Crawford. Agent Goldberg, however, after first denying it, later admitted under oath that he'd received the call from Mordechai Levy.[52]

❖

As they dug, like archaeologists in the dirt, Pitts and his team uncovered the skeleton of a startling narrative. There were a few bones missing and some important connective tissues, but they'd revealed that little about what went down on November 3 should have surprised the police or the Feds. Nothing had been done to prevent the violence, and perhaps, Pitts thought, giving a nod to Nelson's original hunch, the cops had stepped aside to allow the murders to take place, much as they had allowed the Klan to beat the Freedom Riders in 1961.

One could see the shape of a conspiracy on the part of the Klansmen and Nazis to confront the communists, race mixers, and Black rioters they abhorred. But even most of them, if Eddie Dawson could be trusted at all, had expected the police to be present.

Eddie Dawson had acted like a joint, the flexible place where the other pieces of the skeleton plan—the GPD, the FBI, and the Klan and Nazis—converged. Eddie the police informant incited the Klansmen to come to Greensboro, arranged the meeting point at Brent Fletcher's house, refined plans for confronting the CWP with Virgil Griffin, received the parade permit from the GPD, somehow knew that the CWP conference had been moved, kept his former handler at the FBI abreast of the developing violence, drove the parade route with Virgil and two of the shooters, rushed the Klansmen and Nazis to leave Fletcher's house, organized the order of the caravan, led them to Morningside, and shouted the first insults at the marchers.

Afterward, Eddie would claim a police officer berated him for not completing his mission: "How come you didn't kill that damn Johnson? How come you missed him?"[53] "I'll blow the lid off the case if you force me to come out [and testify]," Eddie had told Captain Thomas and the prosecutors when they interviewed him. Later, he'd explain what he meant, referring to what he alleged he'd told Cooper: "how many Klansmen would be there . . . and guns were being brought," and that Cooper had told him the march's "starting point was Carver and Everitt."[54] The fact that Cooper emphasized the starting point of the march to Eddie, rather than the end point, also seemed to contradict another of the GPD's ongoing claims that if trouble were going to happen, it would happen at the end of the march.[55]

❖

With the trial date approaching, Dale Sampson interrupted a strategy meeting with a different concern. "They see us as communists, not as humans," she said. "We have to express to them what hurts inside, like how I held Bill in my arms after he died and checked his heart 50 times to see if it was beating." And, she continued, "We have to admit that some of those leaflets were stupid."[56]

Braced defensively against the torrent of public criticism, racked by grief, and under the sway of Jerry Tung's order to "fight back," Nelson and the CWP family had never directly or collectively faced the mistakes they'd made that put them in the position to be shot down on November 3. It wasn't easy, especially since everyone else from the Klansmen and Nazis to the cops and politicians denied any responsibility for the deaths of five people the CWP members loved, still loved, and for whose memory they continued to fight. When everyone seemed to accept the verdicts of the first two trials as proof that they'd brought the shooting on themselves, facing the press felt, thought Marty, "like being raped."[57]

Dale had cracked something open. "Until we were honest with ourselves," said Marty, the CWP wouldn't be able to "tell the jury exactly why we did what we did . . . to put in court what we believed to be the truth."[58]

"Our mistake," said Dale, "was that we were in a tunnel of third world revolution of taking the streets, of being 'bad' and 'bold' which didn't do any good. It blinded us to what was going on inside the Klan, and it led us to a confrontation. . . . We have to take responsibility for being there that day in the manner that we got there. And that's been the hardest thing to deal with," especially, she believed, because Jerry Tung and the party leadership in New York "refused to face its responsibility."[59]

"Military posturing," observed Signe Waller, can make idealism dangerous.[60] Her thought echoed an observation George Orwell had made back in 1940, when he wrote, "So much of left-wing thought is a kind of playing with fire by people who don't even know that fire is hot."[61] Indeed, the CWP had been "naive," arrogant, and hotheaded; they'd pushed too fast for change. "[We had] emphasized the power of the will to break through objective factors," observed Nelson. "But that has to be balanced with reality. . . . You can run into [a tree], but it will knock you down. I think our organization began to operate outside the laws of consequence. . . . I think a healthy dose of humility would have served me and some of the rest of us. We were doing some good things, but we were losing some balance."[62]

As they traversed the painful process of self-discovery, they kept reminding themselves of something that would have to be made crystal clear to the jury: errors in judgment are not the same as crimes.

Finding this balance would be just one of the challenges facing the legal team in Judge Merhige's courtroom. In addition to presenting the plaintiffs as imperfect humans who were also victims, the lawyers would have to strike a balance between making political points and winning a concrete legal victory. After they had worked with him for nearly five years, the CWP members trusted Pitts to fearlessly and radically "translate law into human rights" and not to compromise their "principled beliefs about the root causes of injustice, oppression, and racism." Pitts had become, in the words of Joyce Johnson, "part of the local fabric."[63]

Pitts and the legal team had scrutinized everything the defendants gave them access to and filled the time Judge Merhige allowed them to prepare. The hour now arrived to test what they knew in the courtroom.

DAMAGES

Spiffed up in suits purchased for them by a supporter, Lewis Pitts and the legal team faced off against a phalanx of defense attorneys representing the BATF, the FBI, and the City of Greensboro. Joe Sher, a pugnacious envoy from the Department of Justice, would lead the defense of the government agencies. This time, under the patient tutelage of Judge Merhige, the Klansmen and Nazis represented themselves.

Defendants from the GPD included Rooster Cooper, Paul Spoon, and Sylvester Daughtry, now a police captain.

Cecil Moses, currently the FBI's top man in Alabama, was forced to share the left side of the courtroom with Virgil Griffin and Roland Wayne Wood, the shape-shifter Eddie Dawson, the cowboy Bernie Butkovich, and the rest of the defendants. He didn't like the association at all. It was exceedingly rare, and personally humiliating, for an FBI man to have to defend himself in court, especially when his bosses believed he'd done good work; in 1980, William Webster had officially commended Moses for his handling of the GreenKil investigation and paid him a $250 bonus.[1] Moses took some comfort from the fact that the Bureau picked up his legal bills and offered moral support; John Mintz, the Bureau's chief counsel, took the seat right beside him. The family still cared for its own. Despite the circumstances, he undoubtedly took some satisfaction in the string of FBI victories connected to GreenKil. The CWP was defunct as an organization; restrictions had been loosened on the FBI's use of informants; and the Bureau's nemesis, Senator Robert Morgan, had lost his 1980 reelection bid while Governor Jim Hunt, an ally, had won a second term in 1981. Moses's star at the FBI, meanwhile, had continued to rise. More remarkable, perhaps, than Moses being forced to suffer through the trial was that the "officious" and ubiquitous Thomas Brereton had been excused as a defendant. But Moses, though inconvenienced, wasn't particularly concerned. During recesses in the proceedings, ever gregarious and charming, he attempted to recruit a Black woman reporter to join the Bureau.

Unusual as this conglomeration of defendants might have seemed to the American public, they were not, in the general sense, strangers to one another. American law enforcement and vigilantes had been collaborating to suppress labor and racial liberation movements in the United States for as long as the new country had existed. Even so, it was rare that these covert alliances burst into public consciousness. In this case, whether the different parties explicitly worked together or not, they'd achieved something significant: together, they'd helped end the Cold War inside the United States, essentially putting out the fire of the homegrown communist, or "ultra-left," movements. This success would inspire white supremacists and white nationalists for generations to come. Now all of them, local cops, federal employees, vigilantes, and the shadowy informants who bound them together, white and Black, would be tried under the 1871 anti–Ku Klux Klan statutes.

In 1986, a year later, the Supreme Court would rule that removing potential jurors from consideration based on their race violated the Equal Protection Clause of the Fourteenth Amendment. Without the benefit of cover from the country's highest court, Judge Merhige took an unusual step: he ruled that defendants could not use their peremptory challenges on Black jurors.

Quickly and efficiently, the judge seated a six-person jury and, for the very first time in a case related to the events of November 3, one Black man joined the jury.

❖

Lewis Pitts and the team had worn themselves to nubs preparing the case. Over the next eight weeks, they would present all they'd discovered, calling seventy-five witnesses. The gavel landed, and Lewis Pitts raised his hill-country tenor to present his arguments and testimony of his clients' grief and pain, guilt and shame, anger and vengeful thoughts, with polite good humor that would earn the judge's respect.

Among the first to be called was Ed Boyd, the Black cameraman who believed he'd filmed a sophisticated military operation.

The plaintiffs' lawyers alternated friendly witnesses, including their CWP clients, with adverse witnesses—the Klansmen, Nazis, cops, federal agents, and city officials they believed had conspired against the CWP. The lawyers' unusual strategy aimed to present the jurors with a stark contrast of "character, action, and motive."

When Nelson Johnson finally took the stand, the defense lawyers were quick to cross-examine his beliefs and ideology, as he'd expected them to.

Lawyer to Nelson: You think that views which you perceive to be racist should not exist?

Nelson: It would be very good if racist views didn't exist, yes.

Lawyer: And to that extent, the first amendment should not protect those ideas.

Nelson: I didn't say that. But again, I don't think that that makes them wholesome views that we necessarily want.

Lawyer: Well, what you're saying now is that you would like to oppose those ideas whereas a minute ago, I thought you said you didn't think those ideas should even exist.

Nelson: Well, the reason to oppose them is to minimize them, and I would hope that at some point there isn't racism in this society, I really would hope that.

Lawyer: Mr. Johnson, all your materials say, "Smash the Klan," "Death to the Klan." Words have meaning. You wanted violence at China Grove and you wanted violence on November third, Mr. Johnson, didn't you?

Nelson: No, that is not true!

❖

After Nelson, Lewis Pitts called Virgil Griffin to the stand to offer a contrasting point of view.

Pitts: You are the Grand Dragon of the Invisible Empire of the Knights of the KKK?

Griffin: Yes, sir, I am.

Pitts: Aren't you a convicted felon, Mr. Griffin?

Griffin: Yes, sir, I am.

Pitts: Can you see this, Mr. Griffin? (Pitts held up a copy of the lynching poster that Eddie Dawson had hung around Greensboro warning Jews, communists, race mixers, and n——s to "beware.")

Griffin: I recognize it.

Pitts: All right sir, don't you talk at your rallies about having a hundred dead people in the street, using a word other than "Black" in those speeches?

Griffin: In my phrases I use a "hundred dead n——s in the street."

. . .

Pitts: And didn't you make a statement to the effect that all of the communists in the US should be executed?

Griffin: I think I said they should be charged for treason against the US, put in front of a firing squad and shot. I believe that's the words I said.

. . .

Pitts: Sir, did you see any guns at the house that morning before you departed on November third for the rally in Greensboro?

Griffin: I believe I saw two shotguns, and a rifle, two long guns or three long guns, I'm not sure, a pistol and the pistol I had in the house.

Pitts: Did you hear Roland Wayne Wood ask you if he ought to take a tear gas grenade with him?

Griffin: Yes, sir, he did.

Pitts: And Eddie Dawson reiterated that if fights and an arrest situation occurred "we'd all go to jail together" and had arrangements for bond?

Griffin: Yes, sir.

Pitts: And you still deny there were plans for violence on November third in Greensboro?

Griffin: Like I said before, we just wanted to stand on the sidewalk and fly the American flag and the Christian Confederate flag and watch the communists march.[2]

❖

When Flint Taylor called Roland Wayne Wood to the witness stand, Wood took the oath by raising his arm in a Nazi salute. As Taylor paused briefly to observe the large Nazi before him, his eyes came to rest on Wood's lapel. Suddenly he realized that five small skulls were pinned there.

Taylor: Do these five skulls stand for the five people
that were killed on the streets of Greensboro?

Wood: No, it stands for the five attacks being
committed against me by communists when I tried to
express my freedom of speech.

Taylor: You are proud that you're a racist, aren't you?

Wood: Yes sir. I believe in the sovereign rights
of the sovereign people of the sovereign states of
the Confederacy that has never surrendered. Lee,
the traitor, surrendered, but not my Confederate
government. I believe that my country is occupied.
And I will fight as my forefathers fought to give me
a free Christian republic.

A few moments later, Wood, the man whose defense attorney in the state murder trial claimed his client had no knowledge of Hitler's persecution of the Jews, burst into song: "Riding through the town / In a Mercedes Benz / Having lots of fun / Shooting Jews down / Rat a tat tat tat / Rat a tat tat tat / Shot the kikes down / Oh what fun it is / To have the Nazis back in town."

No one present would ever hear the tune of "Jingle Bells" the same way. Judge Merhige, stunned, called for a thirty-minute recess.[3]

❖

During the case, Jesse Jackson, fresh off his remarkable presidential campaign, arrived in his college town to show solidarity with the plaintiffs. At a press conference held at Morningside Homes, Jackson stood in the warm spring air, dressed in a trim, double-breasted suit and a politician's striped tie. With Nelson and the others gathered behind him, Jackson articulated his "Mission of Justice":

Greensboro is a city that in 1960 became a beacon for the world when, in peace and in dignity, four students sat down at the lunch counter at Woolworth's. Now, 25 years later, we return. We come back because there has been manifest here an attempt to turn back to the mean times. And we have come to say we will not go back.

We assert non-violent direct action and the full use of the judicial process. Equal protection under the law is a nonnegotiable right. Justice must be swift and sure to be effective.

Death squads must not be allowed in Central America, in North Carolina, in South Africa or anywhere.[4]

The *Greensboro News & Record*—the morning and evening papers had recently merged—quoted little of the speech and nothing from Jackson's line on death squads.

Back in court, the plaintiffs presented their evidence against the police, the BATF, and the FBI. Detective Cooper admitted his use of racial epithets and floundered in his explanations for directing Eddie Dawson to the parade permit and why he hadn't stopped the caravan on its way to Morningside. Paul Spoon fumbled answers about not paying attention to the police radio during the critical minutes from 11 to 11:23 a.m. and why, when Cooper reported the shooting, he'd sent officers to Windsor Community Center instead of Morningside Homes.[5]

Judge Merhige barked at Bernard Butkovich, who, the judge seemed to sense, was perjuring himself on the stand. Despite all the evidence the plaintiffs introduced that suggested Cecil Moses and his colleagues knew—or should have known—there might be violence on November 3, the veteran FBI official, unruffled, confidently stuck to his story: the FBI "had no knowledge at all that we could pass on to the local authorities that there might be that kind of situation brewing."[6]

To prove the police had deliberately vacated Morningside Homes on November 3, the plaintiffs put the former GPD officer April Wise on the stand. Wise recounted for the court how, at around 11 a.m. that morning, she'd been ordered to leave Morningside.

The city lawyer responded that no record of any such call existed. Wise, he said, challenging the former officer's veracity, had never received an order to leave the area. But the plaintiffs were prepared for this: they had discovered a woman who passed her days listening to the police scanner and put her on the stand. She told the jury that she'd heard the command for Wise to vacate her position at Morningside Homes.

On Friday, May 17, the plaintiffs called the former commissioner of the Boston Police Department as their final witness. Robert diGrazia offered his expert opinion that the police had all the probable cause they needed to stop the caravan on the morning of November 3 and that their "low-profile" coverage of the march made no sense at all given what they knew of the white supremacists' plan to confront the march.

After a short break, the attorneys for the Klan, Nazis, FBI, BATF, and City of Greensboro presented their defense in just four days.

With Eddie Dawson on the stand, Jim Moynihan, a Bureau lawyer, asked Dawson what responsibility the FBI bore for protecting the march. "The FBI doesn't do parades," responded Dawson, supporting the argument Cecil Moses had been making all along. The City of Greensboro, not the FBI, was responsible for the march. According to the Levi Guidelines, the FBI was not allowed to run informants; therefore, the Bureau had no information. The 1976 guidelines that angered Moses, which in the wake of the Greensboro events had already been altered in 1983 to loosen restrictions on the FBI's intelligence-gathering activities, now functioned in the court as a shield. Despite the evidence of what the Bureau knew, the FBI personnel insisted that their arguments were technically correct: unofficial, undocumented information did not qualify as knowledge at all.[7]

On June 3, the plaintiffs' lawyers delivered closing arguments. They knew they'd have to convince the jury that "not only did the bad guys do it" but also that the communists were "worthy of being granted a settlement."[8]

"Ladies and gentlemen." Flint Taylor's husky voice, with its New England accent, barely carried to the bench. Judge Merhige asked him to speak up. Flint filled his lungs and continued, "I came down here from Chicago and devoted six months of my life to trying this case. But I had six months of my life to devote: Bill Sampson, Doctor Waller, Sandi Smith, all the others, they don't have a life or six months of a life to devote to justice. But their families, and my co-counsel and I are asking you to stand in their shoes, and to stand up for them, and to stand up for justice, to bring back a verdict and to say the Klansmen and the Nazis and police and federal officials that they can't do this, not in America, not in . . . 1979, no more. No more blaming the victims."

Lewis Pitts complimented Judge Merhige on running an efficient courtroom and then admitting to the jury that he was "nervous as a long-tailed cat," implored the jurors to "think about how many places the police had the opportunity to prevent what happened, how many times one officer could have done one thing that could have prevented the entire tragedy. . . . You know . . . it will take some courage for you to vote against these police officers. Because at first blush, it might be, 'Well, is this an indictment against the system? Am I opposed to law enforcement? Do I oppose police?' Certainly not, that's not at all what we are talking about. . . . We all want and need law enforcement; but none of us want nor should we tolerate irresponsible law enforcement."

Beware, Pitts told the jury, of "efforts to creep into the jury box" and make the case "about whether or not we want communism or don't want communism in this country. You know, the question is about equal protection . . . for black and white, no matter the skin color and no matter the politics."[9]

Carolyn McAllaster, too, asked the jury to look "behind the label" of communism and of "revolution" to focus on the plaintiffs' dreams of good health care, equal and fair pay, good education, and an inclusive democracy.

Then she turned her focus to the plaintiff who, more than any other, had provoked the ire of the Klansmen, the Nazis, the police, the FBI, and the clever defense lawyers: Nelson Johnson. "Now the defendants have put an awful lot of energy and effort into . . . telling you what a dangerous, violent, terrible person Nelson Johnson is; while our own federal government has helped a convicted felon for the Klan and Nazis to make their weapons more lethal than they already were . . . while the city of Greensboro, sworn to uphold the law and protect all citizens of Greensboro, ignored . . . what Eddie Dawson was telling them; and while the city police allowed Dawson to gain custody of the [parade permit] which led them to . . . know where to go. These defendants are trying to tell you that Nelson Johnson is a dangerous, violent person in this case."[10]

As she asked that Nelson be compensated for his injuries and suffering, she flipped that narrative: "Nelson Johnson is really the person in this case who has been most attacked . . . who has gone through the most in terms of blame being placed. . . . And we feel strongly that he should be compensated for that, that what he has gone through has been totally unjustified."

McAllaster asked the jury to "look beyond the innuendo and the labeling to see where the justice truly lies in this case. And I have confidence that when you come to consider damages, you will remember Paul's daily struggle to lead a meaningful life in spite of his handicaps, and Nelson's attempts to stay in the City of Greensboro without constantly being haunted by the innuendo resulting from the events of November 3rd. And I know you'll remember the loss to Sandi's parents of their only child. And I trust that you'll think about Marty coming home each night and eating dinner with Leah [her daughter with Mike Nathan], while Mike's chair stands empty. And Floris forever feeling the pain of losing the first man that she's loved through the violence of another person. And Signe, who is finally now, for the first time since her husband was murdered five years ago, just beginning to come to grips with the reality of having lost her husband. And Dale, who has gone to bed so many nights without Bill to hold her. And I know that you'll think about how all this waste of human life and promise could have been prevented."

The jury retired to deliberate. The old issues surfaced immediately. Four of the six argued that none of the defendants should be found liable for the deaths and injuries. Two of the jurors, the Black man and the woman who'd moved south from New England, argued that the preponderance of the evidence pointed to the guilt of the federal defendants, the local police, and the white supremacists. These two jurors demanded that the families of those killed and wounded be compensated. The issue animating the four in favor of acquittal wasn't that they believed the Klan and Nazis or even law enforcement to be innocent, but rather that a significant settlement would give fresh life to communist organizing. If communists were the enemy, then perhaps Cecil Moses's friend Lee Colwell and Clarence Kelley were right: it was the FBI's job to do the dirty work required to protect "the American way of life" by any means necessary.[11]

The two sides dug in, but this time the two holdouts wouldn't budge. Eventually, the six worked to find a compromise. They agreed to find eight defendants—two police officers, Detective Jerry "Rooster" Cooper and Lieutenant Paul Spoon; five Klansmen and Nazis, Roland Wayne Wood, Mark Sherer, David Matthews, Jack Fowler, and Jerry Paul Smith; and the informant Eddie Dawson—jointly liable for the death of Mike Nathan, awarding his widow $351,000. Additionally, the jurors found Klansmen and Nazis liable for several other assaults, including the attack on Paul Bermanzohn, to whom they awarded $38,359.55. To the families of Sandi Smith, Bill Sampson, Cesar Cauce, and Jim Waller, the jury awarded nothing. And despite Carolyn McAllaster's eloquent plea, neither did Nelson Johnson receive redress.[12]

❖

The lawyers and CWP members huddled together in the courthouse. Had they won or lost? Why had Mike Nathan's been the only death deemed worthy of reward by the jury? Was it because he had not been an official CWP member when he died? Was it that he had been a practicing doctor? That he'd been unarmed when the bullet entered his brain? The plaintiffs were stunned and confused. The settlement, insignificant beside the damages they'd sought, threatened to divide them.

In the tumult of the moment, Lewis Pitts understood his clients' disappointment, but he saw it differently. A southern jury found police officers and Klansmen jointly liable for a wrongful death, something that, quite likely, had never happened before in American history. "Listen," said Pitts, "this is a victory. We have to claim it."[13]

Nelson, Signe, Dale, and Marty gathered themselves. Then they joined hands and walked out the door to the courthouse steps. Crossing the threshold, the press mob came into view. And in that moment, they raised their hands high above their heads. Even if they hadn't achieved the justice they'd sought, a court had found their adversaries culpable for the pain they'd suffered. For now, this would have to stand for victory. Capitalism hadn't collapsed. And the struggle would still tumble and stumble forward through the desert of American inequity, generation after generation.

The next day, in a reversal from Anthony Lewis's 1979 op-ed blaming the CWP for violent speech, a *New York Times* editorial celebrated the victory: "The findings show that North Carolinians understand the need to resist forcible interference with free speech and assembly. Rights are rights, even for radical dissenters. The jury also made clear that police may not yield the streets in the name of neutrality. The verdict set the proper limit: tough talk is permissible; terrorism is not."[14]

After the decision, Judge Merhige, who rarely took vacations, left immediately for a two-week cruise in Alaska with his wife. Physically and emotionally drained by the trial, Merhige and his clerk never debriefed. They'd worked through a difficult trial and, against the odds, managed to preserve the integrity of the court. The lead government lawyer, Joe Sher, thought Merhige had been biased against his government clients. Lewis Pitts believed Merhige had maneuvered to protect the federal agents even as he allowed a couple of city cops to take some blame for wrongful deaths. Merhige's clerk at the trial believed that Sher landed closer to the truth. He thought Pitts and the CWP team had made a compelling case for federal complicity and cover-up and suspected Merhige thought so, too.[15]

There would be no more legal trials resulting from the Greensboro Massacre. Despite all he'd been through, Nelson's words addressed to the citizens of Greensboro hinted at a new spirit animating his voice. He extended both an offer of peace and a renewed commitment to the city: "We ask our city leaders, including the mayor and councilpersons, our civic, political and religious organizations to join in a united effort for social, economic and racial justice," said Nelson. "Together we can heal the scars and wounds of November 3. . . . Greensboro can become . . . a city which turns away from racisms and inequality. Our city can represent jobs, peace and justice for all of its citizens. . . . We seek to work in harmony with all people who share this direction and vision."[16]

Though the City of Greensboro denied any responsibility for the murders, it paid the full $351,000 award to Marty Nathan on behalf of not only the police officers but also the Klansmen, Nazis, and Eddie Dawson. The CWP plaintiffs used a portion of the settlement money to start a foundation that would make small grants to activists fighting for racial and economic justice around the South. Their legacy would continue, even as they struggled with the mysteries of a day that had irrevocably ended and changed lives and life trajectories: How did Dawson know that the march end point had been changed? What role, if any, had the textile mills played in the shooting? Had there been other informants among the Klansmen and Nazis? In the CWP, perhaps? Had there been provocateurs at Morningside Homes that morning? Was there any truth to the shocking claims in Henry Byrd's letter to Nelson? How high in the hierarchy of the federal agencies had knowledge of potential violence gone?

A year after the trial ended, Nelson's picture appeared in the *Greensboro News & Record*. Perhaps for the very first time, it wasn't beside a note covering his activism or anything to do with 1969 or 1979. The caption noted that he'd graduated with honors from North Carolina A&T with a degree in political science.

Even with all the open questions, an excruciating six-year chapter in the lives of Nelson, Joyce, and their friends had ended. If there'd been one more revelation during the agonizing six years since the shooting, it was that wielding communism as a tool to create social change in the United States wouldn't work. Likely with a tremor of exhausted relief, they now faced the terrifying challenge of rebuilding their lives and selecting new philosophies and methods for engaging the world.[17] Even so, they knew that while their lives could begin again, reentering the fast-flowing stream of time, the work to both understand their history and improve the lives of Greensboro's poorest residents would continue.

SECTION IV

RENEWAL: 1986-2006

LIBERATION

At Shiloh Baptist Church one Sunday during the final trial, Reverend Otis Hairston Sr.'s gentle voice floated through the voluminous brick sanctuary, chronicling the parable of the prodigal son who "took his journey into a far country."[1] There the young man fell on hard times, became desperate with hunger, and decided to save himself by returning to his father, saying, "I have sinned against Heaven . . . and am no more worthy to be called thy son." The father, however, rejoiced at the son's return to his house and faith and put on a feast, saying, "My son was dead and is alive again; he was lost, and is found."

Sitting in the oak pew that morning, absorbing Reverend Hairston's homily about family and home, forgiveness and grace and unconditional love, a yearning for connection and community overwhelmed Nelson. He leaned toward Joyce and whispered, "I need to make this move now, I'm going to join." They'd agreed not to commit to a congregation before discussing it as a family, but Joyce, sensing the intensity of Nelson's energy, rose with him and walked to the front of the chapel.[2]

Later, after the trial was over, Nelson and Joyce were changing out of their church clothes when Nelson said he had something to tell Joyce. In a flash, she heard the words he would say before they left his mouth. Sitting beside his wife at the edge of their bed, Nelson confided what Joyce already intuitively understood: "I've been called to the ministry. Will you support me in that journey?" She reached out her arms and embraced him, holding her husband close in unspoken affirmation.[3]

A year later, Reverend Hairston invited Nelson to preach his first sermon. Nelson had graduated from A&T and been accepted into Union Theological Seminary in New York to study for a master's degree in divinity. He planned to study with the distinguished theologian James Cone, who had forged from the words of Jesus and aspirations of Black Power a theology of Black liberation.

On July 13, 1986, congregants filled most of the 816 seats in Shiloh's temple, anxious to hear what Brother Nelson had to say. Joyce and the girls were there. His eldest brother, James, also a reverend, arrived to support his sibling. Signe Waller and Marty Nathan, members of his CWP family, sat together in a pew near the front of the church. Nelson wasted little time in establishing his Christian philosophy. "Some people treat religion as a rationale for selfishness. I'm not interested in being an acceptable, don't-rock-the-boat preacher. The Jesus I know and love rocked the world!"[4] And the Jesus Nelson knew didn't shy away from politics either. From the pulpit, Nelson criticized televangelists who used fear instead of love to draw people to Jesus. He warned against President Reagan's Scripture-cloaked march to militarism and the use of religion to defend and maintain an unequal status quo. Nelson had made no "radical shifts." The man at the front of the church traded in his communist sword for a Christian plowshare sharp enough to break hard ground and "liberate the oppressed." "I've been part of the civil rights movement, the black liberation movement, the socialist movement," he told a local reporter. "I'm less inclined right now to put whole people into categories. I'm no less inclined, however, to be critical of certain ideas, of ideas I believe to be wrong. But I think there's a way to do that that's not condemning other persons."[5]

It had been a long time since Nelson had received a standing ovation in Greensboro, perhaps since the heady days of the Greensboro Association of Poor People and the movement for community control in the early 1970s. The congregants and visitors at Shiloh Baptist boisterously celebrated the return of a man they could still recall with respect and love, but whose ideas for a period of time had outpaced and frightened them. Reverend James Johnson gathered his brother in a bear hug. "He will be one of the great prophets that we have," predicted Reverend Hairston. "I've heard a lot of first sermons, but I've never heard one like this. We thank God that he moved in the heart of Nelson Johnson."[6]

❖

Joyce traveled with Nelson to New York, driving up Riverside Drive and across on 122nd Street to Broadway and Union Theological Seminary. When they arrived, Dr. James Cone was out of town. A tour of the dorms with their coed living arrangements and coed bathrooms caused the couple discomfort and made them feel too far from the safety of home. Nelson at forty-three and Joyce at thirty-nine were older than most of the other students and were still healing, guarding the deep bond that, though frayed and vulnerable, had somehow held through all the years of grief and angst.[7]

They turned around and left New York and drove back south in search of a haven. Half a day later, they arrived in Richmond. Virginia Union University's School of Theology accepted Nelson on the spot. Joyce's mother and stepfather agreed to house their son-in-law, who would share a partitioned room with Joyce's brother. Studying in Richmond—a three-and-a-half-hour drive from Greensboro instead of the nine-hour trip from New York—Nelson would be able to return home each weekend to spend time with his wife and daughters.

As centrifugal force spun burned-out, damaged comrades away from the CWP to struggle with finding meaning in their lives, Nelson, who'd not "drawn any" firm "conclusions" yet about his relationship to faith, worked to rebuild himself in a city that expected nothing of him.[8] Liberated from "the pressure cooker of Greensboro," he buried himself in the library and engaged his professors and classmates in conversation and debate.[9]

At home on weekends, he saw that "not much organizing was going on in Greensboro." He thought that "in a way the shooting had succeeded" at quashing challenges to the status quo.[10] On the other hand, in the tragedy's wake, Jim Melvin had stepped away from elected politics, and the city had finally, after decades of resistance, adopted a district voting system. As anticipated, the complexion of the city council changed quickly. And while the restrictions limiting the covert powers of the FBI had been lifted in 1983, the Supreme Court had made it more difficult for courts to seat all-white juries in its 1986 *Batson* ruling. The Greensboro shooting had had bigger influence, in ways good and bad, on the laws and ways of North Carolina and the United States than most people knew or understood.

As Nelson contemplated his own path and the changes he saw around him, he came to realize that what "man makes, he can also unmake." But that making or unmaking, for good or ill, takes time. Pressing too hard, too fast, as he had with the revolution-minded CWP, wasn't always the best strategy. "I can see errors and weaknesses in my thinking," Nelson had told the *Greensboro News & Record* reporter after his sermon at Shiloh Baptist. But he was "reluctant to second guess where [else] I could've been," still valuing "all of the forces that shaped [his] thought pattern" and carried him to this new intellectual and spiritual stage. Life, he'd come to realize, was "a very long journey," long enough to allow the "possibility that people could change."[11] Even as he held on to Marxian ideas about the function of capital and, in the concept of the common good, identified similarities between Marxist and Christian thought, Nelson came to see the limitations of democratic centralism and the dictatorship of the proletariat.[12] Instead, he began to believe that realizing the goal of "to each according to his needs" depended on Jesus's redemptive spirit, which made it impossible for Nelson to "dismiss whole categories of people." "The word *communism* had been used to turn us into things," Nelson knew; but he and his comrades had done the same thing—especially to the Klansmen and Nazis but also to the police and politicians.[13]

At home, as her husband worked to reinvent himself, Joyce would quip sarcastically to friends that she "turned 40, had two teenage daughters, and became a single mother."[14] Even so, she tenaciously guarded her family's place in the Greensboro fishbowl, took on more responsibility in her job at A&T's Transportation Institute, drove the girls to sports practices and competitions, put healthy meals on the table, and embraced Nelson when he motored home from Richmond on the weekends.

Near the end of his first year of seminary, Nelson, at home for Easter weekend to enjoy a few relaxing days with his Joyce and the girls, was at the dinner table when a knock on the front door echoed through the house. Answering the door, he recognized the Black man standing there, a State Bureau of Investigation agent Nelson had encountered several times over the years. "He's not a bad guy," he thought to himself and stepped outside onto the high porch; "he's half a friend." The two men shook hands and exchanged pleasantries. Then the SBI agent got to what he'd come for.

"The Klan is coming to march in Greensboro. What are you going to do? What's the Communist Workers Party planning?"

Worried that Nelson and his 1979 comrades would try to exact revenge on the Klansmen for killing five of Nelson and Joyce's friends, the man had made the trip from Charlotte to the wood-frame, gabled house on Alamance Church Road, where Greensboro bled into cow pastures and cornfields. But he hadn't come only for information, Nelson believed in the moment; the agent had also come out of one Black man's concern for another.

Nelson didn't bother telling the SBI agent that the CWP had been disbanded quietly two years earlier. Or that he himself had moved on from communism and was finishing his first year of seminary, where he'd discovered a "radical" Jesus who suited his relentless hunger for justice and equality. Instead, he told the man a simpler truth: "We aren't planning anything."[15]

PEACE

Joyce, we need to talk," said Nelson, back again from Richmond the Sunday after the Easter visit from the SBI agent. Most times, the couple would hash out a family consensus around the wide dining room table together with Akua and Ayo. But Nelson beckoned Joyce into the bedroom, away from curious listening ears and the shuffle of stockinged feet at the top of the stairs.[1]

Nelson planted himself at the edge of the couple's bed and, in his deliberate way, told Joyce that if the Klansmen carried out the march they'd planned, their first in Greensboro since the '79 massacre, "it would be like they came just to spit on the graves of our friends. I can't let that happen." Those murderous eighty-eight seconds were clamped to Nelson's shoulders like the whole, immense weight of the world. Awake and asleep, his mind kept those deadly moments near. As the organizer of the ambushed march, he felt responsible to the widows and the children left without fathers, the traumatized residents of Morningside Homes, the frightened citizens of Greensboro. Though he couldn't betray the truth of what he believed happened on November 3, he wanted to help heal the wounds, still raw after all these years. How could he show the people who crossed the street when they saw him coming that he'd been trying to heal the city, not hurt it? He would go ask the Klan, he told Joyce, to cancel the march.

"You are out of your mind," Joyce told him.

If she'd ever had any question about how treacherous the Klan could be, she had no doubts after the 1979 murders. Usually she enjoyed her political debates with Nelson, the give-and-take about organizing strategies or protest tactics, and more recently their discussions about faith. But the fear of that deadly Saturday morning and its aftermath—when they'd become pariahs in the city they called home—remained close, infused everything they did and thought, colored each living day, kept Nelson jobless for nearly a decade, circumscribed their daughters' childhoods.

Despite her acerbic half joke about being single, Joyce's husband came home nearly every weekend. This plan of his, she knew, could make her a widow, orphan her children permanently.

Joyce could hear the tone in her husband's voice that meant he spoke from his heart, that he'd been called to this moment. So, she listened. But she wasn't done with her questions. How, she wanted to know, did this idea occur to him?

Perhaps it was during the drive back to Richmond, he told Joyce, as he turned the conversation with the SBI agent over in his mind.

"There has to be a better, less risky way to stop the Klan than going to see them all by yourself," Joyce insisted. The personal sacrifice we've made as a family is just too great, she thought. The girls would be terrified.

Nelson told Joyce he'd been studying Jesus's imperative to "love thy neighbor"—how Jesus, in response to the question "Who is my neighbor?," conjured fear in the lonely dark. Thieves and bandits stalked the dangerous road between Jericho and Jerusalem. The generous act of the Good Samaritan, the compassionate stranger, said Nelson, teaches us that everyone is our neighbor, even a Klansman. He quoted Jesus's words as they are written in the gospel of Matthew: "Ye have heard it said, Thou shalt love thy neighbor, and hate thine enemy. But I say unto you, Love your enemies, bless them that curse you, do good to them that hate you, and pray for them which despitefully use you, and persecute you, that ye may be the children of your Father which is in heaven: for He maketh his sun to rise on the evil and on the good, and sendeth rain on the just and on the unjust."

Joyce knew these words by heart; the parable of the Good Samaritan was the first Bible verse she'd read aloud in church as a girl in Richmond.

Between the library and the modest Richmond home of Joyce's parents, Nelson lived a monkish life, poring over the pages of theology and philosophy, allowing the words he read to come to life inside him. Nelson remembered his parents' Jesus as a "smart man saying nice things." Now the prophet's words unfurled for him in a new way. When Jesus said to love your enemy, Nelson tried to understand the words not only with his mind but also with his spirit, straining to feel the humanity in people with whom he differed.

"Radical love carries risk," he said.

He'd been reading *Moral Man and Immoral Society* by the Christian realist philosopher Reinhold Niebuhr. Niebuhr explained the tension between society and the individual—how society, by insisting on certain cultural conventions, could constrain an individual person from making a moral choice. Nelson took Niebuhr's idea as a ray of hope. If he could just sit down with one or two of the men who despised him, apart from the pressure of their Klavern crew, maybe, as he showed them that he was no longer a "reckless rebel," he could convince them—his neighbors—that their hate was a dead end.

He poured his heart out to Joyce as they sat together on their bed, revealing the intellectual, political, and spiritual journey that pushed him to make a dangerous drive, alone, into Klan country. He was willing to live in that tension, he told Joyce. He interpreted the concerns Joyce raised less as opposition than an expression of her love and care for him.

A white student had once come through Joyce's department at A&T. She'd encouraged him to pursue his degree and advocated for him to receive financial aid. When he graduated, she'd helped him find a job. Grateful for her support, the student came to her with a confession. After some Black kids threw rocks at his car, he'd planned to blow up the housing project where they lived with explosives provided by Army friends stationed at Fort Bragg in Fayetteville. Instead of turning her back on the young man, Joyce accepted his remorse and engaged him in discussion and prayer.[2]

❖

The conversation between Nelson and Joyce played like a jazz duet: there were long solos, jarring asynchronous moments, riffs and improvisation, tears and smiles.[3] But as usually happened since they began their lifetime conversation back in the winter of 1969, they came back together, finding harmony in a shared desire to make the world a better, more just place.

Joyce began to make her own peace with her husband's act of faith, seeing it as one more leg of the spiritual journey to which they'd both been called. She understood that he needed to put his newly acquired Christian tools to work in the real world. It was what they'd been doing for years: testing theory with practice, then refining the theory and testing it again. Instead of preaching a "dictatorship of the proletariat" and a process for defeating their enemies, they would try to reach them through their common Christian faith. "They say that they are following Jesus Christ," Nelson had said. "That's what I'm trying to do. We—the Klan and I—we should talk it out." She also understood his desire to protect Greensboro. Her job now, a terribly difficult one, would be to wait for Nelson's safe return.

They agreed not to tell any friends from the communist days about Nelson's plan. He didn't wish to debate it with them in the old style of "scientific analysis." This marked the beginning of a new, personal quest. They agreed also not to frighten Akua and Ayo with knowledge of Nelson's upcoming journey.

❖

Five days later, Joyce told Nelson to make sure the car had a full tank of gas. She didn't want him stuck beside the road, looking for assistance on a rural road, dependent on a chance encounter with a Good Samaritan. After giving her husband a last bit of advice and a hug of encouragement, she went back inside to the kitchen. She'd have to keep herself busy to fight off the fear. She thought about what to cook. Maybe some fried chicken. He'd enjoy that when he got home. She prayed to God to protect her husband as she took down the flour. And then she began to sing a hymn: "Guide my feet while I run this race, because I don't want to run this race in vain!"

Nelson climbed into the 1977 Ford Maverick that Cesar Cauce's widow, Floris, had given him after the massacre. Nelson knew that before Cesar died trying to protect terrified protesters from the Klan and Nazi attack, he'd treasured the sporty, cinnamon-colored car, with its long nose and powerful V8 engine. The workingman's toy had given the Cuban immigrant moments of joyous, American-style freedom as he zipped along North Carolina's open roads. Now it would carry Nelson to meet Cesar's killers.

Following Joyce's advice, Nelson checked the Brown Bomber's fuel gauge. It read full. Beside him, on the passenger seat, he set a letter he'd written to Carroll Crawford, the current Klan Grand Dragon, and Virgil Griffin, the Klan leader in '79. Nelson scanned the first few lines:

> *Dear Mr. Carroll Crawford and Mr. Virgil Griffin: I am delivering this letter to you in your capacities of leaders of the Christian Knights of the Ku Klux Klan. Although I strongly disagree with the philosophy of your organization, I feel that a sincere effort should be made to establish some dialog. I hope that my presence and the words in this brief communication will be prayerfully considered.[4]*

If they wouldn't listen or let him speak, he could leave the letter behind. If they were willing to read it, they might understand why he'd come to see them.

Just a few miles outside of Greensboro, the radio crackled and buzzed with nothing but static, so Nelson shut it off to be alone with the thoughts in his head and the scenery along the road as he drove the gently undulating US Highway 29 through farmland and forest, southwest toward Salisbury.

Before he'd last left Richmond, Nelson told two of his professors about his plan. He'd hoped for encouragement, for them to buttress his philosophical and theological argument for going to see the Klan. Instead, they'd discouraged Nelson from making the journey. "Some people," one warned, "are beyond the pale." How could these preachers tell me to give up on these white men if Jesus believed in the possible transformation of every one of us? Nelson wondered. When he visited his pastor in Greensboro, the taciturn Reverend Otis Hairston Sr. gave Nelson all he needed: a nod, the blessing of an elder.

As he drove the spring-bright roads with the radio off, these conversations played in Nelson's head. "Beyond the pale," his professor had said. And with those words fear entered Nelson's body, like ants crawling in his veins, tickling and stinging inside his chest and down his legs. What if the Klan finished the job they'd started in '79? He remembered the rumors that the cops and Klansmen had lamented the fact that he'd walked away from Morningside that morning. Sometimes the scars on his arms, the half-paralyzed finger, reminded him of his faith and the gift of his continuing life. Other times they meant only that people had wanted to kill him. What would happen to his children if he didn't return? What would Joyce do? He conjured shocking images of Jim Crow postcards, white faces grinning under Black bodies hanging from southern trees. What kind of people would send postcards like those? Are they beyond the pale? Would they converse with a Black man coming in the name of Christ? As he passed Salisbury, the last city before he disappeared over a border into what, culturally, became Appalachia, Nelson pulled over onto the shoulder of the road, sweating, his heart racing, his breath coming in shallow gasps.

For a few minutes, he sat there in his car, unable to find a way out of the trap his mind and history had laid for him. At some point, as he fought to collect himself, he looked up and out the car window and began to see the trees around him. The oak, red maple, sycamore, and tulip poplar leaves were beginning to unfurl after a long, bare winter. As he looked closely, it surprised him that these tender, spring leaves weren't green. Nelson noticed ocher, red, yellow, and orange. White swarms of dogwood blooms massed into pillow clouds that floated through the understory beside the country road. The fuchsia flowers of the Judas tree burned in the spring sun. The riot of color reminded Nelson of the beauty of the countryside where he grew up. Sitting in the car, a verse from Philippians came to his mind: "Whatever is true, whatever is noble, whatever is right, whatever is pure, whatever is lovely, whatever is admirable—if anything is excellent or praiseworthy—think about such things . . . And the God of peace will be with you." And there, beside the road, he began to pray.

The terror that had hijacked his body slipped away. Looking again at the leaves and flowers, he thought how each possessed beauty that was neither defined nor negated by the other leaves or flowers. But the garden, the ensemble of diverse woods, was more beautiful than any single leaf or flower. He started up the car, felt the powerful engine rumble to life, and drove on.

A few miles later he came to the crossroads in Mount Ulla. Stores sat on both sides of the road, one store in a wood-frame building, the other store a square stack of cement blocks, both advertising Coca-Cola, cigarettes, and beer. Two white men dressed in overalls and seed caps sat on hay bales beside the road in front of one of the stores, a scene familiar from Nelson's youth in Airlie.

Nelson rolled down the car window, his Black face appearing to the white farmers beside the road. "Can you tell me the way to Carroll Crawford's house?" Nelson asked. He wasn't sure whether they'd tell him, a Black man in a fast car. But they did, gesturing which way to go, saying that Mr. Crawford's trailer was about three-quarters of a mile down the road. You can't miss it, they said.

Nelson covered the distance quickly, passing fields where cows and horses grazed. The men at the crossroads had been right. A big signboard nailed to posts rose from the edge of Carroll Crawford's driveway. In broad, black, hand-painted swipes it read, "No N——s Allowed." A couple hundred yards beyond it, a rusty trailer squatted in a cornfield. Nelson paused, scanning the neatly typed letter on the passenger's seat, then stepped lightly on the gas, and the rubber tires of Cesar's Maverick grabbed the gravel drive.

Nelson climbed the trailer steps and knocked on the door. No one answered, so he slipped the letter under the door.

❖

On the way home, he called Joyce from a pay phone to let her know he was fine and would be home to eat her fried chicken.

Later, he called Carroll Crawford on the phone. The Klansman picked up but didn't believe Nelson had actually been to his home until he discovered the letter lying on the floor just inside the trailer's back door. He swore and shouted at Nelson, outraged that the Black man had disregarded his sign. Read the letter, said Nelson, and call me back. A short time later, Crawford did call back and agreed to meet Nelson a week later at a gas station on the highway outside Salisbury.

For a second time Nelson drove the hour southwest and, when he pulled into the designated meeting spot, saw several men jammed into two pickup trucks. "Follow us," Crawford called to him. And Nelson did follow them, assuming the white supremacists would lead him to some abandoned barn in the countryside. Instead, after a short drive, they pulled into the parking lot of a Holiday Inn on the outskirts of Salisbury just off I-85.

Carroll Crawford and Virgil Griffin led him to a ground-floor room where a table and three chairs awaited. One of them threw open the blinds. Then the Klansmen directed Nelson to the chair facing the window and took their seats, one on either side of him.

Rural white people were not foreign to Nelson, as they were to many of his friends and comrades in Greensboro. He'd grown up around them and trusted that, Black or white, they shared an understanding of country rhythms and life.

Carroll and Virgil knew from Nelson's letter that he'd come to dissuade them from marching in Greensboro. Sitting there, Nelson asked them why they wanted to march, and they launched into a tired litany, beginning with the scourge of Black men raping their women. Nelson pushed back. "You know better than that, man," he said. "You know some of the things y'all did." All the different shades of people, said Nelson, didn't come from Black people raping white people, but from the "nighttime integration" of the slave cabins by white men with unchecked power.

"When it gets in heat, you'll screw a pig," responded one of the Klansmen. It wasn't a joke, but Nelson wanted to laugh. The white supremacist hadn't disagreed with what Nelson said; he'd just justified those visits to the slave cabins in coarse, rural language that Nelson would understand. Nelson had heard white people say things like this, but he'd never debated people who thought this way. A hard reality anchored the surreal scene; these men's friends had murdered his friends and gotten away with it.

Their discussion went back and forth, argument and counterargument. It moved from rape to jobs in the textile mills, to slavery, to the role of women in society.[5] Through it all, Nelson strained to find compassion for the Klansmen, reminding himself that if human culture made them his enemies, together they possessed the power to undo that antagonistic relationship.

After nearly two hours, Nelson brought the conversation back to his reason for coming. "Listen," he said, "I want to ask you not to come to Greensboro."

Carroll and Virgil demurred. They couldn't cancel the march, they said. It would look as though they were taking orders from a Black man. They were willing to promise, however, that they wouldn't start any trouble when they came to Greensboro. However small and incremental their concession, it felt to Nelson like validation. Maybe these men could transform their hate, not by being suppressed or squashed, but by being given the opportunity to trust and, eventually perhaps, love. They were light-years from loving Nelson, but they'd listened to him and offered him something.

"For better or worse," Martin Luther King Jr. had said, "we are all on this particular land together at the same time, and we have to work it out together." As a boy, Nelson had intuitively embraced this generous approach. But somewhere along the line—maybe in the confrontation with the brothers from Norfolk when Nelson was in the military, or during the early grassroots struggles in Greensboro—he'd lost hope in healing and reconciliation. Now he meant to reclaim it.

❖

Before the conversation ended, the men asked Nelson if he knew why they'd placed him in the middle chair facing the window.

No, he said.

They told him that they'd expected him to trick them into a revenge trap. Across the hotel courtyard, they said, pointing toward another window, a sniper had kept his rifle aimed at Nelson's head for the entire two hours. If he'd made a suspicious move, the two men only had to give the sniper a signal.

As the conversation ended, Carroll Crawford said something else. He believed, he told Nelson, that Eddie Dawson, acting on behalf of the Greensboro Police Department and FBI, had manipulated the Klansmen into a conflict with Nelson and the CWP.

On Sunday, June 7, 1987, about 140 members of the Christian Knights of the Ku Klux Klan arrived to march ten blocks through the center of Greensboro.[6]

Five months earlier, at a tick past midnight on January 16, Sylvester Daughtry, the man who'd ordered Nelson's arrest on November 3, had become the first Black police chief of Greensboro and of any major city in North Carolina. When he heard the news, the man who'd been passed over for Daughtry reportedly yelled to his secretary, "I can't believe they gave it to the n—— over me."[7] The change at the top of the department made a few officers so uncomfortable they took early retirement.

Faced with the first Klan demonstration in Greensboro since 1979, the new chief activated nearly the entire force of 388 Greensboro police officers. They were visible at every corner, on rooftops around the city, and every few feet along the Klan walk. The police surrounded Nocho Park, too, where the mayor, John Forbis, led a peace rally. The security effort, which included the state police, Highway Patrol, and State Bureau of Investigation, cost the city some $40,000. But not a single injury was reported. The Klan, as promised, didn't start any trouble.

Nelson, Joyce, and other CWP members steered clear of the event. The press recalled the horrors of 1979, but no one knew about Nelson's drive to Mount Ulla or his meeting in a Salisbury hotel with Carroll Crawford and Virgil Griffin.

BELOVED

By the mid-1980s, CWP members began the perilous rise from years of communist activism back toward the surface of American society, like divers emerging cautiously and in stages from the ocean depths to avoid the bends.

Anxious to engage the world in meaningful ways, yet fearful of red-baiting, many started over in new places as they struggled to process the intensity of the CWP years. Doctors—such as Paul Bermanzohn, who was now in New York—returned to medicine. They remade themselves and continued, in most cases, to advocate for America's working poor even as, for the sake of their own economic survival, many papered over previous, radical affiliations. They lingered in graduate school and fiddled with résumés to hide gaps and incongruities that might provoke awkward questions during job interviews. They carried the brilliance and ambition they'd brought to the dream of disrupting American political and economic systems from the outside into established institutions, becoming lawyers, civil servants, and union leaders. They joined academia and wrote best-selling popular science books. Some earned judgeships; others took jobs as bureaucrats in the administration of American cities, including New York and Washington, DC. At least one would become the mayor of a major US metropolis.

When Nelson graduated from Virginia Union with a degree in theology in 1989, a church in Richmond offered him a position. While he'd grown comfortable in Joyce's hometown, she'd flourished in Greensboro. After nearly twenty years, the family moved from Alamance Church Road to a modest yet comfortable ranch home with a big, sloping backyard on Murrayhill Road, closer to the city's center. Though she'd faced challenges, Joyce had not been vilified as her husband was; she'd been promoted to be the interim director of the Transportation Institute at A&T and, through that job, joined a project to facilitate conversations among citizens from different neighborhoods and circumstances to reimagine Greensboro's future. The VISIONS plan eventually homed in on education, affordable housing, economic development, land use, and transportation. Against the current of a national surge toward privatization, Joyce pushed the city to take the bus system back from the energy company, Duke Power; to establish routes more beneficial to working people; and to reimagine the old train station as a multimodal transit hub.[1]

Nelson hated to leave the city beside the James River and return to face the old resentments. But to begin anew with Joyce and his daughters, he accepted an offer to become an assistant pastor at Shiloh Baptist Church, under the tutelage of his mentor, Reverend Otis Hairston Sr.

❖

A quarter century after Greensboro won an All-America City Award in 1966 and twenty-six years after Nelson arrived in the city to enroll at A&T, leading citizens mustered support to apply for the award again. In addition to VISIONS, they pointed to a renewed public-private collaboration to revitalize the city's downtown and the innovative Challenge Greensboro program, designed to increase minority leadership throughout the city. The city's population had grown to 183,521, an increase of nearly 45,000 in twenty-five years. More dramatic than the population increase, however, was the extraordinary diversity of the team promoting the city. The delegation of white men that had traveled to Boston for the 1966 pitch skirted issues of race and power. The new generation of hopefuls, male and female,

Black and white, imagined the lonely Jefferson Standard building joined by towering neighbors to create "the biggest change on the downtown skyline since the Roaring 20s." They presented Greensboro as a city in the midst of a transition "from its past" of economic dependence on textile mills (rapidly disappearing overseas) and the exclusive leadership of "white male business executives." The "new future" of more affordable housing, accessible public transportation, and an economy based on innovation and technology would be led by women and African Americans, who were beginning to assume leadership of public and private institutions, including the Jaycees. The application highlighted the critical role that the shift from at-large to district voting played in the changes taking place around the city, opening the door to representative leadership. That advance took place in 1982, the year after Jim Melvin stepped down from his ten-year run as mayor. Amid the "changes that rocked the city," one "rallying point" from the 1966 application remained steady: pride in the Greater Greensboro Open Golf Tournament, now called, in the new era of corporate sponsorship, the Kmart GGO.[2]

On July 4, 1991, the *Greensboro News & Record* celebrated the city's second selection as an All-America City, one among ten "best of the best" examples of a forward-looking metropolis.[3] If the winning narrative of social and economic change left something out, it was the courageous pressure, coming largely from the A&T side of Greensboro, that had jolted the "white male executives" enough to force them to make a sliver of room atop the city's hierarchy. Over all the years, that advocacy and resistance had come at the price of careers, reputations, and, in 1969 and '79, lives. And though Greensboro had unquestionably changed since the 1979 shootings, stark inequalities, reinforced by voracious corporate practices, remained in the city. In a country fascinated by mobility—of whalers, soldiers, explorers, pioneers, prophets, and preachers who carry civilization, business, and "the word" to far-flung peoples—Nelson had come home to continue the struggle.

❖

After a brief reintroduction to Black Greensboro through his work at Shiloh Baptist and beside Joyce's high-profile civic engagement, Nelson set out again on his own. He started Faith Community Church to welcome the "homeless, former addicts and prisoners, and others existing on the margins of life."[4] The new church cinched him to the legacy of his grandfather Nelson Thorne Sr., for whom Nelson's mother had named him and who'd raised Lee's Chapel for Airlie's Black farmers and laborers. Through the church door, Nelson became reacquainted with the philosophy of Martin Luther King Jr., whose advocacy of nonviolence and integration he'd rejected in the mid-1960s. From the end of the Montgomery bus boycott in 1956 until his death twelve years later, King posited the fundamental goal of his work to be "beloved community," which he defined as a true "brotherhood," governed by love and arrived at through redemption and reconciliation. As the Soviet Union spun apart, Nelson borrowed King's concept of beloved community and his "abiding faith in mankind and an audacious faith in the future of mankind" through the transformational power of radical love.

Among his founding allies in this new endeavor were two white Presbyterian ministers: Barbara Dua, the pastor at Greensboro's First Presbyterian, and the skinny, independent-minded leader of the Church of the Covenant on Mendenhall Street, Zeb North Holler.[5] Holler, known to all as Z and renowned for his quirky sense of humor, grew up in Greensboro during Jim Crow, in the 1930s and '40s, when, he'd note, "white leaders kept the city under their control." He left for college and a tour as a Navy pilot before entering Union Theological Seminary in Richmond. Confronted with his own racist, middle-class assumptions, he accepted the hard work required to grow and change. At a church in Anderson, South Carolina, despite threats from the Klan, he recalled hosting a group of Freedom Riders as they passed through in defiance of state segregation laws. (The police and FBI would later allow Freedom Riders to be attacked in

Alabama.) In 1968, Z Holler and his congregation in Atlanta served meals to thousands of mourners arriving to grieve the murder of Martin Luther King Jr. In July 1979, Z had been called home to Greensboro and the Church of the Covenant.

Holler had been in Greensboro little more than three months when the November 3 shooting at Morningside Homes fractured the city. The next week, a member of Z's church contacted his pastor for guidance. A funeral director, the man had agreed to transport the bodies of Jim Waller, Bill Sampson, Cesar Cauce, and Mike Nathan to the November 11 funeral march. As the hour approached, the overwhelming presence of police and military troops along East Market Street and the ricocheting rumors of violence terrified the funeral director. Z donned a bulletproof vest, climbed into the lead hearse, and rode along to keep the frightened funeral director company.

Years later, Z Holler came to a meeting with Nelson Johnson fully aware of the man's ossified reputation as an amoral rabble-rouser in Greensboro, kept alive in business meetings and at cocktail parties and sourced to the pages of the *Greensboro News & Record*. The historian Manning Marable wrote that the biggest barrier to Malcolm X's reinvention would be his existing public image.[6] Marable might have said the same of Nelson. Despite the social pressure to toe the line on Nelson Johnson, Z Holler's unusually open mind allowed him to appreciate the incongruity between the person he met and the unrelenting public perception. He trusted his own impression of a "candid," "remarkably gracious," and deeply moral man, interested, as Z was, in the Jesus who said, "Blessed are the poor in spirit: for theirs is the kingdom of heaven."[7]

In Z, Nelson saw someone open to investigating the "spiritual and historical roots" of injustice, beyond the usual "tipping of the hat."[8]

The two became best friends and, with Barbara Dua, formed the Beloved Community Center, a nonprofit hub of community organizing beside Faith Community Church where Nelson would explore Black liberation theology. The two institutions married morality with political action, theory, and practice to advance toward King's shimmering dream, on the far side of a revolution in values and economics.

When a cause arose that threatened this vision of a beloved community, Nelson Johnson and his new comrades were prepared.

❖

During the first half of 1992, nine months after Greensboro celebrated its All-America City Award, Kmart, the nation's number two retailer, opened a new "megadistribution center" on the city's East Side.[9] As its corporate profits sank, Kmart had erected the thirty-five-acre building boasting 12.5 miles of conveyor belts and 8 miles of storage racks to service the retail supercenters it was rushing to open throughout the region.[10] The incentives the city and state dangled only added to the cost-saving benefits the company expected to reap in a "right-to-work" state with a negligible union presence.

The five hundred workers hired to staff the distribution center immediately complained of low pay and poor working conditions. While making five dollars an hour less than counterparts in other Kmart centers around the country, the Greensboro workers were expected to tolerate filthy portable toilets and inadequate air-conditioning and ventilation systems. Some fainted from the dangerous heat, while lax safety measures contributed to more than two hundred worker injuries during the facility's first twenty-four months of operation. Managers bullied laborers with pulled backs and broken fingers back onto the warehouse floor. Rampant sexual harassment and a steady stream of racial jokes and slurs, some scrawled on the walls of the revolting toilets, made the work environment intolerable, especially for the African Americans and women who made up three-quarters of the workforce.[11]

Despite little experience with union organizing and aggressive resistance from management, the workers voted to join the ACTWU Local just eighteen months after the center's opening. Kmart's shrewd lawyers did what they were paid to do: stall. Seven months after the successful union drive, in early 1994, there'd been no progress toward a contract. Then on April 24, under powder-blue skies and a warm, spring sun, a national TV audience looked on as the professional golfers swung toward the finish of the Kmart Greensboro Greater Open at the Forest Oaks Country Club. Suddenly, sixty-four workers, white and Black, stormed the tenth fairway, chanting "No justice, no peace." They sat down in a circle as if intending to picnic on the impeccable grass. Within minutes, a dozen Guilford County sheriff's deputies galloped onto the course in pursuit. "You got your media coverage, so go," shouted a lieutenant. The lieutenant counted off ten seconds. Then another five. When the cops started cuffing the protesters, spectators cheered. One shouted, "Club them like baby seals."[12]

A *Greensboro News & Record* editorial said the protesters made "fools of themselves" and should "whine" about their "wage complaints . . . somewhere other than a golf course." The workers had shanghaied a high-profile moment but failed to win the hearts and minds of Greensboro's citizens.[13]

The plight of the Kmart workers reminded Reverend Nelson Johnson of the early 1970s struggles against the AAA Realty Company and on behalf of the blind workers at Greensboro's Skilcraft plant.

The Beloved Community Center began to host public seminars and discussions about the Kmart fight. To win the battle, Nelson argued, the narrative had to be reframed from a fight between "labor and management" to one about a community standing up for its husbands, wives, brothers, sisters, sons, daughters, friends, and congregants against a ruthless and remote corporation. "Done right," Nelson contended, recalling ideas developed during the heady days of Ford Foundation–funded "community control" organizing, "everything becomes community . . . police abuse of power, labor," housing, and political representation. A job, he'd say, should bestow dignity and self-respect, not abuse and suffering. It should be a chance to "understand one's gifts."[14]

Nelson knew that if he stepped out in front on the Kmart issue, his polarizing reputation could hurt the cause. Patiently and persistently, he worked behind the scenes to bring his colleagues at the Pulpit Forum, the association for Greensboro's Black pastors, around to supporting the workers.[15]

On Thanksgiving Day 1995, outside the Woolworth Building on Elm Street where the 1960 sit-in movement started, pastors and Kmart workers announced a plan for a peaceful demonstration. Two days later, more than one thousand people gathered to chant their solidarity with the Kmart workers. But as the event wound down, four protesters—two of them from out of town—were arrested.

Worried that bad publicity could end the workers' struggle, Nelson decided the time had come to assert his organizing experience. The pastors, rather than the workers, he argued, should engage in civil disobedience on behalf of the community. "We're asking [the workers] *not* to get arrested. The only alternative is for us to get arrested first, so there's no confusion as to who is standing up and speaking out," he told his Pulpit Forum colleagues.[16] Years earlier, on November 2, 1979, he'd demonstrated to his comrades how a provocateur's jacket might swing open to reveal a gun. As he prepared the pastors sixteen years later, he made a similar gesture, showing how a Kmart worker, untrained in civil disobedience, might flail from an arresting cop, unintentionally setting off a riot.

On December 17, under a brown-skinned angel flying brightly atop a Christmas tree, Reverend Johnson informed his Faith Community Church congregation of the plan to block the entrance of the city's new Kmart Supercenter. After church, eight pastors, a state legislator, a governor's aide, and an antipoverty worker knelt in a circle to pray, blocking the entrance to the Kmart.

"Victory today is mine, I told Satan to get thee behind," the spirited crowd belted out as the police bristling in their riot gear loaded the pastors into paddy wagons. "Is this a race struggle or a class struggle?" a reporter called out to Nelson. "If you can tell me if slavery is a class struggle or a race struggle, then I'll answer your question," he replied.[17] On his way to jail, Nelson, the veteran at challenging the legal apparatus, counseled and calmed the other pastors, who were unaccustomed to standing on the wrong side of a cell door.

No one in the All-America City's leadership wanted Greensboro to become the site of a high-profile labor dispute. Nor did becoming known for jailing ministers appeal to leaders. The preachers were quickly set free.

Nelson quietly reached out to city business leaders, inviting them to participate in a Pulpit Forum / Business Work Group at the Beloved Community Center. Curious businesspeople, worried for Greensboro's reputation, showed up. Wary at first, they were as surprised as Z Holler had been to be greeted by Nelson's openness, honesty, and civility.

The civil disobedience continued and expanded. Students and professors from Guilford College joined the protests. On Martin Luther King Jr. Day 1996, the police arrested thirty-nine. On February 12, the number rose to fifty. The next week, thirty-two protesters rode to the jail in paddy wagons. Once again, something that had started in Greensboro began to spread. Solidarity protests sprang up at Kmarts in cities around the country.

Influenced by their conversations at the Pulpit Forum / Business Work Group meetings, the city's business leaders began to see the poor as more than a source of low-wage labor, wholly responsible for their own desperate plights. "I'm not convinced the whole system needs to be changed," said John Lauritzen, a former head of the Greensboro Chamber of Commerce, who attended the meetings, "but we can do a better job helping people."[18]

When the head of a local business group wrote a hysterical letter calling Nelson a "militant dissident" who led "radical fringe elements committed to Kmart's demise . . . [with] no legitimate purpose" other than chaos and vandalism, the alliance Nelson was forming held: Business leaders who frequented the Beloved Community Center remained committed to finding an equitable solution to the Kmart situation. By March 1996, the Pulpit Forum put out a statement that the "struggle has brought workers, union members, preachers, college students and professors, poor people's organizations, civil rights leaders, business people, elected officials, law enforcement officials, and other citizens in our community into dialog about serious life and death issues."[19]

In July 1996, after a three-year battle, the distribution center workers agreed to a union contract with Kmart. Their wages jumped by a third. In the midst of a national climate favoring business, in the state with the weakest union presence in the nation, workers—and their neighbors—had won.

The struggle held another significant outcome: the frigid local opinion of Nelson Johnson began to thaw. The men and women who'd ventured warily to the Beloved Community Center experienced his gift for organizing, his thoughtful intelligence, and, to their great surprise, his willingness to listen to their points of view. He'd given them a glimpse of the man long known to Greensboro's Black community and to the committed activists of different races and backgrounds who'd filtered through the CWP. Preferring to work with him than against him, Nelson's new allies invited him to join the Chamber of Commerce.

Nelson arrived at a private room atop the Greensboro Coliseum with stylish carpets and grand views of the city, a room he'd never imagined existed. For a couple of hours, he mingled with city leaders decked out in their crisp suits. He listened to the clink of ice chilling brand-name hootch in crystal glasses. He smelled the bright hint of cologne. As the minutes ticked away, Nelson felt increasingly uncomfortable. As much as he appreciated the people who'd accepted some social risk to "rehabilitate" his image, his heart, he knew, wasn't up in Greensboro's sky, but down on the city's streets. To function within the Chamber of Commerce, he quickly realized, he'd be required to leave the past behind, to be complicit in sweeping the painful and complicated histories of 1969 and 1979 under the patterned carpet. And, looking forward, he'd have to accept that capitalism could be a neutral or even positive force in shaping the country's racial politics. Nelson never attended a second meeting.[20]

❖

At 11:23 a.m. on November 3, 1999, the bells of the Bennett College chapel tolled for eighty-eight seconds. The people gathered outside in the gusting breeze ducked their heads in prayer or looked up at the fair autumn sky, scanning, it seemed, for a glimpse of "the five spirits," as Nelson referred to his murdered comrades.

On the night of November 6, Joyce Johnson, smiling warmly, her hair set in ringlets, welcomed an overflow crowd into the Bennett College chapel. They'd come to hear Nelson and a panel of invited luminaries, including Columbia University professor Manning Marable; Harvard Law professor Lani Guinier; Robert Meeropol, the son of Julius and Ethel Rosenberg, who'd been executed as Soviet spies; and their constant ally across all the years, Anne Braden.

When Nelson and Joyce were looking for a venue to commemorate the tenth anniversary of November 3, A&T had turned them down. The churches declined, too, though by then Nelson had completed divinity school. Only Bennett College opened its doors, as it had in 1958, when a radical young preacher named Martin Luther King Jr. came to town to tell the story of the Montgomery bus boycott.

Ten years later, Greensboro had become a campus for a weeklong series of events to explore the "tough questions" raised by November 3. Guilford College hosted a presentation by survivors. The University of North Carolina Greensboro offered space for a conversation about the Greensboro Justice Fund's work to fund grassroots activism throughout the South. A special Sabbath service filled the local synagogue. And UNCG's Taylor Theater staged a five-day run of a play about the shooting written by Emily Mann, the decorated playwright and director of Princeton University's McCarter Theater. "*Greensboro: A Requiem*," wrote *New York Times* critic Vincent Canby, "has the potential to become a theatrical event. . . . What emerges," continued Canby, "is a mare's-nest of evil, innocence, fury and sometimes fatally guided impulses to do good. In short, a particularly all-American tragedy . . . less concerned with any 'isms' . . .

than with the climate of ignorance and duplicity that made the confrontation inevitable."[21]

❖

Welcomed to the stage by Joyce, Manning Marable called racial violence the "logical social product of an institutionally racist society." The challenge to inequality, he argued, "comes from the margins . . . from the bottom up." And the most successful struggles, he advised, "build bridges across class and color and gender" toward the society "we seek for ourselves and our children." He noted that "Martin never counseled patience," referring to King's visit to Bennett Chapel some forty years earlier.[22]

Robert Meeropol pointed to the work of the Greensboro Justice Fund as a fine example of making something positive from injustice: "Yes, you got away with killing our sisters and brothers, but we are going to make you pay, by continuing their work and making their work broader and deeper." Lani Guinier called for a "generative, creative, and loving power," a "force that builds community." And Anne Braden, Nelson and Joyce's longtime ally from Louisville, told how after repressive government forces had turned activists against one another in the 1970s, the murders in Greensboro brought them back together, catalyzing a new, more unified movement. "As long as people of color are considered expendable . . . we're going to have to talk about racism until we've built an anti-racist majority," she said.[23]

When Nelson rose to speak, few in the audience knew how close he had come to joining the five slain activists. A few weeks earlier, he'd asked his daughter Ayo to bring him baking soda mixed in water for a bad case of indigestion. When she brought the drink, Ayo noticed her father was sweating profusely. She telephoned her mother. Call an ambulance, Joyce ordered. At the hospital, doctors rushed Nelson into triple bypass surgery, just in time to prevent a massive heart attack.[24] Nor did the audience know about his 1987 journey into the Klan country wilderness.

From the pulpit, Nelson smiled out at "so many marvelous friends who I've not seen for many years." As they beamed back at him, one thought, "I see a different hair cut [than he wore in 1979], but I see Nelson."[25] They noticed the familiar flash in his big eyes, the renewed glint of possibility and hope that pulled people into his orbit like a powerful and rare gravitational force.

❖

As he recounted the power of the narrative they'd faced, that they were "extremists bordering on insanity," he hoped to begin to place the event in "the proper chapter" of the "nation's bloody history." From the pulpit, the grief for what had happened twenty years earlier radiated off him, but it did not submerge him in despair. Instead, he offered commitment. "We are capable of being a much better city. I'm still hopeful for the future of this city. I come not to tear Greensboro down, but to build her up. . . . God has given me an extension, and I don't know what to do with it, except to stay on the battlefield. . . . There is a possibility for equality of life in this nation."

When he finished, the people in the chapel rose, grateful for the fight and the hope he offered. Two decades of excruciating pressure had taken their toll, but a flash of the old confidence had returned, the gift of vision and leadership that had drawn them to him all those years ago.

For the survivors of the shooting in the audience, Nelson's speech allowed them to relax for a moment, to set aside the anger, guilt, fear, and defensiveness that had dogged them for twenty years and to remember the quality of people they'd worked with. "I always thought it was the best of the best of all the people in this country . . . smart people, talented people. . . . I regretted some of the things that happened, but not the people," one would say, echoing a common sentiment.[26] For the first time since the shooting, some felt comfortable being in Greensboro.

After the opening performance of the play, Ayo stood in the crowded theater. "Thank you," she said to her parents, for the example of all they had endured and survived and for continuing to be present as parents through it all.

One reaction to the play sparked Nelson's imagination. The son of a man who'd sat on the jury in the 1980 state trial that acquitted the Klan and Nazis of murder had volunteered to help with the preparations for the twentieth-anniversary events. After a great deal of cajoling, the son had convinced his father to attend a performance. When they walked out of the theater, the former juror thanked his son for bringing him. If he'd seen the play instead of the prosecution's case, the father said, he'd have changed his jury vote to guilty.

In this story, Nelson caught a "glimpse of what the truth might do."[27]

When asked if he planned to catch a performance of *Greensboro: A Requiem*, Jim Melvin still spoke for many local citizens when he said, "It happened, and it's been studied and restudied, studied and restudied. We need to work on the future and not the past."[28] A local newspaper columnist commented, "As if frozen for 20 years and suddenly thawed, old wounds, old prejudices . . . have been revived."

Nelson knew he'd pay a price for revisiting the old history.

TRUTHS

Hurricane Katrina was gathering force, bearing down on Louisiana's Gulf Coast. That Friday evening, August 26, 2005, just before Katrina hit land and, in her spiraling wake, would expose the accumulated devastation of racialized poverty in the United States, Reverend Nelson Johnson donned an off-white suit, a Carolina-blue shirt, and a cherry-red tie to wear onto the stage of the North Carolina A&T auditorium. The man who'd refused to politely accept the city's unspoken rules of civility and commerce, or to expunge the past until all Greensboro's citizens were invited to participate in defining the city's future, tilted toward a microphone. The audience of a few hundred stirred in their seats.

The buzz from the twentieth-anniversary events had led to an engagement with a radical idea spreading across the globe. After generations of human rights abuses in South Africa, Peru, Argentina, and several former Soviet-bloc countries, new governments seeking fresh starts made space for victims of state oppression and violence to tell their stories. These raw forums rested on the idea that the path to a better future ran, not away from the past, but through historical truth. As the injured offered their testimonies and reclaimed dignity, communities and nations could seize the opportunity to renew their social contracts.

The Ford Foundation funded the International Center for Transitional Justice (ICTJ) to develop and replicate truth and reconciliation models, as they'd latched on to Terry Sanford's and President Lyndon Johnson's ideas for unleashing the "maximum feasible participation" of poor US citizens in the mid-1960s.[1] Meanwhile, another New York philanthropic organization, the Andrus Family Fund, appointed resources to test whether a truth and reconciliation approach designed to marshal the past in order to "set an agenda for more equal democracy" could serve a purpose in a rich, future-obsessed "beacon of democracy" such as the United States.[2]

In 2001, with Andrus Family Fund support and ICTJ's expert guidance, the Beloved Community Center and the Greensboro Justice Fund launched a grassroots project in Greensboro they called the Greensboro Truth and Community Reconciliation Project (GTCRP). After twenty-seven years at A&T, Joyce retired as the Transportation Institute's director to join the Beloved Community Center, lending the organization critical operating expertise. An impressive advisory board formed around the new project, which included Vincent Harding, a historian and former adviser to Martin Luther King Jr., and Nelson Mandela's South African prison chaplain, Peter Storey. Two years of meetings and public presentations followed, as organizers methodically garnered support among Greensboro's citizens and civic organizations for the idea of investigating the divided city's past. One local academic summed up the effort's value simply: "The folks in this city don't know what happened" on November 3.[3]

Archbishop Desmond Tutu, who'd led the high-profile South Africa Truth and Reconciliation Commission, visited Greensboro and advised Nelson and Joyce Johnson, the project's supporters, and Greensboro that "you are going to be a crippled community whether you like it or not as long as you refuse to face up to your past. We are all wounded here. We are all needing to be healed. If we want to be a healthy society, vibrant, you aren't going to be able to accomplish it until you look the beast in his eye."[4]

As the Archbishop offered this wisdom, developers were razing Morningside Homes, replacing the fifty-year-old experiment in public housing with a $76 million mixed-income community renamed

Willow Oaks. A reporter visited in late October 2002. Across a chain-link fence, tufts of crabgrass clung to rough dirt and rubble scattered between strips of tarmac, a ghost grid to nowhere, laid over 240-some acres to the east of downtown Greensboro, North Carolina. Since the United States' rightward swerve began in the 1970s, the nation's belief in public housing as a solution for its persistent underclass had deteriorated. Over the next decades, massive complexes were detonated or abandoned in cities around the country. Greensboro reporters called the once-hopeful Morningside Homes a "stalag" that "segregates" and "warehouses" the "poorest of the poor." They described a place where "young men sit on curbs . . . with nowhere else to be," mired in "drug infested," "intractable poverty." Possessing the city's lowest median income and its highest rates of unemployment and violence, the neighborhood had earned a spot on a list of the worst places in the entire United States to live.[5]

The barren plot of land would soon be occupied by the reimagined neighborhood of Willow Oaks. The planned mixed-income development, launched with a $23 million commitment from the Department of Housing and Urban Development and bolstered by more than $15 million from the city and another $37 million in commercial investment, signaled an era of public-private partnerships and an emphasis on individual responsibility for one's circumstances.

At least some, if not most, of the Morningside Homes residents welcomed the opportunity to leave behind the "stigma of living there." In addition to drugs and poverty, the violence of November 3 had marred the neighborhood's image. But there were some in Greensboro who believed the redevelopment project to be, in part, an expensive effort to erase history that the city had never desired to accept any more than America had truly reckoned with the devastation of its racial past.[6] One Greensboro policeman who'd stood duty that fateful November day in 1979 saw in the rubble an attempt to demolish the memory of the event.[7] Willena Cannon squinted over the chain-link fence and said, "Even though they are building this and trying to change the whole neighborhood, that will not remove the blight from '79. This is not covering nothing. The only thing that is going to do that is when the truth come out. They are fighting that tooth and nails."[8]

A toppled street intersection sign waiting to be hauled to the dump lay beside the fence in 2002. The sign read "Carver Drive" and "Everitt Street," the very corner where the shooting took place. Horizontal, it offered no navigational use, but it still pointed toward an unsettled and layered American past—an explosive convergence of race and economics—that like writing on ancient vellum, scrubbed and over-written, can never, despite strenuous efforts, be erased completely.[9]

❖

The city council refused official city participation in the Truth and Community Reconciliation Project, rejecting a petition request signed by some five thousand Greensboro residents.[10] Even so, the truth process ground forward. Following the ICTJ's blueprint, the group named a local task force that included the minister and co-founder of the Beloved Community Center, Z Holler; former Greens-boro mayor Carolyn Allen; and pastor Gregory Headen from the Pulpit Forum. Next, citizens and civic organizations elected a diverse group of seven commissioners. The group sworn in on June 12, 2004, consisted of three businesspeople, two nonprofit activists, an aca-demic, and a woman who grew up in Morningside Homes. The four women of color, two white men, and one white woman were guided by the idea that "there comes a time in the life of every community when it must look humbly and seriously into its past in order to pro-vide the best possible foundation for moving into a future based on healing and hope."[11] The baton of leadership had passed from the Greensboro Truth and Community Reconciliation Project initiated by survivors of November 3 to the Greensboro Truth and Reconcili-ation Commission (TRC) elected by city residents. The commissioners had volunteered for an enormous undertaking, one that would require them to parse, in the words of Paul Bermanzohn, "an enormously complex event with layers and layers of interpretation, misinterpretation and re-misinterpretation."[12]

The TRC's job would be to gather all the evidence and information the commissioners could get their hands on, invite people from all perspectives to participate in a series of public hearings, and, finally, produce a report that, based on the research and testimony, would attempt to explain the "context, causes, sequence, and consequences" of the 1979 shooting. In the spirit of transitional justice, the commissioners were charged with laying out a road map for achieving "community healing."[13]

The Commission hired a small staff, including, as executive director, Jill Williams, a young woman with degrees in religion and conflict resolution, as well as Emily Harwell, a Yale environmental anthropology PhD who'd written the final report for the East Timor Commission for Reception, Truth and Reconciliation on the history and legacy of human rights abuses in that country.

Williams arrived in Greensboro from a job at Davidson College believing that the project entailed little more than sorting out a big misunderstanding. When her aunt and uncle who lived in the city ignored her calls and the Greensboro Police Department began surveilling her movements, Williams realized that she'd signed up to investigate not only a twenty-five-year-old shooting but also Greensboro's institutions and a common narrative of the tragedy that implicated the entire city's social structure. Her relatives, she decided, feared ostracization if they engaged with her work. Meanwhile, the police refused to share department documents, and, according to one officer, destroyed as many as fifty boxes of files related to the November 3, 1979, shooting.[14] People connected to the Truth Commission asserted that the GPD kept them under electronic surveillance and sent undercover officers to Commission meetings.[15] Jill Williams and others suspected the cops when the Commission's locked offices were ransacked, their files dumped on the floor.[16]

"Greensboro's like a 1950s town in a Ziploc bag with the Ziploc closed," observed councilperson Florence Gatten approvingly. When asked about Nelson Johnson, Gatten, who opposed the TRC, mused, "Old Nelson, one of the perpetrators . . . I don't think leopards change their spots." "We don't have much time for these people," agreed Jim Melvin, who threatened to sue the Commission if his name were mentioned in their report. "I don't need somebody to come in and tell me what I don't know," said Melvin, who seemed to feel, as did Gatten, that a new Reconstruction was being imposed on them.[17] Du Bois, in his 1935 book *Black Reconstruction in America*, labored against the widely held view that Reconstruction was "a disgraceful attempt to subject white people to ignorant Negro rule."[18] In the imagination of many of Greensboro's white leaders, one might have neatly replaced the word *Negro* in Du Bois's quote with a single name: Nelson Johnson.

As they fought detractors' cynical assertion that they were Nelson Johnson's puppets and their names and home addresses circulated on right-wing message boards, the commissioners and their staff coaxed participation from unlikely corners. The Klansmen Virgil Griffin and Gorrell Pierce showed up to testify at the first public hearing on July 16, 2005. Griffin, his hair now white, wearing big glasses and a Klan belt, seemed to have changed little over a quarter century. "The truth was proved in the trials," he said. "If you've got the interest of Greensboro and the city and citizens of Greensboro, I think you'd shut this thing down right now and tell the media to get out of here and never bring it up again." When asked why he'd joined the Klan, he responded, "I don't believe in mixed marriages, I don't believe in integration. I don't believe in drugs; I don't believe in the Communist party." As to why he'd come to Greensboro that day, he said simply, "They put the poster out: Death to the Klan, said we's hiding under rocks, we were scum. I'm not scum, I'm as good as any man walks on this earth. . . . I don't hide under a rock from nobody. . . . That's why I'm here today." When asked why, if both sides fired guns, only the marchers died that day, Griffin noted that the Klansmen were country boys and deer hunters. Then he shrugged and added, "Maybe God guided the bullets." The audience sat in stunned silence.[19]

Many key players in history lay beyond the commissioners' reach. Bernard Butkovich, the BATF agent who'd infiltrated Roland Wayne Wood's Nazi cell, died in a plane crash in 1987. The head of the FBI's Greensboro Resident Agency in 1979, Andy Pelczar, retired shortly after the conclusion of the federal civil trial, lauding the FBI's "outstanding relationship with local authorities" in North Carolina.[20] Two years later, he was dead at fifty-one. The controversial agent Tom Brereton passed away in 1993. No one, it seemed, attempted to reach Cecil Moses. Edward Woodrow Dawson had died in 2002 at the ripe old age of eighty-three, leaving his collection of Weary Willie figurines to his wife. In the half dozen or so serious interviews he gave, Dawson always left the impression that he'd carried truths too dark and dangerous to reveal. Whatever his secrets were, they'd been lost to history.

Plump and avuncular, the Klansman and sometime Nazi Gorrell Pierce, who'd been present at the China Grove face-off but hadn't joined the caravan to Morningside on November 3, talked about his pride in the Confederate history he'd picked up "on those porches" where the old-timers "dip[ped] snuff and talked about the Civil War and Reconstruction." Family artifacts reinforced his personal connection to the "War of Northern Aggression"; he noted that "the very frying pan I ate my breakfast on as a child deflected bullets at the Battle of Gettysburg; it had belonged to an ancestor of mine. . . . So it was kind of easy for me to end up on the side of the Ku Klux Klan." Pierce understood, however, that the stories you hear, the versions of history you are taught, matter. "Had I been born in New York City," he mused, "I probably would have made a good Communist."[21]

Pierce recalled helping guide Martha Woodall to Bernard Butkovich and how impressed he'd been when she "dogged it all the way to the end," exposing the federal agent. Back in 1982, Pierce told the federal grand jury he believed the government to be responsible for the shooting. In the intervening twenty-three years, he'd change his opinion; he no longer thought Butkovich or even Eddie Dawson had much to do with what went down at the corner of Everitt and Carver. The communists, the Klansmen, and the Nazis put themselves in the position to spark violence, he said, punctuating this thought with words passed down by his grandmother: "If you're gonna run through the briar patch nekkid don't squall if you get scratched." The shooting "wasn't the city's fault, it wasn't my fault, it wasn't no one person's fault. They don't even know who fired the first shot," Pierce said, repeating a widely held fiction and demonstrating, as he'd noted, the power of a story to shape one's idea of truth.

At the second public hearing, held on August 26 and 27, 2005, three police officers did their best to reinforce the department's official and unofficial talking points. Though the next day's newspaper gave Captain Rick Ball above-the-fold authority under the banner "Officer: Rumors Hide Facts," the commissioners had learned enough to take what the officers said with a grain of salt. Captain Ramon Bell, for example, blamed the Black captain, Trevor Hampton, for the "low-profile" plan for the November 3 parade coverage. Since the afternoon of November 3, the GPD had pointed to the roles played by the Black officers Hampton and Sylvester Daughtry to deflect questions about racial bias in the department. The commissioners found, however, that the "low-profile" plan came not from Hampton, but from Colonel Burch at the very top of the department.

One had to be immersed in the minutiae of history to pick up the relevance of one exchange with Sergeant Mike Toomes. Commissioner Peters, a retired AT&T executive, asked, "If there are a lot of people gathered in the area including a lot of children and firearms are discharged in the air would you consider that hostile or aggressive?" Without any hesitation, Sergeant Toomes responded, "All shots are aggressive as far as I am concerned." Few in the audience were likely to remember that the lawyers who defended the Klan and Nazis had convinced two juries that the first shots fired by their clients into the air were "friendly" warning shots and that this argument had led to community-wide confusion about who'd fired the first shots.

Though they wouldn't testify publicly, the prosecutors Jim Coman, Rick Greeson, and Mike Schlosser agreed to give a private interview. Said Jim Coman, "The CWP were the provocateurs and the wretches from the KKK were so foolish to need to establish their manhood that they came here and fell right into the trap."

"Nelson Johnson is the wheel, spoke, and hub," said Mike Schlosser. "He is a plague on this community."

"[The CWP] won't even admit they did anything wrong," said Coman. "If just one of them had the moral fiber to get up and say publicly that they have regrets for what they did, you can call me up and say I'm full of shit."[22]

That August 26, while the national news tacked with the advance of Hurricane Katrina, Nelson followed the police officers onto the stage. As the truth process advanced, the police had tailed him, too, snapping him back to the paranoia of the weeks and months after the shooting, as if it, too, had been preserved in one of Florence Gatten's Ziploc bags.

"Greensboro is not unique in that something terrible and tragic happened here," Nelson told the audience. "With the United States Senate recently apologizing for 4,700 recorded and largely unexamined lynchings, it is clear that our history is replete with such tragedies. Greensboro, however, might become unique if we humbly and truthfully face the flaws from our past and learn from them."

So I come today with my scars, my wounds, my regrets and my self-criticism, to share my story. It is both a personal and political story; it is an individual and collective story. Seeking authentic truth and understanding around the killings of 1979 is part of my lifelong struggle for democracy and justice. By democracy I mean a real voice, a voice that translates into positive impact on the quality of one's life, especially the lives of the poor. The work that I speak about began in my early years on a farm in Halifax County. That journey has continued over the forty years God has blessed me to live in this city.

First, I deeply regret the use of the slogan "Death to the Klan." In retrospect I am clear that it was an unfortunate, ill-advised slogan. The slogan was meant to convey the weight of our conviction about the damage done by racism, a challenge this nation, especially whites, still needs to face. It would have been more accurate to say "death to racism." . . . We are in large part responsible for whatever misunderstanding arose from that phrase, because it was our decision to use that phrase "Death to the Klan" as a slogan.

Secondly, I very much regret that a flyer was developed in the form of a letter that called the Klan members cowards and challenged them to come from under their rocks and face the wrath of the people. That was wrong. . . . I do apologize for that letter to my brothers and sisters who were and may still be Klan or Nazi members.

Finally, I regret the use of the word *communism*. . . . Let me emphasize that the term *communism*, like the term *Christianity*, means many different things to different people. While I cherish much of what I have learned from my study of Marxism, the word *communism*, however, no longer describes my core beliefs. In addition, because of the fear and confusion associated with the word, it became almost impossible to use that term to convey broadly anything of positive value. I would note in passing that there is a passage in a very broadly read book which says, "Now all who believed were together, and had all things in common and sold their possessions and goods, and divided them among all, as anyone had need." This saying comes from the second chapter of Acts [in the Bible].[23]

But it wasn't only apologies and mea culpas that Nelson had come to discuss. The "plague" on Greensboro came to the stage with detailed questions for the City of Greensboro. "Why didn't Detective Cooper, or any other police officer, warn demonstrators of the impending danger?" he wanted to know. "Why did Detective Cooper and his photographer take pictures and send radio reports but fail to stop the violence once it started?" "Why were all but one caravan vehicle allowed to leave the scene of a known crime scene without a police pursuit?"

Perhaps, these were the "rumors" that Captain Ball had intended and, to a degree, had succeeded in heading off by capturing the following day's newspaper headline. Nelson's words, the words of the man Mike Schlosser called the "wheel, spoke, and hub" of the events of November 3, wouldn't be reported in the newspaper. Perhaps, the printing deadline had passed. Or maybe the cops' words were more comforting to the editors and readers of the *Greensboro News & Record*.

A month later, at the last of the three public hearings, Joyce Johnson took the stage, exhausted from hosting refugees from Hurricane Katrina at the Beloved Community Center. Just two days earlier, the *Greensboro News & Record* had floated the rumor that Nelson planned the November 3 violence with the police captain Trevor Hampton, two Black men conspiring to keep the police from Morningside Homes so the CWP could instigate the "shootout" with the Klan.[24]

"You asked me," said Joyce, "'How were you and your family impacted by November 3, 1979?' We were under great pressure. My husband was vilified in the media, we had to move from our home. . . . I had to constantly explain the truth to our kids. Seven and eight-year-olds want to know things like why did the mean people kill Aunt Sandi? . . . They would ask me questions like 'Why did the Klan get off for murdering people?' when they were chastised for the least little infraction around the house. . . . They had to read characterizations of Nelson as a most dangerous man in Greensboro, from our Mayor, and that he was the one who caused the death of their friends. . . . In many ways their childhood was robbed. . . . [T]hank God I was able to work.

"For those who are moved to continue to cast negative remarks at the old CWP, I forgive them and ask forgiveness from them for similar things that I or others might have done in the past. I urge us all now to bind together to address the great divides that [Hurricane] Katrina has revealed and that are widening each day."

As they analyzed the material, the Commission members struggled with conflicting perspectives among themselves. Commissioner Angela Lawrence had been sent by her parents from a rough neighborhood in Washington, DC, to live with an aunt in Morningside Homes. To her, the green spaces and loving community she discovered there, the playful times with her cousins and the neighborhood kids, were idyllic. The shooting shattered the idyll. She'd seen white people—Jim Waller, Bill Sampson, Cesar Cauce, Mike Nathan—lying dead or dying on the ground and assumed they were Klansmen. No one ever really talked about what happened that morning, but fear and distrust hardened attitudes and lives. She'd grown up harboring rage at Nelson Johnson for not protecting the community and developed a deep distrust of the police. On the Commission, as they discussed the role of the police and federal agents, she'd face off with Bob Peters, the white retired AT&T executive, saying, "The legal system works for you, Bob. It doesn't work for me the way it works for you."[25]

The last day of public hearings took place on October 1, 2005. Eight months later, on May 25, 2006, Commissioner Pat Clark stood before an anxious crowd gathered at Bennett College to read the conclusions she and her colleagues had reached:

The Commission finds that on the morning of Nov. 3, 1979, members of the Klan/Nazi caravan headed for Greensboro with malicious intent. The Commission finds that the WVO [CWP] leadership was very naive about the level of danger posed by their rhetoric and the Klan's propensity for violence, and they even dismissed concerns raised by their own members. However, we also find that this miscalculation was caused in part by the Greensboro Police Department, which did not inform either the WVO or Morningside residents about the Klan's plans and its coordination with other racist groups. Despite the obvious and important roles of the above participants, the majority of commissioners find the single most important element that contributed to the violent outcome of the confrontation was the absence of police. ... While nearly all Commissioners find sufficient evidence that some officers were deliberately absent, we also unanimously concur that the conclusion one draws from this evidence is likely to differ with one's life experience.[26]

Had law enforcement officers conspired to damage the CWP and Nelson Johnson? Or had their bias against him merely justified collective negligence? In Greensboro, no one from a local, state, or federal law enforcement agency breached the blue wall of silence to reveal embarrassing secrets or truths from the inside. Without a whistleblower, the precise degree and quality of law enforcement intent on November 3 would remain a mystery. Instead, the cops continued to intimidate, obfuscate, and tell lies that, after a generation, even they may have believed to be true. Despite this, the Truth and Reconciliation Commission had created something lasting, an edifice more permanent than Morningside Homes. They'd unfolded a blueprint to the past that would guide researchers and journalists not to a single, buried answer, but to a vast network of seemingly disparate events and ideas that converge on a moment to make history.

Humans didn't create fire, but they wrested some control of it. And with that control, Nelson and Joyce knew, humans could choose to use fire for good or for harm. When they were young in Airlie and Richmond, in Durham and Greensboro, change seemed quick, spontaneous, and inevitable. Now, older, after a journey no less daunting than that of Nelson's relatives from Louisiana to North Carolina, they understood change—like democracy—to be a process, a slow grind with advances and setbacks. The lives of their beloved friends had been snuffed out, but Nelson and Joyce had helped protect their friends' memories and arrived nearer to the truth about how this American tragedy and so many like it happened.

Greensboro's city council voted not to read the Truth and Reconciliation Commission's report, as if ignorance could preserve a different truth. In his brief presentation in 1789, Alexander Hamilton had revised General Nathanael Greene's place in the national story, describing how the general's retreat from the battlefield of Guilford Courthouse led to the creation of the United States of America. Now the Commission's report methodically disassembled the self-serving narratives that identified an injured Black man as the shooting's primary culprit and the city's institutions as its victims. In the place of myth, the commissioners left Greensboro with all it needed to begin, over time, to believe in a truer version of its All-America collective identity.

The Truth and Reconciliation Commission and all the people who'd worked to make it possible had also created a model. Once again, something had started in Greensboro. Communities from Maine to California would make pilgrimages to Greensboro to learn how to move through truth toward reconciliation and a brighter future.[27]

The night the Commission released its report, survivors of the shooting and their families gathered in the dark, warm night on the grounds of Bennett College. They lighted candles, and as Nelson and Joyce began to sing, they lifted those small, brave beacons above their heads and raised their voices. "We are marching in the light of truth, we are marching, we are marching, oooooo, we are marching in the light of truth."[28]

EPILOGUE

"One day the South will recognize its true heroes."

—MARTIN LUTHER KING JR.,
"LETTER FROM BIRMINGHAM JAIL"

October 6, 2020, it turns out, was as good a day as any to apologize for the past.

"Are we ready to go?"

The live meeting flickered into focus. This was the first year of the COVID-19 pandemic, and the Melvin Municipal Government Building a block from the police department in downtown Greensboro remained empty. City councilors beamed in, unmasked, from the safety of homes and offices around the city.

Mayor Nancy Vaughan welcomed viewers to this "Special Virtual Meeting of the Greensboro City Council." They quickly agreed to rename the Human Relations Department the Department of Human Rights. Next they concurred unanimously and without any debate to form an Ad-Hoc Committee on African American Disparity, charged in the words of councilwoman Sharon Hightower with determining how to "bring about parity for a race of people that have suffered inequity for quite a long time."

"Item number three," the mayor announced, "is a resolution of apology by the Greensboro City Council for the events that have come to be known as the 'November 3, 1979, Massacre.'" This was the evening's primary business, the reason for the special session, and why I was clicking in, along with activists and journalists from all around the country. Forty-one years earlier, the shooting had exploded

Greensboro's sense of comfort and safety, exposing divisions and fault lines. It had been thirty-five years since Judge Merhige presided over the federal civil trial that found Klansmen, American Nazis, Eddie Dawson, and the police jointly liable for the death of Michael Nathan. And fourteen years had elapsed since the Greensboro Truth and Reconciliation Commission concluded that at least "some officers" had been "deliberately absent" during the deadly eighty-eight seconds at Morningside Homes. Now, in 2020, all of us on the Zoom call were drawn by the chance to witness, in real time, an American city's attempt to reconcile with its violent past.

In 2015, five years before this special meeting and three months after the white supremacist Dylann Roof shot nine members of the Emanuel African Methodist Episcopal Church in Charleston, South Carolina, my wife, Margot, and I had joined my father, Robert, in Greensboro for an exhibit of his *Americans Who Tell the Truth* paintings, hosted by the International Civil Rights Center and Museum. Ellie Richard, the organizer of that exhibit, insisted there were two people we had to meet. We waited in Manny's Universal Cafe, across the train tracks from Elm Street, Greensboro's downtown hub. We'd nearly decided to leave when the café door swung open and a neatly dressed pair hurried out of the bright-white September sun. "I'm sorry we're late," said the man, offering a strong hand. "I'm Nelson Johnson. This is my wife, Joyce."

"Reverend Johnson," called Margarita, the immigrant owner of the Salvadoran café, "I don't see you for a long time!"

His face broke into a wide smile. "I've been running, Margarita."

The Reverend wore an inexpensive suit, white shirt, and the sort of wide, abstract-patterned tie that can be had for a dollar at any thrift store in the country. This was an everyday churchman's attire that offered unquestioned access to a hospital bedside, a clergy meeting, a conference with a city official, a visit to a local jail, or a gathering in protest. Joyce's clothes—an orange blouse adding a dash of color to a brown pantsuit—were the woman's equivalent. The two of them settled into folding chairs around the café table, immediately and intently present, as if that little Latin restaurant on the edge of downtown Greensboro, just blocks from the Woolworth's counter where the 1960s sit-in movement caught fire, was the only place in the world they were meant to be.

Two hours later, when we left the café, I sensed I was teetering at the edge of something essential, something I needed to understand about being American, about how to hold the country's ideals together with its painful contradictions. How did I not know this history? It felt vaguely criminal in that moment, as if by missing these tragic chapters I'd been kept in a state of ignorance—not only about what happened in Greensboro but also about how we are always bound by the past—that robbed our history—*my* history—of meaning.

Two years later, I returned to Greensboro to try to decipher for myself what had happened on November 3, 1979, and how to understand it. The event opened a heavy door to American conflicts around race, class, policing, and ideology, as well as how collective and historical memories figure in our present. As a child of the 1970s, I suspected that what I learned would help me better understand my youth and my present. The shooting was far too close to our current lives for it to be relegated to a self-congratulatory niche in the "we overcame Jim Crow" wing of American history. I began to understand it as one essential—and missing—link between Jim Crow and the racial and cultural violence of our present. Dylann Roof had, in fact, been a follower of Harold Covington, the North Carolina Nazi connected to the 1979 shootings.

And then, shortly after I'd started investigating Greensboro's history, the 2017 Unite the Right rally overwhelmed Charlottesville, Virginia, where Margot and I had recently moved. White nationalists took over the city's public square to defend Civil War monuments. Counterprotesters gathered to denounce white supremacy. The police hung back, seemingly uncertain about how to handle the situation, allowing violence to build. A neo-Nazi sped his car into a crowd of counterprotestors, killing Heather Heyer. Some of Charlottes-ville's leading citizens, blaming the outsiders, resisted calls to reflect on the relationship between local history and the violence. Commu-nities all over the country held vigils. In Greensboro, a thousand people turned out to mourn Heyer. Suddenly, November 3, 1979, had become a prologue.

"Instead of saying Charlottesville might or could happen in Greensboro, we need to say that it did happen here," said a speaker at the Greensboro City Council meeting three days after Heyer was murdered.[1]

Moments later, the city council voted 7–1 to apologize for Novem-ber 3, 1979. It was a dramatic moment. Joyce Johnson's eyes welled with tears. But what, precisely, had the city apologized for? In 2009, the council offered an expression of regret that the November 3 vio-lence had happened. In 2015, officials agreed to place a state historic marker near the site of the shooting. But not once had the city ac-cepted any responsibility for the deaths and injuries that Saturday morning.

In the months and years that followed, I was often in Greensboro or buried in archives up and down the East Coast, sorting through boxes of documents and competing narratives about the shooting. I spent time rummaging through old files and interviewing the John-sons, Lewis Brandon, and others at 417 Arlington Street in Greens-boro, a nondescript, two-story brick building that houses the Beloved Community Center and Faith Community Church. Stepping through a tinted-glass door and onto a worn carpet, I discovered that here the past and the present blur together. Images printed on standard twenty-pound office bond paper are tacked to the walls, telling the story of Black Greensboro's successes and struggles: the ballplayers and musicians, the politicians and businessmen, the activists and ren-egades. The good times and the horrific mingle there, equal parts of the historic fabric. Perhaps no picture captures this inclusive history better than the one of Nelson and Joyce on their wedding day. They are smiling. Behind them lies a toppled, smoldering bus. In the midst of the 1969 rebellion, they've just tied the knot. Love and struggle. Struggle and love.

I doubt I'm the only one who experiences a sense of relief in that space. Here the poor, the powerful, the homeless, the infirm, the radical, the troubled, the contrarian, the comfortable, the strange, the iconoclastic, the traumatized, and those in desperate need of hope are all welcome. All they have to do—all *we* have to do—is accept each other's right to be present. One can sense the hopeful—patriotic even—possibility in this alternative city hall when Nelson Johnson says that "Greensboro is poised to become a moral and justice capital." In that space a more inclusive democracy feels tantalizingly real. As Nelson likes to say, if humans can create society's culture and laws, they can also unmake and remake society's culture and laws.

As I worked on the book, current events proved again and again that the past refuses to be past. In 2018, the Greensboro police hogtied a mentally ill Black man named Marcus Smith and he died on the street. The old team of Nelson Johnson, Lewis Pitts, and Flint Taylor from the People's Law Office in Chicago joined forces with a young lawyer named Graham Holt to hold the city accountable in court. (Four years later, Greensboro would settle with Smith's family, awarding them more than $2.5 million.)[2] And then, as the pandemic locked the country down, the 2020 police murders of Breonna Taylor and George Floyd exploded into the national consciousness, forcing Greensboro to once again reckon with its own history.

All nine city council members of Greensboro, North Carolina, were present on the evening of October 6, 2020: Mayor Nancy Vaughan, Mayor Pro Tem Yvonne Johnson, Nancy Hoffmann, Marikay Abuzuaiter, Justin Outling, Michelle Kennedy, Tammi Thurm, Dr. Goldie Wells, and Sharon Hightower. The cast included eight women and one man. Four, including the man, were African American.

The mayor began to read the long resolution into the record: "Whereas, on November 3, 1979, members of the Ku Klux Klan and the American Nazi Party attacked members of the Communist Workers Party and their supporters as they gathered to engage in a march across the City of Greensboro. These events have come to be known as the 'Greensboro Massacre.'" The result of nearly a year of wordsmithing by members Thurm, Wells, and Mayor Vaughan and careful vetting by the city attorney, the resolution sketched a brief history of the shooting: the event itself that left five dead and ten wounded; two criminal trials that acquitted the Klan/Nazi shooters; the civil trial that found Klansmen, Nazis, and Greensboro police jointly liable for the deaths and injuries; the refusal of the city to sanction or even acknowledge the work of a Truth and Reconciliation Commission that sat from 2004 to 2006; the expression of regret issued by the city in 2009; and then the surprising, spontaneous, yet ambiguous apology issued on August 15, 2017. This document noted that the city's primary law enforcement institution, the police department, and other city personnel "failed to warn the marchers of their extensive foreknowledge of the racist, violent attack" and that, despite this "foreknowledge" the police did not "divert, stop, or arrest the members of the Ku Klux Klan and American Nazi Party."

After laying out this context, the mayor offered the official apology: "That the City Council of the City of Greensboro hereby expresses its apology to the victims, the survivors, their families, and the members of the Morningside Homes community for the events that occurred on November 3, 1979, and the failure of any government action to effectively overcome the hate that precipitated the violence, to embrace the sorrow that resulted from the violence, and to reconcile all the vestiges of those heinous events in the years subsequent to 1979."

The words, uttered publicly and aloud, had power. The mayor's voice wobbled with emotion. As an act of memory and atonement, she continued, the city would offer five scholarships to graduating seniors from Greensboro's historically Black high school who write essays "that [help] this community reconcile the remaining vestiges of the events of November 3, 1979." Each scholarship—for the symbolic amount of $1,979.00—would be given in the name of one of the slain activists—Cesar Cauce, Dr. James Waller, William Evan Sampson, Sandra Neely Smith, and Dr. Michael Nathan.

Spoken out loud the names landed not as code words for an ideological debate, but as incantations for real people, individuals who had lived and died too young fighting, as they thought best, for those left out of America's dream.

You might say that we live in an age of government apologies. Over the past years and around the world there has been a steady stream of apologies for slavery, for the treatment of indigenous people, for the atrocities committed during wars. And the apologies are becoming ever more local and specific. In 2018, for example, the city of Charleston, South Carolina, apologized for its role in the slave trade. There's a form to the official apology: expression of remorse, acceptance of responsibility, admission of wrongdoing, acknowledgment of the suffering caused, promises to do better, and offers to repair. The authors of the Greensboro apology hit all the right notes.

After comments, the mayor called for a vote. "I am a yes," she said. The councilors passed the resolution and the funded scholarships by a vote of 7–2.

❖

It's been said that there are two stories in Greensboro around the November 3 shooting. "A City of Two Tales," one survivor called it. But binaries can be limiting, and perhaps a kaleidoscope is a better metaphor, each person refracting a subset of facts through their own experiences, loyalties, and beliefs. Would the seven people who voted for the resolution all agree on a single narrative of what transpired on November 3, 1979? Certainly not. But they'd read documents with fresh eyes and been moved toward a new vision of the city's reality. "History is written by the victors," Winston Churchill may or may not have said. But who gets to tell the history and who gets to make demands on the history is changing. So much public data exists, not only in books and articles, but in publicly accessible ledgers and diaries, spreadsheets, logs, and government files, that history can be reexamined from the original, primary documents and represented by people other than the creators of the data, the "victors."

The councilors clicked off, drained and exhausted, like actors in a grueling live theater performance. They'd struggled publicly with something difficult in its subject matter and constrained in its form.

News of the apology ricocheted around the fractured state and our divided country, occupying its moment in the relentless rush of information and news. The city had failed to prevent violence in 1979. Now, decades later, a scholarship would be awarded to Greensboro high school students in the names of murdered, communist activists. It was an unprecedented evening in Greensboro. Time will tell if it was a transcendent one.

Nelson and Joyce Johnson have learned a great deal since 1979. One hard lesson is how long it can take to shift the culture of a police force and of a city and its institutions. The resistance to the change they and others call for is still powerful. Though they are tired, they are wiser. And, like our dream of democracy, they refuse to quit. The victory, they will tell you, is found in struggle and in love and, perhaps, in time.

ACKNOWLEDGMENTS

This book wouldn't have happened without the trust that Nelson and Joyce Johnson placed in me. Following their example, I've tried my best to be both compassionate and fair, not only to them, but to every person in this history. But before I won access to the Johnsons, I had to earn the trust of Lewis Brandon, their oldest friend and confidant who, all along the way, insisted on a more nuanced and complex portrait of Black Greensboro than I could have imagined on my own. And I'd never have known about the Johnsons, Lewis Brandon, or the Beloved Community Center if Ellie Richard hadn't introduced me to them in 2015.

I enjoyed the generous hospitality of Spoma Jovanovic and Lewis Pitts who for years shared their home, their Rolodexes, their knowledge, memories, and friendship with me.

John Fox and Leanna Ramsey at the FBI helped me with access to the documents I needed from their Bureau archives. Aaron Smithers went out of his way to find essential materials at UNC's Wilson Library, even during the pandemic. At NYU's Tamiment Library, Tim Johnson (now retired) offered valuable advice on 1970s communist movements. Philip Livingston and William P. Carrell II of the New York State Society of the Cincinnati shared documents and insight into Alexander Hamilton's eulogy of Nathanael Greene. Rebecca Trout and Mike McGrath gave me access to the National Civic League All-America City applications. The digital archive hosted by UNC Greensboro was essential to this project.

The remarkable research of the Greensboro Truth and Reconciliation Commission (GTRC), especially by Emily Harwell, provided me with a guide to sources and a way to test what I believed I was learning along the way. Jill Williams, the GTRC's executive director, helped me understand the local and global significance of the GTRC. Commissioner Angela Lawrence grounded the GTRC's work in her experiences living in Greensboro and growing up in Morningside Homes.

One thing that surprised me as I researched this book was how resilient the blue wall of silence remains. Most of the police officers in Greensboro who know something about November 3, 1979, won't talk about it. Despite this, I received thoughtful guidance on the department's characters and culture from former officer Greg Brooks, to whom I'm indebted.

There are so many people to thank in Greensboro: Brian Lampkin and Steve Mitchell at Scuppernong Books; Beth Sheffield at the Greensboro Public Library; Glenn Perkins and Ayla Amon at the Greensboro History Museum; Gwendolyn Erickson at the Guilford College Library and Quaker Archive; the Bennett College Library staff; and Laura Seel, whose video archive was invaluable.

Beyond Greensboro, my friend Camilo Lund surprised me with helpful connections that led to interviews. Jason Langberg, author of an excellent book about Lewis Pitts, shared files and early drafts with me. Sally Bermanzohn loaned transcripts of her moving interviews with CWP members. Dwight Stone dug into his past to retrieve memories and tapes of interviews he made in 1990 with Eddie Dawson, Lewis Pitts, and Gayle Korotkin when he was working on his Princeton thesis. Brian Balogh made me smarter on 1970s historiography. Andrea Douglas offered the African American Heritage Center at the Jefferson School in Charlottesville as a place to host public conversations with the Johnsons and Flint Taylor.

Three fellowships kept this work going, one from Virginia Humanities, another from the National Endowment for the Humanities, and one from the Virginia Center for the Creative Arts where Kevin O'Halloran and the whole VCCA community gave me the time to finish the book. Charlie Clements and Joe Conforti wrote me the recommendations that helped secure this valuable support.

I interviewed more than seventy people for this book, many of them multiple times. Each deserves a thank-you, though there isn't space here for that. I would, however, be remiss if I didn't specifically thank career FBI man Cecil Moses. His candid, insightful presence in this book makes it better.

A big thank-you to David Patterson and the team—Aemilia Phillips and Chandler Wickers—at the Stuart Krichevsky Literary Agency for all their faith in and support of this project. I'm fortunate that Tracy Sherrod took the leap to sign this book and that editor Patrik Bass, with his North Carolina roots, understood and embraced the story I was reaching for. I'm grateful to the entire team at Amistad and HarperOne for ushering *Morningside* into the world. The support and advice of writer friends Tim Wendel, Jennifer Vanderbes, and Dawn Tripp kept me afloat during the tough days.

The work it took to make this book wouldn't have been possible without the steadfast support of my extended family. My father, Robert, led me to this story and helped me understand the anti-establishment history I was learning. Susan Hand Shetterly, my mother, taught me and encouraged me to write. My sister-in-law Jocelyn listened to early chapter drafts. My parents-in-law came to Greensboro to understand what I was working on and offer me their own valuable insights into the 1960s and 1970s.

And, of course, Margot, my brilliant superhero wife, was there every step of the way, even as she labored on her own book. The privilege of being able to discuss my ideas with her first makes me the luckiest guy in the world. And Giles, who came into the world as I worked on *Morningside*, handled his dad's absences with natural grace and has announced that he's writing his own book about a big cat and an eagle.

NOTES

CHAPTER 1: DEBATE

1. Signe Waller, *Love and Revolution: A Political Memoir* (Lanham, MD: Rowan & Littlefield, 2002), 211; author interviews with Signe Waller (2017–2020) and Joyce Johnson (2017–2022).

2. Waller, *Love and Revolution*, 151, 161; author interviews with Signe Waller (2017–2020).

3. Author interview with Paul and Sally Bermanzohn (May 11, 2018).

4. All the primary books about the Greensboro Massacre and the CWP address their political and revolutionary aspirations: Sally Avery Bermanzohn, *Through Survivors' Eyes: From the Sixties to the Greensboro Massacre* (Nashville: Vanderbilt Univ. Press, 2003); Paul C. Bermanzohn and Sally A. Bermanzohn, *The True Story of the Greensboro Massacre* (New York: Cesar Cauce, 1980); Elizabeth Wheaton, *Codename Greenkil: The 1979 Greensboro Killings* (Athens: Univ. of Georgia Press, 2009); Waller, *Love and Revolution*.

5. Mao Tse-tung, *Quotations from Mao Tse-tung*, "22. Methods of Thinking and Methods of Work," accessed April 14, 2024, https://www.marxists.org/reference/archive/mao/works/red-book/ch22.htm.

6. Dwight Stone, "The 1979 Greensboro Killings: Evidence of Official Complicity" (senior thesis, Princeton Univ., 1990), 1.

7. Author interviews with Paul and Sally Bermanzohn (May 11, 2018), Signe Waller (2017–2020), and Phyllis Jones (July 13, 2018).

8. Bermanzohn and Bermanzohn, *The True Story of the Greensboro Massacre*, 211.

9. All direct quotes from Thomas Anderson are from an unpublished August 3, 1990, interview by Sally Bermanzohn in her personal archive.

10. Sally Bermanzohn interview with Thomas Anderson (August 3, 1990).

11. This letter, "Open Letter to Joe Grady, Gorrell Pierce, and all KKK Members and Sympathizers," dated October 22, 1979, and signed by Nelson Johnson (though it was written by Paul Bermanzohn), is available here (accessed April 16, 2024): https://gateway.uncg.edu/islandora/object/duke%3A65. *Institute for Southern Studies Report: The Third of November* (Durham, NC: Institute for Southern Studies, 1981), 6.

12. Waller, *Love and Revolution*, 211.

13. Author interviews with Nelson Johnson (2017–2022) and Willie Jones (November 3, 2019).

14. Author interviews with Nelson Johnson (2017–2022); Waller, *Love and Revolution*, 211.

15. Causing venues to cancel radical events was an old FBI technique discussed by Director Clarence Kelley in his autobiography. Clarence M. Kelley and James Kirkpatrick Davis, *Kelley: The Story of an FBI Director* (Kansas City: Andrews McMeel Publishing, 1987), 165.

16. Waller, *Love and Revolution*, 214.

17. George M. Taber, "Capitalism: Is It Working . . . ?," *TIME* magazine, April 21, 1980, 40–55.

18. Bermanzohn and Bermanzohn, *The True Story of the Greensboro Massacre*; author interview with Paul and Sally Bermanzohn (May 11, 2018).

19. Jimmy Carter, "Energy and the National Goals: A Crisis of Confidence," speech delivered July 15, 1979, *American Rhetoric: Top 100 Speeches*, https://www.americanrhetoric.com/speeches/jimmycartercrisisofconfidence.htm.

20. *Workers Viewpoint*, July 21–28, 1980, 4.

21. Eddie S. Glaude Jr., *Begin Again: James Baldwin's America and Its Urgent Lessons for Our Own* (New York: Crown, 2020), 47.

22. *TIME* magazine, April 21, 1980, 40–55.

23. Sally Bermanzohn interview with Nelson Johnson (October 9, 1989), 6.

24. Bermanzohn, *Through Survivors' Eyes*, 4.

25. Sally Bermanzohn interview with Signe Waller (October 31, 1989).

26. Sally Bermanzohn interview with Shirley (August 1991), 11.

27. Sally Bermanzohn interview with Roz (undated).

28. Waller, *Love and Revolution*, 214.

29. Sally Bermanzohn interview with Nelson Johnson (October 9, 1989).

CHAPTER 2: SHADOWS

1. Edward W. Dawson's deposition testimony, June 13, 14, and 15, 1984, taken in US District Courthouse in Greensboro, North Carolina, University of North Carolina collection no. 4630, Greensboro Civil Rights Fund Records, 1971–1987 (hereafter "GCRF Records"), folder 1565; PBS, "88 Seconds in Greensboro," *Frontline*, aired January 24, 1983; *The Third of November*, 15.

2. "Dukes of Hazzard Lyrics (Good Ol' Boys by Waylon Jennings)," *Musixmatch*, accessed April 9, 2024, https://www.musixmatch.com/lyrics/The-Hazzard-County-Boys/Good-Ol-Boys. *Dukes of Hazzard* debuted on January 26, 1979.

3. Kathleen Belew, *Bring the War Home: The White Power Movement and Paramilitary America* (Cambridge, MA: Harvard Univ. Press, 2018), 110–13.

4. *Greensboro Record*, "Hines-Clements Reality, Inc." advertisement, October 20, 1960, D9, column 1.

5. PBS, "88 Seconds in Greensboro"; Eddie Dawson deposition testimony; *The Third of November*, 15.

6. Greensboro Truth and Reconciliation Commission (GTRC) Archive, Bennet College Library, Greensboro, Emily Mann and Mark Wing-Davy interview with Eddie Dawson (November 1994).

7. Eddie Dawson deposition testimony.

8. Eddie Dawson deposition testimony; *The Third of November*, 25.

9. For an excellent overview of the Klan in North Carolina and its place in the national story, read David Cunningham, *Klansville, U.S.A.: The Rise and Fall of the Civil Rights–Era Ku Klux Klan* (Oxford: Oxford Univ. Press, 2012).

10. "Black power and civil rights are not true issues in America today. They are a taken for granted means of the international communist conspiracy spreading frustration, animosity, and ill will." Robert Shelton, quoted in Cunningham, *Klansville, U.S.A.*, 3.

11. Cunningham, *Klansville, U.S.A.*, 3.

12. Cunningham, *Klansville, U.S.A.*, 158–59.

13. Patsy Sims, *The Klan* (Lexington: Univ. Press of Kentucky, 1996), 68–72.

14. Cunningham, *Klansville, U.S.A.*, 63.

15. Sims, *The Klan*, 68–72.

16. *The Third of November*, 25.

17. PBS, "88 Seconds in Greensboro"; James Reston Jr. interview with Robert Morgan.

18. Richard F. Shepard, "Emmett Kelly, the Mournful Clown, Dead," *New York Times*, March 29, 1979, D23, https://timesmachine.nytimes.com/timesmachine/1979/03/29/issue.html.

19. *Greensboro Daily News*, "TV Today," November 2, 1979, D2.

20. PBS, "88 Seconds in Greensboro," transcript, 17; Eddie Dawson deposition testimony; *The Third of November*, 27.

21. PBS, "88 Seconds in Greensboro," transcript, 18.

22. Wheaton, *Codename Greenkil*, 110–12.

23. PBS, "88 Seconds in Greensboro," transcript, 18.

24. PBS, "88 Seconds in Greensboro," transcript, 18.

25. *The Third of November*, 6.

26. GCRF Records (4630), folder 2555, Wilson Library, University of North Carolina, "Plaintiffs' Closing Arguments Before the Honorable Robert R. Merhige, Jr., Winston-Salem, North Carolina," June 3, 1985.

27. Eddie Dawson deposition testimony.

28. GCRF Records (4630), folder 1760, Jerry Paul Smith grand jury hearing.

29. Eddie Dawson deposition testimony; *The Third of November*, 8; Jim Schlosser, "Shootout Figure Takes His Own Life," *Greensboro News & Record*, July 9, 1984, B1, B2.

CHAPTER 3: MORNING

1. Gayle Hicks Fripp, *Greensboro: A Chosen Center; an Illustrated History*, 2nd ed. (New York: Windsor Publishing, 1983), 31.

2. GCRF Records (4630), folder 2394, batch 13, Nelson interview by SAs Thomas Brereton and Horace Beckwith. The scene here is set through author interviews with Nelson and Joyce Johnson (2017–2022) and personal observation of the property and landscape (2017–2024).

3. Byron McCauley, "Bowling Engineered Disco into New Career," *Greensboro News & Record*, March 5, 1990, 4.

4. Details from listings and announcements in the *Greensboro Daily News*, November 2, 1979; from the *Carolina Peacemaker*, November 3, 1979; and from author interviews with FBI agents William Schatzman (April 8, 19, 2019) and George Alznauer (April–May 2019).

5. Author interview with Afrique Kilimanjaro (2019).

6. "Jim Melvin to Debate Jacobs on Issues," *Carolina Peacemaker*, November 3, 1979, 16.

7. "Jim Melvin to Debate Jacobs on Issues," 16.

8. William March, "Quest for the Best Makes Melvin Tick," *Greensboro Daily News*, November 3, 1979, B1, B7.

9. "For Mayor: Melvin," editorial, *Greensboro Daily News*, November 4, 1979, G2.

10. B. J. Battle, "25 Years in Review," *Carolina Peacemaker*, June 16, 1979, 16.

11. Tom Dent interview with Sol Jacobs (February 1, 1991), Tulane Digital Library, https://digitallibrary.tulane.edu/islandora/object/tulane%3A53909.

12. Waller, *Love and Revolution*, 218.

13. GCRF Records (4630), folder 2394, batch 13, Nelson interview by SAs Thomas Brereton and Horace Beckwith. Paradise Drive-Inn is referenced in Otis L. Hairston, *Greensboro, North Carolina* (Mount Pleasant, SC: Arcadia Publishing, 2003), 7.

14. For description of Paradise Drive-Inn, see Amílcar Cabral / Paul Robeson Collective and Greensboro Collective, "The Greensboro Massacre: Critical Lessons for the 1980's," *Encyclopedia of Anti-revisionism On-Line*, accessed April 9, 2024, https://www.marxists.org/history/erol/ncm-1a/greensboro/part1.htm.

15. "Announcement of Morningside Homes," *Greensboro Record*, September 11, 1951, A5.

16. Allen Johnson, "'A Beautiful Cage'? Stunted Growth at Willow Oaks," *Greensboro News & Record*, January 15, 2017, https://greensboro.com/blogs/allen-johnson-a-beautiful-cage-stunted-growth-at-willow-oaks/article_f2f55b22-66b7-56da-a40f-f99f98ab4aa6.html.

17. GCRF Records (4630), folders 1349–63, Nelson Johnson (November 19–21, 1984) and Joyce Johnson (October 2–3, 1984) deposition testimony.

18. GCRF Records (4630), folder 2907, video logs for rally footage, November 3, 1979.

19. Waller, *Love and Revolution*, 196; GCRF Records (4630), folders 1590–91; FBI file CE 44-3527, vol. II, "Beckwith Report," February 1, 1980: 5–17.

20. Bermanzohn, *Through Survivors' Eyes*, 212.

21. Bermanzohn, *Through Survivors' Eyes*, 210.

22. Waller, *Love and Revolution*, 219.

23. Bermanzohn, *Through Survivors' Eyes*, 213.

24. *The Third of November*, 8–9. In this account Eddie mentions calls at 7 a.m. and 8:30 a.m. Eddie Dawson deposition testimony, 667–88. Eddie says he called Cooper's house at 7 a.m. and around 10 a.m. In his deposition, Jerry Cooper (*Waller v. Butkovich*, June 25, 1984) acknowledges the 8:30 a.m. call but denies receiving either the call around 7 a.m. or the one at 10 a.m. Cooper would also deny telling either of his superiors, Lieutenant Talbott

and Captain Thomas, that he'd seen guns being loaded into the Klan and Nazi cars. Talbott, however, provides this detail in his grand jury testimony. R. L. Talbott federal grand jury testimony, August 5, 1982, 41.

25. Eddie Dawson deposition testimony.

26. Schlosser, "Shootout Figure Takes His Own Life." Fletcher's is an incredibly sad story. His life was ruined by the Vietnam War and the injuries he sustained there. He was thirty-eight when he committed suicide. "Brent Fletcher," obituary, *Greensboro News & Record*, July 9, 1984, B4.

27. Frazier Glenn Miller Jr. died in federal prison on May 3, 2021. He was on death row for murdering three people outside a Jewish community center in Kansas. He dedicated his life to violent white supremacy and was a high-profile leader of the movement for white power. For a more complete history of his life, see the Southern Poverty Law Center site: https://www.splcenter.org/fighting-hate/extremist-files/individual/frazier-glenn-miller.

28. Belew, *Bring the War Home*, 19–32.

29. Eddie Dawson deposition testimony; GCRF (4630), folder 1341, Virgil Griffin deposition testimony.

30. Eddie Dawson deposition testimony, 717.

31. Eddie Dawson deposition testimony; *The Third of November*, 29.

32. Eddie Dawson deposition testimony, 667–88.

33. Jerome Adams, *Old Conflicts, Young Deaths: The Greensboro Killings*, unpublished manuscript, 1985, 36–60, Greensboro Truth and Reconciliation Commission Archive, Emily Mann Files, Bennet College Library.

34. Virgil Griffin deposition testimony.

35. Eddie Dawson deposition testimony; Virgil Griffin deposition testimony.

36. Eddie Dawson claims he didn't direct the Ford Fairlane into the spot ahead of the van. Photographic evidence and other testimony, however, suggests that he did just that.

37. GCRF Record (4630), folder 1903, interview with A. D. [April] Wise, November 3, 1979.

CHAPTER 4: SHOOTING

1. Author interview with Ed Boyd (April 4, 2019).

2. From author interview with Ed Boyd (April 4, 2019); GCRF Record (4630), folder 2247, Ed Boyd testimony.

3. Greensboro Truth and Reconciliation Commission (GTRC) Final Report, chap. 7, "Sequence of Events on Nov. 3, 1979," May 26, 2006, 176.

4. Author interviews with Signe Waller Foxworth (2017–2020).

5. Waller, *Love and Revolution*, 221.

6. *The Third of November*, 27.

7. Paul Bermanzohn, GTRC statement, July 15, 2005, Greensboro, North Carolina. See also Bermanzohn, *Through Survivors' Eyes*, 214.

8. Bermanzohn, *Through Survivors' Eyes*, 214.

9. The Klan claimed that the demonstrators initiated the fight by attacking Klan cars. On film it's difficult to discern, but the claim by members of the CWP that they hit the cars when the cars lurched and veered at them seems credible. Regardless, the arrival at Morningside by the Klan was aggressive, threatening, and not officially sanctioned. And the young man in the truck, Mark Sherrer, was loading his gun before any altercation or contact between the groups took place.

10. GTRC Final Report, chap. 7, "Sequence of Events on Nov. 3, 1979," 179.

11. FBI file CE 44-3527, vol. II, "Beckwith Report."

12. GCRF Records (4630), folder 2907, video logs for rally footage, November 3, 1979.

13. The man would be identified as Charles Finley. GCRF (4630), file 2394, "Nelson Johnson Grand Jury," 20–21; interview conducted by police detective J. D. Batten (January 18, 1980).

14. White men who were part of the Greensboro media and law enforcement in 1980, and even the state prosecutors of the Klan and Nazis, have cast doubt on Nelson Johnson's claims that he was stabbed. They insinuated in interviews with the author that he made up the story about being stabbed. Not only have I seen how, to this day, he cannot hold the ring finger on his left hand straight, but I've seen the medical records, the photographs of his arm and hand in a splint, and the descriptions of the blood gushing from his wound. GCRF Records (4630), folder 2392, 12 (Nelson Johnson's injuries described by a doctor).

15. Bermanzohn, *Through Survivors' Eyes*, 208–27; author interviews with Nelson Johnson (2017–2022); GTRC Final Report, chap. 7, "Sequence of Events on Nov. 3, 1979," 188.

16. Bermanzohn, unpublished interview with Signe Waller (October 31, 1989), 13.

17. Bermanzohn, *Through Survivors' Eyes*, 217.

18. James Baldwin, *The Evidence of Things Not Seen*, reissued ed. (New York: Holt, 1995 [1985]), xvi.

19. Author interview with Ed Boyd (April 4, 2019).

20. GCRF Records (4630), folder 1903, "Police Interviews," Captain Trevor Hampton interview (November 14, 1979).

21. GCRF Records (4630), folder 2907, video logs for rally footage, November 3, 1979.

22. Author interview with Sylvester Daughtry (author interviewed Daughtry three times in person between 2018 and 2019 at the Bob Evans restaurant in Chantilly, Virginia).

23. In interviews with the author, Sylvester Daughtry admits trying to step on Nelson Johnson's shoulder. Nelson Johnson showed the author scars on his neck that he says are from being kicked in that moment. The video of the incident supports Johnson's claims.

24. Bermanzohn, *Through Survivors' Eyes*, 220.

25. GCRF Record (4630), folder 1903, interview with A. D. [April] Wise (November 3, 1979).

26. I discovered in my research that the uncle of Greensboro Police Department officer W. D. Comer was at one time a member of the same Klan Klavern in Greensboro as Eddie Dawson. I don't know whether the uncle was a true believer, an informant, or both. And I don't know how this fact informed the attitudes of his nephew. However, it does support what everyone always claimed: that the police and the Klan were never far apart.

CHAPTER 5: JURISDICTION

1. Multiple author interviews with FBI agent Cecil Moses are the primary sources for this chapter (2018–2021).

2. Garrett Epps, "Wanted By the FBI: A Better Class of Criminal," *Washington Post*, January 28, 1979, https://www.washingtonpost.com/archive/lifestyle/magazine/1979/01/28/wanted-by-the-fbi-a-better-class-of-criminal/ade9714a-0e5a-4299-b869-0b2429a62f07/.

3. Max Fraser, "Down in the Hole: Outlaw Country and Outlaw Culture," *Southern Cultures*, accessed August 23, 2020, https://www.southerncultures.org/article/down-in-the-hole/.

4. Fraser, "Down in the Hole."

5. John T. Elliff, *The Reform of FBI Intelligence Operations* (Princeton, NJ: Princeton Legacy Library, 1979). Or as another student of government bureaucracy—Harvard professor James Q. Wilson, author of the "broken windows" theory of policing, who'd spent the mid-1970s interviewing FBI employees including Cecil Moses—wrote with detached, patrician understatement, the Bureau had been "beset by *controversy.*"

6. James T. Wooten, "Carter 'Would Have' Ousted Kelley, but Won't Say He Will if President," *New York Times*, September 8, 1976, https://www.nytimes.com/1976/09/08/archives/new-jersey-pages-carter-would-have-ousted-kelley-but-wont-say-he.html.

7. The FBI doesn't give out information about how many agents work in each Bureau office. This is an estimate based on names I've learned from talking with various special agents who worked in Greensboro.

8. Author interview with Mickey Michaux (January 16, 2018).

9. Kathy Hoke interview of Dargan Frierson (November 10, 1989; January 9, 1990), University of North Carolina Greensboro Digital Archive, https://gateway.uncg.edu/islandora/search?type=dismax&f%5B0%5D=dc.contributor%3AFrierson%2C%5C%20Dargan%5C%20%5C%28Interviewee%5C%29.

10. Author interviews with former GPD officer Greg Brooks provided background on the relationship between the GPD and the FBI. As a young officer, Brooks was assigned the task of guarding the seized yellow van in the GPD parking garage on November 3, 1979. (The author talked with Brooks dozens of times in person and by phone between 2018 and 2024.)

11. Moses isn't 100 percent sure whether this call took place the night of November 3 or the morning of November 4.

12. Ronald Ostrow, "Others Also Under Consideration to Succeed Webster: Ex-FBI Man Candidate to Head Agency," *Los Angeles Times*, March 19, 1987, https://www.latimes.com/archives/la-xpm-1987-03-19-mn-14128-story.html.

13. Internal FBI files show just how seriously not only Moses but the whole FBI bureaucracy took Senator Morgan's breach of confidence. Morgan, however, did not back off talking about his distrust of the FBI. National Archives and Records Administration, file no. 62-116395, https://www.archives.gov/files/research/jfk/releases/docid-32989589.pdf.

14. In this role, Mitchell oversaw and ran coordination between the approximately fifteen thousand North Carolina National Guardsmen, the three thousand members of the Highway Patrol, and the smaller Alcohol Law Enforcement agency, a vestige of the

Prohibition era. This account of the call to Governor Hunt is from an author interview with Burley Mitchell (May 25, 2018).

15. The name *Beijing* had not yet been adopted internationally. So all the US press releases and news about Governor Hunt's trip referred to *Peking*.

16. North Carolina State Archives, Governor James B. Hunt Jr. Press Secretary's Files, 1979, Speeches, November 1–30, 1979, "Chinese Say 'Future Bright' for N.C.–China Trade," press release, November 4, 1979.

17. Author interview with Governor James B. Hunt Jr. (January 25, 2018).

18. Michael Myerson, *Nothing Could Be Finer* (New York: International Publishers, 1978), https://archive.org/stream/nothingcouldbefi00myer_0/nothingcouldbefi00myer_0_djvu.txt.

19. For a definitive account of the history of the Wilmington Ten, see Kenneth Robert Janken, *The Wilmington Ten: Violence, Injustice, and the Rise of Black Politics in the 1970s* (Chapel Hill: Univ. of North Carolina Press, 2015).

20. Howard E. Covington Jr., *Once Upon a City: Greensboro, North Carolina's Second Century* (Greensboro, NC: Greensboro Historical Museum, 2008), 148.

21. Covington, *Once Upon a City*, 170; Lindsey Gruson, "After Violence, Community Leaders Ask for Calm," *Greensboro Daily News*, November 4, 1979, A4.

22. Covington, *Once Upon a City*, 170.

23. Covington, *Once Upon a City*, 170.

24. W. J. Cash, *The Mind of the South* (New York: Vintage Books, 1991 [1941]), 363.

25. Gruson, "After Violence, Community Leaders Ask for Calm"; "City Police Officers Cited for Training in Council Session," *Greensboro Daily News*, November 28, 1974, C7.

26. This section is taken from author interviews with Joyce Johnson (2017–2022).

27. This is a reference to the 1919 Palmer Raids. For more background on the Palmer Raids, see Beverly Gage, *The Day Wall Street Exploded: A Story of America in Its First Age of Terror* (Oxford: Oxford Univ. Press, 2009); Adam Hochschild, *American Midnight: The Great War, a Violent Peace, and Democracy's Forgotten Crisis* (Boston: Mariner Books, 2022).

28. Joyce Johnson deposition testimony.

29. Joyce Johnson, GTRC statement, September 30, 2005, Greensboro, North Carolina, https://greensborotrc.org/hear_statements.php.

30. Joyce Johnson, GTRC statement.

CHAPTER 6: NARRATIVES

1. Author interviews with Susan Kidd (December 2018) and Joyce Johnson (2017–2022).

2. Charles Babington, "Police Near Scene Not Told Klan Was Approaching," *Greensboro Daily News*, November 4, 1979, A1–A7.

3. Author interview with Bill Dill (January 4, 2019).

4. There are multiple hearsay accounts in Greensboro of State Bureau of Investigation agents watching the shooting at Morningside.

5. Author interview with Susan Kidd (December 2018).

6. Greg Lewis, "WVO in Struggles for 'Oppressed People,'" *Greensboro Daily News*, November 4, 1979, A6.

7. "Klan Ambush Kills 4 WVO People," *Greensboro Record*, November 3, 1979, A1.

8. Author interviews with Nelson Johnson (2017–2022); Sally Bermanzohn, unpublished interview with Nelson Johnson (October 9, 1989).

9. *Through Survivor's Eyes*, 198. Later, Nelson told a similar version of events to the Greensboro Truth and Reconciliation Commission. GTRC Final Report, chap. 6, 151. Author interviews with Nelson Johnson confirmed his version of events relating to the parade permit. In Larry Gibson's grand jury testimony (August 23, 1982) he discusses the unprecedented restriction prohibiting the CWP from carrying arms. Gibson also claimed that when he had his initial conversation with Johnson on October 19, 1979, he had no knowledge that the Klan and Nazis intended to come to Greensboro. In his depositions and testimony, Gibson said he was aware of the November 1 intelligence and admitted he had trouble with "Nelson and other black groups," but claimed he wasn't the officer to give Nelson Johnson the parade permit. In an author interview, he said he "doesn't think" he delivered the parade permit to Johnson. GCRF Records (4630), folder 1338, Larry Gibson deposition; GCRF Records (4630), folders 2357–58, Larry Gibson testimony.

10. GCRF Records (4630), folder 2394, batch 1, memo written by "E. Welch, Detective" on November 9, 1979. This document also confirms that the officials took him from the cell to an interrogation room late on the night of November 3, 1979, and that he said nothing of substance to them. Beyond that, I've accepted Nelson Johnson's version of not only his state of mind but what the officers said to him in that room.

11. Author interview with the ex-wife of a GPD officer (2019).

12. This account is based on author interviews with former FBI agents William Schatzman and George Alznauer (April–May 2019).

13. Martha Woodall, "Rules Differ for ATF Agents Involved in Undercover Work," *Greensboro Record*, July 14, 1980, A1, A3: "Although tighter surveillance restrictions were placed on the FBI and CIA in recent years, most of the limitations have not been extended to the Treasury Department's Bureau of Alcohol, Tobacco and Firearms."

14. William Schatzman told the author this is what he said to the BATF agents (April 8 and 19, 2019).

15. Mae Israel, "Some Hearts Are Swollen with Anger," *Greensboro Daily News*, November 5, 1979, A7.

16. See student letters in *A&T Register*, November 6, 1979. Also Israel, "Some Hearts Are Swollen with Anger," A7.

17. PBS, "88 Seconds in Greensboro," transcript, 21, 98.

18. Jack Scism, "Four Die in Klan-Leftist Shootout," *Greensboro Daily News*, November 4, 1979, A1, A6.

19. Steve Berry, "Violence Not New to Leader of Rally," *Greensboro Daily News*, November 4, 1979, A4.

CHAPTER 7: NAMESAKE

1. "Sit-ins," Martin Luther King Jr. Research and Education Institute, Stanford University, accessed April 14, 2024, https://kinginstitute.stanford.edu/encyclopedia/sit-ins.

2. Kathye Hoke interview of Dag Frierson, Interview 1, UNCG Digital Archive, (November 10, 1989), 6.

3. Dwight F. Cunningham, "Marker to Remind of Quaker Pioneers," *Greensboro Daily News*, November 2, 1979, A9.

4. Alexander Stoesen, "Clyde and Ernestine's College: Gilford, 1930–1965, Patterns of Power," *Southern Friend: Journal of the North Carolina Friends Historical Society* (Fall 2001), 2.

5. Hal Sieber, *Holy Ground: Significant Events in the Civil Rights-Related History of the African-American Communities of Guilford County, North Carolina, 1771–1995* (New York: Tudor Publishing, 1995), 25.

6. Gwendolyn Erickson, "Fit for Freedom but Not for Friendship?: Introductory Exploration of Quaker Education, African-American Opportunity, & HBCUs," Universities Studying Slavery Conference, Tougaloo College, October 2018.

7. Greensboro Monthly Meeting Minutes, October 1, 1952, provided by Gwendolyn Erickson, archivist, Guilford College, Greensboro, North Carolina.

8. For background on Nathanael Greene, see John Hairr, *Guilford Courthouse: Nathanael Greene's Victory in Defeat, March 15, 1781*, Battleground America Guides (Cambridge, MA: Da Capo Press, 2008); Gerald M. Carbone, *Nathanael Greene: A Biography of the American Revolution* (London: Palgrave MacMillan, 2008). Also see John Morgan Dederer, "Making Bricks Without Straw: Nathanael Greene's Southern Campaigns and Mao Tse-Tung's Mobile War," *Military Affairs* 47, no. 3 (October 1983): 115–21.

9. New York State Society of the Cincinnati Archives Proceedings 1783–1803, provided by Philip Livingston, secretary. See also a complete version of Alexander Hamilton's eulogy from the National Archives, accessed April 9, 2024: https://founders.archives.gov /documents/Hamilton/01-05-02-0141.

10. Cokie Roberts, *Founding Mothers: The Women Who Raised Our Nation* (New York: HarperCollins, 2004).

11. Ethel Stephens Arnet and Walter Clinton Jackson, *Greensboro, North Carolina* (Chapel Hill: Univ. of North Carolina Press, 1955).

12. New York State Society of the Cincinnati Archives Proceedings 1783–1803. See also a complete version of Alexander Hamilton's eulogy from the National Archives.

13. "Unveiling of a Fine Monument," *Greensboro Daily Record*, July 3, 1915, 1, 2.

14. "Unveiling of a Fine Monument," 1, 2.

15. "Unveiling of a Fine Monument," 1, 2.

16. "The Birth of a Nation," *Greensboro Daily Record*, October 30, 1915; advertisement for *Birth of a Nation*, *Greensboro Daily Record*, November 6, 1915, 7.

17. "Ask Mayor to Stop 'Birth of a Nation': Negroes and Their Friends Call Production 'Cruel and Untrue,'" *Greensboro Daily News*, April 4, 1915, 9.

18. "Monday Night Is First of a Series: 'The Birth of a Nation' Will Draw Great Crowds in This City," *Greensboro Daily Record*, November 6, 1915, 7.

19. Linda Gordon, "When the Ku Klux Klan Was a Mass Movement," *History Extra*, November 27, 2019, https://www.historyextra.com/period/20th-century/ku-klux-klan -mass-movement-organisation-secret-society-rise-american-south-1920s/.

20. W. E. B. Du Bois, *Black Reconstruction in America: Toward a History of the Part Which Black Folk Played in the Attempt to Reconstruct Democracy in America, 1860–1880* (New York: Routledge, 2017 [1935]), 182.

21. Du Bois, *Black Reconstruction in America*, 713–14.

CHAPTER 8: THORNE

1. Bermanzohn, *Through Survivors' Eyes*, 17–18. According to author David Cunningham, "Only seven percent of Blacks in eastern NC owned their own land." *Klansville, U.S.A.*, 107.

2. Author interviews with Nelson Johnson (2017–2022); his brother Ivan Johnson (December 14, 2017; January 20, 2019); and his sister Alma "Mickey" Monk (January 20, 2019). Nelson's father, James Ransom Johnson, died in 2003 at the age of ninety-four.

3. A sketch of this history is available in the Annie Blackwell Thorne Papers, 1769–1965, Collection No. 04521, University of North Carolina at Chapel Hill, Wilson Special Collections Library.

4. Gleaned from family obituaries and grave records. See "Rev. Nelson T. Thorne Sr.," *Find a Grave*, accessed April 10, 2024, https://www.findagrave.com/memorial/156466981 /nelson-t-thorne.

5. Author interviews with Ivan Johnson (December 14, 2017; January 20, 2019).

6. A great deal has been written about Rosenwald Schools that is publicly available. The best resource for Halifax County is Marvin A. Brown, Principal Investigator, *Research Report: Tools for Assessing the Significance and Integrity of North Carolina's Rosenwald Schools and Comprehensive Investigation of Rosenwald Schools in Edgecombe, Halifax, Johnston, Nash, Wayne, and Wilson Counties*, URS Corporation–North Carolina for the Office of Human Environment, North Carolina Department of Transportation and Federal Highway Administration, December 2007. Good information about Rosenwald Schools exists also at the North Carolina Government and Heritage Library's ncpedia.org page: https://www.ncpedia.org/rosenwald-fund.

7. Author interviews with Nelson Johnson (2017–2022). See also Bermanzohn, *Through Survivors' Eyes*, 14.

8. Bermanzohn, *Through Survivors' Eyes*, 21.

9. Bermanzohn, *Through Survivors' Eyes*, 17.

10. Bermanzohn, *Through Survivors' Eyes*, 13–14.

11. Author interviews with Nelson Johnson (2017–2022).

12. Author interviews with Ivan Johnson (December 14, 2017; January 20, 2019).

13. See Adam Clayton Powell Jr. talk about the "new breed of cats" here: https://www .youtube.com/watch?v=DSYQGrGthGM&ab_channel=AfroMarxist. Martin Luther King Jr., "The Montgomery Bus Boycott," speech, 1955: https://www.blackpast.org /african-american-history/1955-martin-luther-king-jr-montgomery-bus-boycott/. Malcolm X, "The Ballot or the Bullet," April 3, 1964, Cleveland, Ohio (Howard Fuller was present at this speech), http://www.edchange.org/multicultural/speeches/malcolm _x_ballot.html.

14. Bermanzohn, *Through Survivors' Eyes*, 57.

15. Author interviews with Nelson Johnson (2017–2022).

CHAPTER 9: ALL-AMERICA

1. Irwin Smallwood, "City Submits Bid for All-America Designation," *Greensboro Daily News*, November 15, 1966, B1, B12.

2. "Official Entry of Greensboro, North Carolina for a 1966 All-America City Award," National Civic League Archives. Provided to the author by the National Civic League, January 31, 2020.

3. William March, "Quest for the Best Makes Melvin Tick," *Greensboro Daily News*, November 3, 1979, B1, B7.

4. Covington, *Once Upon a City*, 13.

5. Covington, *Once Upon a City*, 84.

6. Thomas I. Storrs, "Presentation on Greensboro Before All-America Cities Award Jury," Boston, Massachusetts, November 14, 1966. Provided to the author by the National Civic League, January 31, 2020.

7. Joseph Knox, "Greensboro Becomes All-America City," *Greensboro Daily News*, March 24, 1967, B1, B7.

8. Storrs's presentation to the All-America City Committee.

9. Knox, "Greensboro Becomes All-America City," B1, B7.

10. During the sit-in years, Melvin and his fellow Jaycees could, in fact, claim credit for inviting Charlie Sifford to play the 1961 Greater Greensboro Open, the first PGA Tour stop in the South to permit a Black entrant.

11. Sieber, *Holy Ground*.

12. Author interviews with Lewis Brandon (2017–2020).

13. Du Bois quotes are from *The Souls of Black Folk* (New York: Free Press, 1998 [1903]) and "The Georgia Negro: Occupations of Negroes and Whites in Georgia," graph displayed at the Negro Exhibit of the American Section at the Paris Exposition Universelle in 1900, https://www.loc.gov/item/2005676812/.

14. North Carolina Advisory Committee to the United States Commission on Civil Rights, *Trouble in Greensboro: A Report of an Open Meeting Concerning the Disturbances at Dudley High School and North Carolina A&T State University*, March 1970, https://gateway.uncg.edu/islandora/object/duke:441#page/1/mode/1up.

15. William H. Chafe, *Civilities and Civil Rights: Greensboro, North Carolina, and the Black Struggle for Freedom*, rev. ed. (Oxford: Oxford Univ. Press, 1981), 108.

16. Joe Chavis, Patrisha Tulloch, and Robert Spruill, "The Dudley–A&T Rebellion," *Carolina Peacemaker*, June 16, 1979, 1, 3, 16.

17. All data are from the University of North Carolina Greensboro digital collection "Postwar Greensboro: Urban Renewal and Development," accessed April 10, 2024, https://gateway.uncg.edu/postwargso.

18. Cunningham, *Klansville, U.S.A.*; "Ku Klux Klan Rally Is Held," *Greensboro Daily News*, September 4, 1966, A10. Interestingly, the note, though it mentions a "cross burning," doesn't mention that the cross was found on the lawn of a Black homeowner.

19. David Neal, "Hiding in Plain Sight," *Scalawag*, July 8, 2015, https://scalawagmagazine.org/2015/07/hiding-in-plain-sight/.

20. Kelso Gilenwater, "Race Relations Inadequate," *Greensboro Daily News*, October 5, 1969, A1, A4.

CHAPTER 10: FUND

1. Quote from Du Bois, *Black Reconstruction in America*, 14.

2. Author interviews with Lewis Brandon (2017–2020).

3. North Carolina Advisory Committee to the United States Commission on Civil Rights, *Black/White Perceptions: Race Relations in Greensboro*, November 1980, https://gateway.uncg.edu/islandora/object/mss%3A146536#page/1/mode/1up.

4. Author interviews with Nelson Johnson (2017–2022).

5. Robert Korstad and James L. Leloudis, *To Right These Wrongs: The North Carolina Fund and the Battle to End Poverty and Inequality in 1960s America* (Chapel Hill: Univ. of North Carolina Press, 2015), 63–64.

6. James L. Leloudis, "Leadership and Politics in the War on Poverty: The Case of the North Carolina Fund," *Popular Government* (Spring/Summer 2003): 2–13, https://www.sog.unc.edu/sites/default/files/articles/article1_18.pdf.

7. George Esser claims that the first use of the phrase "war on poverty" was in the press release announcing the incorporation of the North Carolina Fund in July 1963. The phrase was used in a meeting with the Ford Foundation in December 1963, just weeks before Johnson's State of the Union address. George Esser with Rah Bickley, *My Years at the North Carolina Fund: 1963–1970; an Oral History* (self-published, 2007), 42, 58.

8. Once the "community-controlled" grassroots organizations were structured and funded in the state's poorest regions, Sanford believed, the need for the NCF would cease to exist, emphasizing that the Fund would close its doors after five years. The intervention was meant to shift the economic paradigm, not to establish long-term dependence.

9. Lyndon B. Johnson, "Annual Message to the Congress on the State of the Union, January 8, 1964," *American Presidency Project*, https://www.presidency.ucsb.edu/documents/annual-message-the-congress-the-state-the-union-25.

10. The Economic Opportunity Act of 1964, Public Law 88–452, 78 Stat. 508–516 (1965), https://college.cengage.com/history/ayers_primary_sources/economicopportunity_1964.htm.

11. News Conference of President Lyndon Johnson, March 13, 1965, *Public Papers of Lyndon B. Johnson*, vol. 1, 274 (1965).

12. Korstad and Leloudis, *To Right These Wrongs*, 2.

13. Esser, *My Years at the North Carolina Fund*, 145.

14. Howard Fuller, *No Struggle, No Progress: A Warrior's Life from Black Power to Education Reform* (Milwaukee: Marquette Univ. Press, 2014), 59.

15. Malcolm X, "The Ballot or the Bullet."

16. Nathan Garrett, *A Palette, Not a Portrait: Stories from the Life of Nathan Garrett* (Bloomington, IN: iUniverse, 2010), loc. 3133, Kindle.

17. Korstad and Leloudis, *To Right These Wrongs*, 194.

18. Author interviews with Ivan Johnson (December 14, 2017; October 20, 2019).

19. Bill Morris, "If the Walls Could Talk, They'd Tell This Story," *Greensboro News & Record*, January 28, 1991, updated January 24, 2015, https://greensboro.com/if-the-walls-could-talk-theyd-tell-this-story/article_5cdf1aef-ded6-5883-824e-5ca863140e6c.html.

20. "Integrated Group Heckled," *Greensboro Daily News*, August 21, 1966, A15.

21. Author interviews with Nelson Johnson (2017–2022).

22. Gillet Rosenblith, "'Community Control': Residential Carcerality in Greensboro, North Carolina," master's thesis, 2015, https://libraetd.lib.virginia.edu/public_view/41687h67m.

23. Korstad and Leloudis, *To Right These Wrongs*, 212; see also Osha Gray Davidson, *The Best of Enemies* (Chapel Hill: Univ. of North Carolina Press, 2007), 177. The local NCF project was called the Choanoke Area Development Association (CADA).

24. Fuller, *No Struggle, No Progress*, 76–77.

25. Roy Reed, "Roy Reed Walked Across Hell," *Arkansas Times*, August 29, 2012, https://arktimes.com/news/cover-stories/2012/08/29/roy-reed-walked-across-hell.

26. Wikipedia, s.v. "Stokely Carmichael," accessed April 10, 2024, https://en.wikipedia.org/wiki/Stokely_Carmichael.

27. Peniel Joseph, "Stokely Carmichael's Call for 'Black Power' Spoke Real Truth to a Flawed Nation," *Andscape*, June 16, 2016, https://theundefeated.com/features/stokely-carmichaels-call-for-Black-power-spoke-real-truth-to-a-flawed-nation/.

28. Fuller, *No Struggle, No Progress*, 74.

29. This history is covered in great detail in this excellent book: Timothy Tyson, *Radio Free Dixie* (Chapel Hill: Univ. of North Carolina Press, 2001).

30. Korstad and Leloudis, *To Right These Wrongs*, 306.

31. Korstad and Leloudis, *To Right These Wrongs*, 291, 297, 301; Fuller, *No Struggle, No Progress*, 76.

32. Fuller, *No Struggle, No Progress*, 91. Fuller claims a Black Durham police officer told him about his white colleagues' betting pool.

33. Esser, *My Years at the North Carolina Fund*, 172.

34. Frederick Douglass, "If There Is No Struggle, There Is No Progress," 1857, https://www.blackpast.org/african-american-history/1857-frederick-douglass-if-there-no-struggle-there-no-progress/.

35. Garrett, *Palette, Not a Portrait*, loc. 2831.

36. Korstad and Leloudis, *To Right These Wrongs*, 310.

37. Chafe, *Civilities and Civil Rights*, 175.

38. Korstad and Leloudis, *To Right These Wrongs*, 288; author interviews with Nelson Johnson (2017–2022) and Lewis Brandon (2017–2020).

CHAPTER 11: LOVE

1. *The Orangeburg Massacre*, by Jack Bass and Jack Nelson (Macon, GA: Mercer Univ. Press, 2017), provides background on this event. In 1970, Cleveland Sellers was scapegoated and convicted of "not dispersing when ordered to" and sentenced to a year in prison. He was pardoned twenty-five years later. His legal issues were very similar to Nelson Johnson's in Greensboro and took place at the same time.

2. Author interviews with Nelson Johnson (2017–2022). See also Bermanzohn, *Through Survivors' Eyes*, 101.

3. Author interviews with Nelson Johnson (2017–2022).

4. *Report of the National Advisory Commission on Civil Disorders*, February 29, 1968, https://belonging.berkeley.edu/sites/default/files/kerner_commission_full_report.pdf ?file=1&force=1.

5. This was a line that King used frequently in speeches, particularly in 1965 and 1966, as he argued against the ends justifying the means.

6. "Memphis Sanitation Workers' Strike," Martin Luther King Jr. Research and Education Institute, Stanford University, accessed April 10, 2024, https://kinginstitute.stanford .edu/memphis-sanitation-workers-strike.

7. "'I've Been to the Mountaintop' by Dr. Martin Luther King Jr.," American Federation of State, County and Municipal Employees, AFL-CIO (AFSCME), accessed April 10, 2024, https://www.afscme.org/about/history/mlk/mountaintop.

8. Richard F. Weingroff, "The Greatest Decade 1956–1966: Part 1; Essential to the National Interest, Celebrating the 50th Anniversary of the Eisenhower Interstate System," US Department of Transportation, Federal Highway Administration, accessed April 10, 2024, https://highways.dot.gov/highway-history/interstate-system/50th-anniver sary/greatest-decade-1956–1966-part-1-essential; "Interstate Highway System: The Myths; Defense Was the Primary Reason for the Interstate System," US Department of Transportation, Federal Highway Administration, accessed April 10, 2024, https:// highways.dot.gov/highway-history/interstate-system/50th-anniversary/interstate -highway-system-myths#question2.

9. David Cecelski, "We Hear That You Are Sending Your Child to Youngsville School," June 17, 2020, https://davidcecelski.com/2020/06/17/we-hear-that-you-are-sending-your -child-to-youngsville-school/.

10. Nicholas Graham, "April 1968: Carolina Reacts to the Assassination of Dr. Martin Luther King, Jr.," *For the Record* (blog), University of North Carolina Libraries, April 4, 2018, https://blogs.lib.unc.edu/uarms/2018/04/04/april-1968-carolina-reacts -to-the-assassination-of-dr-martin-luther-king-jr/.

11. *Technician* (Raleigh, NC), vol. 47, no. 63 [vol. 48, no. 63], April 5, 1968, NC State University Libraries, https://d.lib.ncsu.edu/collections/catalog/technician-v47bn63-1968 -04-05#?c=&m=&cv=&xywh=-5060%2C-434%2C16003%2C8657; *Technician* (Raleigh, NC), vol. 7, no. 64 [vol. 48, no. 64], April 8, 1968, https://d.lib.ncsu.edu/collections/catalog /technician-v47bn64-1968-04-08#?c=&m=&cv=&xywh=-8804%2C-388%2C23490 %2C8531.

12. "The Four Days in 1968 That Reshaped D.C.," *Washington Post*, March 27, 2018, https://www.washingtonpost.com/graphics/2018/local/dc-riots-1968/.

13. "Negroes March Here; National Guard Called," *Greensboro Daily News*, April 5, 1968, 1, 4.

14. Charlotte Field Office Report to FBI Headquarters, April 7, 1968, Black Panther Party–North Carolina, FBIHQ file 105-165706-8, sections 1 and 2, *FBI Records: The Vault*, accessed April 10, 2024, https://vault.fbi.gov.

15. A portion of Nelson Johnson's FBI file is in the GCRF Records (4630), folder 1025. GTRC Final Report, chap. 4, "Federal Investigations of White Supremacists and the

WVO," May 26, 2006; "Federal Investigations of White Supremacists and the WVO Locates a Reference to Nelson Johnson's Inclusion in the FBI's ADEX Here," FBI SA Boland, "Nelson Johnson, EM–ALSC," to US Secret Service, Charlotte 157–9855, FD-204 (May 12, 1976), 1, 24.

CHAPTER 12: SMOKE

1. This section is based primarily on author interviews with Joyce Johnson (2017–2022).

2. Jonathan Capehart, "How MLK's Famous Letter Was Smuggled out of Jail: 'Voices of the Movement' Episode 3," *Washington Post*, April 18, 2019, https://www.washington post.com/opinions/2019/04/18/how-mlks-famous-letter-was-smuggled-out-jail-voices -movement-episode/.

3. Martin Luther King Jr., "Letter from a Birmingham Jail [King, Jr.]," April 16, 1963, https://www.africa.upenn.edu/Articles_Gen/Letter_Birmingham.html.

4. Martin Luther King Jr., "Why I Am Opposed to the War in Vietnam," speech delivered April 4, 1967, at Riverside Church, New York, transcript available at https://guides .lib.berkeley.edu/c.php?g=819842&p=5924547.

5. William Johnson, "The Timid Generation," *Sports Illustrated*, March 11, 1968, https://vault.si.com/vault/1968/03/11/the-timid-generation.

6. Joyce Johnson, GTRC statement.

CHAPTER 13: FUSION

1. Garrett, *Palette, Not a Portrait*, loc. 3140.

2. James Baldwin, *No Name in the Street*, reprint ed. (New York: Vintage, 2007 [1972]), 88.

3. Garrett, *Palette, Not a Portrait*, loc. 3144; GAPP statement and internal documents viewed at the Beloved Community Center archives at the Beloved Community Center, 417 Arlington Street, Greensboro, North Carolina.

4. Author interviews with Nelson Johnson (2017–2022) and Lewis Brandon (2017–2020); "Shots Are Exchanged Near A&T Campus," *Greensboro Daily News*, March 14, 1969, A1, A7.

5. "Optimism Limited on Racial Issues," *Greensboro Record*, October 11, 1969, A6, A7.

6. "A&T Cafeteria Dispute Is Tentatively Settled," *Greensboro Daily News*, March 13, 1969, A18; "Shots Are Exchanged Near A&T Campus"; "A&T Dispute Settled; Food Service Resumes," *Greensboro Daily News*, March 15, 1969, B1, B7; "Police Release Eight on Bonds Following Disorders Near A&T," *Greensboro Daily News*, March 15, 1969, B1, B7.

7. North Carolina Advisory Committee to the United States Commission on Civil Rights, *Trouble in Greensboro*.

8. Author interviews with Nelson Johnson (2017–2022) and Lewis Brandon (2017–2020).

9. Joyce Johnson, GTRC statement.

10. Author interviews with Joyce Johnson (2017–2022).

11. Sally Hicks, "Talking 'Bout My Generation: the Middle-Age Bulge," *Duke Magazine*, June 1, 2005, https://alumni.duke.edu/magazine/articles/talking-bout-my-generation.

12. Chafe, *Civilities and Civil Rights*, 125.

13. Author interviews with Joyce Johnson (2017–2022).

14. Author interviews with Nelson and Joyce Johnson (2017–2022) and Lewis Brandon (2017–2020). Also, FBI files in *FBI Records: The Vault*, Black Panther Party–North Carolina: FBIHQ file 105-165706-8, sections 1 and 2, which offer a physical description of Harold "Nunding" Avent as well as evidence of his violent rhetoric.

15. Michael Zwerin, "Everybody's Stepchild," *Village Voice*, March 30, 1967, 18.

16. Author interviews with Nelson Johnson (2017–2022); *FBI Records: The Vault*, Black Panther Party–North Carolina: FBIHQ file 105-165706-8, sections 1 and 2.

17. *FBI Records: The Vault*, Black Panther Party–North Carolina: FBIHQ file 105-165706-8, sections 1 and 2.

18. Author interviews with Nelson and Joyce Johnson (2017–2022).

19. This episode about "Nunding" and the car comes from author interviews with Nelson and Joyce Johnson (2017–2022).

CHAPTER 14: TRUE BLUE

1. David Lamm, "Littler Wins 4-Way Playoff for GGO Title," *Greensboro Record*, April 7, 1969, B2, B4.

2. Richard Benson II, *Fighting for Our Place in the Sun: Malcolm X and the Radicalization of the Black Student Movement 1960–1973* (New York: Peter Lang, 2015), 191–222; Martha Biondi, *Black Revolution on Campus* (Berkeley: Univ. of California Press, 2012), 142–73.

3. Author interview with Milton Coleman (January 15, 2019).

4. Cohen N. Greene, "Johnson Assails Student Press," *A&T Register*, September 26, 1969, 3. Greensboro would be SOBU headquarters. College and university chapters around the country would pay a membership fee of $200 to fund the newsletter and the speaker's bureau, which sent Nelson Johnson around the country to talk and organize new chapters.

5. *FBI Records: The Vault*, Black Panther Party–North Carolina: FBIHQ file 105-165706-8, sections 1 and 2, Document D20550072, 54.

CHAPTER 15: WAR

1. Claude Barnes has given various accounts of these events. See Claude Barnes, "Bullet Holes in the Wall: Reflections on the Dudley/A&T Student Revolt of 1969," in *American National and State Government: An African American View of the Return of Redemptionist Politics*, ed. Claude W. Barnes, Samuel A. Moseley, and James D. Steele (Dubuque, IA: Kendall Hunt, 1997/2000), 91–100.

2. North Carolina Advisory Committee to the United States Commission on Civil Rights, *Trouble in Greensboro*; Chafe, *Civilities and Civil Rights*, 185–95; author interviews with Lewis Brandon (2017–2020).

3. William Chafe interview with Jack Elam, UNCG Digital Archive, 17, accessed April 10, 2024, https://gateway.uncg.edu/islandora/object/duke%3A2; William Chafe interview with Lewis Brandon III, UNCG Digital Archive, 22, accessed April 10, 2024, https://gateway.uncg.edu/islandora/object/duke%3A31.

4. North Carolina Advisory Committee to the United States Commission on Civil Rights, *Trouble in Greensboro*.

5. "Police Arrest Student Leader," *Greensboro Daily News*, May 15, 1969, B9.

6. Chafe, *Civilities and Civil Rights*, 21.

7. North Carolina Advisory Committee to the United States Commission on Civil Rights, *Trouble in Greensboro*, 13.

8. Joe Chavis, Patrisha Tulloch, and Robert Spruill, "The Dudley–A&T Rebellion," *Carolina Peacemaker*, June 16, 1979, 1.

9. Nancy Price, "Open Hearing," letter to the editor, *A&T Register*, October 16, 1969, 4; Cohen N. Greene, "Student Legislature Fills Key Positions," *A&T Register*, October 16, 1969, 1.

10. Chavis, Tulloch, and Spruill, "The Dudley–A&T Rebellion," 1, 3, 16.

11. Chavis, Tulloch, and Spruill, "The Dudley–A&T Rebellion," 16.

12. David Newton, "The Day the National Guard Swept A&T's Scott Hall," *Greensboro Daily News*, May 20, 1979, G1, G6.

13. Kelso Gillenwater, "Police Quell Disorder After Dudley Protest," *Greensboro Daily News*, May 22, 1969, C1, C3.

14. John Marshall Stevenson, editorial, *Carolina Peacemaker*, November 30, 1968, 4.

15. Robert Stephens, "Witnesses Describe Grimes Death," *Greensboro Daily News*, July 7, 1969, B1, B10.

16. Stephens, "Witnesses Describe Grimes Death," B1, B10.

17. Chavis, Tulloch, and Spruill, "The Dudley–A&T Rebellion," 1, 3, 16.

18. Author interviews with Nelson Johnson (2017–2022). See also *FBI Records: The Vault*, Black Panther Party–North Carolina: FBIHQ file 105-165706-8, sections 1 and 2.

19. Author interviews with Nelson Johnson (2017–2022).

20. Author interviews with Nelson Johnson (2017–2022).

21. Kelso Gillenwater, "A&T Campus is Cleared After Extended Violence," *Greensboro Daily News*, May 24, 1969, A1, A2; Robert Stephens, "Bullet Scarred A&T Campus Quiet, Empty," *Greensboro Daily News*, May 24, 1969, A9; "Scott Raps Militants for Violence in City," *Greensboro Daily News*, May 24, 1969, B1; Nat Walker, "Outsiders Seen in Dorm Before Shooting Begins," *Greensboro Daily News*, May 24, 1969, B1; Joe Knox, "School Board Backs Dudley Principal in Disorder Action," *Greensboro Daily News*, May 24, 1969, B1; Chafe, *Civilities and Civil Rights*, 190.

22. Kelso Gillenwater, "Police Quell Disorder After Dudley Protest," *Greensboro Daily News*, May 22, 1969, C1, C3.

23. Chavis, Tulloch, and Spruill, "The Dudley–A&T Rebellion," 1, 3, 16.

24. Author interviews with police officers Art League (2018), Greg Brooks (2018–2024), and Marc Ridgill (2021) support Chief Paul Calhoun's testimony at the "Riots, Civil and Criminal Disorders" hearings: "Hearings Before the Permanent Subcommittee on Investigations of the Committee on Government Operations, United States Senate, 91st Congress," June 26 and 30, 1969, 4858–86.

25. Jack Elam would claim that President Dowdy was unreachable. It stretches credulity that the mayor who brought Nelson Johnson into the GPD command center couldn't—with the help of the police and FBI—find the A&T president if he needed to, or that he didn't delay the operation until he found the university president.

26. George D. Adams Jr., "Adams Takes a View of His Impressions of '69," *A&T Register*, December 18, 1969, 3; Chavis, Tulloch, and Spruill, "The Dudley–A&T Rebellion," 1, 3, 16.

27. Chavis, Tulloch, and Spruill, "The Dudley–A&T Rebellion," 1, 3, 16.

28. Stan Swofford, "Dudley Student Sparks 'Greensboro Rebellion,'" *Greensboro News & Record*, January 1, 2000, A7.

29. Author interviews with Sylvester Daughtry (2018–2019).

CHAPTER 16: HEARINGS

1. Greene, "Johnson Assails Student Press," 3.

2. Chavis, Tulloch, and Spruill, "The Dudley–A&T Rebellion," 1, 3, 16.

3. The *New York Times* called the invasion of A&T the largest military operation that had ever taken place on an American campus. The following reporting comes from the transcript of "Riots, Civil and Criminal Disorders—Hearings Before the Permanent Subcommittee on Investigations of the US Senate Committee on Government Operations, 91st Congress."

4. If Eastover, South Carolina, sounds familiar, it may be because it was the home of Dylann Storm Roof, the neo-Nazi who massacred Black parishioners in the Emanuel AME Church in Charleston, South Carolina, on June 17, 2015. Roof admired American Nazi Harold Covington, who's connected to the 1979 Greensboro Massacre.

5. See President Lewis Dowdy's bio on the A&T website: "Lewis C. Dowdy," North Carolina Agricultural and Technical State University, accessed April 11, 2024, https://www.ncat.edu/honors/dowdy-scholars-program/dowdy-bio.php. The author learned more about him in his interviews with Nelson Johnson and Lewis Brandon.

6. For more background on Adlerman, see "Jerome S. Adlerman, 73, Dead; Lawyer Aided Senate Inquiries," *New York Times*, October 2, 1975, 41, https://www.nytimes.com/1975/10/02/archives/jerome-s-adlerman-73-dead-lawyer-aided-senate-inquiries.html.

7. See the University of North Carolina Greensboro digital collection, which includes letters Chief Calhoun sent to area universities in April 1969 requesting their help in moderating student activism: http://libcdm1.uncg.edu/cdm/ref/collection/CivilRights/id/1217.

8. This history, including Nixon's quote about Rumsfeld, comes from the remarkable book by Korstad and Leloudis, *To Right These Wrongs,* 338.

9. See *Washington Star* reporting on the Senate hearings, riots, and related topics, 1969.

10. "Riots, Civil and Criminal Disorders, Hearings Before the Permanent Subcommittee on Investigations of the Committee on Government Operations, United States Senate, 91st Congress," 4858–86.

11. Korstad and Leloudis, *To Right These Wrongs*, 335; Roy Wilkins, letter to the editor, *New York Times*, August 8, 1969, 32.

12. From Johnson's memoir. "Lyndon Johnson," *Alpha History*, accessed April 11, 2024, https://alphahistory.com/vietnamwar/lyndon-johnson.

13. North Carolina Advisory Committee to the United States Commission on Civil Rights, *Trouble in Greensboro*.

14. David Lee Brown, "Malcolm X University Opens to Liberate Black People," *A&T Register*, May 17, 1969: "The existence of racial opposition [at Duke University] made it imperative that a counter institution be established . . . in direct response to the vacuum created by the existing educational system, which does not provide an ideological or practical methodology for meeting the physical, social, psychological, economic, and cultural needs of Black people." Footage from the Malcolm X Liberation University is available on YouTube: Hezakya Newz & Films, "1969 Special Report: 'Malcolm X Liberation University,'" video uploaded May 8, 2021, https://www.youtube.com/watch?v=f0B-eUTBKjk.

15. See the tax law: Tax Reform Act of 1969, H.R. 18270, https://www.finance.senate.gov/imo/media/doc/Prttax17.pdf. Not even "community capitalism" would satisfy Jesse Helms and other North Carolina segregationists, who attacked the founding of an all-Black community called Soul City, supported by Nixon's Office of Economic Opportunity.

16. See Flint Taylor, *The Torture Machine: Racism and Police Violence in Chicago* (Chicago: Haymarket Books, 2019).

17. Imogene Jones, "Blacks Ask Aid for Pair," *Greensboro Record*, August 12, 1970, B1.

18. Nikki Giovanni, "Adulthood," January 1, 1968, https://genius.com/Nikki-giovanni-adulthood-annotated.

CHAPTER 17: DEMANDS

1. Wilson Elkins, "The History of L. Richardson Memorial Hospital, Greensboro, North Carolina," *Journal of the National Medical Association* 61, no. 3 (May 1969): 205–12, https://www.ncbi.nlm.nih.gov/pmc/articles/PMC2611706/pdf/jnma00517-0005.pdf.

2. Benjamin Briggs, "The Secrets of Nocho Park, Clinton Hills, and Benbow Park," Preservation Greensboro, accessed April 14, 2024, https://preservationgreensboro.org/the-secrets-of-nocho-park-clinton-hills-and-benbow-park/.

3. Chafe, *Civilities and Civil Rights*, 178–98.

4. Langston Hughes, *Good Morning Revolution: Uncollected Writings of Social Protest* (New York: Citadel Press, 1992).

5. Jack Elam interview by Bill Chafe (undated), digital collections, accessed April 14, 2024, https://gateway.uncg.edu/islandora/object/duke%3A2.

6. Chafe, *Civilities and Civil Rights*, 174–86.

7. Author interviews with Joyce Johnson (2017–2022), who quoted Coretta Scott King. Manseen Logan, "3 Speeches from Coretta Scott King That Commemorate MLK and Cement Their Family's Lasting Legacy," *Blavity*, January 17, 2020, https://blavity.com/blavity-original/3-speeches-from-coretta-scott-king-that-commemorate-mlk-and-cement-their-familys-lasting-legacy?category1=culture.

8. Rosenblith, "Community Control."

9. Tom Dent, *Southern Journey: A Return to the Civil Rights Movement* (Athens: Univ. of Georgia Press, 2001), 50.

10. Ned Cline, "Housing Strike Settled," *Greensboro Daily News*, April 4, 1970, B1, B6.

11. Milton Coleman, "Blind Black Workers Strike at N.C. Skilcraft," *Pittsburgh Courier*, November 7, 1970, https://www.newspapers.com/clip/9765603/the-pittsburgh-courier/; "Say Blind Workers Are 'Little Short of Slavery,'" *Jet*, October 1, 1970, https://books

.google.com/books?id=xzcDAAAAMBAJ&printsec=frontcover&source=gbs_ge
_summary_r&cad=0#v=onepage&q&f=false.

12. Coleman, "Blind Black Workers Strike at N.C. Skilcraft."

13. C. A. Paul, "Albright Blasts SAC Report Bias," *Greensboro Daily News*, April 3, 1970, A5.

14. Imogene Jones, "Blacks Ask Aid for Pair," *Greensboro Record*, August 12, 1970, B1, B4.

15. North Carolina Advisory Committee to the United States Commission on Civil Rights, *Trouble in Greensboro*.

16. Paul, "Albright Blasts SAC Report Bias," A5.

CHAPTER 18: NATION TIME

1. Nelson Johnson letter, August 14, 1970. The author read this four-page letter in the Beloved Community Archives in Greensboro.

2. "Judge Signs Order Releasing Nelson Johnson," *Greensboro Daily News*, August 20, 1970, A17.

3. Author interviews with Joyce Johnson (2017–2022).

4. This August 19, 1970, statement is in the Beloved Community Center Archives.

5. Howard E. Covington Jr., *Henry Frye: North Carolina's First African American Chief Justice* (Jefferson, NC: McFarland & Company, 2013), 156–57.

6. Author interviews with Nelson Johnson (2017–2022); see also Willena Cannon, unpublished interview with Sally Bermanzohn (November 1, 1989), 7.

7. As quoted here: https://www.cpusa.org/article/james-baldwin-anti-communism-and -white-supremacy/. Baldwin, apparently, said this during a 1961 speech to the Liberation Committee for Africa, arguing that anticommunism was a form of white supremacy.

8. Fuller, *No Struggle, No Progress*, 149–59.

9. Bermanzohn and Bermanzohn, *The True Story of the Greensboro Massacre*, 103. See also a pamphlet for the SOBU/YOBU Pan-African Work Program, Cleveland L. Sellers, Jr. Papers, 1934–2003, Avery Research Center, Charleston, South Carolina, accessed April 11, 2024, https://lcdl.library.cofc.edu/lcdl/catalog/lcdl:102684?tify.

10. See the documentary on the Gary Conference: William Greaves, dir., *Nationtime*, written by Amiri Baraka, Langston Hughes, and William Greaves, 1972. See also Leonard N. Moore, *The Defeat of Black Power: Civil Rights and the National Black Political Convention of 1972* (Baton Rouge: Louisiana State Univ. Press, 2018). Gary Mayor Richard Hatcher made the reference to Indian Territory in his convening speech.

11. All quotes are taken from William Greaves's documentary *Nationtime*.

12. "Gary Declaration, National Black Political Convention," 1972, https://www .Blackpast.org/african-american-history/gary-declaration-national-Black-political -convention-1972.

13. From William Greaves's documentary *Nationtime*.

14. Fuller, *No Struggle, No Progress*, 149–59.

15. Cynthia Bellamy, "African Liberation Day," *Harvard Crimson*, July 14, 1972, https:// www.thecrimson.com/article/1972/7/14/african-liberation-day-pibetter-come-here/.

16. Quoted from Frederick Douglass's 1857 speech "If There Is No Struggle, There Is No Progress," accessed April 14, 2024, https://www.blackpast.org/african-american -history/1857-frederick-douglass-if-there-no-struggle-there-no-progress/.

17. Author interviews with Nelson and Joyce Johnson (2017–2022); see also Africa Information Service (ed.), *Return to the Source: Selected Speeches of Amílcar Cabral* (New York: Monthly Review Press, 1973).

18. Author interviews with Nelson and Joyce Johnson (2017–2022).

CHAPTER 19: TABOO

1. Author interviews with Nelson Johnson (2017–2022).

2. Bermanzohn and Bermanzohn, *The True Story of the Greensboro Massacre*, 107–10.

3. The author received large batches of FOIA docs from the FBI pertaining to the ALSC on June 14 and 17, 2019, from Bureau file 157-25073. These included not only documents pertaining to FBI intelligence gathering, but internal ALSC and SOBU documents collected by the FBI through informants.

4. Andrew Lanham, "When W. E. B. Du Bois Was Un-American," *Boston Review*, January 13, 2017, https://www.bostonreview.net/articles/when-civil-rights-were-un -american/.

5. Paul Robeson, "Unread Statement before the House Committee on Un-American Activities (June 12, 1956)," *History Is a Weapon*, https://www.historyisaweapon.com /defcon1/robesonunamericanactivities.html.

6. Robeson, "Unread Statement."

7. See Robin D. G. Kelley, *Hammer and Hoe: Alabama Communists During the Great Depression* (Chapel Hill: Univ. of North Carolina Press, 1990).

8. Peter Dreier, "The Red Scare Took Aim at Black Radicals Like Langston Hughes," *Jacobin*, March 31, 2023, https://jacobin.com/2023/03/langston-hughes-red-scare-Black -radicals-leftists-huac-red-baiting.

9. Richard Wright, "I Tried to Be a Communist," *The Atlantic*, August 1944, https:// www.theatlantic.com/magazine/archive/1944/08/richard-wright-communist/618821/.

10. "Black Leaders '73: A Black Journal Special," *Black Journal*, episode 332, WNET, aired May 15, 1973, American Archive of Public Broadcasting, http://americanarchive .org/catalog/cpb-aacip-512-cr5n873x76.

CHAPTER 20: FROGMORE

1. Peoples College, "Selected Documentary History of Peoples College in the African Liberation Support Committee (1973–74 and 1977)," accessed April 11, 2024, http:// alkalimat.org/114%201973-74%20and%201977%20selected%20documentary%20history %20of%20peoples%20college%20in%20the%20african%20liberation%20support%20 committee.pdf.

2. Martin Luther King Jr., "Beyond Vietnam: A Time to Break Silence," speech delivered April 4, 1967, at Riverside Church, New York, https://www.americanrhetoric.com /speeches/mlkatimetobreaksilence.htm.

3. Afi-Odelia Scruggs, "Beyond Vietnam: The MLK Speech That Caused an Uproar,"

USA Today, updated February 16, 2018, https://www.usatoday.com/story/news/nation-now/2017/01/13/martin-luther-king-jr-beyond-vietnam-speech/96501636/.

4. Quoted from Martin Luther King Jr.'s controversial speech "Beyond Vietnam: A Time to Break Silence."

5. They included Gene Locke, Houston; Brenda Paris, Montreal; John Warfield, Austin, Texas; Abdul Alkalimat, Nashville; Nelson Johnson, Greensboro; Kwadwo Akpan, Detroit; Owusu Sadaukai, Greensboro; Imamu Baraka, Newark; Don Lee, Chicago. African Liberation Support Committee, "Statement of Principles," accessed February 18, 2024, https://www.marxists.org/history/erol/ncm-2/statement-principles.pdf.

6. The best archive of material from this meeting was kept by the FBI, per FOIA documents received by the author: FBI D2050069, 21.

7. Devin Fergus, *Liberalism, Black Power, and the Making of American Politics, 1965–1980* (Athens: Univ. of Georgia Press, 2009), 55: "In short, chronicling Fuller's ideological sojourn into Marxist-Leninism and the forces contributing to it is a sine qua non for charting the movement's national demise." See also Leonard N. Moore, *The Defeat of Black Power: Civil Rights and the National Black Political Convention of 1972* (Baton Rouge: Louisiana State Univ. Press, 2018).

8. FBI, Bureau File 157-25073.

9. FBI, Bureau File 157-25073.

10. FBI, Bureau File 157-25073.

11. FBI, Bureau File 157-25073.

CHAPTER 21: BUREAU

1. Author interviews with Cecil Moses (2018–2022); Christopher Lydon, "J. Edgar Hoover Made the F.B.I. Formidable with Politics, Publicity and Results," obituary, *New York Times*, May 3, 1972, https://archive.nytimes.com/www.nytimes.com/learning/general/onthisday/bday/0101.html.

2. *Newsweek*, January 12, 1970.

3. Betty Medsger, *The Burglary: The Discovery of J. Edgar Hoover's Secret FBI* (New York: Knopf, 2014).

4. For a thorough background on COINTELPRO, see Ward Churchill and Jim Vander Wall, *The COINTELPRO Papers: Documents from the FBI's Secret War Against Dissent in the United States* (Boston: South End Press, 1990); US Senate, *Report of the Senate Select Committee to Study Governmental Operations with Respect to Intelligence Activities* (hereafter Church Committee Report), April 29, 1976.

5. Author interviews with Cecil Moses (2018–2022).

6. Hoover famously refused to hire Black agents. When forced to do so by JFK, Hoover promoted his chauffeur, among others, but did not assign these agents field duties.

7. For a description of Hoover's life and rise, see Beverly Gage, *G-Man: J. Edgar Hoover and the Making of the American Century* (New York: Viking, 2022).

8. Author interviews with Cecil Moses (2018–2022).

9. UPI, "J. Edgar Hoover: Black Panther Greatest Threat to U.S. Security," July 16, 1969,

https://www.upi.com/Archives/1969/07/16/J-Edgar-Hoover-Black-Panther-Greatest-Threat-to-US-Security/1571551977068/.

10. To see a reproduction of the original document, go to *FBI Records: The Vault*, Black Extremist-100-448006, section 1, accessed April 11, 2024, https://vault.fbi.gov/cointel-pro/cointel-pro-black-extremists/cointelpro-black-extremists-part-01-of.

11. Andrea May Sahouri, "Then and Now: A Look at the 50+ Years Between Des Moines Civil Rights Protests," *Des Moines Register*, updated July 4, 2020, https://www.desmoinesregister.com/story/news/2020/06/15/history-of-civil-rights-protests-in-des-moines-iowa-george-floyd-death-Black-lives-matter/3151476001/.

12. US Congress, "Black Panther Party—Hearings before the Committee of Internal Security of the House of Representatives," 1970, https://www.google.com/books/edition/Black_Panther_Party_Hearings_Before/193zTOIPNwMC?hl=en&gbpv=0; Bruce Fehn and Robert Jefferson, "North Side Revolutionaries in the Civil Rights Struggle: The African American Community in Des Moines and the Black Panther Party for Self-Defense, 1948–1970," *Annals of Iowa* 69 (Winter 2010): 51–81, https://pubs.lib.uiowa.edu/annals-of-iowa/article/14696/galley/123095/view.

13. For an overview of the Black Panther Party in Des Moines, Iowa, see this archival resource at New York University: https://wp.nyu.edu/gallatin-bpparchive2021/midwest-chapters/des-moines-iowa/. Also see the *Des Moines Register* from 1968–1970. Author interviews with Cecil Moses (2018–2022).

14. "City Hall Bombing Aftermath," Ames History Museum, accessed April 12, 2024, http://www.ameshistory.org/tribunearchives/city-hall-bombing-aftermath.

15. Michael Richardson, "J. Edgar Hoover and the Framing of the Omaha Two," *Crime Magazine*, December 28, 2011, http://www.crimemagazine.com/j-edgar-hoover-and-framing-omaha-two.

16. *FBI Records: The Vault*, https://vault.fbi.gov/cointel-pro/cointel-pro-black-extremists/cointelpro-black-extremists-part-01-of/view.

17. Elaine Brown, "'A Taste of Power': The Woman Who Led the Black Panther Party," *Longreads*, March 3, 2015, https://longreads.com/2015/03/03/a-taste-of-power-the-woman-who-led-the-Black-panther-party.

18. Nicholas Goldberg, "How the FBI and the Los Angeles Times Destroyed a Young Actress' Life 50 Years Ago," *Los Angeles Times*, June 7, 2020, https://www.latimes.com/opinion/story/2020-06-07/fbi-los-angeles-times-jean-seberg-50-years.

19. Author interviews with Cecil Moses (2018–2022).

20. According to author interviews with Cecil Moses (2018–2022) and Lee Colwell (February 14–15, 2020), FBI agents learned to keep the messy things inside the organization and to be compassionate when their colleagues were suspended for one infraction or another (in most cases, they viewed even the infractions as being in the interest of national security). When that happened, fellow agents passed the hat, collecting a full paycheck "down to the cent" and slipping the vital envelope into a colleague's home mailbox.

21. As winds of scandal gathered velocity in Washington, DC, a handful of journalists continued to push for access to more information about COINTELPRO and began winning court battles that required the reluctant FBI to make public additional secret documents.

22. Kelley and Davis, *Kelley*, 149.

23. Mark Felt would claim to be Deep Throat in a 2005 interview he gave with *Vanity Fair* magazine. John D. O'Connor, "'I'm the Guy They Called Deep.Throat,'" *Vanity Fair*, July 2005. However, other FBI sources would say that Deep Throat was a composite and that several FBI agents were leaking, not just one.

24. Kelley and Davis, *Kelley*, 152.

25. House Judiciary Committee, "Articles of Impeachment [July 27, 1974]," https:// watergate.info/impeachment/articles-of-impeachment.

26. For a thorough treatment of the Kent State Massacre, read Joseph Kelner and James Munves, *The Kent State Coverup* (New York: Harper & Row, 1980).

27. Author interviews with Cecil Moses (2018–2022).

28. Through a FOIA request, the author received FBI documents pertaining to the "Group of 12" (Bureau File 1404103-1) on November 15, 2019. This information is from a 1973 memo from Clarence Kelley.

29. Author interviews with Cecil Moses (2018–2022).

30. FBI FOIA, Group of 12 (Bureau File 1404103-1).

31. Author interview with Lee Colwell (February 14–15, 2020).

32. Jeremiah Kim, "James Baldwin, Anti-communism, and White Supremacy," Communist Party USA, May 14, 2020, https://www.cpusa.org/article/james-baldwin -anti-communism-and-white-supremacy/.

33. See the definitive account of Gary Thomas Rowe's work with the FBI in Gary May, *The Informant: The FBI, the Ku Klux Klan, and the Murder of Viola Liuzzo* (New Haven, CT: Yale Univ. Press, 2005). Also, there's an account of Rowe's activities in the Church Committee Report.

34. Church Committee Report, 127.

35. See the FBI's files on George Dorsett and Senator Robert Morgan (Bureau File: 62-116395). During his time as an informant, Dorsett had said, among other inflammatory things, "We don't intend to have any violence if we have to kill every n—— in America."

36. Office of the Inspector General, *The Federal Bureau of Investigation's Compliance with the Attorney General's Investigative Guidelines (Redacted)*, chap. 2, September 2005, https://oig.justice.gov/sites/default/files/archive/special/0509/chapter2.htm.

37. Kelley and Davis, *Kelley*, 312.

38. Office of the Inspector General, *The Federal Bureau of Investigation's Compliance with the Attorney General's Investigative Guidelines*.

39. Author interviews with Cecil Moses (2018–2022).

40. GTRC Final Report, "Greensboro Police Department and the 'Communist Problem,'" 125, cites a July 19, 1984, deposition with B. S. Ford in which he admits the department shredded files and specifically those related to Nelson Johnson.

41. US Senate, *COINTELPRO: The FBI's Covert Action Programs Against American Citizens*, April 1976, https://www.hsdl.org/?abstract&did=479830.

42. Kelley and Davis, *Kelley*, 177.

43. Author interview with Lee Colwell (February 14–15, 2020). This point of view was echoed also in interviews with Cecil Moses.

44. Colwell and Moses both expressed this opinion to the author. It's touched on at the end of Kelley and Davis, *Kelley*, 298–315.

45. Author interviews with Cecil Moses (2018–2022). Despite the OPE's significant work and Kelley's steadying hand, morale at the Bureau remained low. This, in combination with a new mandatory retirement age of fifty-five, led to an exodus of nearly three thousand agents in 1977.

46. Mark Felt—who later claimed to be Deep Throat—and Ed Miller were convicted and fined for authorizing agent break-ins at the homes of friends and family members of the Weather Underground.

47. Horace Beckwith's voice is heard on tape, trying to recruit Malcolm X, in the Netflix documentary *Who Killed Malcolm X?*, directed by Rachel Dretzin and Phil Bertelsen (2020).

48. Charles R. Babcock, "Agent Who Aided FBI's Self-Probe Escapes Firing," *Washington Post*, January 26, 1979, https://www.washingtonpost.com/archive/politics/1979/01/27/agent-who-aided-fibs-self-probe-escapes-firing/f291e6ba-2b1b-4c49-ae91-d3f76d0df341/.

CHAPTER 22: ELECTRIC

1. Author interviews with Nelson and Joyce Johnson (2017–2022) and Howard Fuller (January 23, 2019; February 20, 2019).

2. Author interviews with Nelson and Joyce Johnson (2017–2022), Signe Waller Foxworth (2017–2020), and Paul and Sally Bermanzohn (May 11, 2018). See also Waller, *Love and Revolution*, 81–84.

3. Author interviews with Nelson Johnson (2017–2022) and Howard Fuller (January 23, 2019; February 20, 2019); see also Bermanzohn and Bermanzohn, *The True Story of the Greensboro Massacre*, 116–17.

4. Author interviews with Nelson and Joyce Johnson (2017–2022).

5. Waller, *Love and Revolution*, 82; author interviews with Signe Waller Foxworth (2017–2020).

6. In addition to author interviews with Nelson and Joyce Johnson and Dennis Torigoe (April 1, 2020), the WVO's position on busing is laid out in this article: "The Boston Forced Busing Plan: The Dialectics of Bourgeois Formal Democracy and Fascism," *Workers Viewpoint* 2, no. 1 (May 1975), https://www.marxists.org/history/erol/ncm-1a/wvo-busing.htm.

7. Waller, *Love and Revolution*, 82–85; Fuller, *No Struggle, No Progress*, 159.

8. Fuller, *No Struggle, No Progress*, 159. Author interviews with Howard Fuller and Nelson Johnson confirmed the threats and paranoia of the time.

9. Bermanzohn, *Through Survivors' Eyes*, 134; author interview with Paul and Sally Bermanzohn (May 11, 2018).

10. Bermanzohn, *Through Survivors' Eyes*, 122. Nelson would, in fact, say he'd been racist against white people.

11. Author interviews with Paul and Sally Bermanzohn (May 18, 2018) and Nelson and Joyce Johnson (2017–2022).

12. Author interview with Paul Bermanzohn (May 11, 2018).

13. Author interview with Paul and Sally Bermanzohn (May 11, 2018).

14. Kelley and Davis, *Kelley*, 163.

15. International Workingmen's Association, "Address of the International Working Men's Association to Abraham Lincoln, President of the United States of America," presented to US Ambassador Charles Francis Adams, January 28, 1865, https://www .marxists.org/archive/marx/iwma/documents/1864/lincoln-letter.htm.

16. Du Bois, *Black Reconstruction in America*, 345.

17. Rob Christensen, *The Paradox of Tar Heel Politics* (Chapel Hill: Univ. of North Carolina Press, 2010). See also Nick Martin's illuminating "State of Union" 2018 series of articles on North Carolina politics in *Splinter News*, https://www.splinter.com/state-of -the-nation. Both trace the long positive and negative legacies of Southern Democrat policies in North Carolina.

18. Du Bois, *Black Reconstruction in America*, 26.

19. Author interview with Burley Mitchell (May 25, 2018).

20. Nelson Johnson FBI file, GCRF Records (4630), folder 1025, 24.

21. Author interviews with Nelson, Joyce, and Ayo Johnson (2017–2022); WVO Bolshevik Committee article in Beloved Community Center Archive.

CHAPTER 23: LABOR

1. Author interviews with Joyce Johnson (2017–2022).

2. Author interview with Sally Bermanzohn (May 11, 2018).

3. Waller, *Love and Revolution*, 122.

4. Bermanzohn, *Through Survivors' Eyes*, 139–42; Waller, *Love and Revolution*, 118–24.

5. A summary of Joe Judge's trial is found here, accessed April 14, 2024: https://archive .org/stream/nummonews4197unse/nummonews4197unse_djvu.txt.

6. Hicks Fripp, *Greensboro: A Chosen Center*, 100–101; Arnet and Jackson, *Greensboro, North Carolina*.

7. "Mill Village Way of Life Is Bygone Era," *Greensboro News & Record*, May 18, 1991, updated January 25, 2015, https://greensboro.com/mill-village-way-of-life-is-bygone-era /article_34be617d-b2ad-5b55-a4f8-698e1bc6752d.html.

8. Neal, "Hiding in Plain Sight"; Elizabeth Gillespie McRae, "White Patriots of North Carolina," *Encyclopedia of North Carolina*, ed. William S. Powell (Chapel Hill, NC: Univ. of North Carolina Press, 2006), https://www.ncpedia.org/white-patriots-north -carolina.

9. Author interview with former mill executive Chip Berry (February 12, 2021).

10. Author interview with Chip Berry on how the city actually operated (February 12, 2021). As a young man working in those country club rooms, Chip Berry witnessed the mill executives' fear of the WVO.

11. Barry Hirsch, David Macpherson, and William Even, "Union Membership, Coverage, and Earnings from the CPS," January 16, 2024, https://www.unionstats.com/.

12. Bermanzohn, *Through Survivors' Eyes*, 148–51; Bermanzohn and Bermanzohn, *The True Story of the Greensboro Massacre*, 135–68.

13. Waller, *Love and Revolution*, 142.

14. See Signe Waller, *A City of Two Tales: The Greensboro Massacre of November 3, 1979, in Fact, Context, and Meaning* (2005), 137, https://gateway.uncg.edu/islandora/object

/mss%3A232693#page/1/mode/1up. This self-published piece establishes a link between Cone's private security and the police.

15. Author interview with Chip Berry (February 12, 2021). Author interviews with former GPD officer Greg Brooks confirmed the relationship between the police and private security at the mills (2018–2024).

16. Rick Gray, "Cone, ACTWU Both Opposed to ROC," *Greensboro Daily News*, May 22, 1977, C3.

17. Waller, *Love and Revolution*, 151. Jim had been on the ground offering medical support at major protests around the United States for a decade, including the Democratic National Convention in Chicago in 1968 and Wounded Knee in South Dakota in 1973.

18. Waller, *Love and Revolution*, 154–58; Bermanzohn, *Through Survivors Eyes*, 154–58.

19. Bermanzohn, *Through Survivors' Eyes*, 154–58; Waller, *Love and Revolution*, 152–60.

20. Waller, *Love and Revolution*, 157.

21. Waller, *Love and Revolution*, 180–81; Bermanzohn, *Through Survivors' Eyes*, 153; author interview with Chip Berry (February 12, 2021).

22. Waller, *Love and Revolution*, 160; author interview with Sally Bermanzohn (May 11, 2018).

23. Author interviews with Nelson Johnson (2017–2022), Paul and Sally Bermanzohn (May 11, 2018), and Signe Waller Foxworth (2017–2020).

24. Waller, *Love and Revolution*, 187.

25. Copies of these flyers are in the Beloved Community Center archive and the GCRF archive at UNCG. Compelling arguments have been made that Lyndon LaRouche may have been an intelligence asset for the CIA or other US intelligence agencies, particularly in Matthew Sweet's book *Operation Chaos: The Vietnam Deserters Who Fought the CIA, the Brainwashers, and Themselves* (New York: Henry Holt & Company, 2018).

26. City Council of Greensboro meeting minutes, June 18, 1979.

27. Author interview with Martha Woodall (March 13, 2018). The author tried multiple times to interview Jim Melvin. When I finally got him on the phone in January 2018, he ranted at me, questioning why anyone would dig up this history, but declined to sit for a formal interview.

28. Chip Berlet, *The Hunt for Red Menace: How Government Intelligence Agencies and Private Right-Wing Groups Target Dissidents and Leftists as Subversive Terrorists and Outlaws*, revised ed. (Somerville, MA: Political Research Associates, 1994), 67.

29. Waller, *Love and Revolution*, 188. Also, the Institute for Southern Studies, in *The Third of November*, and Dwight Stone, in "The 1979 Greensboro Killings" (thesis, Princeton University, 1990), argue that the Revolutionary Communist Party's violent confrontations caused confusion and urgency within the Greensboro Police Department.

CHAPTER 24: CHINA GROVE

1. Stone, "The 1979 Greensboro Killings," 83.

2. Wayne King, "Klan Fights Leftists and Nazis at Its Exhibit," *New York Times*, February 27, 1979, https://www.nytimes.com/1979/02/27/archives/klan-fights-leftists-and

-nazis-at-its-exhibit-called-it-endorsement.html; Natalie Wexler, "Klan Exhibit Closed by Violence," *Winston-Salem Journal*, February 27, 1979, 1.

3. Lindsey Gruson and Charles Babington, "The Shootout: Many Roads Led to Armed Conflict Here," *Greensboro Daily News*, A1, A12; Mae Israel and Dwight Cunningham, "Johnson Traces Struggles from Equality for Blacks to Battling Capitalism," *Greensboro Daily News*, December 9, 1979, A12; Lindsey Gruson, "District Attorney Says He's 'Caught In Middle of a No-Win Situation,'" December 9, 1979, A12.

4. Brenda A. Russell, "Southern Justice: 1978," *Harvard Crimson*, October 21, 1978, https://www.thecrimson.com/article/1978/10/21/southern-justice-1978-pbtbommy-lee-hines/.

5. Wayne King, "2 Klansmen and a Black Woman Are Shot in a Street Clash in Alabama," *New York Times*, May 27, 1979, 26.

6. Wayne King, "Klan and Blacks March Through Tense Decatur," *New York Times*, June 10, 1979, 26; Waller, *Love and Revolution*, 192–93; Bermanzohn, *Through Survivors' Eyes*, 182.

7. *Robinson v. State*, 430 So. 2d 883 (Ala. Crim. App. 1983), https://casetext.com/case/robinson-v-state-2131.

8. Waller, *Love and Revolution*, 191.

9. Author interviews with Nelson and Joyce Johnson (2017–2022) and Paul and Sally Bermanzohn (May 11, 2018).

10. GCRF Records (4630), file 1797, "Series 3 Grand Jury Hearings: Section X– Interview of Witnesses–China Grove." In his FBI interview on April 15, 1982, Paul Luckey accuses Nelson Johnson of being more aggressive and confrontational. His accusations appear out of character and like a smear on Nelson Johnson's character. Nelson Johnson, meanwhile, says Luckey proposed violence. Confidential interviews by the Truth and Reconciliation Commission with residents of China Grove support Nelson Johnson's version of events. Luckey would later be called as a defense witness for the Klan and Nazis in both the federal criminal and federal civil trials.

11. According to the TRC researchers, the FBI interviewed a Klansman named James Mason who said that Klansman Joe Grady had friends in the China Grove Sheriff's department. Special Agents Brereton and Lowe, interview with James Allen Mason at Cleveland Field Office, CE 44A-3527 (November 12–13, 1981), 3–4.

12. Waller, *Love and Revolution*, 195.

13. "Bad Medicine for the Klan: North Carolina Indians Break Up Ku Kluxers' Anti-Indian Meeting," *Life*, January 27, 1958, 26–28, https://books.google.com/books?id=5VUEAAAAMBAJ&pg=26#v=onepage&q&f=false.

14. David Cunningham quotes Key on page 26 of his book *Klansville, U.S.A.* He sources the quote to Key's seminal book, *Southern Politics in State and Nation* (Knoxville: Univ. of Tennessee Press, 1984).

15. See Cunningham, *Klansville, U.S.A.*

16. Waller, *Love and Revolution*, 193–99; Bermanzohn, *Through Survivors' Eyes*, 185–91; *The Third of November*, 3–4; "Film Screening Prelude to Klan/Nazi Shooting, 1979," North Carolina Department of Natural and Cultural Resources, July 8, 2016, https://www.dncr.nc.gov/blog/2016/07/08/film-screening-prelude-klannazi-shooting-1979.

17. Waller, *Love and Revolution*, 197.

18. Joseph Gorrell Pierce, GTRC statement, July 16, 2005, Greensboro, North Carolina, https://greensborotrc.org/hear_statements.php.

19. Joseph Gorrell Pierce, GTRC statement; Bermanzohn, *Through Survivors' Eyes*, 4; Waller, *Love and Revolution*, 203.

20. Joseph Gorrell Pierce, GTRC statement.

21. Bermanzohn, *Through Survivors' Eyes*, 188.

22. Wheaton, *Codename Greenkil*, 88.

23. Author interviews with Joyce Johnson (2017–2022).

24. Sally Bermanzohn, unpublished interview with May (August 1990), 9, 11.

25. *The Third of November*, 4.

26. Sally Bermanzohn, unpublished interview with Marty Nathan (January 1990), 15.

27. Sally Bermanzohn, unpublished interview with Marty Nathan (January 1990), 15.

CHAPTER 25: BANNERS

1. Waller, *Love and Revolution*, 250.

2. Scism, "Four Die in Klan-Leftist Shootout."

3. Waller, *Love and Revolution*, 257.

4. Bermanzohn and Bermanzohn, *The True Story of the Greensboro Massacre*, 222.

5. Adam Zucker, dir., *Greensboro: Closer to the Truth* (2007).

6. Wikipedia, s.v. "Nightline," updated February 4, 2024, https://en.wikipedia.org/wiki/Nightline; "News Summary," *New York Times*, November 5, 1979, https://www.nytimes.com/1979/11/05/archives/news-summary-international.html.

7. Governor James B. Hunt Jr. Speeches, November 1, 1979–November 30, 1979, "Statement: November 17, 1979, News Conference—Carter, Iran," North Carolina State Archives.

8. Du Bois, *Black Reconstruction in America*, 713.

9. For an authoritative account, see Stephen Kinzer, *All the Shah's Men: An American Coup and the Roots of Middle East Terror*, 2nd ed. (Hoboken, NJ: John Wiley & Sons, 2008).

10. Reuters, "Teheran Students Seize U.S. Embassy and Hold Hostages," *New York Times*, November 5, 1979, https://www.nytimes.com/1979/11/05/archives/teheran-students-seize-us-embassy-and-hold-hostages-ask-shahs.html.

11. Editorial, "Let It Pass," *Greensboro Daily News*, November 9, 1979, A4.

12. Waller, *Love and Revolution*, 279.

13. Waller, *Love and Revolution*, 257.

14. Author interview with Earl Tockman (December 12, 2017).

15. Waller, *Love and Revolution*, 264; Jack Scism, "Funeral March Is Peaceful," *Greensboro Daily News*, November 12, 1979, A1, A5.

16. Author interview with Burley Mitchell (May 25, 2018).

17. Author interview with Burley Mitchell (May 25, 2018).

18. Author interview with Burley Mitchell (May 25, 2018).

19. Author interviews with Cecil Moses (2018–2022) and with people who were arrested and wish to remain anonymous; Wheaton, *Codename GreenKil*, 177.

20. Sally Bermanzohn, unpublished interview with Liz (November 1, 1989), 10.

21. Sally Bermanzohn, unpublished interview with Nelson Johnson (October 9, 1989), 8.

22. Rosie Stevens, "Johnson Poses an Enigma in Struggle," *Carolina Peacemaker*, November 24, 1979, 1.

23. Stevens, "Johnson Poses an Enigma in Struggle."

24. Bermanzohn, *Through Survivors' Eyes*, 248.

25. Author interviews with Nelson Johnson (2017–2022).

26. Author interviews with Nelson Johnson (2017–2022).

27. Sally Bermanzohn, unpublished interview with Shirley (August 1991), 19.

28. Kenwin Coranna, "Memories of Morningside: Decades Later, Deadly Clash in Greensboro Community Still Resonates," *Greensboro News & Record*, December 6, 2020, https://greensboro.com/news/crime/memories-of-morningside-decades-later-deadly-clash-in-greensboro-community-still-resonates/article_0d323948-1867-11eb-b103-dfe501bb6382.html.

29. Bermanzohn and Bermanzohn, *The True Story of the Greensboro Massacre*, 231–38.

30. Associated Press, "Klansman Turns Self In," *Greensboro Daily News*, November 12, 1979, A5.

31. Anthony Lewis, "Free Speech and Provocation Can Be Hard to Separate," *New York Times*, November 11, 1979, https://www.nytimes.com/1979/11/11/archives/free-speech-and-provocation-can-be-hard-to-separate.html.

32. Joyce Johnson, GTRC statement.

33. Author interviews with Ayo Johnson (2017–2022).

CHAPTER 26: POLITICS

1. Howard Troxler and David McKinnon, "5th Shootout Victim Dies; 14 Defendants Denied Bail," *Raleigh News and Observer*, November 6, 1979, 1, 6.

2. Mae Israel, "Abuse Charged, Denied," *Greensboro Daily News*, December 15, 1978, A1, A14.

3. Brent Hackney, "Rumors of Divorce Floated During DA Race," *Greensboro Daily News*, December 16, 1978, B1, B11; Steve Berry and Mae Israel, "Judge Kivett Orders Return of Schlosser Divorce Complaint," *Greensboro Daily News*, December 15, 1978, A1, A14; Israel, "Abuse Charged, Denied."

4. Editorial, "Schlosser for DA," *Greensboro Daily News*, November 1, 1978, A6.

5. Steve Berry, "Schlosser Blames Alexander for 'Justice Maze,'" *Greensboro Daily News*, April 26, 1978, D1.

6. Editorial, "Schlosser for DA," A6. Guilford County wouldn't elect its first African American district attorney until 2018. When she was elected, Avery Crump also became the first woman district attorney of Guilford County.

7. Mae Israel, "Schlosser Praises Staff at Swearing-In Ceremony," *Greensboro Daily News*, January 3, 1979, B2.

8. Jennifer Fernandez, "Jim Coman, Former SBI Director Prosecutor in Klan-Nazi Shootings, Has Died," *Greensboro News & Record*, September 2, 2018, https://greensboro .com/news/local_news/jim-coman-former-sbi-director-prosecutor-in-klan-nazi -shootings-has-died/article_bd05c813-3be2-51ec-ade4-d2d814c36783.html.

9. Author interviews with Rick Greeson (May 3, 2019) and Michael Schlosser (2018–2020).

10. Wheaton, *Codename Greenkil*, 3; author interviews with Cecil Moses (2018–2022).

11. Author interviews with Rick Greeson (May 3, 2019) and Michael Schlosser (2018–2020).

12. TRC interview with Jim Coman, Rick Greeson, and Mike Schlosser (August 4, 2005).

13. TRC interview with Jim Coman, Rick Greeson, and Mike Schlosser (August 4, 2005).

14. Lindsey Gruson, "The Shootout: Many Roads Led to Armed Conflict Here," *Greensboro Daily News*, December 9, 1979, A1, A12.

15. All letters referenced in this section can be found in the North Carolina State Archives, Governor James B. Hunt Jr. General Correspondence, 1980. Unfortunately, Governor Hunt's communications with the FBI and SBI around the November 3, 1979, shooting have been removed from the files, though the folders themselves remain, indicating that they held documents at some point.

16. Author interview with Governor James B. Hunt Jr. (January 25, 2018).

17. Allen W. Trelease, *White Terror: The Ku Klux Klan Conspiracy and Southern Reconstruction*, reprint ed. (Westport, CT: Praeger, 1979 [1971]), 63.

18. Governor James B. Hunt Jr. Speeches, North Carolina State Archives; Jack Betts, "Hunt Ousts Protesters at Briefing," *Greensboro Daily News*, July 24, 1980, D1, D14.

19. Associated Press, "Grand Dragon Says Klan Endorsing Hunt Re-election," *Greensboro Daily News*, January 7, 1980, B1.

20. Author interview with Rick Greeson (May 3, 2019).

21. Author interview with Rick Greeson (May 3, 2019).

22. Author interviews with Michael Schlosser (2018–2020).

23. Bermanzohn, *Through Survivors' Eyes*, 251; see also Wayne Slater, "Sampson: Did Early Promise Go Wrong?," *Greensboro Daily News*, November 20, 1979, A1, A5.

24. Author interviews with Nelson Johnson (2017–2022); see also Sally Bermanzohn's unpublished interviews with Marty Nathan (January 1990) and Dale Sampson Levin (October 7, 1989).

25. Sydney Nathans, "Case Deserves a Special Prosecutor," *Greensboro Daily News*, December 12, 1979, A6.

26. Waller, *Love and Revolution*, 289. Some hoped this march would be the beginning of a new age of civil rights activity.

27. Waller, *Love and Revolution*, 297.

28. "Greensboro Anti-Klan March Attracts 3,500," *Gastonia Gazette*, February 3, 1980, A4; Lindey Gruson, "Marchers: Leftist 'Iceberg' Emerges, Unites," *Greensboro Daily News*, February 4, 1980, A1, A8.

29. Staff, "CWP Head Plans Write-In Candidacy For Governor," *Greensboro Daily News*, May 17, 1980, A13.

30. William March, "Justice Clears Police of Criminal Wrongdoing," *Greensboro Daily News*, April, 30, 1980, A1, A9.

31. March, "Justice Clears Police of Criminal Wrongdoing," A1, A9. At least one Greensboro City Council member, John Forbis, expressed disappointment that the DoJ didn't "tell the citizens . . . their police had performed well. . . . We've got a heck of a good police department here. . . . Everything I've seen indicates to me that our folks acted properly, in a wartime situation."

32. March, "Justice Clears Police of Criminal Wrongdoing," A1, A9.

33. Steve Berry, "6 CWP Members, 2 Klansmen Indicted on Rioting Charges," *Greensboro Daily News*, May 3, 1980, A1, A9. Klansmen and Nazis in the state murder trial included David Wayne Matthews, Roland Wayne Wood, Jerry Paul Smith, Lawrence Gene Morgan (likely Nelson's assailant), Coleman Blair Pridmore, and Jack Wilson Fowler Jr.

34. Waller, *Love and Revolution*, 305.

35. Nathans, "Case Deserves a Special Prosecutor," A6.

36. The CWP argued against the simplistic, black-and-white narrative of "Klan versus communist." This did not mean the CWP members thought that the Klan and Nazi shooters were innocent, but convicting a few poor white men wasn't going to solve the real issues at hand. But now the prosecution's charges against the six CWP members put them in a difficult situation regarding the trial against the killers. Even if the CWP members saw some value, however incomplete, in convicting the shooters, any testimony they might provide in that trial against the Klan and Nazis could, they believed, be used against them in a felony riot trial, making it too risky for them to participate in the "sham" trial.

CHAPTER 27: CHARGED

1. Waller, *Love and Revolution*, 309.

2. Jim Schlosser and Rick Stewart, "CWP Stirs Up Battle Outside Courtroom," *Greensboro Record*, June 16, 1980, A1, A2.

3. Author interview with Rick Greeson (May 3, 2019).

4. Schlosser and Stewart, "CWP Stirs Up Battle Outside Courtroom," A1, A2; Waller, *Love and Revolution*, 309–12.

5. Schlosser and Stewart, "CWP Stirs Up Battle Outside Courtroom," A1, A2.

6. Schlosser and Stewart, "CWP Stirs Up Battle Outside Courtroom," A1, A2.

7. Author interviews with Nelson Johnson (2017–2022).

8. Author interview with Rick Greeson (May 3, 2019).

9. GTRC Final Report, chap. 10, "Injustice in the Justice System," May 26, 2006, 264.

10. TRC interview with Jim Coman, Rick Greeson, and Mike Schlosser (August 4, 2005).

11. Author interview with Rick Greeson (May 3, 2019).

12. Waller, *Love and Revolution*, 313.

13. Waller, *Love and Revolution*, 284.

14. Author interviews with Nelson Johnson (2017–2022).

CHAPTER 28: REVELATIONS

1. Author interview with Martha Woodall (March 13, 2018).

2. Martha Woodall, "Nazis Shift to Raleigh—but Add a Threat to City," *Greensboro Record*, February 20, 1980, A1, A3. See also Lindsey Gruson, "Covington's Strong Showing Disturbs GOP," *Greensboro Daily News*, May 8, 1980, A1, A13, for primary election results.

3. Woodall, "Nazis Shift to Raleigh—but Add a Threat to City," A1, A3.

4. Author interview with Martha Woodall (March 13, 2018).

5. This whole scene with Wood is drawn from Woodall's article: Martha Woodall, "Death Detours Wood in His Cause Pursuit," *Greensboro Record*, March 25, 1980, A1, A8.

6. Information on Wood's alleged violent and illegal activity from the Bureau of Alcohol, Tabacco, and Firearms report (October 2, 1978) found in the GCRF Records (4630), file 990. In fact, according to the BATF, it was Wood's activity that led them to open the investigation and put Bernard Butkovich undercover with the Winston-Salem Nazi unit. These white power advocates also discussed overthrowing the US government. Jerome Adams's unpublished book on the Greensboro Massacre, *Old Conflicts, Young Deaths: the Greensboro Killings*, found in the TRC Archives at Bennett College, also provides valuable background on Roland Wayne Wood, including the information on his time selling "second-hand pornographic magazines," 139.

7. Author interview with Martha Woodall (March 13, 2018).

8. Bob Raissman, "Organizer Says Victims Were Marked," *Winston-Salem Journal*, November 6, 1979, 2.

9. Author interview with Martha Woodall (March 13, 2018).

10. Author interview with Martha Woodall (March 13, 2018); author interview with Larry Gibson (July 3, 2024).

11. Martha Woodall, "Top ATF Officials Gave Infiltration OK," *Greensboro Record*, July 28, 1980, A1, A2.

12. Martha Woodall, "Nazis Say Federal Agent Infiltrated Unit, Knew of Plans for Nov. 3 Motorcade," *Greensboro Record*, July 14, 1980, A1, A2; Martha Woodall, "Rules Differ for AFT [*sic*] Agents Involved in Undercover Work," *Greensboro Record*, July 14, 1980, A1, A3: "It is against the law for undercover agents to act as provocateurs. Recent, stringent guidelines have been imposed to cover FBI undercover activities, but many of the restrictions have not been extended to the ATF. Reports of past abuses by FBI agents and their paid informers led to the tighter controls."

13. Meredith Barkley, "Judge Studying Allowing Documents as Evidence," *Greensboro News & Record*, May 17, 1985, D6.

14. Betts, "Hunt Ousts Protesters at Briefing," D1, D14.

15. Waller, *Love and Revolution*, 319.

16. GTRC Final Report, chap. 10, "Injustice in the Justice System," 262.

17. Lindsey Gruson, "Klan Rally Planners Included Police Informant," *Greensboro Daily News*, August 3, 1980, A1, A9.

18. *The Third of November*, 31; author interview with Rick Greeson (May 3, 2019).

19. GCRF Records, audiocassette C-4630/5 and 6, "Ed Dawson Tape." The author also listened to Eddie Dawson's recording of this call in the GCRF archives at the University of North Carolina Greensboro.

CHAPTER 29: PITTS

1. Silkwood's story would be made into the 1983 movie *Silkwood*, starring Meryl Streep and directed by Mike Nichols.

2. Author interviews with Lewis Pitts (2017–2024); draft of Jason Langberg, *The Life of a Movement Lawyer: Lewis Pitts and the Struggle for Democracy, Equality, and Justice* (Columbia: Univ. of South Carolina Press, 2024).

3. Author interviews with Lewis Pitts (2017–2024).

4. Langberg, *Life of a Movement Lawyer.*

5. Jack Betts, "Greensboro CWP Members Disrupt Convention," *Greensboro Daily News*, August 15, 1980, 1, 10.

6. Waller, *Love and Revolution*, 328.

CHAPTER 30: TRIAL

1. Waller, *Love and Revolution*, 319.

2. Michael Schlosser, Jim Coman, and Rick Greeson interview with the Greensboro Truth and Reconciliation Commission, August 4, 2005. Steve Berry, "Defense: Clients Ambushed," *Greensboro Daily News*, August 5, 1980, A1, A3.

3. Author interview with Rick Greeson (May 3, 2019).

4. Berry, "Defense: Clients Ambushed," A1, A3.

5. Berry, "Defense: Clients Ambushed," A1, A3.

6. Berry, "Defense: Clients Ambushed," A1, A3.

7. Author interview with Rick Greeson (May 3, 2019).

8. FBI file CE 44-3527, vol. II "Beckwith Report," 31–72; GCRF Records (4630), folders 1590–91.

9. Author interview with Rick Greeson (May 3, 2019).

10. Author interview with Rick Greeson (May 3, 2019).

11. Steve Berry, "Jurors View Videotape of Witness Under Hypnosis," *Greensboro Daily News*, August 20, 1980: A1, A16.

12. The widows would claim that the prosecutors never invited them to testify. Greeson and Coman would angrily contradict this, saying they certainly had. It's possible that the CWP lawyers never passed along the request.

13. Author interview with Rick Greeson (May 3, 2019); GTRC Final Report, chap. 10, "Injustice in the Justice System," 267.

14. Waller, *Love and Revolution*, 340; Jim Wicker, "Jailer: Killings Admitted," *Greensboro Record*, August 28, 1980, A1.

15. GTRC Final Report, chap. 10, "Injustice in the Justice System," 272–74.

16. Author interview with Rick Greeson (May 3, 2019).

17. Steve Berry, "Defense Argues Communists' Shots Began Fatal Battle," *Greensboro Daily News*, October 30, 1980, B5.

18. Author interview with Rick Greeson (May 3, 2019); Michael Schlosser, Jim Coman, and Rick Greeson interview with the Greensboro Truth and Reconciliation Commission (August 4, 2005).

19. Steve Berry, "Witness Says Waller Wanted 'Martyr,'" *Greensboro Daily News*, October 14, 1980, B1.

20. Waller, *Love and Revolution*, 345–46.

21. GCRF Records (4630), folder 1999; *Waller v. Butkovich*, Plaintiff's Second Amended Complaint, 4; author interviews with Lewis Pitts (2017–2024).

22. Jack Scism, "CWP Files Lawsuit Charging Conspiracy," *Greensboro Daily News*, November 4, 1980, B2.

23. Author interview with Robert Lackey (July 8, 2019).

24. Author interview with Robert Lackey (July 8, 2019).

25. Author interview with Octavio Manduley Almaguer, the son of the juror (June 17, 2019).

26. Author interview with Octavio Manduley Almaguer (June 17, 2019).

27. Author interview with Robert Lackey (July 8, 2019).

28. Author interview with Robert Lackey (July 8, 2019).

29. GTRC Final Report, chap. 10, "Injustice in the Justice System," 276; author interviews with Robert Lackey (July 8, 2019) and Octavio Manduley Almaguer (June 17, 2019).

30. Author interview with Robert Lackey (July 8, 2019).

31. Wicker, "Jailer: Killings Admitted," A1.

32. Steve Berry, "Shootout Verdict: Not Guilty," *Greensboro Daily News*, November 18, 1980, A1, A13.

33. Berry, "Shootout Verdict: Not Guilty," A1, A13.

34. Author interviews with Nelson Johnson (2017–2022).

35. GTRC Final Report, chap. 10, "Injustice in the Justice System," 279.

36. Author interviews with Rick Greeson (May 3, 2019) and Jim Coman (January 22, 2018).

37. Author interview with Rick Greeson (May 3, 2019).

38. Author interviews with Nelson Johnson (2017–2022).

CHAPTER 31: KLAN ACTS

1. Ronald Reagan, "Inaugural Address 1981," January 20, 1981, https://www.reagan library.gov/archives/speech/inaugural-address-1981.

2. "Hearing before the Subcommittee on Crime of the Committee on the Judiciary, House of Representatives, Ninety-Sixth Congress, Second Session, on Increasing Violence Against Minorities" (hereafter referred to as "Conyers Hearings"). Hearings were held on

December 9, 1980, March 4, 1981, June 3, 1981, and November 12, 1981. Arthur Kinoy testimony, December 9, 1980, 25; Althea T. L. Simmons statement, December 9, 1980, 116.

3. Conyers Hearings, Kinoy testimony, 27.

4. Drew S. Days III, "Turning Back the Clock: The Reagan Administration and Civil Rights," *Harvard Civil Rights–Civil Liberties Law Review* 19 (1984): 309.

5. In other words, the DoJ denied that it had a role in affirming and increasing Americans' rights and was willing only to correct current, demonstrably intentional biases, not legacy wrongs.

6. *The Third of November*, 33.

7. Ed Hatcher, "Nov. 3 Rally Indictments Are Asked," *Greensboro Daily News*, June 25, 1981, A1, A12.

8. See Bermanzohn, *Through Survivors' Eyes*, 281, for the backstory.

9. Larry King, "Johnson on Jail Hunger Strike?," *Greensboro Daily News*, August 4, 1981, B1.

10. "Letter from Nelson Johnson to Editor," July 29, 1981, https://gateway.uncg.edu /islandora/object/mss%3A146650#page/2/mode/1up.

11. Bob Hiles, "CWP Leader Nelson Johnson Leaves Jail," *Greensboro Daily News*, August 18, 1981, B2.

12. "U.S. Attorney Recommends Prosecution in Greensboro Massacre Case," press release, Greensboro Justice Fund, June 25, 1981, https://gateway.uncg.edu/islandora /object/mss%3A146509#page/1/mode/1up.

13. Conyers Hearings, William Van Alstyne testimony, November 12, 1981, 399.

14. Conyers Hearings, Van Alstyne testimony, 399.

15. Conyers Hearings, November 12, 1981, 362–63.

CHAPTER 32: COAT

1. GCRF Records (4630), Series 4, folder 2865, internal GCRF documents.

2. Author interviews with Michael Johnson (April–May 2018).

3. "Letter from Attorney Lewis Pitts to U.S. Attorney General William Smith," March 24, 1982, https://gateway.uncg.edu/islandora/object/mss%3A146496#page/1/mode /1up.

4. Author interviews with Michael Johnson (April–May 2018).

5. Waller, *Love and Revolution*, 398.

6. Meredith Barkley, "Judge Studying Allowing Documents as Evidence," *Greensboro News & Record*, May 17, 1985, D6.

7. Sally Bermanzohn, unpublished interview with Marty Nathan (January 1990), 33.

8. GCRF Records (4630), folders 1349–63, grand jury depositions of Joyce Johnson and Nelson Johnson.

9. Henry C. Byrd Sr.'s letter, February 14, 1983, provided to the author from Lewis Pitts's personal archive.

10. Henry C. Byrd Sr.'s letter, February 14, 1983; Larry King, "Man Charged with Perjury Will Get Hearing," *Greensboro Daily News*, June 14, 1983, A4.

11. The name of this officer in the trial transcript of *United States of America v. Henry C. Byrd, Sr.* and when he was a member of the GPD was Raymond Neil Bell. He now goes by Ramon Neil Bell.

12. These details are from Henry C. Byrd Sr.'s letter to Nelson Johnson in Lewis Pitts's personal archive. These details are reproduced in the affidavit read into the record in *United States of America v. Henry C. Byrd, Sr.*, US Court of Appeals, Middle District of North Carolina, Greensboro Division, 449–52.

13. Author interviews with Lewis Pitts (2017–2024).

14. Author interviews with Lewis Pitts (2017–2024). A copy of the affidavit can be found in the record in *United States of America v. Henry C. Byrd, Sr.*

15. *United States of America v. Henry C. Byrd, Sr.*, trial transcript.

16. Larry King, "Nine Indicted in Nov. 3 Probe," *Greensboro Daily News*, April 22, 1983, A1, A8.

17. Author interview with Henry C. Byrd Sr.'s lawyer, Robert Warren (2018).

18. *United States of America v. Henry C. Byrd, Sr.*, record, 84.

19. Author interviews with Lewis Pitts (2017–2024). In an affidavit dated March 17, 1985 (GCRF Records [4630], folder 2700), Byrd said that he was bullied and tricked by Brereton into giving inconsistent and contradictory statements to the grand jury.

20. Author interviews with Michael Johnson (April–May 2018).

21. GTRC Final Report, chap. 10, "Injustice in the Justice System," 287–88.

22. Despite this important admission, Michael Johnson still didn't consider applying statute 241, which would have required proof of conspiracy but not racial malice.

23. Rebecca Ragsdale, "Sherer Gives Testimony in Klan Trial," *Greensboro Daily News*, February 1, 1984, B1, B8. This article discusses Mark Sherer's retractions on the witness stand of his grand jury testimony. Larry King, "Klan Pair Plotted to Kill Witness," *Greensboro Record*, May 5, 1983, A1, A3. This article discusses how Virgil Griffin and Dave Matthews intimidated potential Klan witnesses, which might have caused Sherer to change his testimony. Rebecca Ragsdale and Donald Patterson, "Sherer Says Klan Plotted Assassination," *Greensboro Record*, February 2, 1984, C1, C2.

24. *United States of America v. Virgil L. Griffin, et al.*, closing argument by Jim D. Cooley, Esq., before the Honorable Thomas A. Flannery, Winston-Salem, North Carolina, April 11, 1984, record, 80.

25. *United States of America v. Virgil L. Griffin, et al.*, closing argument by Cooley, 112.

26. *United States of America v. Virgil L. Griffin, et al.*, closing argument by Cooley, 113.

27. Author interview with Rick Greeson (May 3, 2019).

28. Vincent Taylor, "250 Hold Greensboro March to Protest Klan-Nazi Acquittals," *Greensboro News & Record*, May 6, 1984, C2. US Representative John Conyers, in a letter read at a mass rally in Greensboro on May 5, 1984, said that the acquittals made a "mockery of our judicial system."

29. Author interviews with Nelson Johnson (2017–2022).

30. Bermanzohn, *Through Survivors' Eyes*, 312.

31. Joyce Johnson, GTRC statement; author interviews with Joyce Johnson (2017–2022).

32. Author interviews with Nelson Johnson (2017–2022).

33. "The New Communist Movement: Collapse and Aftermath," *Encyclopedia of Anti-revisionism On-Line*, accessed April 13, 2024, https://www.marxists.org/history/erol/ncm-7/index.htm.

34. Author interviews with Nelson and Joyce Johnson (2017–2022).

CHAPTER 33: DISCOVERY

1. Ronald Bacigal, *May It Please the Court: A Biography of Judge Robert R. Merhige, Jr.* (Lanham, MD: University Press of America, 1992).

2. Author interview with Adeeb Fadil (March 13, 2021); Mary Kelly Tate, "Personal Reflections on the Honorable Robert R. Merhige, Jr.: A Judge, Mentor, and Friend," *University of Richmond Law Review Online* 52 (2017): 17, https://lawreview.richmond.edu/2017/09/28/personal-reflections-on-the-honorable-robert-r-merhige-jr-a-judge-mentor-and-friend/.

3. Marty Nathan, as quoted in Langberg, *Life of a Movement Lawyer*.

4. Author interview with Robert Warren (2018).

5. Waller, *Love and Revolution*, 388.

6. GCRF Records (4630), folder 1999, *Waller v. Butkovich*, Plaintiff's Second Amended Complaint.

7. GTRC Final Report, chap. 10, "Injustice in the Justice System," 290–91.

8. Tate, "Personal Reflections on the Honorable Robert R. Merhige, Jr."

9. *Waller v. Butkovich* (Civil Action No. C-80-605G), April 17, 1984, Judge Merhige opinion.

10. Author interviews with Lewis Pitts (2017–2024); Waller, *Love and Revolution*, 441.

11. Sally Bermanzohn, unpublished interview with Marty Nathan (January 1990), 31.

12. Grady's threat was captured by television cameras. The Truth and Reconciliation Commission reviewed the footage and cited it in their final report, 132.

13. GCRF Records (4630), folders 1291–92, Bernard W. Butkovich deposition.

14. These details are from Butkovich's and Mark Sherer's testimony in the *US v. Griffin* federal criminal trial and *US v. Mark J. Sherer* trial. See GRCF Records (4630), folders 2779, 2280–81, 2095.

15. Waller, *Love and Revolution*, 340. See also Michael Massoglia, "Smith's Scrapbook Withheld from Jury," *Winston-Salem Journal*, October 3, 1980, 9.

16. Mark J. Sherer plea agreement, GCRF Records (4630), file 2002.

17. Roy Clinton Toney grand jury testimony, GCRF Records (4630), files 1763, 1806.

18. The cars driving away and leaving the two cars behind is evident from the video footage in the GCRF Records (4630).

19. GPD, Statement of Brent Fletcher (December 28, 1979), who admits to firing shot 2; GPD, Statement of Mark Sherer (May 12, 1980), in which Sherer admits to firing shots 1, 3, and 4. Toney admits to firing shot 5. Roy Toney testimony in *US v. Griffin* and grand jury in GCRF Records (4630), file 1806. This accounts for all the "mystery" shots that were vague in the FBI analysis.

20. Wheaton, *Codename Greenkil*, 162. These are direct quotes from Matthews's interview with the police in the aftermath of the shooting.

21. Chris Benson grand jury deposition, GCRF Records (4630), file 1682.

22. Mark Sherer plea bargain, 2.

23. Author interviews with Sylvester Daughtry (2018–2019). Daughtry remembered all these absences vividly. All but those of Major Conrad Wade are mentioned in the TRC report.

24. Byron Thomas grand jury testimony, *US v. Griffin*, 11–12. GCRF (4630), folders 2521–22.

25. Jerry Cooper testimony, GCRF Records (4630), folders 2323–33.

26. T. L. Burke, internal GPD interview, June 3, 1980; Larry Gibson, internal GPD interview, November 29, 1979.

27. Larry Gibson deposition, GCRF Records (4630), folder 1338.

28. R. L. Talbott federal grand jury testimony, August 5, 1982, 41.

29. Dawson deposition, *Waller v. Butkovich*, June 12–14, 1984, 493; Jerry Cooper testimony.

30. R. L. Talbott deposition, GCRF Records (4630), folders 1416–17, and also as quoted in GTRC Final Report, 271; Jerry Cooper testimony.

31. Jerry Cooper deposition, GCRF Records (4630), folders 1303–4.

32. Chief William Edward Swing deposition, GCRF Records (4630), folders 1413–15.

33. Sylvester Daughtry grand jury testimony, August 19, 1982, 25; Paul Spoon deposition, *Waller v. Butkovich*, August 14, 1984.

34. Greensboro Police Department, "History of the Greensboro Police Department," accessed April 16, 2024, https://www.greensboro-nc.gov/home/showpublisheddocument/43813/637038917960430000.

35. Greg Brooks told the author this story (2018–2024). He was a member of the same training class and witnessed this event.

36. Author interviews with Art League (2018) and Greg Brooks (2018–2024).

37. Author interviews with Sylvester Daughtry (2018–2019).

38. Author interviews with Marc Ridgill (October 7, 2021) and Greg Brooks (2018–2024).

39. The radio transcript information is from William E. Swing, Chief of Police, *An Administrative Report of the Anti-Klan Rally, Greensboro, North Carolina*, November 3, 1979, Greensboro Police Department, November 19, 1979.

40. Jerry Cooper deposition.

41. Stone, "The 1979 Greensboro Killings," 61.

42. Stone, "The 1979 Greensboro Killings," 65.

43. John Westra deposition, GRCF (4630), folders 1422–23, 155.

44. Raeford Milano Caudle grand jury file, GCRF (4630), folder 1703, 56; Roland Wayne Wood deposition, GCRF (4630), folders 1428–29, 217–18.

45. Barkley, "Judge Studying Allowing Documents as Evidence," D6.

46. As it turned out, at least three law enforcement agencies—the FBI, the GPD, and the Durham Police Department—were gathering intelligence on the CWP prior to Novem-

ber 3. This information gave credence to Joyce Johnson's assertion that she'd been tailed around The Grove by an unmarked car driven by a man who looked like Tom Brereton.

47. *The Third of November*, 28.

48. H. M. Michaux Jr. deposition, GCRF (4630), folder 1376.

49. To this day, documents from the preliminary investigation have never been released.

50. See Daisy Ferguson and Mordechai Levy affidavits, Greensboro TRC Archive, Bennett College, in Emily Mann files.

51. Daisy Ferguson and Mordechai Levy affidavits.

52. Richard Goldberg testimony, GCRF (4630), folders 271, 2360–2361.

53. Dwight Stone telephone interview with Eddie Dawson, cited in Stone, "The 1979 Greensboro Killings," 100.

54. Author interview with Rick Greeson (May 17, 2019). A version of this is also recounted in Dawson's interview with Dwight Stone.

55. "You made a good decision. We knew we could count on you," Captain Thomas said when Eddie refused to testify in the state trial. One detail Pitts and his team didn't seem to notice in the deluge of discovery materials was that when the GPD provided them with a transcript of Captain Thomas's call with Eddie, the transcriber attributed Captain Thomas's words to Eddie and Eddie's to Captain Thomas, turning the conversation into incomprehensible gibberish. Improbable as a clerical error, it was likely just one more attempt at obfuscation.

56. Sally Bermanzohn, unpublished interview with Dale Sampson (October 7, 1989).

57. Sally Bermanzohn, unpublished interview with Marty Nathan (January 1990), 35.

58. Sally Bermanzohn, unpublished interview with Marty Nathan (January 1990), 34.

59. Sally Bermanzohn, unpublished interview with Dale Sampson (October 7, 1989), 30.

60. Waller, *Love and Revolution*, 477.

61. Thomas Ricks, *Churchill and Orwell: The Fight for Freedom* (New York: Penguin Books, 2017), 127.

62. Bermanzohn, *Through Survivors' Eyes*, 325.

63. Langberg, *Life of a Movement Lawyer*.

CHAPTER 34: DAMAGES

1. Author interviews with Cecil Moses (2018–2022). The commendation from William Webster is in the FBI "GreenKil" documents released to the author under the FOIA.

2. The trial transcripts reproduced here are taken from Bermanzohn, *Through Survivors' Eyes*, 304–6. Sally Bermanzohn's source was Emily Mann's play *Testimonies*. Mann did extensive research into the shooting and collected a massive archive of trial documents.

3. Waller, *Love and Revolution*, 460; Bermanzohn, *Through Survivor's Eyes*, 308.

4. Bermanzohn, *Through Survivors' Eyes*, 301, 364; Brian Shaw, "Jackson Wants Justice in Klan-Nazi Lawsuit," *Greensboro News & Record*, April 14, 1985, C6.

5. Jerry Cooper testimony; Paul W. Spoon testimony, GRCF (4630), folders 2509–10.

6. Author interview with Adeeb Fadil (March 8, 2021).

7. Author interviews with James Moynihan (February 1, 2018; April 27, 2018).

8. Sally Bermanzohn, unpublished interview with Marty Nathan (January 1990), 35.

9. GCRF Records (4630), folder 2555, Wilson Library, University of North Carolina, "Plaintiffs' Closing Arguments Before the Honorable Robert R. Merhige, Jr., Winston-Salem, North Carolina," June 3, 1985.

10. GCRF Records (4630), folder 2555, "Plaintiffs' Closing Arguments," June 3, 1985.

11. Author interview with Flint Taylor (December 7, 2018).

12. See Truth and Reconciliation Commission Final Report, 305.

13. Author interview with Lewis Pitts (December 7, 2018).

14. Editorial, "Even Radicals Have Rights," *New York Times*, June 14, 1985, A30.

15. Author interview with Adeeb Fadil (March 8, 2021).

16. Waller, *Love and Revolution*, 462.

17. Author interviews with Nelson and Joyce Johnson (2017–2022).

CHAPTER 35: LIBERATION

1. "Hairston, Otis L.," *Civil Rights Digital Library*, Digital Library of Georgia, October 9, 2008, https://crdl.usg.edu/people/hairston_otis_l.

2. Author interviews with Nelson and Joyce Johnson (2017–2022).

3. Author interviews with Joyce Johnson (2017–2022).

4. Cecile Holmes White, "Winds of Change Blow Nelson Johnson to God," *Greensboro News & Record*, July 14, 1986, B1.

5. White, "Winds of Change Blow Nelson Johnson to God," B1.

6. White, "Winds of Change Blow Nelson Johnson to God," B1.

7. Author interviews with Nelson and Joyce Johnson (2017–2022).

8. Sally Bermanzohn, unpublished interview with Signe Waller (October 31, 1989), 17.

9. Author interviews with Nelson Johnson (2017–2022).

10. Author interviews with Nelson Johnson (2017–2022).

11. Bermanzohn, *Through Survivors' Eyes*, 339; White, "Winds of Change Blow Nelson Johnson to God," B1.

12. "Crossing the line between being a communist and a follower of the radical gospel is a very fine line." Sally Bermanzohn, unpublished interview with Jean (August 1990), 15.

13. Author interviews with Nelson Johnson (2017–2022); Sally Bermanzohn, unpublished interview with Nelson Johnson (October 9, 1989), 11.

14. Author interviews with Joyce Johnson (2017–2022).

15. Author interviews with Nelson Johnson (2017–2022).

CHAPTER 36: PEACE

1. Author interviews with Nelson and Joyce Johnson (2017–2022).

2. Joyce Johnson, GTRC statement.

3. This image of the "duet" comes from Ayo Johnson in interviews with the author (2017–2022).

4. The author viewed this letter dated April 24, 1987, in the Beloved Community Center archive.

5. Nelson's private debate with the Klansmen in 1987 mirrored debates that had been going on for decades: Marcus Garvey with the Klan in the 1920s; Elijah Muhammad and Klan debates in the 1950s and '60s. White rape or Black rape? White jobs or Black jobs? Whom does separation benefit? See Les Payne and Tamara Payne, *The Dead Are Arising: The Life of Malcolm X* (New York: Liveright, 2020), 336–39.

6. Elizabeth Coady and Steve Berry, "5 Arrests in Klan Parade," *Greensboro News & Record*, June 8, 1987, A1, A4; Kimberly J. McLarin, "Peace Festival Draws 500 to Park," *Greensboro News & Record*, June 8, 1987, B1, B4.

7. Author interview with former GPD officer Greg Brooks, who recounted the story about Dave Williams. Williams had led the internal investigation of GPD officers in the wake of the November 3, 1979, shooting and was responsible for assembling Chief Swing's administrative report.

CHAPTER 37: BELOVED

1. Joyce Johnson statement to the TRC, 2005.

2. Greensboro's official All-America City application, 1991, National Civic League archives, sent to the author electronically by the National Civic League.

3. Donald W. Patterson, "The Best of the Best," *Greensboro News & Record*, July 4, 1991, 1–16 (special section); Virginia Demaree, "On a Roll with New Bus System," *Greensboro News & Record*, July 4, 1991, 13 (special section), highlighting Joyce Johnson's work on the bus system.

4. Z Holler, *Jesus' Radical Message: Subversive Sermons for Today's Seekers* (Eugene, OR: Wipf & Stock, 2010), loc. 81, Kindle.

5. "Obituary for Rev. Z. N. Holler, August 2, 1928–December 8, 2016," Forbis & Dick Funeral Service, https://www.forbisanddick.com/obituaries/Z-Holler/#!/Obituary.

6. Manning Marable, *Race, Reform, and Rebellion* (Jackson: Univ. Press of Mississippi, 1984), 89.

7. Z Holler, *Jesus' Radical Message*, loc. 407.

8. Z Holler, *Jesus' Radical Message*, loc. 54.

9. Kmart was second only to Walmart.

10. Peter Krouse, "Lesson Learned: Kmart Fight Leads to More than Satisfactory Labor Contract—It Spawns New Attitude Toward Encouraging Social Change," *Greensboro News & Record*, September 29, 1996, E1, E2; Penda D. Hair, *Louder than Words: Lawyers, Communities and the Struggle for Justice* (New York: Rockefeller Foundation, March 2001), 102–119. The Beloved Community Center Archives offer a rich source of communications and strategy documents relating to the Kmart labor dispute.

11. Hair, *Louder than Words*, 102–19.

12. Jim Schlosser, "Kmart Workers Disrupt GGO," *Greensboro News & Record*, April 25, 1994, A1, A7.

13. Editorial, "Union Lost Credibility in Protest to Jaycees," *Greensboro News & Record*, April 16, 1994, A8.

14. This phrase recalled the "I am a man" slogan that defined the 1968 sanitation workers strike in Memphis.

15. Author interviews with Nelson Johnson (2017–2022).

16. Krouse, "Lesson Learned," E1, E2.

17. Krouse, "Lesson Learned," E1, E2. While the activists hoped to ignite the civil rights energy of the 1960s and early 1970s, they avoided putting race at the center of the story.

18. Krouse, "Lesson Learned," E1, E2.

19. Letter from David A. Daniel to the Piedmont Associated Industries, December 5, 1995; Pulpit Forum press statement, March 27, 1996. Both documents are in the Beloved Community Center archives.

20. Author interviews with Nelson Johnson (2017–2022).

21. Vincent Canby, "Theater Review: When Communists Clashed with Nazis and the Klan," *New York Times*, February 12, 1996, https://www.nytimes.com/1996/02/12/theater /theater-review-when-communists-clashed-with-nazis-and-the-klan.html.

22. Thanks to the private video archive of Laura Seel, the author was able to watch all of the speeches referenced here.

23. Braden at Bennett College, November 6, 1999, also said, "All through our history whenever this country has moved in a humane direction toward a democratic society, it's because there has been a movement from the African American community."

24. Author interviews with Ayo Johnson (2017–2022).

25. Sally Bermanzohn, unpublished interview with Al, August 1991, 17.

26. Sally Bermanzohn, unpublished interview with Shirley (August 1991), 24.

27. Author interviews with Nelson Johnson (2017–2022). "If only the community had a way of knowing the truth, it could help the city," Nelson thought.

28. Cathy Gant-Hill, "Play About Dark Day in 1979 Comes Home to the Gate City," *Greensboro News & Record*, October 31, 1999, D1; Cathy Gant-Hill, "Play Tells Story Greensboro Has Needed to Hear," *Greensboro News & Record*, November 18, 1999, D1; Jim Dodson, "Citizen Jim's Latest Hurrah," *O. Henry Magazine*, February 28, 2022, https://www.ohenrymag.com/citizen-jims-latest-hurrah/.

CHAPTER 38: TRUTHS

1. The Economic Opportunity Act, 1964, 78 Stat. 508–16 (1965), https://college.cengage .com/history/ayers_primary_sources/economicopportunity_1964.htm.

2. Spoma Jovanovic, *Democracy, Dialogue, and Community Action: Truth and Reconciliation in Greensboro* (Fayetteville: Univ. of Arkansas Press, 2012), 79; Brian Klaas, "America's Self-Obsession Is Killing Its Democracy," *The Atlantic*, July 21, 2022, https://www .theatlantic.com/ideas/archive/2022/07/american-democracy-breakdown-authoritarianism -rise/670580/.

3. Jovanovic, *Democracy, Dialogue, and Community Action*, 63.

4. Transcript created from video shared by Laura Seel from her personal archive.

5. Lorraine Ahearn, "At Morningside, Ribbon-Cuttings to Wrecking Balls," *Greensboro News & Record*, November 3, 2002, B1; editorial, "A New Morningside: Rethinking Community," *Greensboro News & Record*, September 3, 1998, A12.

6. Margaret Moffett Banks, "Combination of Residences, and the Troubled Past of Morningside Homes Is Lost in the Mix," *Greensboro News & Record*, July 17, 2005, A1, A6.

7. Author interviews with Greg Brooks (2018–2024).

8. Zucker, *Greensboro: Closer to the Truth.*

9. Ahearn, "At Morningside, Ribbon-Cuttings to Wrecking Balls," B1.

10. Jovanovic, *Democracy, Dialogue, and Community Action*; Lisa Magarrell and Joya Wesley, *Learning from Greensboro: Truth and Reconciliation in the United States* (Philadelphia: Univ. of Pennsylvania Press, 2010).

11. GTRC Final Report, "Executive Summary," May 26, 2006, 2.

12. Paul Bermanzohn, GTRC statement.

13. GTRC Final Report, "Executive Summary," 2.

14. Editorial, "City Must Look into Files Claim," *Greensboro News & Record*, February 28, 2008, A8.

15. GTRC Final Report, "Executive Summary," 25.

16. Author interviews with Jill Williams (2019–2023).

17. Zucker, *Greensboro: Closer to the Truth.*

18. Du Bois, *Black Reconstruction in America*, 713.

19. Video recordings of Greensboro Truth and Reconciliation Commission open meetings are at the TRC Archive at the Bennett College Library.

20. Meredith Barkley, "Supervisor Ends Varied FBI Career," *Greensboro News & Record*, December 30, 1985, B1, B3.

21. Video recordings of Greensboro Truth and Reconciliation Commission open meetings are at the TRC Archive at the Bennett College Library.

22. TRC interview with Jim Coman, Rick Greeson, and Mike Schlosser (August 4, 2005).

23. Nelson Johnson, GTRC statement, August 26, 2005.

24. Margaret Moffett Banks, "Testimony Lacks New Information," *Greensboro News & Record*, September 28, 2005, A1, A4.

25. Author interview with Angela Lawrence (February 23, 2022).

26. GTRC Final Report, "Executive Summary," 10.

27. In 2006, two months after the Greensboro Truth and Reconciliation Commission Report was released, the International Truth and Reconciliation conference came to Greensboro, including people from around the United States and five continents and representatives from South Africa, Peru, Northern Ireland, and Sri Lanka.

28. Zucker, *Greensboro: Closer to the Truth.*

EPILOGUE

1. Lauren Barber, "Greensboro City Council Apologizes for 1979 Greensboro Massacre," Triad City Beat, August 15, 2017; https://triad-city-beat.com/greensboro-city-council -apologizes-citys-role/.

2. See Ian McDowell's incisive book *I Ain't Resisting: The City of Greensboro and the Killing of Marcus Smith* (Scuppernong Editions, September 2023).

ABOUT THE AUTHOR

ARAN SHETTERLY is a writer and editor. He is the author of *The Americano*, a cofounder of the Mexico City–based magazine *Inside Mexico*, and a collaborator with the arts and education organization Americans Who Tell the Truth. He has received numerous fellowships, including a Virginia Humanities Fellowship and a 2019 National Endowment for the Humanities grant. He lives in Charlottesville, Virginia, with his son and wife, *New York Times* bestselling author Margot Lee Shetterly.